QNAP Setup Guide

5

Nicholas Rushton, BA Hons.
Callisto Technology and Consultancy Services
QTS 5.0 © 2022 CTACS

QTS Version 5.0.1, Updated November 2022
Copyright © Nicholas Rushton 2022

The right of Nicholas Rushton to be identified as the author of this work has been asserted by him in accordance with the Copyright, Designs and Patents Act 1988.

All rights reserved. No part of this publication may be reproduced, stored in or introduced into a retrieval system, or transmitted, in any form, or by any means (electronic, mechanical, photocopying, recording or otherwise) without the prior permission of the author. Any person who does any unauthorized act in relation to this publication may be left liable to criminal prosecution and civil claims for damages. An exception is granted in that up to 750 words in total may be quoted for the purpose of review. The information in this publication is provided without warranty or liability and it is up to the reader to determine its suitability and applicability to their own requirements. This book and its author are unconnected with QNAP Systems Inc. and this is an independently produced publication.

This book is sold subject to the condition that it shall not, by way of trade or otherwise, be lent, resold, hired out, or otherwise circulated without the author's prior consent in any form of binding or cover other than that in which it was published and without a similar condition including this condition being imposed on the subsequent purchaser.

All copyrighted terms and trademarks of the registered owners are respectfully acknowledged.

Table of Contents

1 GETTING STARTED — 12

1.1 OVERVIEW — 13
1.2 CHOOSING A QNAP NAS MODEL — 17
1.3 DISK DRIVES — 20
1.4 SWITCH AND WIRELESS ACCESS POINTS — 22
1.5 LOCATION AND ELECTRICAL CONSIDERATIONS — 23

2 INSTALLING QTS — 24

2.1 OVERVIEW — 25
2.2 INSTALLATION — 27
2.3 FIVE MINUTE TOUR OF QTS — 35
2.4 SETTING UP STORAGE — 40
2.5 NETWORK SERVICES — 48
2.6 HARDWARE & POWER OPTIONS — 50
2.7 OTHER INSTALLATION OPTIONS — 55

3 SHARED FOLDERS — 58

3.1 OVERVIEW — 59
3.2 CREATING A SHARED FOLDER — 61
3.3 MAKING CHANGES TO A SHARED FOLDER — 65
3.4 ENABLING HOME FOLDERS — 66
3.5 LOADING EXISTING DATA INTO SHARED FOLDERS — 67

4 MANAGING USERS — 68

4.1 OVERVIEW — 69
4.2 CREATING USERS — 70
4.3 MODIFYING, DISABLING AND DELETING USER ACCOUNTS — 73
4.4 ADDING MULTIPLE USERS — 75
4.5 USER GROUPS — 78

5 ACCESSING THE SERVER — 82

5.1 OVERVIEW — 83
5.2 USING A BROWSER AND FILE STATION — 83
5.3 CONNECTING MACS — 86
5.4 CONNECTING WINDOWS COMPUTERS — 89
5.5 CONNECTING LINUX & UNIX COMPUTERS — 96
5.6 CONNECTING SMARTPHONES AND TABLETS — 97
5.7 CONNECTING CHROMEBOOKS — 99

6 SECURITY — 101

6.1 OVERVIEW — 102
6.2 SECURITY COUNSELOR — 102
6.3 SECURITY CHECKUP — 105
6.4 ANTIVIRUS APPLICATION — 106
6.5 MALWARE REMOVER — 108
6.6 ALLOW/DENY LIST — 110
6.7 IP ACCESS PROTECTION — 111
6.8 ACCOUNT ACCESS PROTECTION — 112
6.9 SSL CERTIFICATE & PRIVATE KEY — 113
6.10 PASSWORD POLICY — 115
6.11 2-STEP VERIFICATION — 117
6.12 QUFIREWALL — 119
6.13 QULOG CENTER — 121
6.14 DISALLOW USB DEVICES — 122

7 BACKUPS — 123

7.1 OVERVIEW — 124
7.2 HYBRID BACKUP SYNC — 126
7.3 BACKUP TO EXTERNAL DRIVE — 128
7.4 RESTORE FILES FROM EXTERNAL DRIVE — 137
7.5 USB ONE TOUCH COPY — 140
7.6 SYNC TO CLOUD — 142
7.7 NAS TO NAS BACKUPS USING RYSNC — 147
7.8 BACKING UP WINDOWS PCS USING QNAP NETBAK REPLICATOR — 154
7.9 BACKING UP COMPUTERS USING BUILT-IN WINDOWS BACKUP PROGRAMS — 160

7.10 BACKING UP MACS	162
7.11 BACKING UP SYSTEM SETTINGS	165

8 HOUSEKEEPING & MAINTENANCE — 166

8.1 OVERVIEW	167
8.2 CHECKING FOR QTS UPDATES	167
8.3 DASHBOARD	170
8.4 NOTIFICATION CENTER	171
8.5 CHECKING THE HEALTH OF THE DISKS	178
8.6 RAID DATA SCRUBBING	181
8.7 SYSTEM STATUS	183
8.8 RESOURCE MONITOR	184
8.9 QBOOST	186
8.10 USING QMANAGER	189
8.11 LOCATING THE NAS	191
8.12 MANAGING MULTIPLE SERVERS	193

9 MULTIMEDIA & STREAMING — 195

9.1 OVERVIEW	196
9.2 MULTIMEDIA CONSOLE	198
9.3 DLNA MEDIA SERVER	206
9.4 MUSIC STATION	209
9.5 QUMAGIE	213
9.6 PHOTO STATION	217
9.7 VIDEO STATION	222
9.8 CAYIN MEDIASIGN PLAYER	225
9.9 CINEMA28	227
9.10 HYBRIDDESK STATION	229
9.11 MEDIA UPLOAD FROM QFINDER PRO	232
9.12 OTHER MULTIMEDIA APPS	233

10 PRODUCTIVITY & PERSONAL APPS — 234

10.1 OVERVIEW	235
10.2 QSIRCH	236
10.3 QCONTACTZ	239

10.4 QcalAgent	242
10.5 Notes Station	244
10.6 Download Station	245
10.7 Text Editor	248
10.8 Web Server	249

11 REMOTE ACCESS & CLOUD   251

11.1 Overview	252
11.2 myQNAPcloud	253
11.3 Accessing with an Internet Browser	256
11.4 Qsync	257
11.5 HybridMount	264
11.6 Virtual Private Networks (VPN)	268
11.7 QuFTP Service	277

12 STORAGE   279

12.1 Overview	280
12.2 RAID	280
12.3 Increasing Pool Free Space	284
12.4 Snapshots	286
12.5 SSD Caching	297
12.6 SSD Trim	303
12.7 iSCSI	304
12.8 What is Qtier?	310

13 SURVEILLANCE   311

13.1 Overview	312
13.2 Setting Up QVR Elite	312
13.3 QVR Pro Client	321

14 VIRTUALIZATION   325

14.1 Overview	326
14.2 Virtualization Station and Installing Windows	328

14.3 CONTAINER STATION	**333**
14.4 UBUNTU LINUX STATION	**337**

15 MISCELLANEOUS & ADVANCED TOPICS — 339

15.1 OVERVIEW	**340**
15.2 APP CENTER	**340**
15.3 HELP CENTER & HELPDESK	**344**
15.4 LICENSE CENTER	**345**
15.5 PERSONALIZATION SETTINGS	**346**
15.6 CUSTOMIZING THE LOGIN SCREEN	**349**
15.7 PRINTING	**350**
15.8 ACL (ACCESS CONTROL LISTS)	**351**
15.9 INTERNET ROUTER DOES NOT SUPPLY DHCP	**353**
15.10 INTERNET ACCESS USING A PROXY SERVER	**356**
15.11 PORT TRUNKING	**357**
15.12 USING AN EXTERNAL NTP SERVER	**361**
15.13 ADDITIONAL NETWORKING FEATURES	**362**
15.14 THE ADMIN ANOMALY	**363**
15.15 RESETTING THE ADMIN PASSWORD	**364**
15.16 PREPARING THE NAS FOR DISPOSAL	**365**

INDEX	**366**

Comments & Reviews From Other Purchasers

You are in good company - thousands of people have used guides from CTACS to help them setup their home and business networks. This is what purchasers of the *QNAP NAS Setup Guide* have written in their reviews:

"Excellent book. If you're new to QNAP NAS, this is the book to get. Really like it. Easy to read and understand." – HD

"Excellent step by step guide, especially for newbies. The guide is a very-well organized and carefully written document that should be of great help to beginners in the Qnap universe. It covers all the basic aspects and also provides hand-holding for the Windows, Mac and the Linux user with small, but insightful remarks. Highly recommended!" – Fred2yu

"Nice distillation of important setup concepts. I was struggling with getting my SAN up and running by simply using the available manuals and QNAP community. This guide provided a methodical and easy-to-understand set of instructions and explanations which has me feeling pretty good about where I'm at now. I'm glad I got this before going too far with my installation..." – Verified Purchaser

"In Layman's Terms. This is a well-organized guide highly recommended for novices who are considering or have just purchased a QNAP NAS. It is written in layman's terms so you do not need to be an IT specialist to understand it. Great supplement to the QNAP user's manual but easier to understand and in some cases more thorough." – 'G'

"Welcome clarity. The author has a refreshingly simple and clear style of writing which guides the uninitiated reader through this unfamiliar territory. The book is not aimed at an expert user, rather is it designed to help anyone who has met the equipment and various menus for the first time. It is a friendly guide. I strongly recommend it and I thank the author." – Dr D.E.L.

"Four Stars. Very good for beginner..." – BM*

A Good How To Guide. I have had a TS-451 for about four years. I was able to use it but I really did not understand all the QTS software offered until I purchased this book. I highly recommend this book if you have a QNAP product." – Verified Purchaser

"A valuable guide for new QNAP owners. I purchased this very affordable guide to help me get acquainted with my new QNAP 453 Pro. There is no user's guide on the box. While one can be downloaded, I liked the coaching provided by this Setup Guide - by a fellow user who has done this before. Now I feel ready to tackle the QNAP guide for reference now that I have the NAS up and running." – DL

"Welcome clarity. The author has a refreshingly simple and clear style of writing which guides the uninitiated reader through this unfamiliar territory. The book is not aimed at an expert user, rather is it designed to help anyone who has met the equipment and various menus for the first time. It is a friendly guide. I strongly recommend it and I thank the author". – Dr L

"Four Stars. Clear, easy to follow and up to date." – David

"Great overview of the basic operation of a NAS. It took me about 2 hours to go through it, reading most of it and skimming part of it. I now have a much better understanding of what the NAS will do, how it's organized and how to configure it. I'm ready to start using it. Nice job!" – DP

About This Book

With superb functionality and ease of use through the acclaimed QTS operating system, QNAP is the NAS device of choice for discerning purchasers: great hardware able to provide shared storage, backups, cloud services, multimedia streaming, run applications and more. But this power and flexibility comes at a price and setting up a QNAP NAS for the very first time can seem a daunting prospect for someone who has not done so before. This guide is based around the latest version of QTS and with copious illustrations, easy-to-follow instructions and based on years of real-world experience, will take you through it from start to finish and help ensure that your home or small business (or church, charity, school) network is a success. It is written according to the Goldilocks Principle: not too little information, not too much information, but just the right amount.

The guide is structured into three main parts:

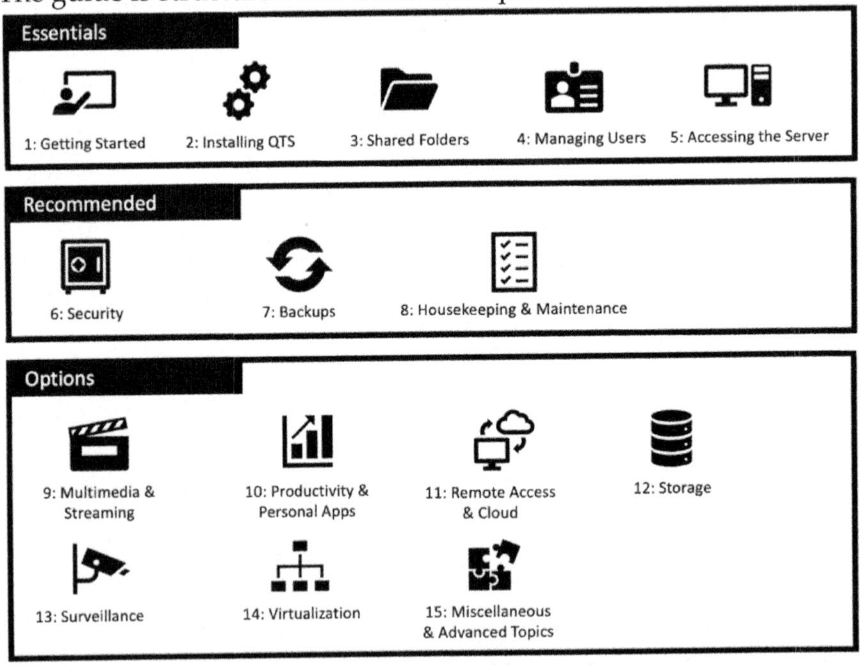

Essentials
- 1: Getting Started
- 2: Installing QTS
- 3: Shared Folders
- 4: Managing Users
- 5: Accessing the Server

Recommended
- 6: Security
- 7: Backups
- 8: Housekeeping & Maintenance

Options
- 9: Multimedia & Streaming
- 10: Productivity & Personal Apps
- 11: Remote Access & Cloud
- 12: Storage
- 13: Surveillance
- 14: Virtualization
- 15: Miscellaneous & Advanced Topics

Figure 1: Structure of this guide

Chapters 1 to 5 cover the essentials, the things you absolutely must do, which consists of setting up the hardware, installing QTS, creating some shared folders, creating the users and then connecting your computers and mobile devices to the NAS.

Chapters 6 to 8 comprise things which are strongly recommended: setting up security; organizing backups for the server and the connected computers; learning about housekeeping and maintenance to keep the server in good health.

Chapters 9 through 15 are other topics to investigate and includes ways to make your system more capable and useful, such as multimedia and setting up remote access for using the server from outside the home or office. Other subjects covered include personal and productivity applications, surveillance and virtualization.

In a hurry? The first five chapters will get you up and running ASAP. Then return and explore at leisure.

About the Author

The author has worked in IT for four decades, on systems of all sizes and types throughout the world, from the largest companies to the smallest and including several of his own. He currently runs his own independent consultancy and is the author of numerous networking guides, published through CTACS as eBooks and paperbacks. Titles include: *QNAS Setup Guide; Windows Server 2022; Windows Server 2019 Essentials; Little Book of macOS Server; Synology Setup Guide; Little Book of Synology; Using Windows 10 as a Server; Using Windows 11 as a Server*.

1
GETTING STARTED

1.1 Overview

If you are reading this, then it is likely you already know what Network Attached Storage (NAS) is and may have purchased or are about to purchase a QNAP NAS unit. But for those who do not, or by way of recap:

When two or more computing devices are connected together, a network is created. The Internet is a worldwide, public network comprising billions of users, computers and servers.

A private, or local area network, is typically intended for the use of a household, business or educational establishment. Such networks are commonly built around a NAS unit.

The keyword here is 'storage'. A NAS device consists of a large amount of disk storage contained in its own box. Unlike most external drives, which typically connect to a single computer with a USB or Thunderbolt connection, a NAS links to a router or network switch using an Ethernet cable and this enables it to be accessed and shared by computers and other devices on the local network.

The NAS can also be accessed remotely from anywhere via the Internet. It is protected by user accounts, passwords, encryption and other security measures so that only authorized people can access it, not the world at large.

A NAS device runs its own operating system. This is not Windows or macOS, rather, it is a proprietary system and in the case of QNAP is called QTS. Often, the term *firmware* rather than operating system is used to describe it. Although specifically designed for file sharing and managing clients, QTS is also able to run apps that provide many additional capabilities.

A NAS does not need its own screen, keyboard and mouse. Rather, it is interacted with using a browser such as Chrome, Firefox, Safari etc. from any computer on the network. At the simplest level it can simply be thought of as a 'black box' or computing appliance.

What can a NAS do? Many things, but some popular uses include:

- Providing extra storage for computers
- A backup system for computers

- Providing a shared, common area where a business or family can store their documents and other files
- Being the heart of a home entertainment system, providing a central library for music, photos and videos, with the ability to stream them to computers, tablets and smartphones
- Running a private cloud system, with controlled remote access to your data. Similar in principle to services such as Dropbox, OneDrive and iCloud, but totally under your own control and with effectively unlimited usage plus no subscription charges
- A sophisticated video surveillance system for the home, office or other premises
- A comprehensive development platform for software developers
- An alternative to a traditional business file server running Windows Server or Linux, along with productivity applications

QNAP are one of the leading and most innovative suppliers of NAS worldwide and have sold millions of units. They offer a wide range of hardware, suitable for individual users all the way through to the largest of enterprises. For many years, QNAP referred to their NAS systems as *Turbo Stations* and then, more latterly, as *Turbo NAS*. These names have partially been abandoned but are reflected in the fact that most model numbers continue to begin with the designator 'TS' e.g. TS-328, TS-451+, TS-677 and so on. For reference, Turbo Station, Turbo NAS, QNAP and NAS all refer to one and the same thing. An alternative name for a NAS box is *server* and we will use both terms interchangeably in this book.

A typical small network based around a NAS is depicted below. The key components are:

NAS (server) - this is the heart of the network, running QTS and upon which data is stored
Backup device – for example, an external USB drive connected to the server
Internet connection - this may be a separate router or an all-in-one wi-fi router
Switch and Wireless Access Point(s) – to provide expansion in larger networks

Printer(s) – may be networked or plugged into the server with a USB cable

Desktops PCs – running Windows, macOS or Linux, connected using Ethernet or wireless

Laptops, Chromebooks, Tablets and Smartphones – connected wirelessly

Whilst it may not match your own setup exactly, it should be broadly similar. Further information about the components is given in the following sections and later sections of the guide.

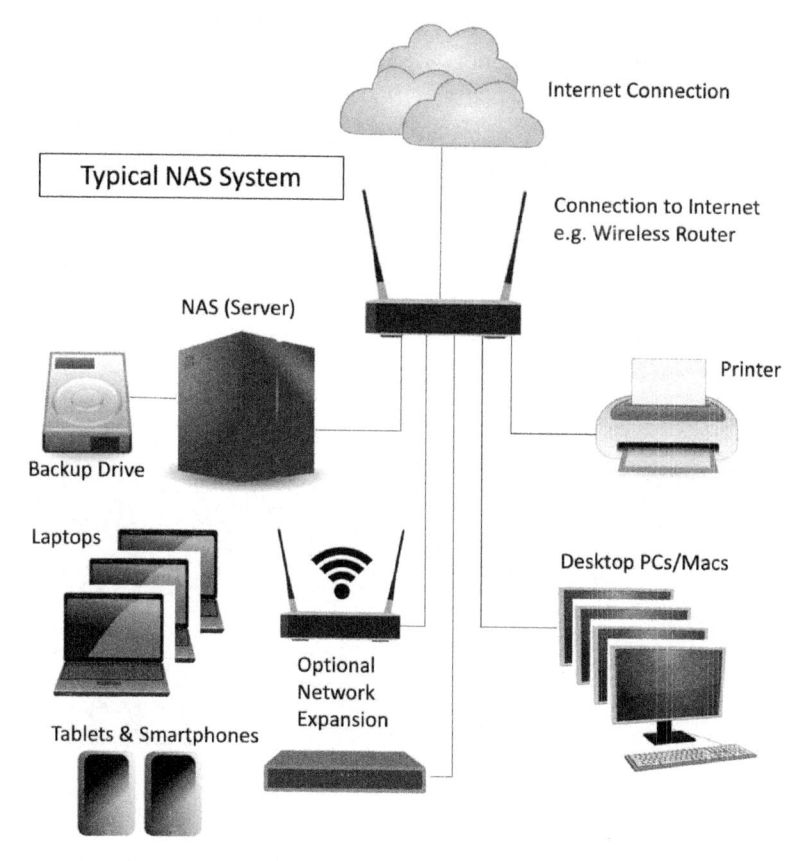

Figure 2: Typical NAS System

Any modern computer can be used with the NAS. The computers can be running any mixture of Windows 11/10, Windows 8/8.1, Windows 7, Windows Vista or Windows XP. Home or Professional versions of Windows are equally suitable.

Apple Macintosh computers running macOS and older versions of OS X can be connected, as can Linux PCs. Devices running iOS (iPad, iPhone) and Android (tablets and Smartphones) can be connected, as can many smart televisions and gaming boxes. Chromebooks can also be used and, unusually amongst NAS vendors, QNAP provides some specific support for them.

Note: QuTS Hero Edition, QuTS Cloud NAS and QES are close variants of QTS for use by enterprise users but are not specifically covered in this guide. QuTS Hero Edition and QES use the advanced ZFS filing system, whilst QuTS Cloud NAS is a virtualized version of QTS running on private cloud services such as Azure and Amazon EC2. However, for the most part they feature the same user interface and features as regular QTS.

1.2 Choosing a QNAP NAS Model

QNAP offer many different models of their NAS hardware, designed to cater for everyone from single and home users, through to the largest of enterprises with thousands of users and high availability requirements. The models vary according to form factor, number of disk drives that can be used, network adapters, performance, expandability and price:

Form Factor – QNAP NAS boxes come in two basic varieties. Some are standalone units designed to sit on top of a cupboard or desk, whereas others are designed to be mounted in standard computer cabinets (racks) that take devices that are 19 inches/48cm wide. There are also a handful of models that do not fit these categorizations, including a domestic model that resembles a set-top box or DVD player and a laptop-style device. Home and small business users will typically use a standalone unit, although larger organizations may prefer rack-mounted units.

Number of Disk Drives – QNAP NAS units can hold between 1 and 30 disk drives, depending on the model. Having more drives allows greater storage capacity and permits the use of RAID to improve resilience and throughput. Many models can be expanded using external cases and units to provide more drives.

Networking – all models feature at least Gigabit Ethernet and many models have multiple network adapters. QNAP have led the way to higher speeds by offering 2.5 Gbe, 5 Gbe and 10 Gbe network adapters for increased network throughput. There are also some models with Thunderbolt ports, enabling them to be connected to Macs and other suitably equipped computers, providing the high-speed data links that are particularly beneficial in tasks such as 4K video editing.

Performance - Some models have more powerful processors (Intel or AMD rather than ARM) plus more memory (RAM). These are typically aimed at business users and home users with more demanding requirements. Some advanced features, mainly of interest to enterprise rather than home or small business users, require models with Intel/AMD processors. One advantage of ARM is lower power consumption. Lower-cost QNAP models are usually ARM-based.

Expandability – Some models feature PCIe expansion slots, enabling M2 SSD cache memory or additional network adapters to be added. Sometimes the main memory (RAM) is upgradeable.

QNAP have grouped their ranges into three main groups:

Home & SOHO – aimed at personal, home and Small Office Home Office users

SMB – designed for small and medium businesses

Enterprise – targeted at larger organizations and enterprise users

Choosing the right model can be confusing as there is often overlap between them, but in general you want to buy the most capable model you can afford. If you have or are planning to have large amounts of data, then you should buy a model with multiple drive bays, particularly one that supports SSD caching as this can give a good performance boost. If you are particularly interested in multimedia and home entertainment, a number of models feature HDMI output for direct connection to a television set.

A previously used QNAP might be an option in some instances, provided it is in good condition and not so old than it cannot run the current version of QTS. It depends upon the model, but in general QNAP support the current version of QTS on their hardware for in excess of 5 years. There are relatively few parts that can go wrong on a NAS; most commonly it is the fan or power supply that might develop a fault and these are generally easy to replace. If the unit is supplied with disk drives already installed, confirm that they are healthy. For instance, the drives in a NAS that has been used 24x7 for, say, three years may be becoming worn out and in need of replacement and you should budget accordingly.

Typical Usage Scenarios

These are some examples of how people are using QNAP NAS and the equipment choices they made:

Individual – Sue has a Windows desktop PC as well as a MacBook. She wanted additional storage space and the ability to share files between them, along with the ability to backup her MacBook using Time Machine. She was also curious about exploring the other possibilities offered by NAS, such as surveillance cameras, whilst minimizing the costs.

Her choice was a 1-bay TS-128A. The portable USB hard drive she was using previously was re-positioned as an external backup drive for the NAS.

Enthusiast – Andy had previously owned a very basic NAS device from another manufacturer but had outgrown it and wanted something more capable. As a semi-professional photographer, he was concerned about data safety and wanted a unit with multiple drives. As an IT enthusiast, he also wanted to be able to run other operating systems such as Windows and Linux. His choice was a 4-bay TS453D, with upgraded memory to run virtualization software.

Family – The Palmer family comprises two adults and two children. All have computers, plus tablets and smartphones. They are very keen on movies and music and wanted the ability to store their large collections in a single location, then stream to any device in the household. Their choice was the 4-bay TS451D2, which has a HDMI socket for direct connection to the family television set.

Small Business – Helen Translation Services Inc. wanted a capable in-house network, but without the costs and complexity associated with traditional Windows or Unix-based file servers. As they have several offsite and home-based staff, they also wanted full remote access, but without the ongoing costs associated with commercial cloud services. They also felt more comfortable with the idea of their data being under their direct control, rather than with a third party. Their solution was the 8-bay TVS-872N, which is backed up to a separate TS-253Be located elsewhere in the premises.

1.3 Disk Drives

NAS devices are not supplied by QNAP with disk drives already installed in them. Rather, the idea is that the customer buys the drives separately and installs them, which is quite easy to do, else buys a ready-populated unit from a reseller. This approach is generally better because it offers more choice.

QNAP NAS units are very flexible in terms of the brand and type of disk drives that can be used in them. However, it is strongly recommended to use drives that have been specifically designed for use with NAS, as such drives are optimized for continuous 24x7 operation over several years and consider the heat and vibration characteristics of NAS enclosures, along with other requirements. Although such drives are slightly more expensive than the regular disk drives as used by desktop PCs, the investment can easily be justified given the importance of data integrity. The main NAS-specific drives are as follows:

Western Digital Red – these are available in three variants. WD Red are intended for use in NAS systems with 1 to 8 bays. WD Red Plus are similar, but better suited to more heavily utilized RAID systems (the technical difference is that they do not use Shingled Magnetic Recording or SMR). For systems with more drive bays, up to 24, WD Red Pro drives are recommended.

Seagate IronWolf – intended for NAS systems with 1 to 8 bays. Iron Wolf Pro drives are available for systems with up to 24 drive bays. For larger systems, Seagate have the enterprise-level Exos series.

Toshiba N300 – designed for use in NAS systems with 1 to 8 bays. For larger systems, Toshiba have their MG Enterprise series.

Disk drives are manufactured in 3.5" (8.9cm) and 2.5" (6.4cm) form factors and most NAS models can use either, although some may require adaptor brackets to use 2.5" drives. The 3.5" drives offer higher capacities and better price performance, but 2.5" drives use less power, generate less vibration, are generally quieter in operation and increasingly popular. For systems with more than one drive, it is preferable that all the drives are the same model and capacity.

In a NAS equipped with multiple drives, they can be configured for *RAID*, short for *Redundant Array of Independent (or Inexpensive) Disks*. There are various types of RAID, referred to using a numbering system i.e. RAID 0, RAID 1, RAID 5 and so on. The basic idea is to improve reliability and performance through the use of multiple drives to provide redundancy and share the workload; a comprehensive description of the different levels be found in section **12.2 RAID**.

Although most disk drives are mechanical, solid-state drives based around flash memory, known as SSDs, are increasingly being used in laptop computers and elsewhere and will probably become the norm in all computing devices. Besides fast performance, SSDs have reduced power consumption and no mechanical noise, which makes them more suitable for some environments. NAS-specific SSDs are available from Seagate and Western Digital. At present, SSDs are more expensive than their mechanical counterparts, especially for the high-capacity ones that would be of most use in NAS, although prices are expected to fall.

QTS can take full advantage of SSDs for regular storage but can also use them to boost performance in two other ways: *caching*, where they act as a high-speed buffer to the mechanical hard drives, and *tiering*, whereby data is initially stored on SSD but if it is not accessed for a while, then it is migrated to slower mechanical drives for longer term storage. Depending on the model, caching can be done using 2.5" SSD (SATA) drives, or with M.2 or M.2 NVMe drives in dedicated slots or PCIe expansion cards. As drives used for caching take a lot of hits, it is recommended to use high quality ones, rather than low-cost consumer units. This topic is discussed in section **12.5 SSD Caching**.

1.4 Switch and Wireless Access Points

The devices in a network are connected using Ethernet cabling and wireless access points (WAPs). In a domestic setting or small business, everything might link back to an internet-connected all-in-one wireless router, whereas in a larger business setup there may be a separate router and possibly a separate firewall. Ethernet switches and wireless access points can be used to expand the network and provide greater capacity. The following points can be usefully observed:

- The NAS should be connected to the main network switch or combined wireless router using an Ethernet cable or a high-performance wireless connection. Wired connections should be of Gigabit (1Gb) specification or better. An increasing number of models support higher speed Ethernet connections such as 2.5 Gbe, 5 Gbe, 10 Gbe or 25 Gbe, as standard or via add-in cards. If so, it is worthwhile connecting at least the NAS to a high-speed switch, even if the rest of the infrastructure runs at slower speeds.
- For wireless devices such as laptops and tablets, make sure they operate at 801.11n, 801.11ac or 801.11ax ('Wi-Fi 6') specification.
- Check the specification of the combined wireless router if you are using one. Many ISPs (Internet Service Providers) supply relatively low-cost models, often free of charge when you take out a contract with them. These are often of average quality, for instance the Ethernet ports may not be Gigabit or the latest wireless standards may not be supported. Spending money on professional or prosumer ("professional consumer") routers and switches will usually give better performance and reliability.

In some scenarios, it might not be possible to connect the NAS using a wired Ethernet connection. QNAP fully support wireless connectivity within QTS and a list of suitable wireless adaptors can be found on the QNAP website. They also sell high-performance PCIe adapters that can be installed in some models. The NAS should be located as close to the wireless router as possible.

1.5 Location and Electrical Considerations

The server should be placed away from direct sunlight and any source of heat, such as a radiator. Avoid locations that are wet or damp. As little physical access is required the unit can be located out of sight and reach, for instance in a cupboard or a locked room. Most models generate very little noise and can usually be operated in an office or family room without too much disruption, although larger units are noisier.

It is possible that data loss can occur if the electrical mains power fails whilst the NAS is running. The best way to mitigate against this is to use an intelligent UPS (Uninterruptible Power Supply) with the NAS; in the event of power problems this will enable it to continue operating for short periods and then to shut it down in an orderly manner if necessary. Most popular brands work with QNAP (e.g. APC, CyberPower, Powercom) and a list of supported UPSs' can be found on the QNAP website. In a business environment, the use of an UPS should be considered essential.

If a UPS is not used, which is commonly the case in a domestic environment, then the NAS should at least be connected to a clean electrical power supply via a surge protector.

2
INSTALLING QTS

2.1 Overview

QTS is the operating system or firmware and one of the key things that differentiates QNAP from all the other brands of Network Attached Storage. It has such familiar features as a Desktop, taskbar and a drag-and-drop interface, analogous to what people are accustomed to with Windows, Mac and Linux PCs. The current version at the time of writing is QTS 5.0.1 and this guide is based around it; however, if you have a slightly different version you should still find most of it applicable, although possibly with minor variations (usually cosmetic) in some areas.

The assumption in this chapter is that you are installing a brand new QNAP NAS. If this is not the case – maybe you have obtained a previously used model, for instance – you might find it helpful to first take a quick look at sections **15.15 Resetting the Admin Password** and **15.16 Preparing the NAS for Disposal**, which will help you re-initialize it.

The installation process consists of loading the QTS firmware, defining some essential network settings, then setting up storage. Having done so, you will then be able to create shared folders (**3 SHARED FOLDERS**), setup the users (**4 MANAGING USERS**) and connect computers and other devices (**5 ACCESSING THE SERVER**).

Begin by physically installing the disk drive(s) in the NAS. The specifics of this varies according to the model; in some instances, the drives are held in removeable caddies which are inserted into the NAS, whereas in others the case must be opened and the drive(s) inserted into an internal frame or cage. However, the process is straightforward and often does not even require a screwdriver.

The NAS should then be connected to the network using an Ethernet cable. If the NAS has more than one network adapter, connect only the first one for now; usually, at least in a domestic or small business setting, the cable will lead directly from the NAS to the router. If you intend or need to connect the NAS wirelessly to the router, it is suggested that you still use a cable initially and then switch to the wireless adaptor once it is up and running.

To perform the installation, you will require a computing device with a browser, such as a desktop PC, laptop computer, Chromebook or tablet. It does not matter whether the device is running Windows, macOS, Linux, iOS or Android. QNAP recommend the Chrome, Safari or Firefox browsers; Microsoft Edge and Internet Explorer are not officially supported, although do seem to work in practice. The device needs to be connected to the same local network as the NAS.

The QTS installation process described in this chapter should work without problems in 99% of cases. In the rare event that difficulties are encountered, which would generally be at the very first stage, refer to section **2.7 Other Installation Options** for alternatives.

2.2 Installation

Enter the address of *install.qnap.com* into the browser and on the screen that appears, the NAS should appear in the *Uninitialized QNAP Device List* box. It is suggested you make a note of the MAC Address, which consists of six pairs of numbers and letters, separated by colons e.g. 12:34:56:78:90:AB, as this may be needed in some circumstances. Click the **Initialize** button.

If the NAS was not found, click **Rescan**. If it still does not appear, and you have satisfied yourself that there is no problem with the network cabling, click the link underneath marked **install the firmware by using the "Cloud Key"**. This will initially take you to a different screen, but you will still end up with the screens subsequently described below.

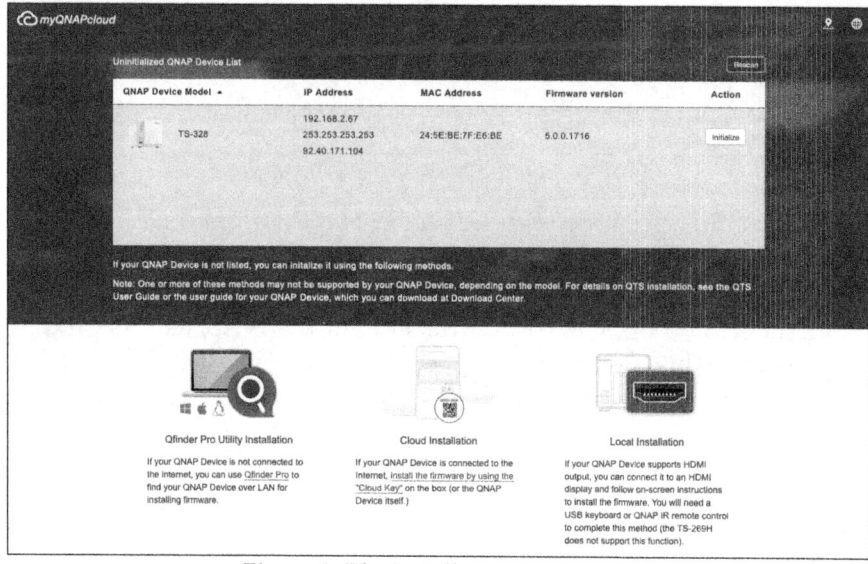

Figure 3: The install.qnap.com screen

QNAP's *myQNAPcloud* is a simple-to-use mechanism for setting up cloud and remote access and which eliminates many of the technical issues that can be associated with this topic. The next screen wants you to sign-in using a *QNAP ID* to help set it up. If you are an existing QNAP customer you can enter your details, otherwise click the **Create QNAP ID** link.

You could defer this step until later by clicking the **create later** link in the 'Tip' section, although this is not recommended as myQNAPcloud is so integral to the operation of the NAS.

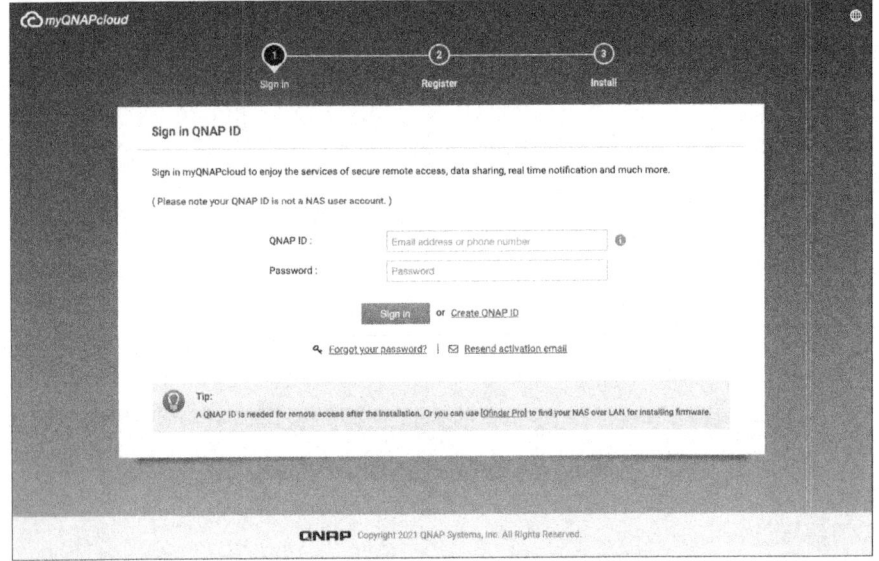

Figure 4: Sign in/Create QNAP ID account

As part of this process, you register a *myQNAPcloud Device Name*. This can generally be whatever you wish, although all the obvious names have long since been taken. One option is to use the *Cloud Key*, which is printed on a sticker on the side of the NAS, as it is unique. Having done this, the remote (i.e. internet) address of your server will be that device name with *myqnapcloud.com* as a suffix e.g. *q99999999.myqnapcloud.com*.

Once this has been done you will be returned to the main screen and may receive a panel asking you to check your warranty. This is a sales pitch and does not have to be done, so you may prefer to just close it by clicking **Close** button.

On the main screen, click the large **Start Smart Installation** button:

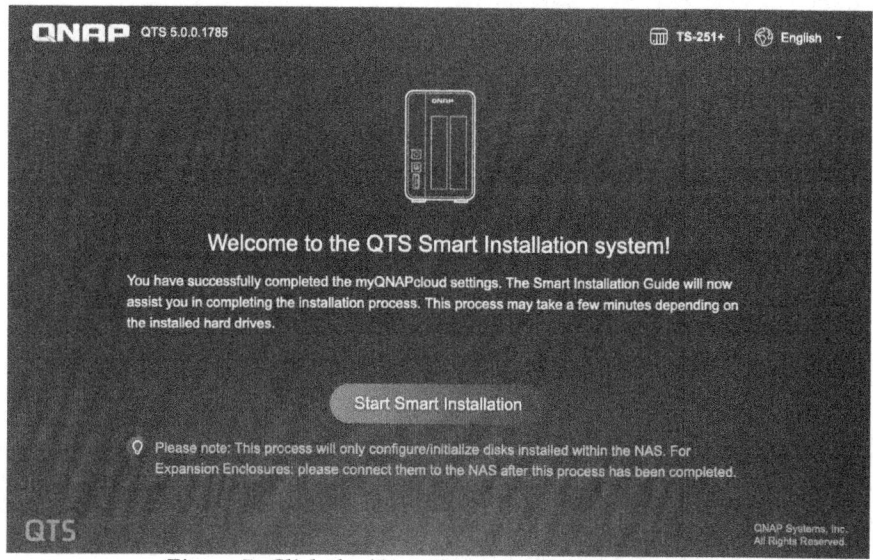

Figure 5: Click the 'Start Smart Installation' button

You may see a screen for specifying the firmware version (if the NAS has previously been used you will certainly see this). You can check for any update or click **Browse** and manually load a copy of the QTS firmware that was downloaded earlier - you might do this is you had reason to load a specific version of QTS, for instance. Or, just click **Next** to continue with the installation.

Note: if you receive an error message stating that "a valid myQNAPcloud Device cannot be found", go back to the beginning and this time register for the QNAP ID account.

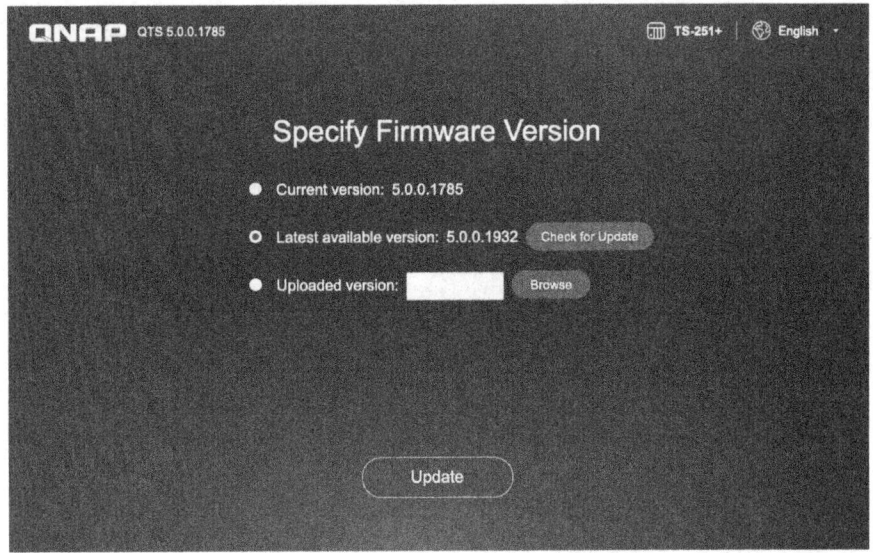

Figure 6: Specify firmware version

On the subsequent screen, change the NAS Name, which will currently be set to something seemingly random e.g. *NAS1FB6BC*, and make it something more meaningful, such as *server*. If you have or envisage having multiple servers, you may want to adopt a naming convention such as *server1, server2, server3* or something applicable to your organization, such as departmental names, locations, classroom numbers etc. The NAS Name can be up to 14 characters in length and include letters, numbers and dashes (-), although spaces and periods (full stops) are not allowed.

The *Username* will become the main (i.e. administrative) user of the system. Choose something suitable (not 'administrator' or 'admin') – in this example we have chosen *systemadmin*. Specify and confirm the password for the user. The best passwords are non-obvious and comprise a lengthy mixture of letters, numbers and symbols. As you type, QTS will advise on the strength of the password. You can click the mini 'eye' icons so you can check what you are typing. Click **Next**. Note: if you do not see the screen below, switch to section **2.7 Other Installation Options** and follow the Qfinder Pro Installation Option.

Figure 7: Specify the NAS Name, username and password

The subsequent screen is for setting the date and time. Check that the correct *Time Zone* has been identified, otherwise change it using the dropdown. Select the **Synchronize with an Internet time server automatically** option and click the **Test** button; after a few seconds the correct time should be picked up. It is recommended to use an NTP (time) server, as accurate time keeping is required for cloud and synchronization services to work correctly. Click **Next**:

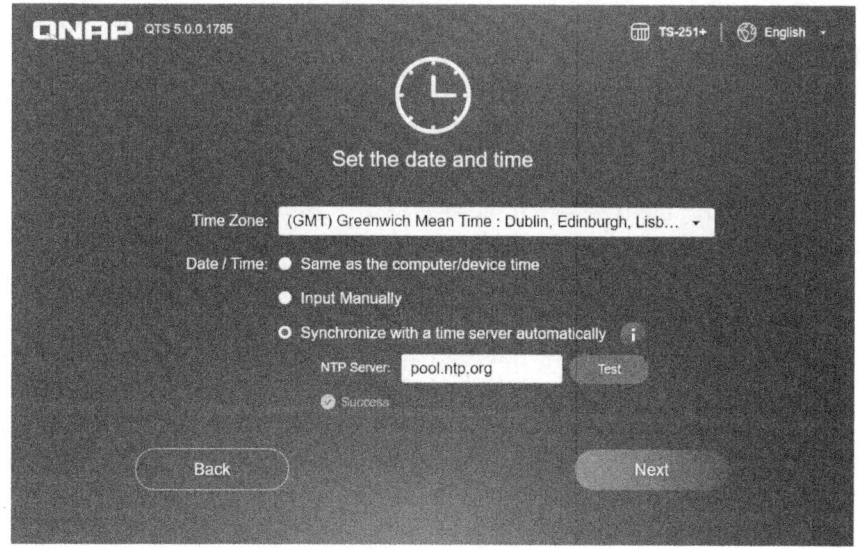

Figure 8: Date and time settings

The next screen is for configuring the network settings. If you understand about IP addresses, you can skip the next four paragraphs and continue with the one that begins 'Click the Use static IP address option...'

Every device within a network is represented by a unique number, known as the *IP address*. This consists of four sets of three digits, separated by periods, ranging from 000.000.000.000 through to 255.255.255.255. Most of these IP addresses are reserved for websites and other internet applications, although they are not generally used in a direct manner thanks to the Domain Naming System or DNS, which removes the need to memorize them (for instance, it is easier to remember *google.com* rather than 216.58.210.238). These addresses are known as *public IP addresses*. However, a limited set of numbers are not routable over the internet, making them 'invisible' to it, and these private IP addresses are used within local area networks. The sequences which must be used are 10.0.0.0 to 10.255.255.255, 172.16.0.0 to 172.31.255.255 and 192.168.0.0 to 192.168.255.255. As these addresses are isolated, they can safely be used by anyone without risk of duplication and the same numbers are used worldwide in millions of separate networks.

Much of the equipment intended for use in small businesses and homes tends to assume a 192.168.nnn.nnn numbering scheme; for instance, internet routers commonly have addresses such as 192.168.1.1 or 192.168.0.254 or similar pre-defined, depending on the brand. However, devices such as computers, printers and NAS boxes do not come with pre-defined IP addresses; instead, they need to be configured with a suitable address and there are two ways of doing so: you can use *static IP addresses* or *dynamic IP addresses*.

With static IP addresses, it is necessary to visit each device and individually configure it. For instance, you might set the first computer to *192.168.1.101*, the second to *192.168.1.102*, the third to *192.168.1.103* and so on. You have to be careful to keep track of everything and above all make sure there are no duplicates. If this sounds like hard work then that's because it is – you might get away with it if there are only a handful of devices, but beyond that it rapidly becomes unmanageable. With dynamic IP addresses, the numbers are assigned automatically by a DHCP (*Dynamic Host Configuration Protocol*) server and it keeps track of everything.

This is not usually a separate device or physical server (although it could be in a large network) and most all-in-one routers of the sort used in small businesses and homes have DHCP server software built in. During the installation of QTS, the server will have received a dynamic IP address from the router's DHCP server. Although dynamic IP is more practical for devices such as computers and tablets and smartphones, NAS boxes work better with fixed or static addresses so we need to assign one.

Click the **Use static IP address** option. If the NAS has more than one **Interface** (Ethernet adaptor), use the first one. The IP address of the router is listed as the **Default Gateway** (this is simply an alternative name for it), and you should specify an **IP Address** that is close to that of the router. In this example, the **Default Gateway** (router) is on 192.168.1.1, so we have chosen an adjacent **IP Address** of 192.168.1.2 for the NAS. The **Subnet Mask** is invariably 255.255.255.0. The **Primary DNS Server** should be 127.0.1.1, or the address of the router. The **Secondary DNS Server** can be ignored, but by default will be 8.8.8.8 and which is Google's DNS server, although you could set it to something different if you wanted. Click **Next** to continue.

Note: if the address of the Default Gateway has not been picked up automatically e.g. it is listed as 0.0.0.0, you cannot proceed and will need to refer to the router manufacturer's documentation to determine what it is.

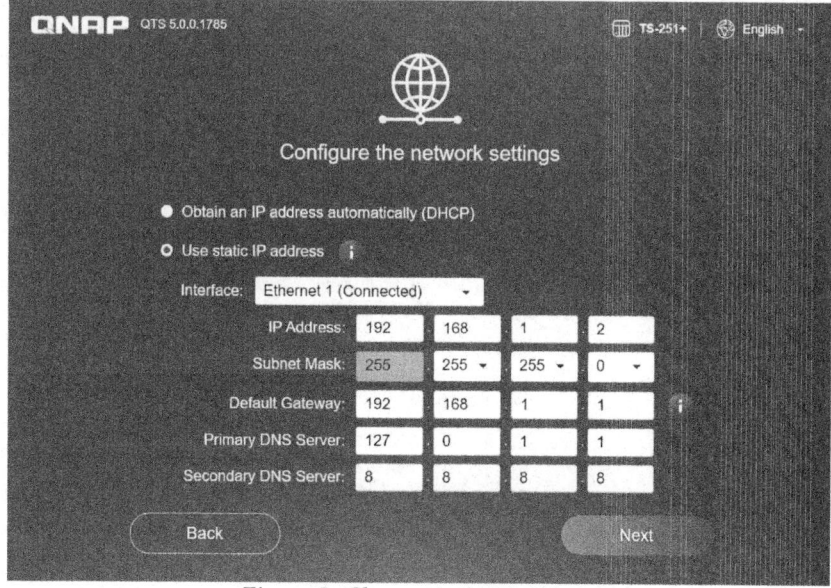

Figure 9: Choose static IP address

33

A *Summary* screen is then displayed; click **Apply** to continue, then click the **Initialize** button on the warning message about clearing all drive data. Installation, which typically takes around 10-15 minutes, will now proceed and whilst it does so a status screen is displayed.

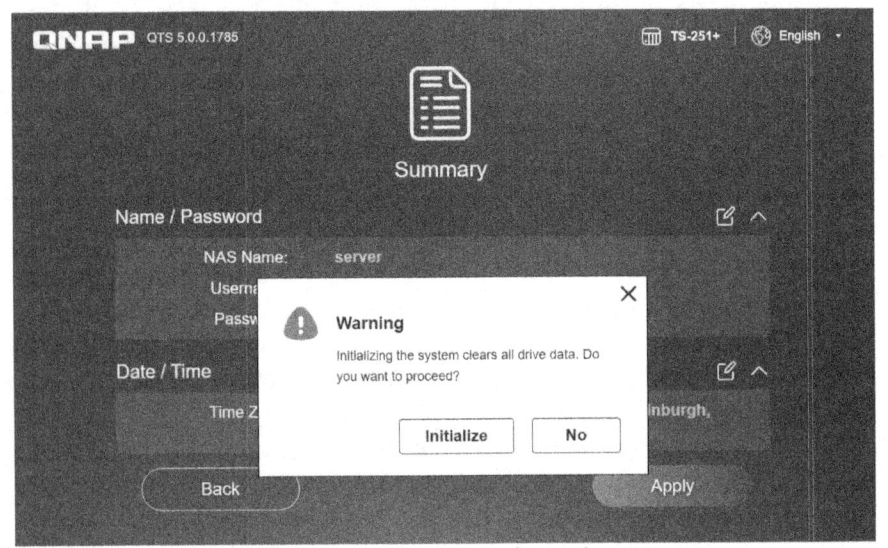

Figure 10: Summary screen and warning message

Upon completion, you should be presented with the standard QTS logon screen. However, if you chose not to register or enter a valid QNAP ID at the start of the installation screen you will receive an error screen, but this is not a problem. Either way, continue with the **2.3 Five Minute Tour of QTS** below.

2.3 Five Minute Tour of QTS

If the login screen is not being displayed, enter *https://server* in the address bar of the browser (assuming you called your NAS *'server'*, otherwise enter the name you specified). If it cannot be found, try entering the IP address of the server instead e.g. *https://192.168.1.2*. If the browser generates a message stating that there is a security risk (you might see this with Firefox), then it is misleading and can be ignored. If the browser states that the site is 'forbidden', then you have most likely typed *http* rather than https. Enter the administrative user name along with the password you defined earlier.

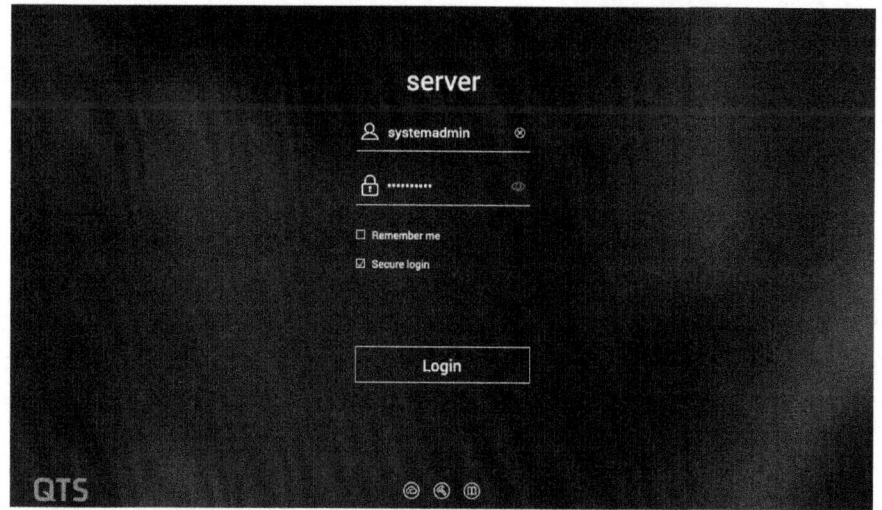

Figure 11: QTS Login screen

The initial logon is intrusive, with several panels and pop-ups. A statement about *Data & Privacy* is shown – work through and accept it. There is a quick tour of the screen – click repeatedly until it closes. There is a *Data Collection Agreement* whereby you agree to share anonymous data with QNAP and its business partners – reply Yes or No depending on how you view such matters.

A screen to configure *Storage & Snapshots* is displayed, close it by clicking on the cross in its top right-hand corner; it is important and you cannot do anything useful with the NAS until storage has been configured, but we will return to it shortly.

The main QTS screen will now be visible. It is easy to use and slightly reminiscent of an iPad or other tablet. There is the *Desktop*, which can be customized e.g. the background wallpaper can be changed. There are multiple icons on the Desktop, the selection of which can vary slightly depending upon the model. Some of these are for running system functions and some are for running applications. The icons can be distributed over multiple screens if there are too many to fit on a single screen. After installation, QTS may automatically download and install additional icons, such as the one for *Malware Remover*.

In the bottom left-hand corner is a trash can, which holds deleted files. At the top of the screen is a menu bar and task bar that provides searching, various options, controls, status information and notifications. On some models, there is also a volume control. Clicking the top left-hand corner of the screen will temporarily hide any items on the desktop.

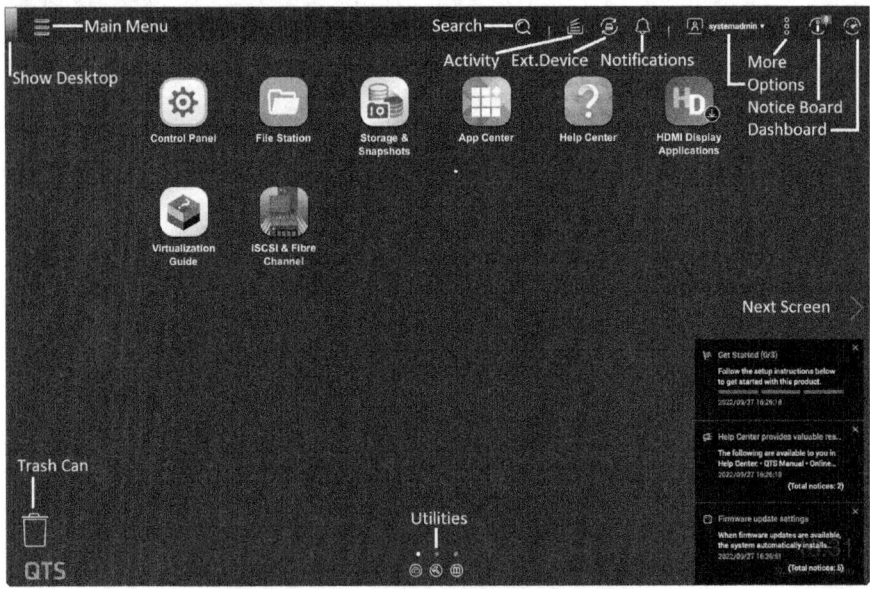

Figure 12: Overview of the QTS Desktop

The *Main Menu* provides access to important programs. When clicked it expands down the left-hand side of the screen, displaying all icons. These icons are clicked to run the underlying programs and duplicate some that are already on the Desktop, for example *Control Panel*, *File Station* and *App Center*. Depending on your QNAP model there may be some minor differences in the selection:

Figure 13: Main Menu

The *Control Panel* provides options to setup and customize the server, organized into four groups: *System, Privilege, Network & File Services* and *Applications*. As with the Main Menu, there may be some minor differences, depending on your QNAP model e.g. the HDMI Display Applications icon is only present if the NAS has a HDMI port.

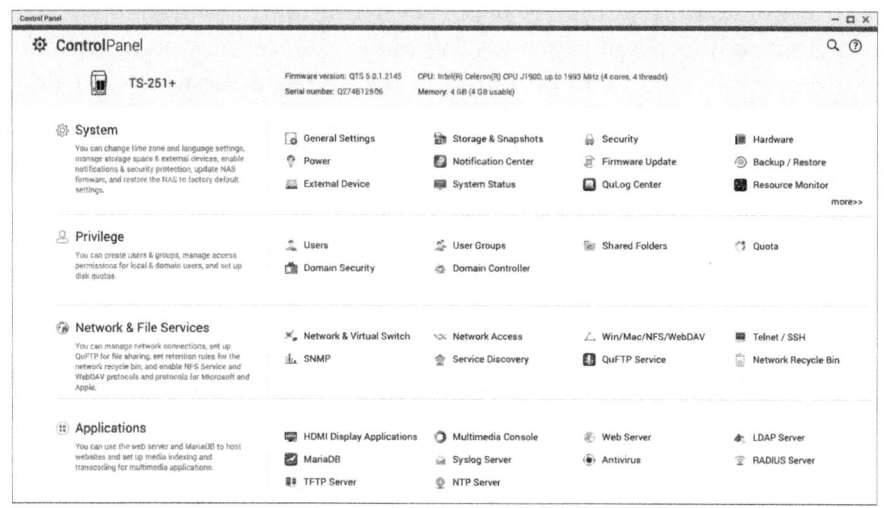

Figure 14: Control Panel

37

When an icon is clicked, the Control Panel view changes, with the main groups listed as a column, all icons for the highlighted group listed in a second column, and with the specifics for the option displayed in the main part of the screen, sometimes organized into tabs. In some instances, clicking an icon causes a separate app to run. Most apps and features run in resizable windows on the Desktop, although some open in a new browser tab.

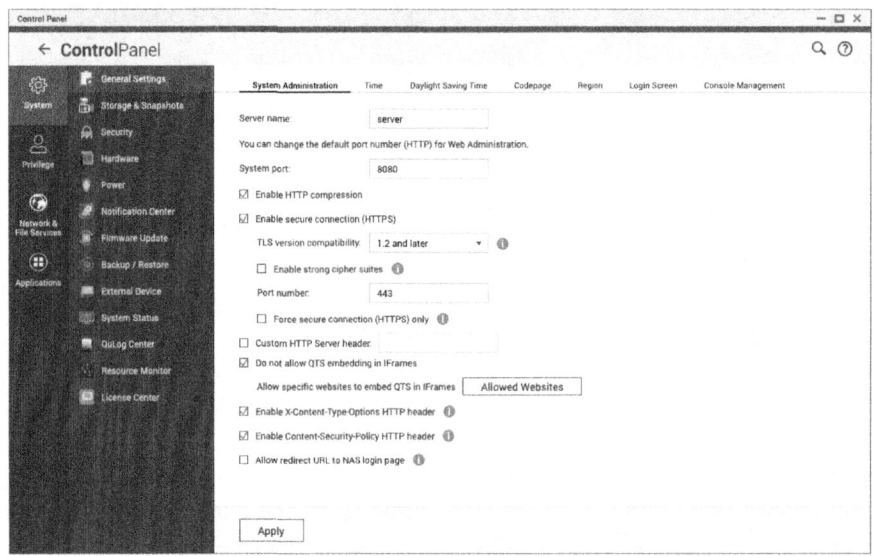

Figure 15: Control Panel, expanded view (General Settings)

Returning to the Desktop, *File Station* displays the contents of the disk volumes and folders and is used for manipulating files, similar in principle to File Explorer on a Windows PC or Finder on a Mac (further information can be found in **5.2 Using a Browser and File Station**). The *App Center* icon provides access to a portal ('app store') from where applications can be downloaded to provide additional functionality. Both of these features are covered later on in this guide.

In the top right-hand corner of the screen is an icon that looks like a small dial or speedometer and which, when clicked, shows the *Dashboard*. The Dashboard provides an 'at a glance' overview of the health and status of the server. The Dashboard is made up of several smaller panels; these panels can be dragged temporarily onto the Desktop on an individual basis if desired or clicked to launch a corresponding utility. To put the Dashboard away, click the icon for a second time:

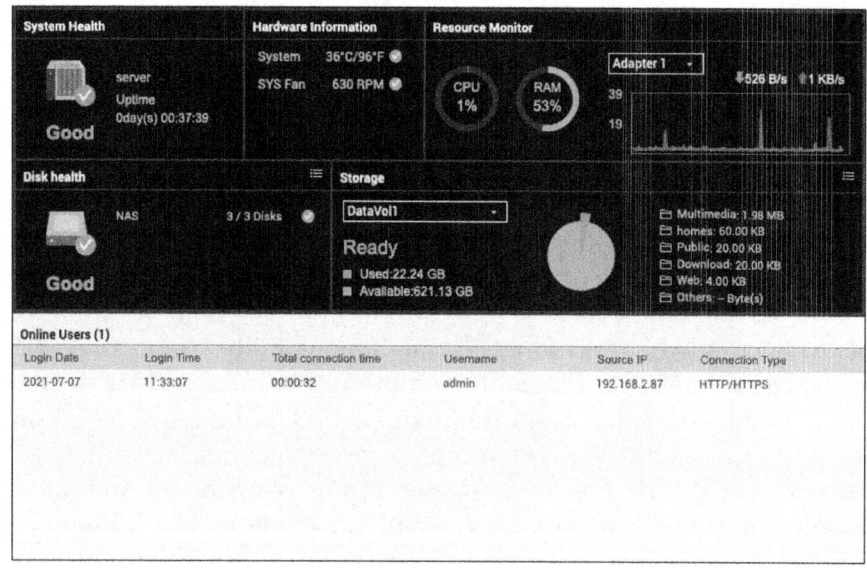

Figure 16: Dashboard

To the immediate left of the Dashboard icon is the *Notice Board*. This is a slide-out panel which displays system notifications. In some instances, individual notifications can be expanded to display further information. Recent notifications also appear at the bottom of the screen in the right-hand corner. Following a new installation of QTS, the Notice Board will display a set of steps to follow to configure the system. These can be worked through, although are only a small subset of what needs to be done (hence the need for this manual). One of the notices which will continue to 'nag' is to 'Enable 2-step verification to add an extra layer of protection for your account'. However, this is optional and how to do so is described later in section **6.11 2-Step Verification**.

The remainder of the top line of the main QTS screen provides status information, such as background tasks and any external drives that are connected. There are some configuration options, mainly concerned with the current user rather than the system as a whole. You can also logout, restart and shutdown the system from here (provided you have administrative rights, standard users cannot do so). Normally, a NAS is left running 24x7, but can be scheduled to shut down automatically out-of-hours and how to do so is described later in this chapter. At the bottom of the screen are several small icons which act as useful links to downloadable resources, including utilities and mobile applications.

2.4 Setting up Storage

During the installation of QTS the hard drives in the NAS will have been formatted, but they still need to be configured before they are ready for use. Before continuing, it is necessary to appreciate that QNAP NAS units are designed to cater for a vast range of users and requirements. Some people may have a device at home with a single hard drive; a small business may have a server with multiple drives; a large business may have several dozen servers, with huge amounts of storage and the need to ensure high availability. Somehow, QTS must cater for these disparate requirements in a consistent and understandable manner and it has succeeded, although some of the methods may seem over-complicated for people who just want to 'get on with it'. Whilst the focus in this guide is on home and small business systems, corporate users will hopefully be able to gain an appreciation of some of the extensive storage capabilities of QTS.

The key concepts are that the hard drives in a system constitute a *storage pool*, upon which one or more *volumes* can be created, and that these volumes can be configured into *RAID groups*, whereby multiple drives are used to provide redundancy and improve performance (further information can be found in section **12.2 RAID**). Most aspects of storage are managed through the *Storage & Snapshots* app, which can be started from the Main Menu or Control Panel. The first time it is run, a quick tour is displayed, else it can be viewed subsequently by clicking on the magic wand icon in the top right-hand corner of the panel.

Click on **Storage** within the **Overview** section of the app to display this screen, although some details will vary depending on your system. In this example we have a fresh installation of QTS, currently with two unconfigured drives. Drives are indicated at the topic of the screen, with round icons indicating conventional mechanical hard drives (HDD), square icons indicating solid state drives (SSD) and hexagon icons showing any drive adapters.

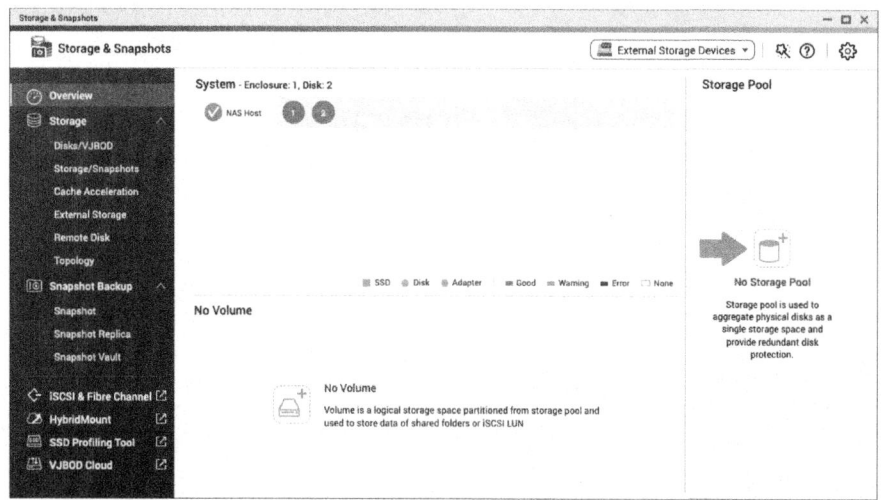

Figure 17: Storage & Snapshots

There are several sections, listed down the left-hand side of the screen: *Overview*, which gives an 'at a glance' summary of the setup; *Storage*, used for configuring drives and volumes and managing any SSD caches; *Snapshot Backup*, which generates space-efficient backups 'on the fly'; *iSCSI & Fibre Channel*, which launches a separate app for creating virtual or remote disks; *HybridMount*, a separate app which integrates public cloud services with the server, plus *SSD Profiling Tool* and *VJBOD Cloud* (some of these options are not loaded by default and initially these are only links to the App Center, from where they are downloaded). Snapshots, iSCSI and HybridMount are more advanced facilities and are covered in section **12 STORAGE**. Whilst available on all current models, Snapshots may not be available on some older systems.

The first thing to do is create a storage pool. In the right-hand panel, marked *Storage Pool*, click the icon of a disk (indicated by an arrow in the above screenshot). Or, you can click **Storage/Snapshots** in the *Storage* section, followed by the **New Storage Pool** button. The *Create Storage Pool Wizard* will launch. You would not normally tick the *Enable Qtier* box, which is a more advanced feature, not commonly used in a home or small business setting (it is overviewed in **12.8 What is Qtier?**). Click **Next** to begin.

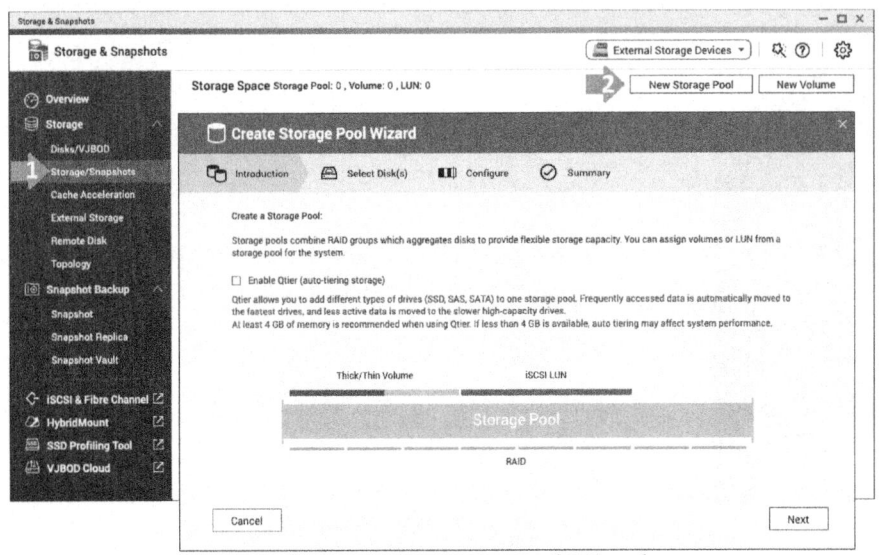

Figure 18: Create Storage Pool Wizard

On the subsequent screen, select the disk(s) to be used in the Storage Pool and choose the RAID level e.g. RAID 1, RAID 5 etc - any options which are unavailable will be grayed out. If the server has three or more drives, you can designate one disk as a *Hot Spare* – a spare drive on standby that can quickly be used to replace a failed drive. If self-encrypting drives are being used, although this is uncommon in a home or small business, a SED secure storage pool can be created, otherwise do not tick this option. In this example, three hard drives will be used for a storage pool with RAID 5 protection:

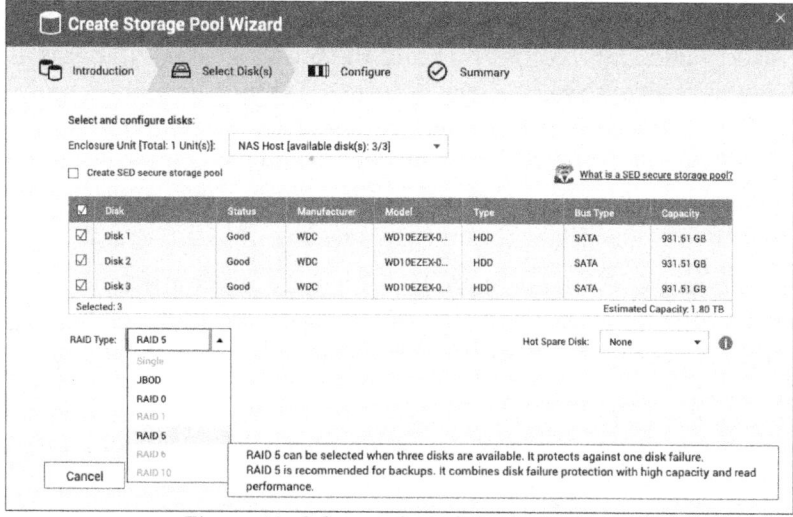

Figure 19: Select and configure the drives

A configuration screen with some additional options is displayed. You may want to remove the tick from the **Alert Threshold** box, as this can result in confusing/misleading notifications about how much storage space is available. The **Enable Pool Guaranteed Snapshot Space** option reserves space for snapshots; this is a mechanism for 'on-the-fly' backups and is described more thoroughly in section **12.4 Snapshots**. A value between 5%-20% can be selected using the dropdown. Click **Next** to reach a summary screen, where you click **Create** to proceed. Note that you will always lose some disk space due to storage and system overheads, described as *Estimated Reserved Space*:

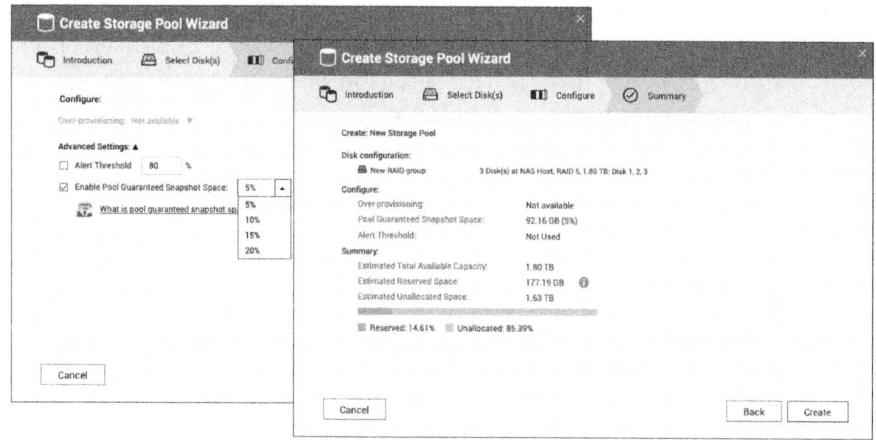

Figure 20: Summary Screen

43

There will be a warning message that existing data on the disks will be erased – click **OK** to continue and the Storage Pool will be created, which will typically take several minutes. When complete, a message is displayed, advising that a *Volume* now must be created, so click the **New Volume** button and the *Volume Creation Wizard* will run. The first decision is to choose the type of volume and there are three possibilities:

Thin volumes ('On-demand space') - which are most efficient at using space, as they allocate it on demand, rather than by reserving space up-front as the other two options do. They also support *Snapshots*.

Thick volumes ('Preconfigured space') - which have greater flexibility and performance, and also support *Snapshots* on suitable NAS models.

Static volumes ('Traditional configuration') - which offer the best performance and are the most straightforward. They can be thought of as 'normal' disk volumes, analogous to what you would have on a PC or Mac.

The Wizard defaults to Thin volumes. In general, this is the most flexible type, and of particular benefit in larger environments, but also requires the most management. However, if you are a typical home or small business user, Thick volumes may prove more suitable. Static volumes are also a good option, especially on smaller systems or where maximum performance is required, and provided that more advanced features such as Snapshots or LUNs are not required (Static volumes can only exist on RAID groups, so are not an option for single-drive systems). Unable to decide? Choose Thick volumes. If the NAS has more than one storage pool, specify its *Location* using the dropdown. Click **Next**:

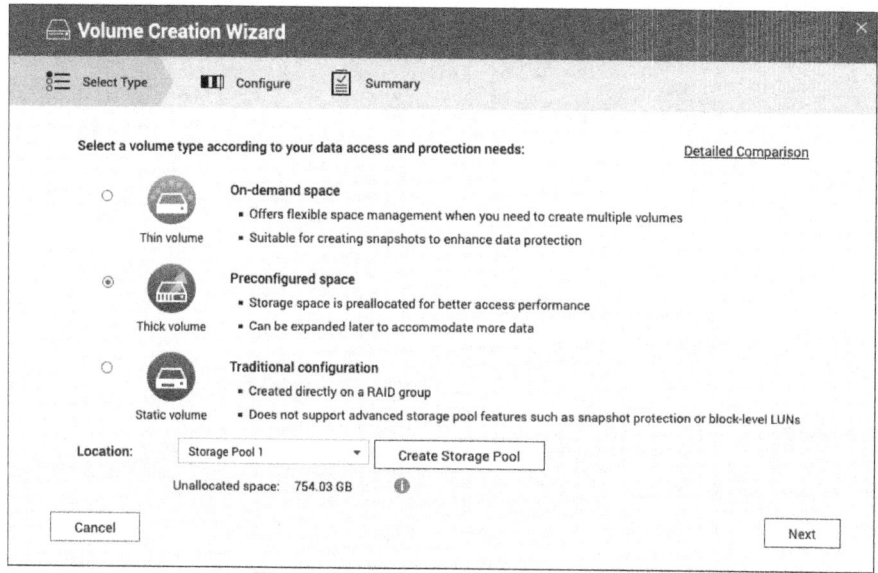

Figure 21: Volume Creation Wizard

The contents of the next screen depend on what volume type you selected. If you chose the Thick volume option, it will be as shown below. You need to decide the capacity of the volume i.e. how much of the Storage Pool is allocated for normal data storage. The suggested default value may be too low, causing you to quickly run out of space. You could choose *Set to Max* i.e. use all of it, but this may have some untoward implications. Instead, manually choose a value that is around three-quarters of the maximum available. In this example, our Storage Pool capacity is 754 GB, so we have chosen to set the volume capacity at 560 GB. The assumption is that encryption is not being used; if you wish to encrypt the volume it needs to be done now, as it cannot be done retrospectively. Click **Advanced Settings** to expand the panel. Check that the **Alert threshold** box is still unticked. The File system option does not need to be changed unless you have specific requirements. Click **Next**.

45

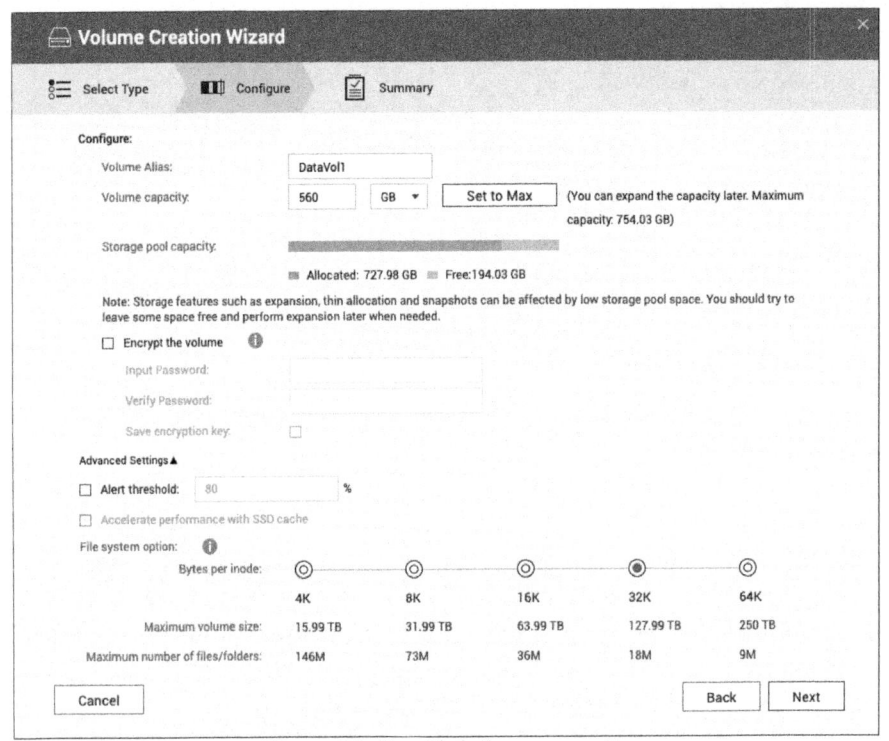

Figure 22: Specify volume capacity

A Summary screen is displayed - click **Finish** and the volume will be created. The time taken for this depends on the size and type of the storage pool, but may range from a few minutes to several hours. Once the system recognizes that it has usable storage space, it will create some default folders automatically and download several supporting apps (this only occurs when the first storage pool that is created). Upon completion, returning to the Overview section will show that it has been updated and it is from here that the status and space utilization can subsequently be monitored.

Figure 23: Overview of newly configured Storage

2.5 Network Services

Network Services refers to the means or *protocols* by which QTS provides access to files and folders for different types of client devices. These clients can be Windows PCs, Macs, or Linux machines and other Unix variants. Other devices, such as tablets and smartphones, may be able to access files on the server if they understand the underlying protocols associated with these computer types or are equipped with suitable apps.

By default, QTS assumes that you will be using Windows PCs and Macs and it is not usually necessary to change any of the settings in Network Services. So, most people reading this can simply skip to the next section. However, if any of the following conditions apply, then you may need to make changes: the Windows workgroup is not actually called *Workgroup*; you want to backup Macs to the server using Time Machine; you need to make a shared printer available to Mac clients; older Macs are being used (pre-macOS 10.9); you wish to use Linux or other Unix-based computers in a manner which uses features specific to those operating systems. In such cases, launch **Control Panel** and click the **Win/Mac/NFS/WebDAV** icon under **Network & File Services**. There are four tabs: *Microsoft Networking, Apple Networking, NFS Service* and *WebDAV*:

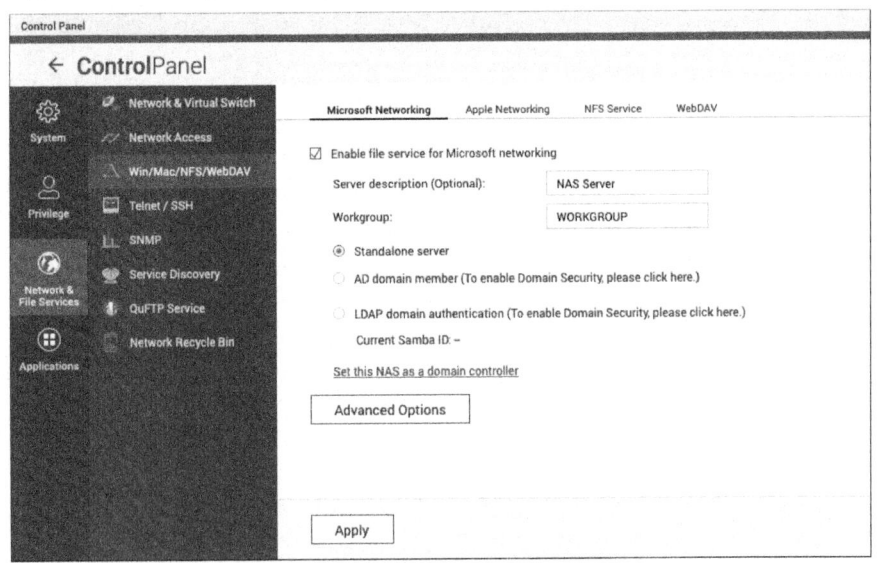

Figure 24: Network file services

Windows Computers

If your workgroup is not called *Workgroup*, although it usually is, change the name of the **Workgroup** to match that of your computers on the **Microsoft Networking** tab. Optionally, a *Server description* can be specified. Having made any changes, click the **Apply** button.

There are some further options. These are not typically used in a home or small business setting but allow a QNAP server to be configured for working in an Active Directory environment, as a client or as a domain controller. The **Advanced Options** button is for configuring WINS and changing the SMB version. These features may be applicable where the server is being used in conjunction with or as an alternative to a Windows Server environment.

Macs

Historically, Apple computers used a network protocol called AFP (*Apple Filing Protocol*) whilst Windows computers used SMB (Server Message Block), but eventually Macs switched to SMB for their default network protocol, too. Although you can operate without AFP support, it is suggested that you keep the AFP service enabled, and you will certainly need it if you are still using versions of macOS prior to 10.9 (Mavericks). It can be checked/enabled by ticking the **Enable AFP (Apple Filing Protocol)** box on the **Apple Networking** tab. If you are using macOS 10.7 or later, you need to make sure the **DHX2 authentication support** box is ticked. Having made any changes, click the **Apply** button.

Linux/Unix Computers

Most Linux/Unix distributions include the ability to connect to SMB-based systems, such as QTS. Unless you have a specific need, you may find it easier to use SMB, in which case you do not need to do anything additional. However, if you use Linux or other Unix-type variant computers in an 'advanced' manner – defined here as using the NFS protocol – you will need to enable NFS on the server. On the **NFS Service** tab, tick the **Enable NFS v2/v3 Service** and **Enable NFS v4** Service boxes. There are further options and advanced settings, which may be of interest to experienced Linux/Unix administrators. Having made any changes, click the **Apply** button.

2.6 Hardware & Power Options

QNAP units have several power management options, some of which are concerned with energy saving and can be used to reduce power consumption and potentially save energy costs. The options available depend on the model, so there can be minor variations in these screens.

Disk Standby Mode

The disk(s) can be configured to go into standby mode after a set period. This saves energy but will result in a short delay when somebody next accesses the server, typically in the order of about 15-30 seconds while the disks spin up again, unless you are using SSDs – *Solid State Drives* – which have no spin time and are instantly available. To control this feature, go to **Control Panel** and click on **Hardware**, then click the **General** tab. Make sure the box marked **Enables hard disk standby mode** is ticked. Underneath it the standby time can be selected from the drop-down; if the server is used infrequently it can be set to a short interval (e.g. 5 minutes), but if it is constantly in use then a higher value (e.g. 30 minutes or an hour) might be more suitable. Choose a value and click **Apply All**.

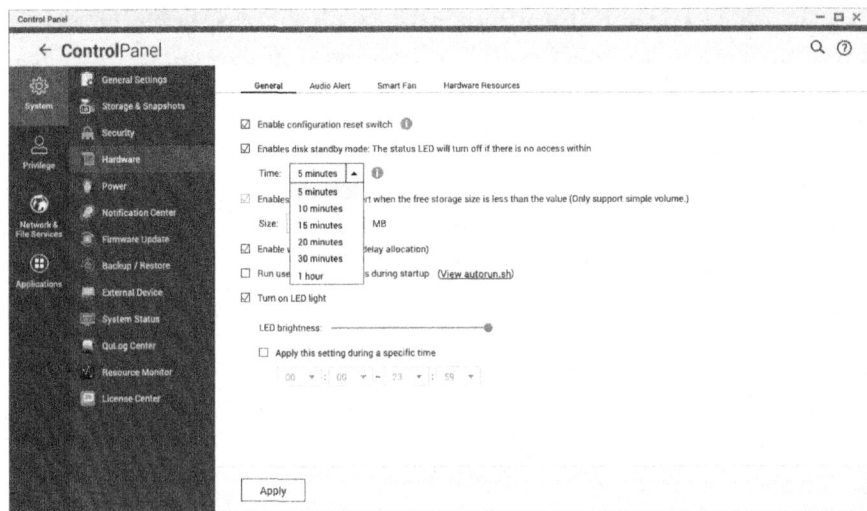

Figure 25: Settings for hard disk standby mode

Controlling the LED Lights

On some models it is possible to set the brightness of the LED indicators on the unit, using the slider on the **General** tab within **Control Panel > Hardware**, which is located underneath the hard disk standby option described above on supported models. This can reduce power consumption, plus reduce distraction if the server is in a bedroom or next to a television set. A schedule can be defined so this happens at a particular time e.g. overnight, by clicking the **Apply this setting during a specific time** box and using the dropdowns to specify the start and end times. Having made any changes, click **Apply**.

Audio Alert

When a serious error occurs on the NAS – such as a disk problem – and when the system starts up and shuts down, it will make a bleeping noise. If required, this can be switched off. Additionally, a small number of models have a built-in loudspeaker and can announce system events in English or Chinese, controllable from the **Audio Alert** tab. Having made any changes, click **Apply**.

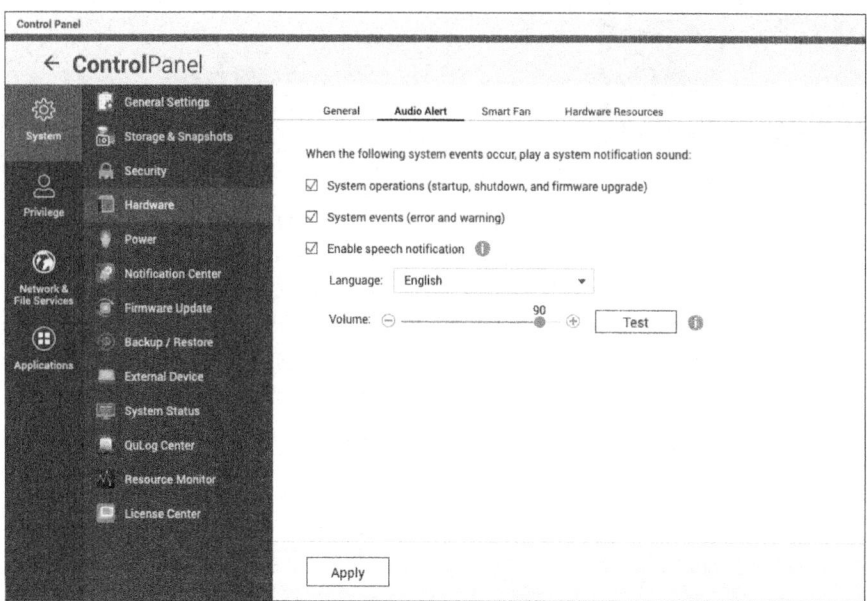

Figure 26: Settings for Audio Alerts

Smart Fan

Most QNAP models have fans in them to keep them running cool and the settings can be adjusted to reduce noise levels and/or cope with warmer environments. To adjust, go to **Control Panel** and click on **Hardware** within the **System** section, followed by the **Smart Fan** tab:

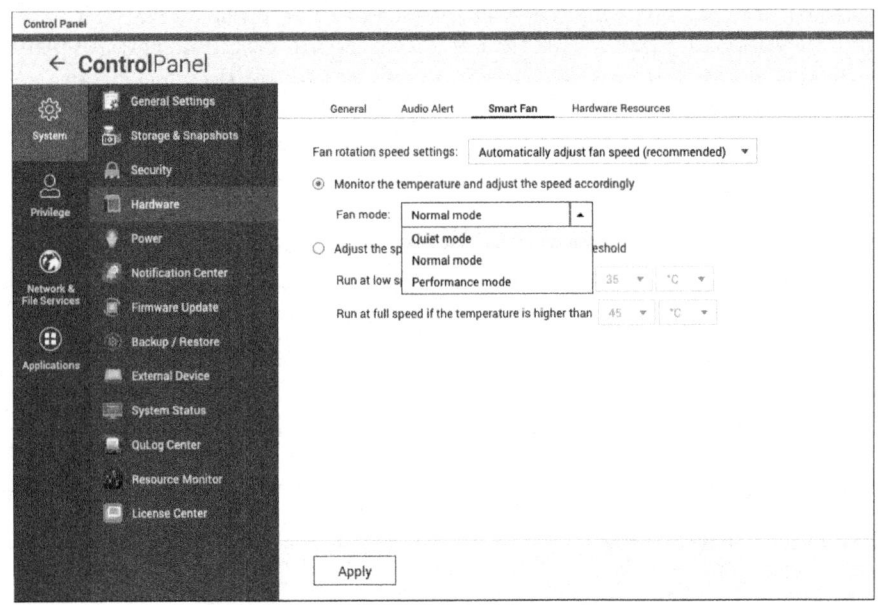

Figure 27: Settings for Smart Fan

The default settings are for the *Fan rotation speed settings* set to **Automatically adjust fan speed (recommended)** and *Monitor the temperature and adjust the speed accordingly* with a *Fan mode* of **Normal**. The latter is controlled using a dropdown; in a domestic environment you might wish to have the fan on *Quiet mode* to minimize noise, whereas in a warm office during the Summer you might want the *Performance mode*. Another option is to *Adjust the speed according to the temperature threshold*.

After making any changes, click the **Apply** button.

Hardware Resources

Some QNAP models can take expansion cards to increase storage or improve performance. The settings for any such cards can be managed from the **Hardware Resources** tab.

Power Schedule

Unlike desktop and laptops, NAS boxes are usually left running continuously. However, the server can be scheduled to power itself on and off automatically and doing so can save on energy costs and possibly enhance security (as security problems cannot occur when the server is switched off). If this is done, then it is important to arrange that the NAS will not be powered down when an activity such as backup or an anti-virus scan is scheduled to take place.

To create a schedule, go to the **Control Panel** and click the **Power** icon in the **System** section, followed by the **Power Schedule** tab. Tick the **Enable schedule** and **Postpone the restart/shutdown schedule when a replication job is in progress boxes.** Click the **Add** button and an initial 'Shutdown' event will appear. The events are listed in a table format and by clicking on the individual part of the entry the parameters can be changed i.e. the action, schedule type and times. If you are going to use this facility, you want to create events to both turn on and shutdown the server. Having defined the events click the **Apply** button. In this example, the server is being scheduled to turn on at 7:00am/0700 every day and shutdown at 11:00pm/2300 hours.

Suggestion: a server typically takes several minutes to startup, possibly much longer if you have many apps installed. If, for example, you wanted to be able to use it starting at 7:00am, you might want to schedule it to turn on 10 minutes before that time.

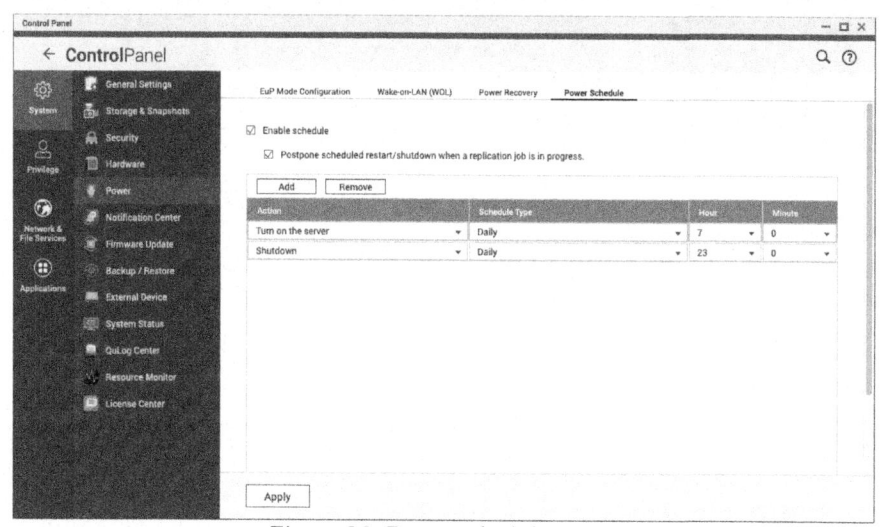

Figure 28: Power schedule screen

Uninterruptible Power Supply

The use of an Uninterruptible Power Supply (UPS) is advisable, particularly in a business environment or if you live in a part of the world where there may be electrical outages or brownouts.

There are several ways of connecting the UPS, but the most common method in a small business or domestic environment is with USB so we will assume that. Connect the cable from the UPS to one of the USB sockets on the server. Wait one minute for it to be recognized then go into the **Control Panel** and click the **External Device** tab. Choose the **USB Connection** option. There is a choice as to what happens when power is lost, but the default value of shutting down after 5 minutes will be suitable in many circumstances. Click the **Apply** button.

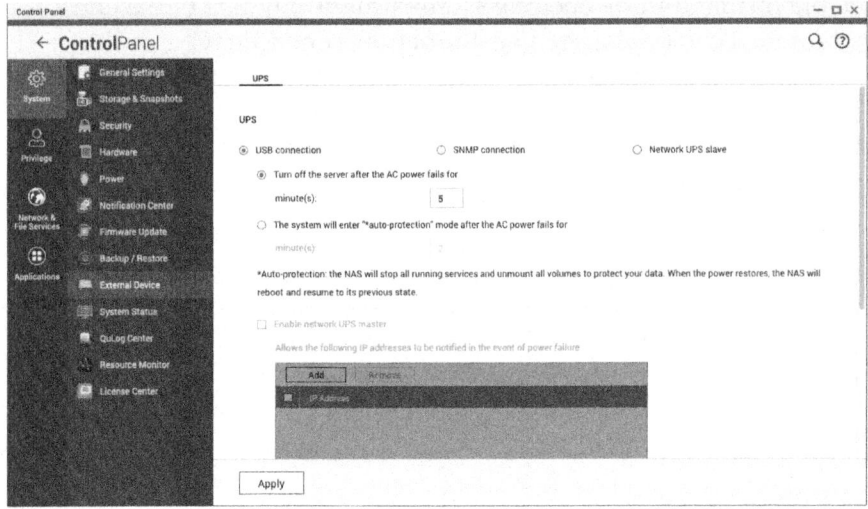

Figure 29: UPS Support

2.7 Other Installation Options

The installation method described earlier in this chapter is the easiest and preferred technique for installing the QTS firmware and is recommended in most cases. However, there are two other methods for installing QTS:

Qfinder Pro Installation – this method can be used in situations where the NAS is not currently connected to the internet, enabling the installation to take place offline provided the QTS software has previously been downloaded. It can also be used in some rare situations where the standard installation method does not work.

Local Installation – some QNAP models feature a HDMI output for connecting them to suitable-equipped computer screens or televisions. If so, you can install QTS by using the QNAP Infra-Red remote-control handset or a USB keyboard (with optional mouse). QNAP refers to this as a *Local Installation*. However, this installation is only partial and most of the configuration work still must be performed using a browser as described in this chapter. For this reason, it offers no advantage and hence is not described here.

Qfinder Pro Installation Option

This requires that the *Qfinder Pro* utility program and a copy of the QTS firmware are downloaded onto the installation computer. If the computer does not have an internet connection, it can be done elsewhere and then transferred across using, say, a USB memory stick/thumb drive.

Go to the QNAP website, **www.qnap.com** and click **Support** followed by **Download Center**. Using the three dropdowns of *Product Type, Bay* and *Model,* select your NAS. Unlike Windows or macOS, where a single version of the operating system runs on all computers, QTS is finely optimized for each QNAP model and you need the correct version. The latest release is at the top of the listing within the *Operating System* section – click on the appropriate download link for your location (USA, Europe, or Global for anywhere else).

When the download of QTS is complete, click the *Utility* section and download the *Qfinder Pro* software, which is available in Windows, Mac and Linux (Ubuntu 32-bit and 64-bit) formats. Install and run it on your computer; if you receive a message from the computer's firewall, allow access for the *Qfinder Pro* software. After a few seconds it should find the NAS:

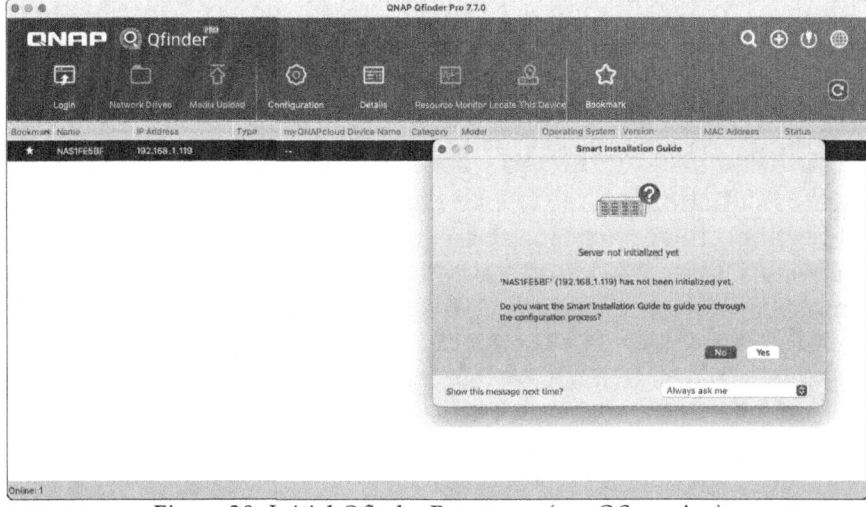

Figure 30: Initial Qfinder Pro screen (macOS version)

Click **Yes** to the message 'Server not initialized yet' and your internet browser will launch. You may initially receive a panel asking you to check your warranty - this is basically a sales pitch and does not have to be done. Close the browser and return to Qfinder Pro. A second message, advising 'SMTP server not configured yet' may also be displayed. Click **No** to this. You will be returned to the main QNAP Qfinder Pro screen. Right-click the NAS and click **Update Firmware**. You may be prompted to login to the NAS. The first field is for the user name, which is *admin*. The second field is for the password and the default for this is the 12 numbers and letters of the MAC Address, but without the dashes. This is displayed by Qfinder Pro and can also be found on a sticker on the rear or underneath of the NAS. For example, if the MAC Address was 12-34-56-78-90-AB then the password would be 1234567890AB (the letters are always in upper case). Click **OK**.

On the resultant panel, navigate to the firmware file you loaded beforehand, select it and click **Start**.

When the firmware has been loaded, a Welcome screen is displayed by the browser. If this does not happen, right-click the server within Qfinder and choose **Login**. Click the large **Start Smart Installation** button and follow the standard instructions starting with Figure 3 in section **2.2 Installation**.

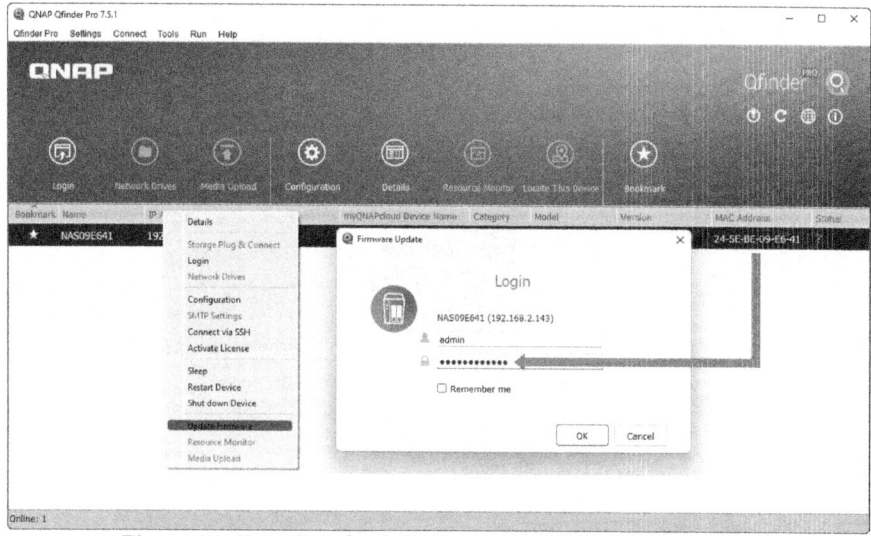

Figure 31: Entering the default password (Windows version)

3
SHARED FOLDERS

3.1 Overview

The main purpose of a local network is to provide an environment for users to store and share information. This is done by creating folders on the server, some shared and some private, then defining access rights to control who sees what. The structure of these folders will depend upon the requirements of the household or organization, but a typical arrangement might be a shared folder that everyone has access to, folders for music, photos and videos (particularly on a home system), plus individual private home folders for each user.

QTS will have already created several suitable folders when you created a disk volume in section **2.4 Setting up Storage** and in some instances these may be sufficient for your purposes. But if they are not, then it is easy to create additional ones.

The default shared folder is called *Public*. In this instance, 'public' means everyone in the household or organization, not the rest of the world. The private folders for each user are known as *home folders* and are for each user to do with as they please, as what is stored in them does not affect anybody else.

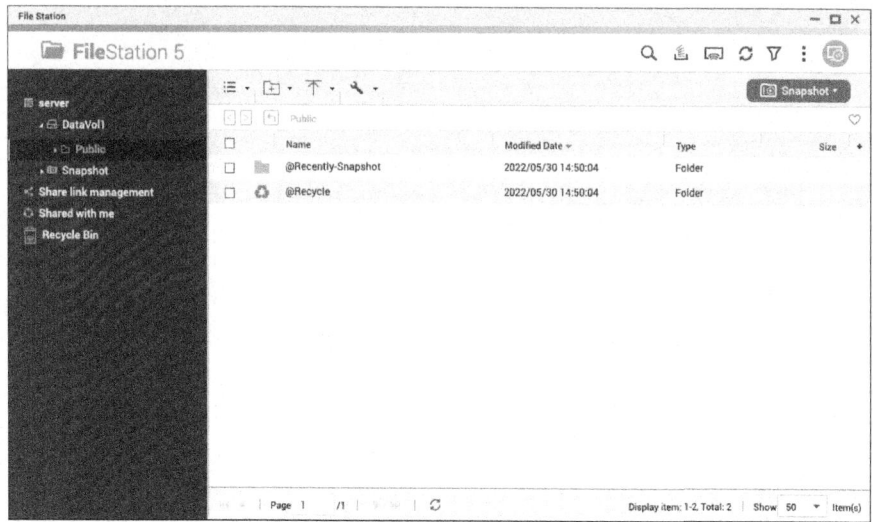

Figure 32: Default folder structure

The above screenshot shows the folder structure on a freshly installed system as viewed using *File Station*, which can be thought of as the QTS equivalent to Windows File Explorer or macOS Finder. If the NAS does not support the Snapshot mechanism, or it was not enabled during the creating of the Storage Pool, then the Snapshot folder will not be listed.

A detailed explanation of working with File Station can be found in section **5.2 Using a Browser and File Station**.

3.2 Creating a Shared Folder

To create a new shared folder, go to **Control Panel** and click **Shared Folders**. Click the **Create** button and from the dropdown choose **Shared Folder**. Specify the **Folder Name** and optionally give it a descriptive **Comment** – in this example we will create a folder called *Media* that will subsequently be used for holding photos, videos and music. If there is more than one Disk Volume in your system, choose the one you want to use from the dropdown. Do not change the *Path*. Optionally, you can choose to encrypt the folder if it is holding sensitive information. Click **Next**:

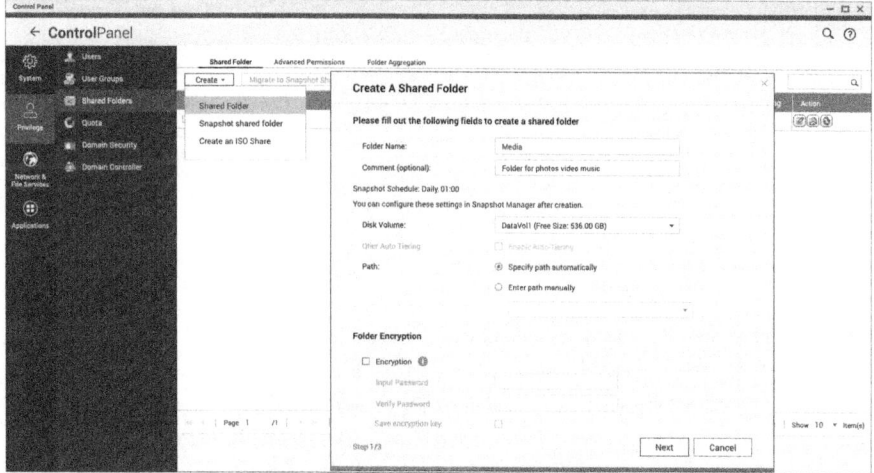

Figure 33: Creating a Shared folder

It is necessary to specify which users have access to the folder and what type of access it is. This is something of a chicken-and-egg situation as we have yet to create any users; this topic is discussed in **4 MANAGING USERS** and you may therefore wish to read that section if you are ready to create additional shared folders at this time. Against each user name, tick the box that defines what access they should have:

RO or Read Only - meaning users can access items in the folder but not update them

RW or Read Write - meaning users have full access to items in the folder and can do as they wish

Deny - meaning they have no access at all

For instance:

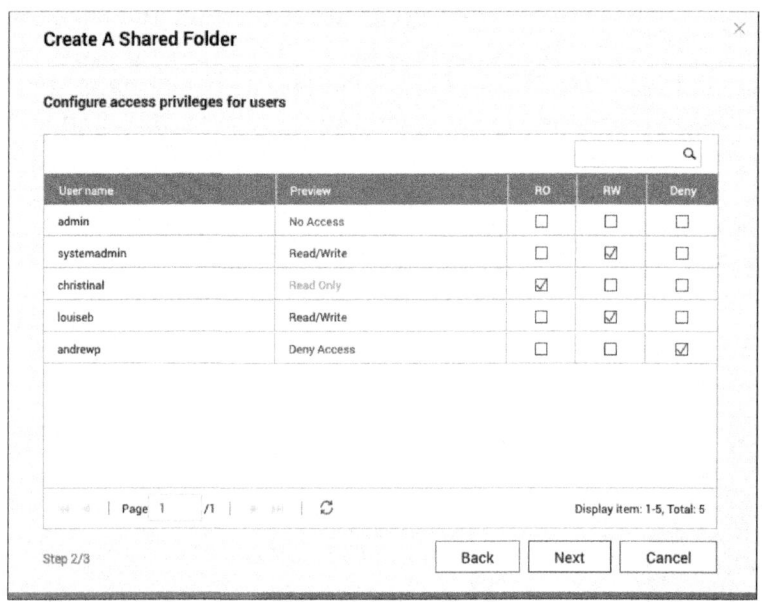

User name	Preview	RO	RW	Deny
admin	No Access	☐	☐	☐
systemadmin	Read/Write	☐	☑	☐
christinal	Read Only	☑	☐	☐
louiseb	Read/Write	☐	☑	☐
andrewp	Deny Access	☐	☐	☑

Figure 34: Creating a Shared folder – Configure access privileges

Click **Next**. There are a few items that you may want to change on the third panel. The first one relates to *Guest* access; a guest is someone who can connect to the server without having to provide a user name or password. By default, guest users should not get any access so check that the **Deny Access** option has been selected. The second setting is an option to *Hide network drive* (i.e. the shared folder) from general view; this is only a security measure in a limited sense, as anyone who knows the name of the folder can still find it. However, it does prevent the share appearing in Windows Explorer or the macOS Finder, thus reducing the amount of clutter if there are many shared folders. Ignore the *Lock File* option. The next significant option is whether the *Network Recycle Bin* is enabled for the folder. If it is, then files that been deleted, whether accidentally or intentionally, can be recovered. The folder can optionally be designated for use by Time Machine/Mac backups, although it is suggested you explore this topic separately in **7.10 Backing Up Macs**.

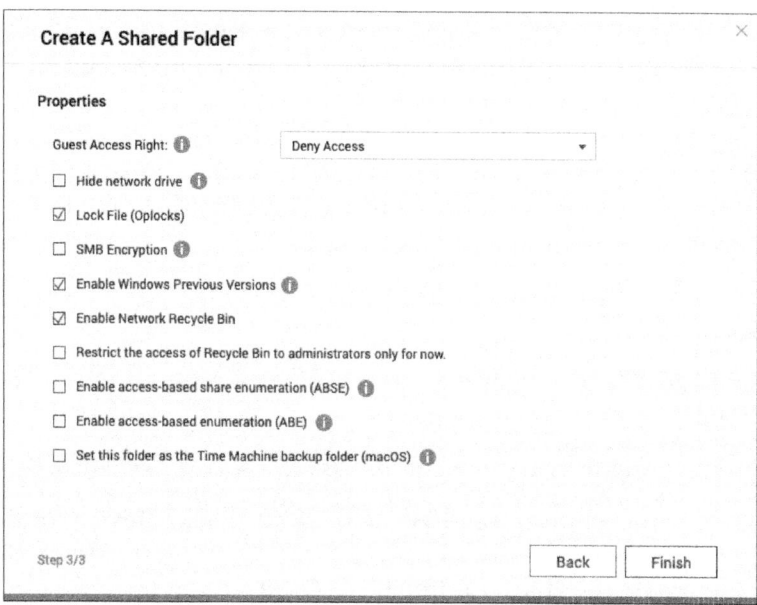

Figure 35: Creating a Shared folder – Properties

Once the settings are the way you want them, click the **Finish** button. Upon doing so a message is displayed, advising that 'Shared folders can also be configured as content source folders' i.e. for use as multimedia folders. This topic is explored in chapter **9 MULTIMEDIA & STREAMING**. As this message is not very useful, you may want to tick the **Do not show this message again** box and click **OK**. The folder will be created in a few seconds and the list of shared folders within Control Panel will be updated.

Creating a Shared Folder with Qmanager

If the Qmanager app is being used on a mobile device (see section **8.10 Using Qmanager** for an overview), shared folders can be created as follows:

Tap **Privileges Settings** from the menu in the top left-hand corner. Tap the **Shared Folders** icon at the bottom of the screen. Tap the three dot 'snowman' menu in the top right-hand corner of the screen and choose **Create A Shared Folder**. Specify the **Folder Name** and optionally give it a **Description** – in this example we will create a folder called *Media* that will subsequently be used for holding photos, videos and music. If there is more than one Disk Volume in your system, choose the one you want to use.

It is necessary to specify which users have access to the folder and what type of access. This is something of a chicken-and-egg situation as we have yet to create any users; this is discussed in **4 USERS** and you may therefore wish to read that section if you are ready to create additional shared folders at this time. Tap **Access control (By User)**. Against each user name in turn, tap the right-hand side of the screen and choose the option that defines what access they should have:

RO or Read Only - meaning users can access items in the folder but not update them

RW or Read Write - meaning users have full access to items in the folder and can do as they wish

Deny - meaning they have no access at all

In this example, choose **Read/Write** then tap **Back**. Having returned to the original screen, tap **Apply** in the right-hand corner of the screen to create the shared folder.

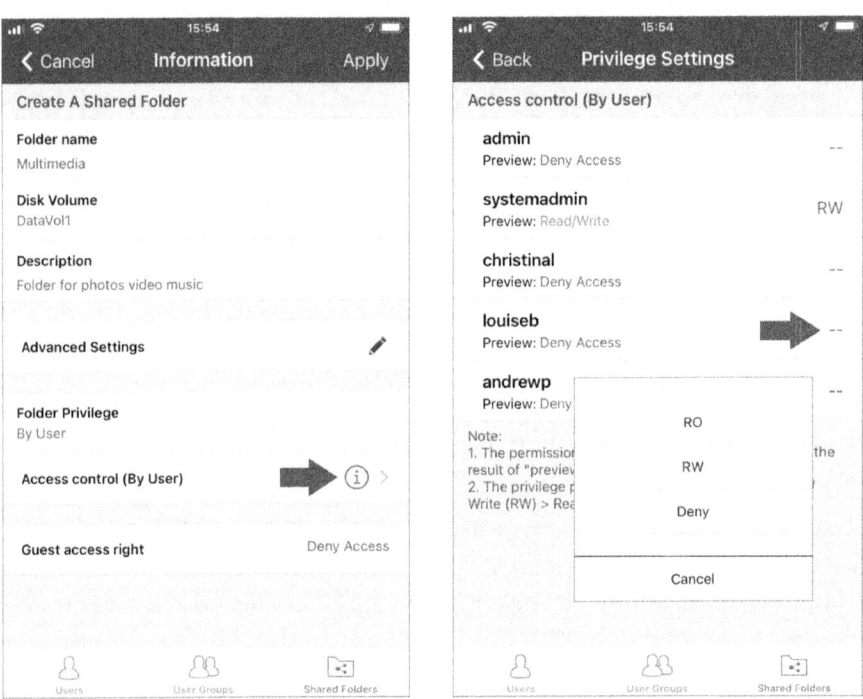

Figure 36: Creating a Shared folder with Qmanager (iOS)

3.3 Making Changes to a Shared Folder

To make changes to an existing shared folder, go to **Control Panel** and click **Shared Folders**. A list of folders is displayed; on the right-hand of the screen is an *Action* column, with three mini-icons against each folder:

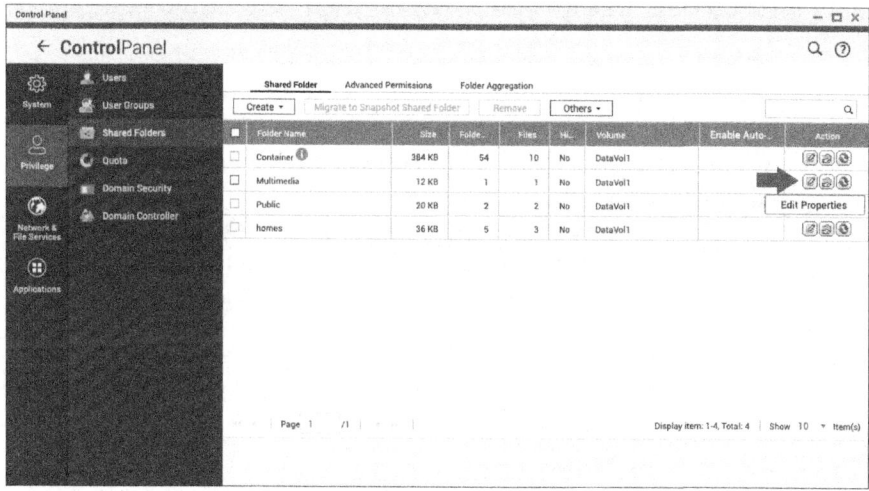

Figure 37: Changing a shared folder

The first mini icon, looking like a pencil writing on paper, is **Edit Properties**. Click it to change such elements as the *Comment* (description), whether the folder is designated a *Media Folder*, to *Enable Network Recycle Bin* etc. Having made any changes click **OK**.

The second mini icon, which looks like a hand holding a cardboard folder, is for editing the user permissions of the folder i.e. whether individuals have Read Only, Read/Write or are denied access. Having made any changes click **Apply** and **Close**. The third mini icon, looking like a recycling symbol, refreshes the screen display following any changes.

To delete a shared folder, go to **Control Panel** and click **Shared Folders**. Place a tick in the box to the left of the folder name then click the **Remove** button. Acknowledge the warning message and click **Yes**.

Note: in some instances, an App will create its own shared folder for special purposes and it might only be possible to manage and delete it from within that App. Such folders are indicated, as in the Container folder in the above screenshot. Also, most aspects of the system-generated Public folder cannot be modified.

3.4 Enabling Home Folders

Most folders on a server are shared folders, potentially for the use of everyone on the network subject to access privileges. There is also the option to have *home folders* for each user, where they can store things that nobody else needs access to, analogous to the *My Documents* or *Documents* folders that people have on their individual computers. To enable it:

Click **Control Panel** followed by **Users**. Click the **Advanced Settings** button followed by **Home Folder**. On the pop-up panel, make sure that the **Enable home folder for all users** option has been ticked. This will cause home folders to be created automatically for any users that subsequently login (the individual folders are not created prior to their first login). If the server has multiple disk volumes, the dropdown can be used to select which one will be used.

Conversely, if you did not want users to have home folders for some reason, you would remove the tick. This scenario is sometimes required in education institutions or businesses that employ temporary staff, for example.

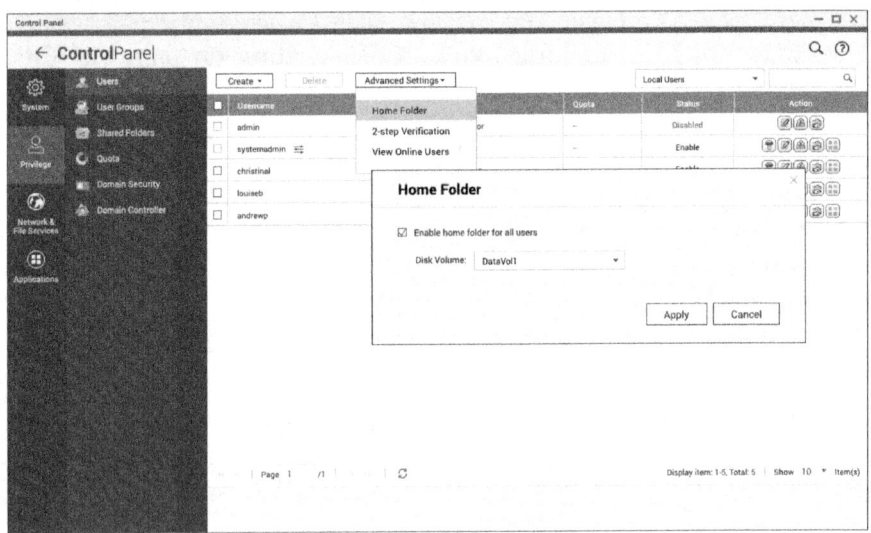

Figure 38: Enable Home folders

3.5 Loading Existing Data into Shared Folders

There may be a requirement to load data from existing computers or systems onto the NAS and into the new shared folders that have been created and there are several ways to do so:

Method One: Wait until the network is up and running i.e. shared folders have been created, users have been defined, computers are connected and able to access the server. Then, login from each computer and copy data from the user's local folders to the appropriate folders on the server.

Method Two: Visit each individual computer and copy data from the user's folders to an external plug-in drive. Then, connect the drive to the server and copy the data to the appropriate folders on the server. The advantages of this method are that it can be started before or in parallel with setting up the server, plus it can be retained as a long-term archive.

Method Three: The Qfinder Pro utility has a special facility for uploading media files from a computer to the NAS. How to use it is described in section **9.11 Media Upload from Qfinder Pro**.

Method Four: Some QNAP models feature *Direct Attached Storage* (DAS) capability, whereby the NAS can be plugged directly into a computer using a USB or Thunderbolt cable, whereby it appears as a regular external hard drive. Data can then be copied to it from the computer.

Regardless of which method is used, an anti-virus/malware check should be run on the computers *before* copying any data. It is also a good idea to first review the data on the computers and delete any unrequired and duplicate data, rather than carry it forward to the new environment.

4
MANAGING USERS

4.1 Overview

To access the NAS, it is necessary to have *user accounts* for it. During the installation of QTS, an initial administrator account had to be created. If you are the only person who will ever use the NAS, you can use that account for everything and skip this chapter altogether. However, if other people will also be using it, as is typically the case in a home, business or educational environment, then you will need to create user accounts for them.

You should decide a naming convention and this is one area where a different approach can be taken depending on whether it is a home or business network. In the case of a home network the user names can be anything you want, although there is some merit in following a scheme. For instance, you could use the first names of the family or household members. In a business or educational environment a more formal approach may be more appropriate. As a general point, the greater consistency there is then the better. For user names, two common conventions are to use the first name plus the initial of the surname, or the initial of the first name plus the surname, although in some parts of the world other conventions might be more appropriate. In the case of particularly long names and double-barreled names, one option is to abbreviate them. For example:

Name of Person	User Name	User Name
Nick Rushton	nickr	nrushton
Jasveen Kumar	jasveenk	jkumar
Ian Smith	ians	ismith
Amber Williams	amberw	awilliams
Daniela Petrova	danielap	dpetrova

4.2 Creating Users

To create a user, go into **Control Panel** and click **Users**; alternatively click **Main Menu** followed by **Users**. Click the **Create** button, which is a drop-down with three entries: *Create a User* – for creating individual users, one at a time; *Create Multiple Users* – for creating users in bulk, such as might be done in a large organization like a business or school, using an automated naming scheme e.g. *pupil001, pupil002, pupil003* etc.; *Import/Export Users* – also for creating users in bulk, using a spreadsheet containing names extracted from another computer system e.g. a registration or HR application.

As a household or typical small business will have a relatively small number of users, we will create them one at a time using the first option, so click **Create a User**.

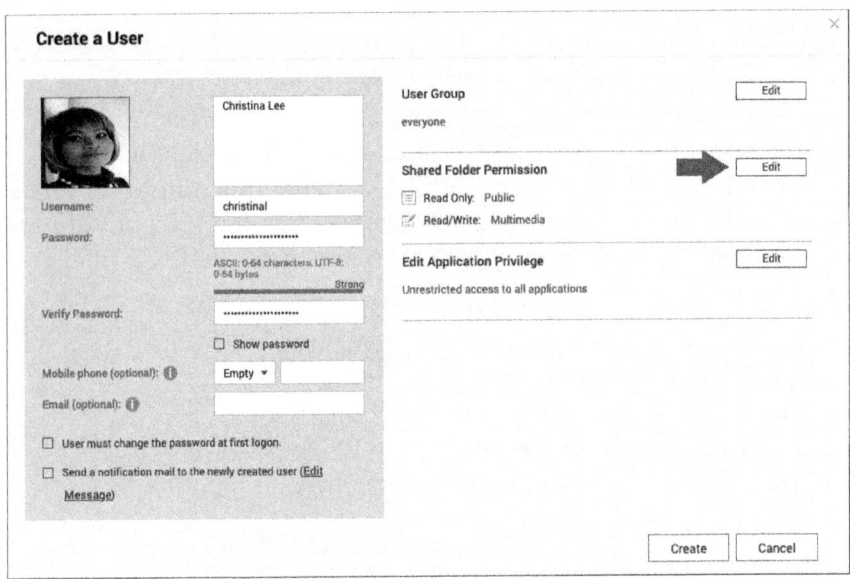

Figure 39: Create a User

Enter the *Username* by which they will be known to the system, along with a *Password* and its confirmation. The password should be at least 8 characters in length and include both letters and numbers; as the password is entered, QTS will advise how strong it is. If desired, password requirements can be changed (see **6.10 Password Policy**). To force the user to change their password when they use the system for this first time, tick the **User must change the password at first logon** box.

Optionally, specify the email address and send a notification to the newly created user (the SMTP server settings must first be configured in **Control Panel > System > Notification Center** to do this. See section **8.4 Notification Center**). You can also optionally enter a *User Description* and a small photograph of the user (*jpg* format is suitable, with a file size of no more than a few hundred KB).

The right-hand side of the panel defines what the user can and cannot do, as in what shared folders and applications they can use. The default settings are generally fine, but with one possible exception relating to the shared folders. Specifically, a new user only has *Read Only* access to the *Public* folder, whereas it may be more convenient if they have *Read/Write* access. To change this, click the **Edit** button in the *Shared Folder Permission* section. Put a tick in the RW column against *Public*, click the **Create** button and the user will be created and with the appropriate permissions.

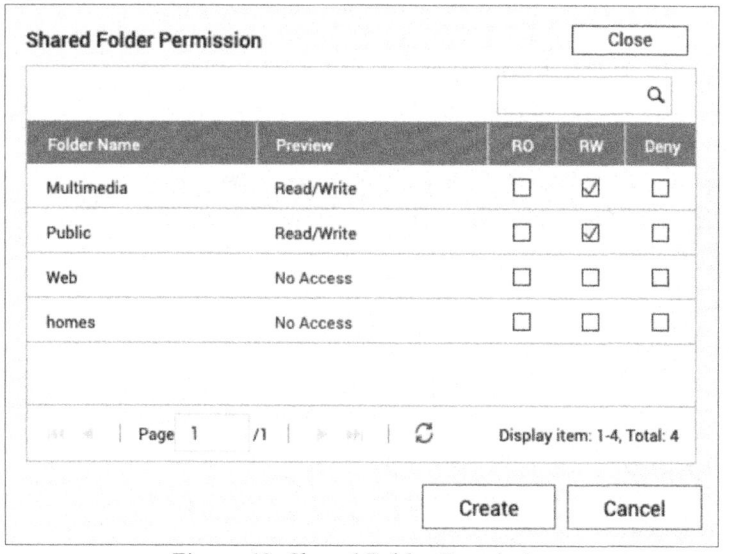

Folder Name	Preview	RO	RW	Deny
Multimedia	Read/Write	☐	☑	☐
Public	Read/Write	☐	☑	☐
Web	No Access	☐	☐	☐
homes	No Access	☐	☐	☐

Figure 40: Shared Folder Permission

This process should be repeated until all the users have been created. If you have a relatively large number of users to be created, you might find it helpful to first create a checklist of names and passwords to work through. As the users are created, the main *Users* screen will be populated with their details.

Creating a User with Qmanager

If the Qmanager app is being used on a mobile device (see section **8.10 Using Qmanager** for an overview), users can be created as follows:

Tap **Privileges Settings**, followed by the **Users** icon at the bottom of the screen. Tap the three dot 'snowman' menu in the top right-hand corner of the screen and choose **Create a User**. Enter the *Username* by which they will be known to the system, along with a *Password* and its confirmation. The password should be at least 8 characters in length and include both letters and numbers. Enter an optional description, such as the user's full name.

The bottom part of the screen defines the user's access to shared folders and applications. The default settings are generally fine, but with possible exceptions relating to the shared folders. Specifically, a new user only has *Read Only* access to the *Public* folder, whereas it may be more convenient if they have *Read/Write* access. To change this, tap **Shared Folder Privilege** then tap the right-hand side of the entry for the *Public* folder and select **RW** from the popup. Returning to the original screen, tap **Apply** in the top right-hand corner to create the user.

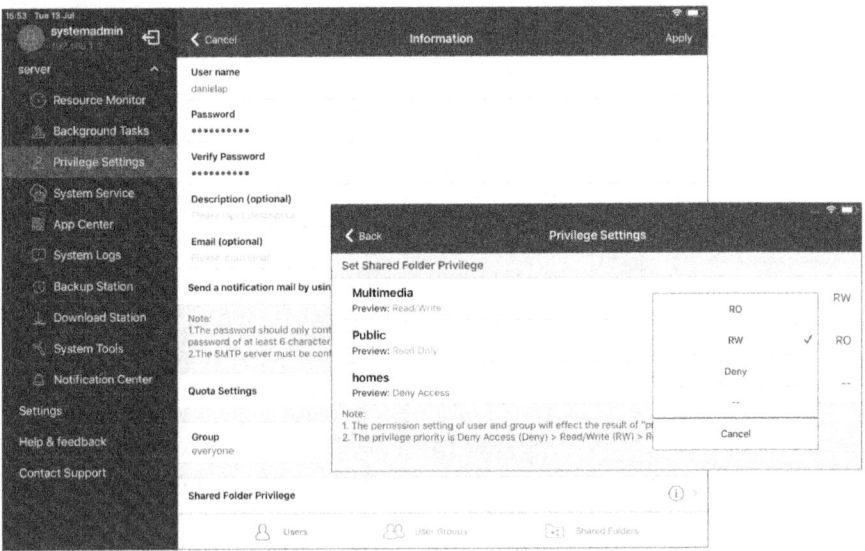

Figure 41: Creating a user with Qmanager

4.3 Modifying, Disabling and Deleting User Accounts

To modify an existing user, go into **Control Panel** or the **Main Menu** and click **Users**. Place a tick against the username and then the small icons on the right-hand side of the panel can be used. Note that to fully understand the meaning of some of these options it may be necessary to refer to other sections of this guide and they are mentioned here primarily for reference purposes:

☐	Username	Description	Quota	Status	Action
☑	stevew	Steve Williams	–	Enable	

- Change Password
- Edit Account Profile
- Edit User Group
- Edit Shared Folder Permission
- Edit Application Privilege

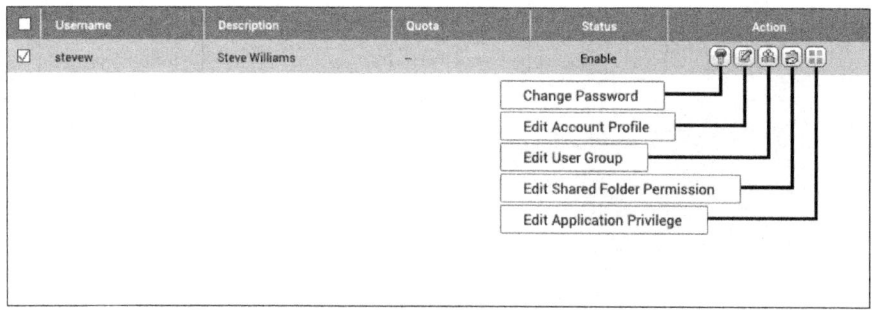

Figure 42: Icons for modifying a user's settings

Change Password – for changing the user's password

Edit Account Profile – change the description and email details for the user

Edit User Group – change group membership. This will make more sense after reading the next section of this book

Edit Shared Folder Permission – defines the user's access to the various shared folders. This will make more sense if you have read section **3 SHARED FOLDERS**.

Edit Application Privilege – defines the applications and services that the user has access to.

When a user leaves the organization, their account should in the first instance be disabled to prevent it being used. It is preferable to do this rather than immediately delete the account, as there may subsequently be a need to access it or the user may return at a later date e.g. they are on maternity/paternity or sick leave. To disable an account, place a tick against the username, click the **Edit Account Profile** mini icon then tick the **Disable this account** box.

Optionally, you can specify an *Expiry date* for the account, after which it will no longer be valid. Click **OK**. This step can subsequently be reversed if required.

To permanently delete a user, place a tick against their name in the list of users and click the **Delete** button at the top of the panel. Acknowledge the confirmation message by clicking **OK**.

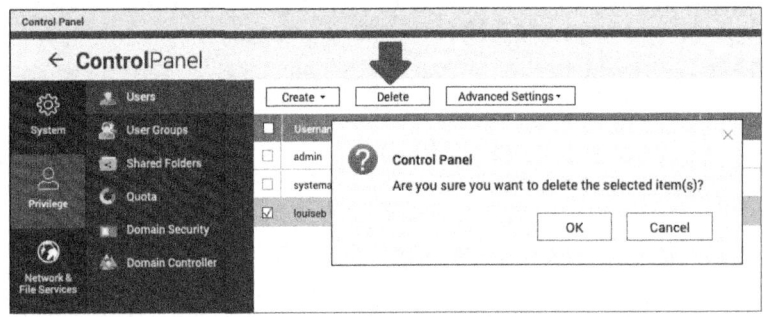

Figure 43: Deleting a user

4.4 Adding Multiple Users

In a domestic or small business setting, creating users one at a time is unlikely to be problematic. But when many need to be created, such as in a larger business or an educational setting, it can be time consuming. Fortunately, QTS has two mechanisms to create users in bulk.

Method One – Create Multiple Users

Go into **Control Panel** > **Users**. Click the **Create** button and choose **Create Multiple Users** to launch the *Multiple Users Creation Wizard*. Click **Next** and the following panel is displayed. In this example, we are setting up users for a classroom in a school.

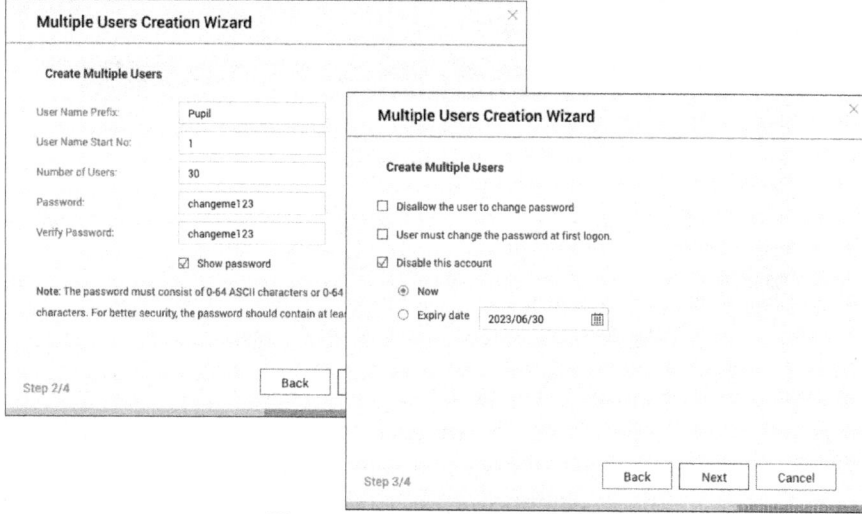

Figure 44: Create multiple users

The way it operates is that user names are created in the form of a prefix plus a numeric value. For the *User Name Prefix* we are using 'Pupil', the *User Name Start No.* is 1 and the *Number of Users* is 30. The *Password* is set as *changeme123* in this example. Click **Next**. On the following panel, the users can be forced to change their password at first logon, or prevented from changing it. An expiry date for the accounts can be specified, for instance in the case of a school it might be set to the end of the academic year. Click **Next** and the users will be created, with a confirmation screen displayed when the process is complete. Click **Finish**. In this example, 30 users, named *Pupil01* through *Pupil30*, will be created.

Method Two – Import/Export Users

QTS has the ability to create users from a file in CSV format, which can be created using Microsoft Excel or it might be possible to generate it from another computer system, such a school registration or human resources application.

The spreadsheet needs to be formatted as follows:

Column A – Username
Column B – Password
Column C – Quota in MBytes - optional, otherwise set to 0
Column D – Group Name – suggest make members of *everyone*
Column E – Email name – optional
Column F – User description e.g. full user name

It needs to be saved in CSV format with UTF-8 encoding.

	A	B	C	D	E	F
1	danielap	Bulgaria1234		everyone		Daniela Petrova
2	stevew	France5678		everyone		Steve Williams
3	ians	Canada9012		everyone		Ian Smith
4	jasveenk	India3456		everyone		Jasveen Kumar
5	gustavh	Germany7890		everyone		Gustav Hansa
6	maryo	Ireland1234		everyone		Mary Ohara
7	andrewp	America5678		everyone		Andrew Palmer

Figure 45: Example spreadsheet format for creating users

Go into **Control Panel > Users**. Click the **Create** button and choose **Import/Export Users**. Select the **Import user and user group settings** option, click **Browse** and locate and select the CSV file. To force the users to change their password upon first logon, tick the appropriate box. Click **Next**.

A preview will be displayed. The *Status* fields should all be blank; any errors will be displayed in red and the underlying problem in the CSV file should be corrected before proceeding. When everything is suitable, click **Next** and the users will be created. The time taken for this depends on how many users there are.

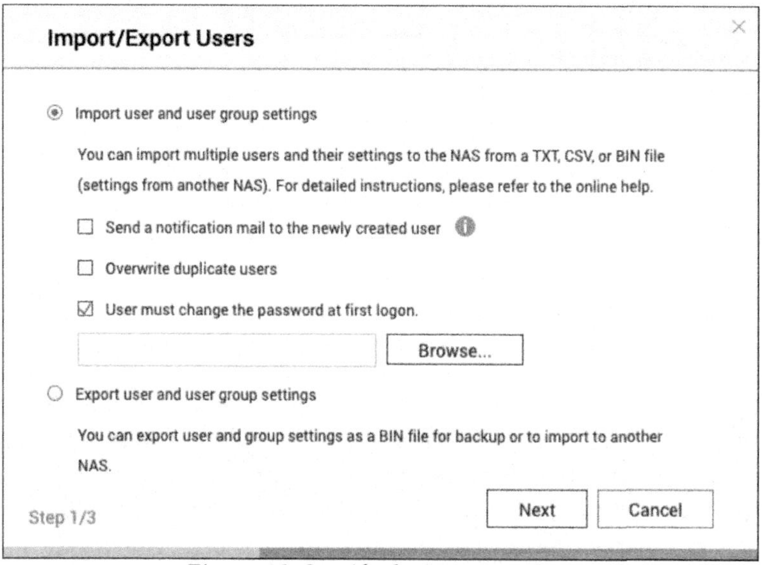

Figure 46: Specify the import options

4.5 User Groups

In a home environment or an organization with a small number of users, specifying who has access permissions to folders is relatively easy to manage. But as the number of users increases it becomes more time consuming; for example, consider having to define the access rights for, say, 50 users. Such organizations are usually large enough that they contain departments or teams to carry out the different functions. For instance, there might be several people working in accounts, several in sales, several in marketing and so on.

To support these typical organizational structures, QTS features the concept of *groups*. A group consists of a number of users who have something in common within the organization, such as they are all members of the same department, the same classroom etc. Access rights can be specified once for the group, which means they then apply to all members of that group. If a new person joins, they just have to be specified as a member of the group, at which point they inherit all the relevant access rights. There is a built-in group in QTS called *everyone*, which all users are automatically members of, but you can create additional ones to reflect the needs of the organization. An individual user can be a member of multiple groups.

In this example, we will create a group called *sales* whose members alone have access to a corresponding folder of the same name, although the folder does not have to match the group name and can be called anything you wish. Begin by creating a shared folder called *sales*. The method for creating shared folders is described in detail in **3.2 Creating a Shared Folder**, but in summary: **Control Panel > Shared Folders > Create > Shared Folder**, name the folder *sales* and click the **Create** button.

Within the **Control Panel** click the **User Groups** icon, followed by the **Create** button. Name the group *sales,* optionally provide a *Description* then click the **Create** button.

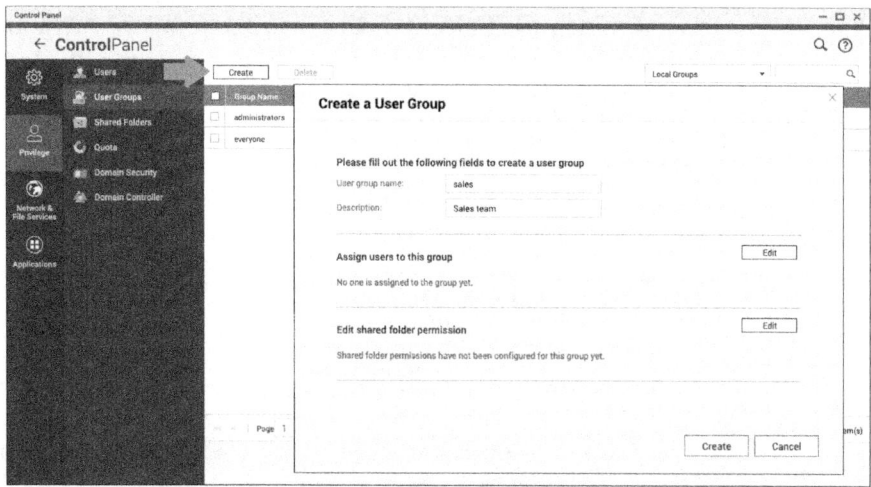

Figure 47: Creating a new User Group

Having done that, the *sales* group will be listed alongside the built-in ones (*administrators, everyone*) that are present on every system:

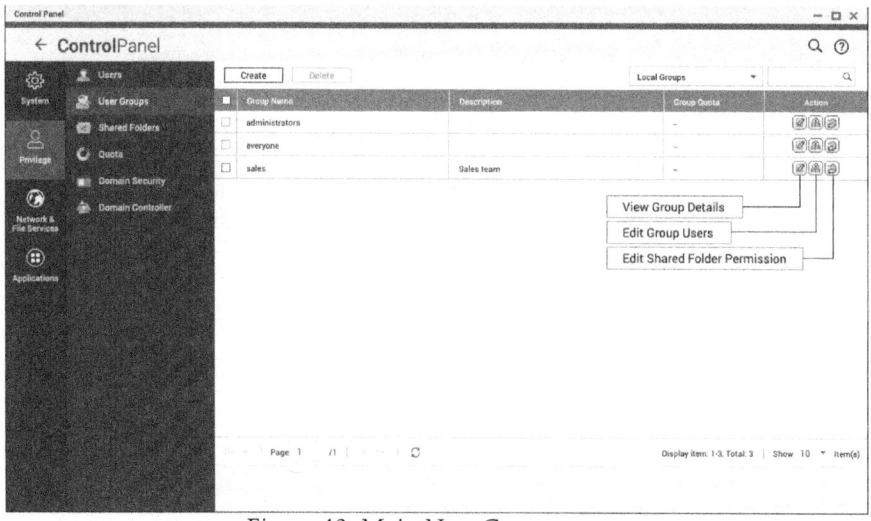

Figure 48: Main User Groups screen

On the right-hand side of the screen against each group name are three action icons: *View Group Details*; *Edit Group Users*; *Edit Shared Folder Permission*. What we are about to do now could have been done as we were creating the group, but it is useful to know how to edit a group in this way in case you ever need to modify it subsequently.

Place a tick against *sales* and click the **Edit Group Users** icon, which is used for specifying the members of a group. Tick the users who are to be members of *sales* and click the **Apply** button when finished:

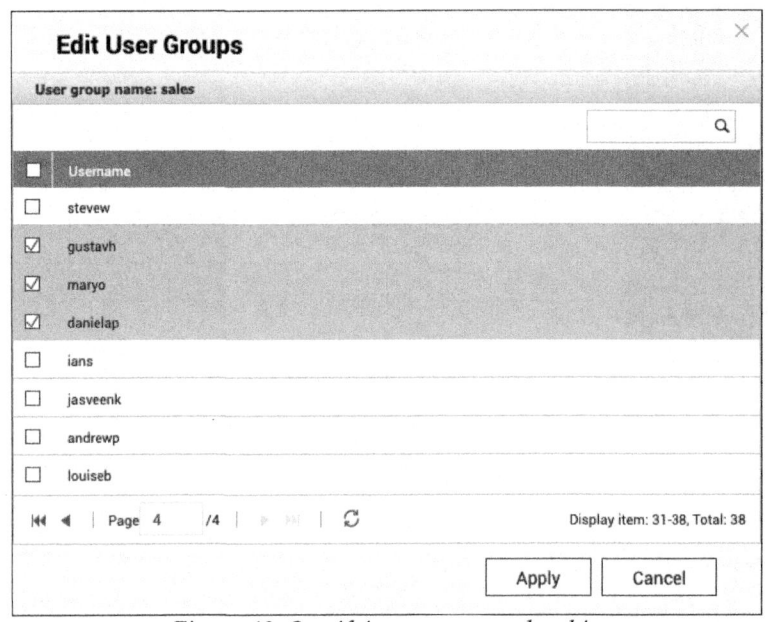

	Username
☐	stevew
☑	gustavh
☑	maryo
☑	danielap
☐	ians
☐	jasveenk
☐	andrewp
☐	louiseb

Edit User Groups — User group name: sales — Page 4 /4 — Display item: 31-38, Total: 38

Figure 49: Specifying group membership

Now click the **Edit Shared Folder Permission** icon. The screen lists the shared folders and by placing a tick in the appropriate box, the access to each folder for the group is specified. The choices are *RW* (Read Write), *RO* (Read Only) or *Deny* (i.e. no access). For the *sales* folder specify **RW**. It is not necessary to specify anything for the other folders as whatever settings the individual users already have for them will be retained. When finished click **Apply**:

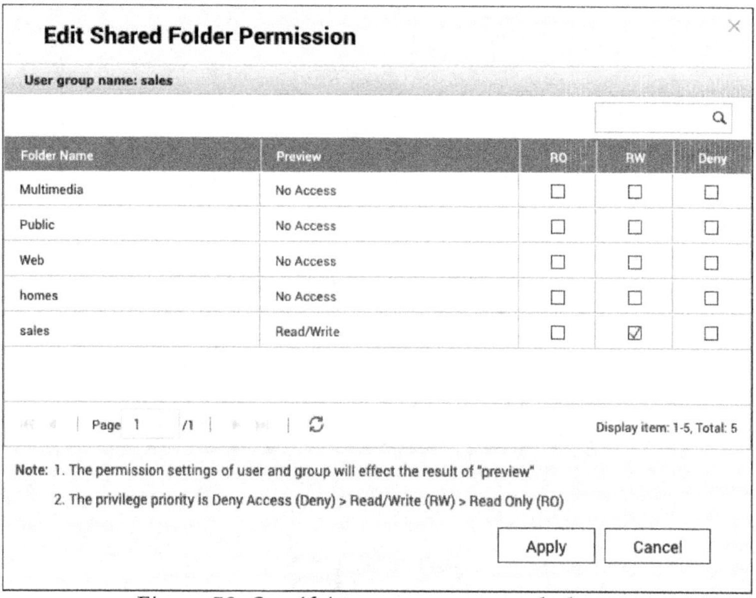

Figure 50: Specifying access to network shares

The advantage of this is that the creation of additional users or changes to existing users becomes easier. For instance, when a user is created they only have to be defined as being a member of a particular group to automatically inherit all the rights associated with that group. The larger and more structured the organization, the more benefits accrue from this approach.

5

ACCESSING THE SERVER

5.1 Overview

There are multiple methods for accessing the NAS, some of which are available to Windows users only, some to Mac users only, whereas others are available for most platforms. There are also apps available for portable devices such as smartphones and tablets.

5.2 Using a Browser and File Station

This is ae universal method for accessing the NAS and works for Windows PCs, Macs, Linux computers and Chromebooks. Using any computer on the local network, launch a browser such as Firefox, Chrome, Edge or Safari and type in the name of the server (which is "*server*" in our example) or its IP address. The standard QTS login screen is displayed; the user should enter their name and password and they will be presented with a minimalist Desktop; in essence, all they can access is *File Station* and a handful of applications (unless additional options have been granted to them).

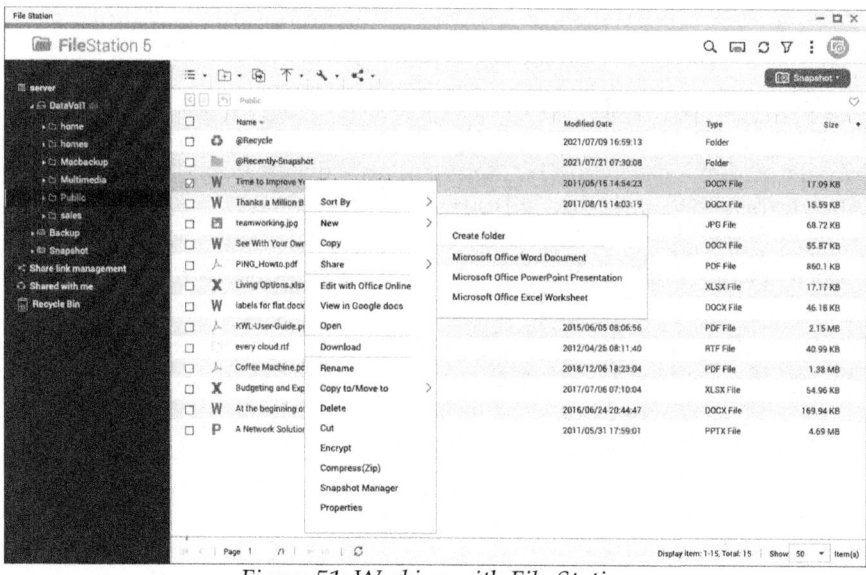

Figure 51: Working with File Station

Within *File Station* they can see the folders and files that belong to them or to which they have been granted access, such as their *home* folder plus the *multimedia* and *public* folders. To work with a file or folder, right-click it and a pop-up menu will appear with the various available options.

Alternatively, click the spanner tool icon at the top of the screen. Most graphic files and photographs can be viewed by double-clicking them, as can PDF files, and MP3 music files can be played. There are also common file manipulation commands for copying, renaming, deleting files and so on. Some features, such as uploading files and folders, are only supported in the Chrome browser.

There are options to view documents, spreadsheets and presentations using *Google Docs*, or edit and create new ones directly in Microsoft *Office Online* (it is necessary to have myQNAPcloud enabled for this feature to work). Another way to edit a file is to choose the **Download** option to first download it to the local computer, make the changes to the document using Word, Excel or other preferred application, then use the **Upload** button in File Station to return the new version back to the server.

Options

To adjust the settings of File Station, click the three-dot 'snowman' menu in the top right-hand corner of the screen and choose **Settings**. There are six tabs, with the administrator having more options than regular users:

General – show hidden files and network recycle bins.

File Transfer – options over copying and uploading files, including what happens when using files from Google Drive.

Multimedia – enables the 360º panoramic view button.

Documents – provides options for editing and viewing Microsoft Office files.

File Operations – control over SMB file attributes.

Third-party Service - control over converting Apple iWork file formats to Microsoft Office using a third-party online service.

Logging Out

When the user has finished using the NAS, they should logout. This is done by clicking their user name in the top right-corner of the screen and choosing the **Logout** option. Note: the administrator has additional menu options, related to managing the NAS.

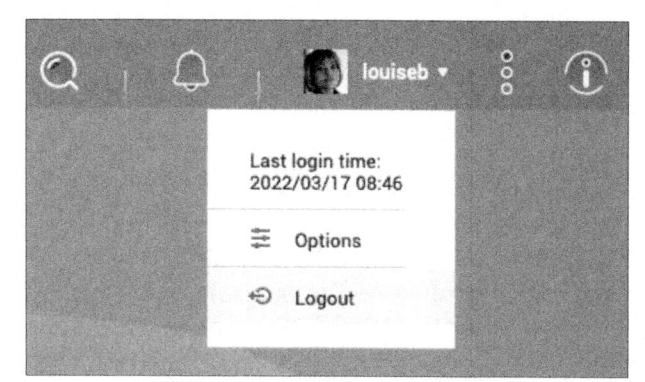

Figure 52: User Options menu

5.3 Connecting Macs
With Qfinder Pro
Download and install *Qfinder Pro* onto each Mac, which needs to be running macOS 10.14 (Mojave) or later. An icon will be placed in the *Applications* folder. Run it and the server should be listed, although *Qfinder Pro* may take a few seconds to find it. If it does not appear then there is a problem of some description, such as the Mac is not connected to network or the NAS is not powered on. Highlight the server and click the **Network Drives** icon; there will be a prompt to logon to the server - enter the details of a user previously defined on it. If you are the only person using the Mac, you could choose to tick the *Remember me* box.

A pop-up appears giving a choice of protocols. You would usually accept the default one – **SMB/CIFS** – but if you are using very old versions of macOS you might have to use **AFP** instead, with **NFS** available for Linux/Unix users. It is possible you may receive a message to the effect that QTS can optimize the performance of SMB, in which case answer **Yes**. Optionally, you can choose to *Add mounted folders to Favorites in Finder*. Click **OK**:

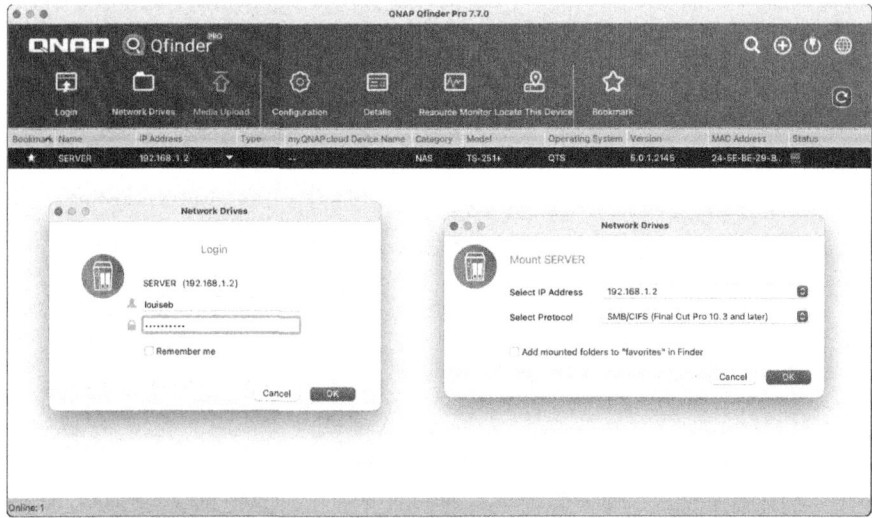

Figure 53: Enter username and password, then select the protocol

The next panel lists the available volumes i.e. shared folders. Choose the volume(s) to mount and click **OK**. To mount multiple volumes in one go, hold down the **Command key** and click each of the required volumes in turn:

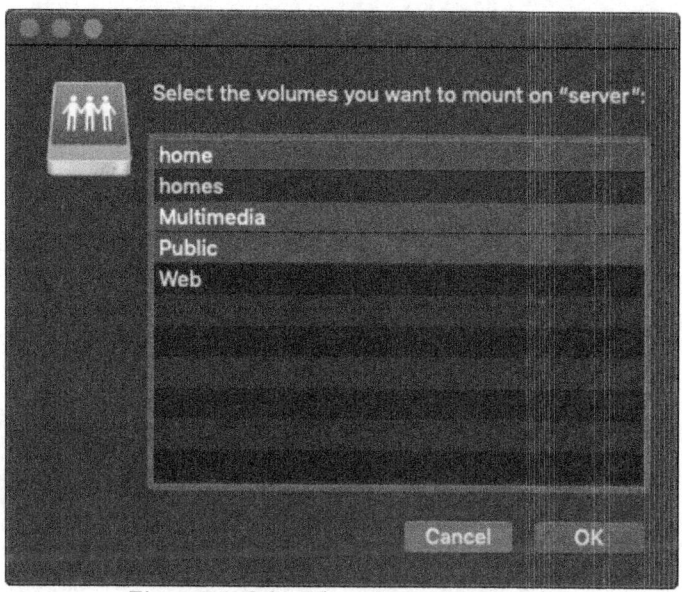

Figure 54: Select the volume(s) to mount

The chosen volume(s) will be opened and folder icon(s) placed on the desktop, assuming you have Finder configured appropriately (see **Finder > Preferences > General**). The contents of the shared folders can then be used in the normal way.

Note: if you receive a message from Qfinder Pro, advising that it wants to change some settings to improve performance, then allow it to do so.

From Finder

*Note: if you are using older versions of macOS (before 10.9 Mavericks), you should check that the Apple File Service (AFP) is enabled on the NAS, as described in section 2.5 **Network Services**.*

On the menu bar of the Mac, click **Go** followed by **Connect to Server**; alternatively, press **Command K**. A dialog box is displayed. Enter the name or IP address of the server preceded with *smb://* or *afp://* e.g. *smb://192.168.1.2* or *smb://server* or *afp://server*. To add the server to your list of Favorites for quick access, click the **+** button. Click **Connect**. Enter the user name ('Registered User') and password as previously defined on the NAS and click **Connect**. You can also tick the **Remember this password in my keychain** box if you are the only person who uses the computer:

Figure 55: Enter the user name and password

A list of available shared folders (*volumes*) is displayed. Choose the volume to mount and click **OK.** To mount multiple volumes at once, hold down the **Command key** and click on the required folders in turn. Icon(s) for the folder(s) will appear on the Desktop (assuming you have set Preferences in Finder to show Connected Servers). Click an icon to display the contents - they behave the same as standard Mac folders.

Alternatively, click Finder, navigate to the server in Locations, click the **Connect As** button and then login and mount one or more volumes/shared folders.

5.4 Connecting Windows Computers
With Qfinder Pro
Qfinder Pro is a flexible piece of software that can do multiple things, one of which is accessing shared folders. Download and install *Qfinder Pro* onto each computer, which needs to be running Windows 8 or later. If you receive a message from the computer's firewall, grant access to *Qfinder Pro*. An icon will be in placed on the computer's desktop – double-click to run it. You may receive a message advising that 'SMTP server not configured yet' – this is not required, although configuring SMTP (email) if required is covered in section **8.4 Notification Center**. The server should be listed, although *Qfinder Pro* may take a few seconds to find it. If it does not appear then there is a problem of some sort, such as the computer is not connected to the network, the NAS is not powered on, or the firewall needs configuring on the computer.

Click the **Network Drives** icon. The resultant pop-up panel will default to the IP address of the server (if you have multiple servers, you can choose a different one from the dropdown) and **SMB/CIFS** protocol. Click **OK**.

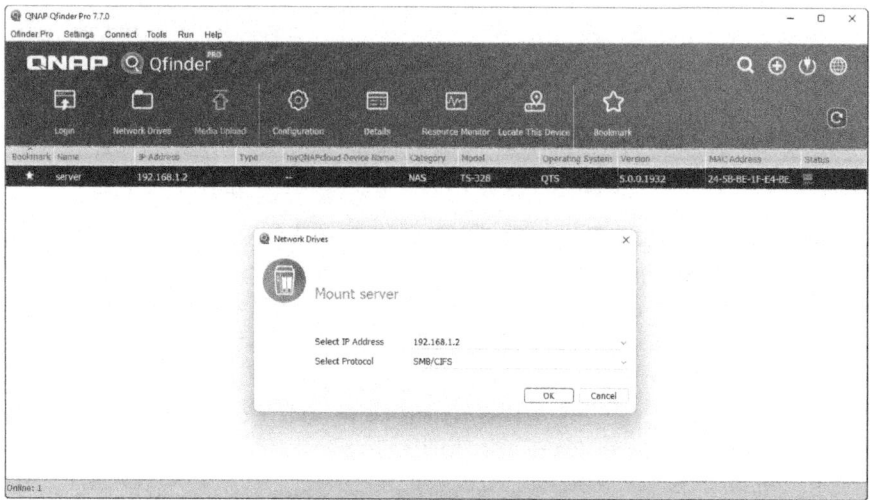

Figure 56: Mount server

You will be prompted to enter your network credentials i.e. user name and password as previously defined on the server.

If you are the exclusive user of the computer you can also tick the **Remember my credentials** box. Click **OK**. Windows File Explorer will now open, displaying the list of shared folders.

Windows Explorer/File Explorer

A simple way to access the server is by going into File Explorer/Windows Explorer, which is on the taskbar in most versions of Windows. Expand the left-hand panel to view the Network and down the left-hand side the server should be visible. Click it and the list of shared folders will be displayed:

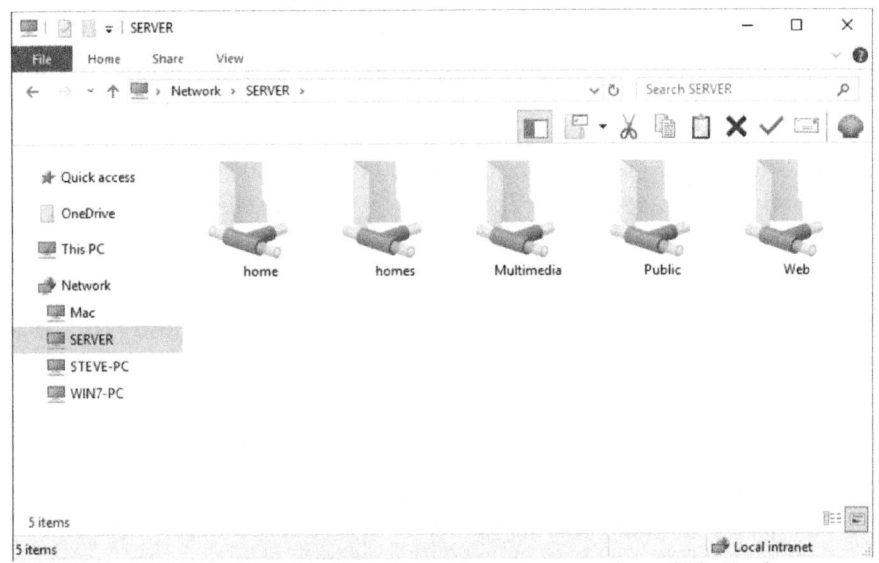

Figure 57: List of shared folders from Windows Explorer/File Explorer

To access a shared folder, double-click it and you will be prompted to enter a user name and password as previously defined on the server. If you wish, tick the option box to remember the login details, although you should only do this if you are the sole user of the computer. Although all the shared folders may be visible, you can only access the ones to which you have privileges. With a fresh installation that has not been modified in any way this would include the *Public* and *Home* folders.

Accessing Shared Folders Using the Run Command

To access a shared folder from a Windows computer, right-click the **Start** button and choose **Run** if using Windows 11, 10 or 8.1, else click **Start** and **Run** if using Windows 7. Alternatively, hold down the **Windows key** and press the letter **R**. In the small dialog box that appears, type in the name of the shared folder using the format *server**name_of_folder* e.g. *server**public* and click **OK**.

The contents of the folder will be displayed in File Explorer/Windows Explorer, from where the files can be used in the standard way. Note that you may be prompted to enter a user name and password as defined previously on the server.

Mapping Drives Manually

The techniques described so far provide access to shared folders from Windows computers by referring to them using what are called UNC or *Universal Naming Convention* names and which take the form *server**shared*. However, many Windows users are accustomed to and prefer to use drive letters, such as C:, D: and so on. The process by which a UNC name can be turned into a drive letter is known as *mapping* and this can be done using File Explorer. You can use whatever drive letters you wish, provided they are not already in use (for instance you cannot choose C as that is always in use on a Windows computer). However, using corresponding letters makes things easier. For example, map *multimedia* to M, *public* to P and *home* to H.

Windows 11

Open File Explorer, which appears on the Taskbar by default. Expand the left-hand panel to view the Network and click the server to display the list of shared folders. You may be prompted to enter a valid user name and password as previously defined on the server; if you wish, tick the option box to remember the login details, although you should only do this if you are the sole user of the computer. Right-click the shared folder and choose **Show more options**, followed by **Map network drive**. On the resultant panel, specify the Drive letter using the dropdown and click **Finish**. Upon a successful connection, the contents of the newly mapped drive will be displayed. The process should now be repeated for each shared folder that is needed.

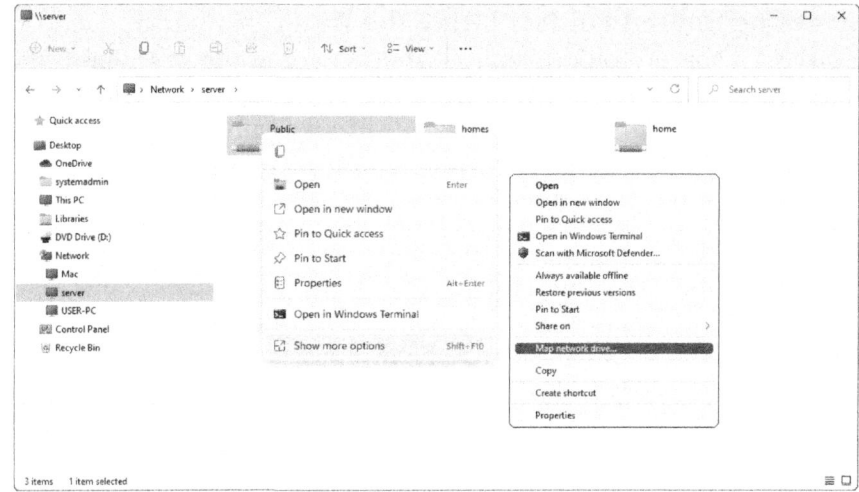

Figure 58: Mapping a drive in Windows 11

Windows 10

Open File Explorer, which usually appears on the Taskbar by default. Expand the left-hand panel to view the Network and click on the server to display the list of shared folders. You may be prompted to enter a valid user name and password as previously defined on the server; if you wish, tick the option box to remember the login details, although you should only do this if you are the sole user of the computer. Right-click on the shared folder to highlight it. On the menu bar click **Home** and in the *New* section click the small icon and choose **Map as drive**. On the resultant panel, specify the Drive letter using the dropdown and click **Finish**. Upon a successful connection, the contents of the newly mapped drive will be displayed. The process should now be repeated for each shared folder that is needed.

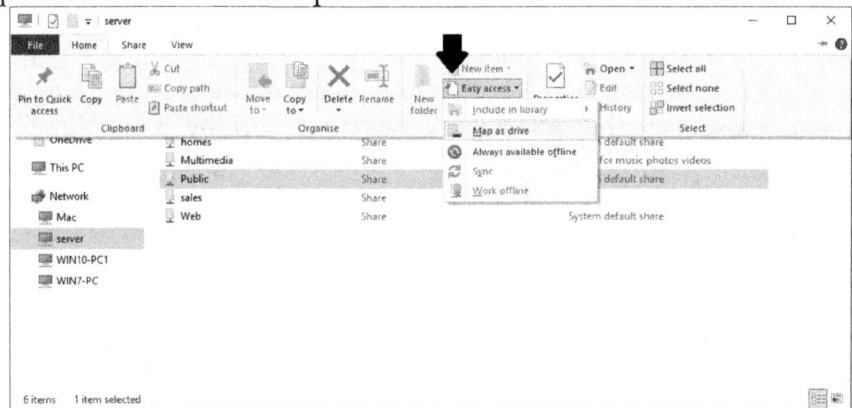

Figure 59: Mapping a drive in Windows 10

Windows 7

Open Windows Explorer, which usually appears on the Taskbar by default, else click **My Computer** on the Start menu. If the menu bar is not displayed, click **Organize > Layout > Menu bar** to display it. Expand the left-hand panel to view the Network and click on the server to display the list of shared folders. You may be prompted to enter a valid user name and password as previously defined on the server; if you wish, tick the option box to remember the login details, although you should only do this if you are the sole user of the computer. Right-click the shared folder and choose **Map network drive**. On the resultant panel, specify the Drive letter using the dropdown and click **Finish**. Upon a successful connection, the contents of the newly mapped drive will be displayed. The process should now be repeated for each shared folder that is needed.

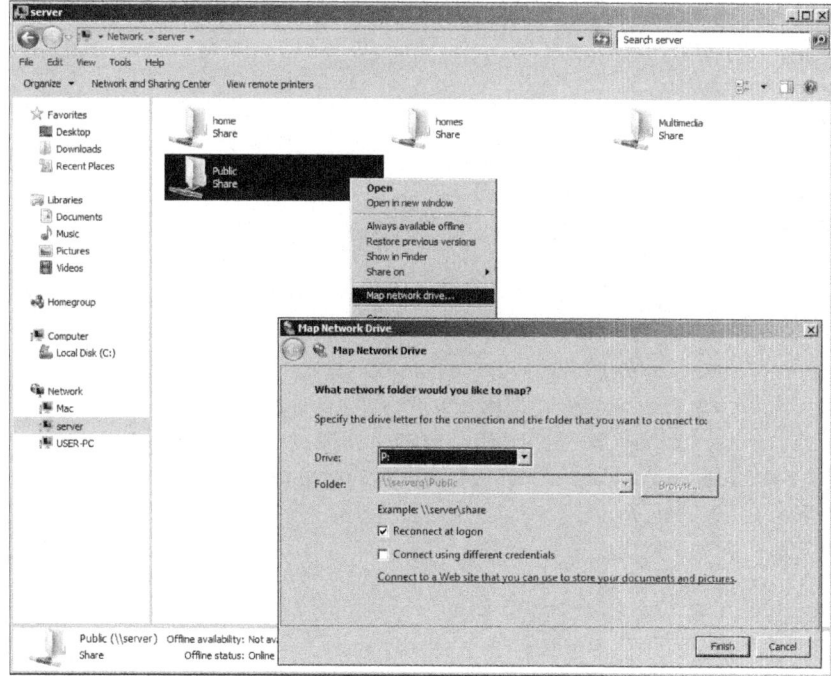

Figure 60: Mapping a drive in Windows 7

Using a Batch File (Windows)

Setting up a batch file is a more advanced technique for Windows PCs but can be useful when a particular computer is used by more than one person. As such, it is possibly more applicable to a small business or educational environment rather than to a home system. Start off by using Notepad or WordPad to create a plain text file called *Connect-to-NAS.cmd*. The contents of the file will vary depending on the folders to be mapped. In this example each user has a personal *home* folder and there are two shared folders called *multimedia* and *public*:

@echo off
ping server -n 1 > nul
if errorlevel 1 goto offline
:online
: remove drive mappings if already present
net use * /delete /y > nul
: map the drives
net use h: \\server\home /persistent:no
net use m: \\server\multimedia /persistent:no
net use p: \\server\public /persistent:no
goto end
:
:offline
cls
echo You are not connected to the network.
echo If you are outside the office then this is expected.
echo If you are inside the office then it means there is a problem.
echo Data stored on the network is not currently available.
pause
:end

The file should be placed on the Desktop of each computer. After the computer starts up, the user should run it by double-clicking its icon. A window is displayed prompting for the user name, followed by a prompt for the password. After the user has successfully entered their details, the mapped drives will be available until the computer is shutdown or they logoff from the Start menu. The drive mappings can be verified by launching Windows Explorer/File Explorer, which appears by default on the Taskbar in Windows 7 and later versions.

If the NAS is not available, the drives will not be mapped and a warning message is displayed. It is to be expected that this message will appear if using, say, a laptop computer outside of an office, but if it appears when inside then it indicates a problem. This could be a connectivity issue on the computer e.g. Ethernet cable unplugged or wireless switched off. If everyone in the office is receiving it, then it would suggest that the server is powered off or otherwise out of action.

When a particular user has finished with a computer, they should logoff or restart the computer.

Ideally, computers should be setup with only one Windows user defined on them. If this is not the case, then the *Connect-to-NAS.cmd* file needs to be placed in *C:\Users\Public\Public Desktop*, which will cause it to appear on the Desktop for all users. The Public Desktop folder is a hidden folder and will therefore first need to be made visible before it can be used. To do this, go to **Control Panel** on the computer and choose **Folder Options** or **File Explorer Options** depending on your version of Windows. Click on the **View** tab, enable **Show hidden files, folders and drives** and click **OK**. Copy the *Connect-to-NAS.cmd* file to the Public Desktop folder, then make the Public Desktop folder hidden again.

Unfortunately, *Connect-to-NAS.cmd* is not tolerant of errors. If the user enters the wrong logon details there will be a brief error message and the drives will fail to map. The user will need to run the cmd file and try again.

5.5 Connecting Linux & Unix Computers

Although QTS includes comprehensive support for the NFS filing system used by Linux and Unix computers (see **2.5 Network Services**), Linux and Unix distributions inevitably include support for the SMB filing system used by QTS. Unless you have specific reason not to, it is suggested that you use SMB for connecting. The ability to do this is usually inherent, although in some cases it may have to be added by downloading what is commonly described as a *Samba client*. In this example, we are using the popular Ubuntu Linux distribution.

Click on the **Files** icon, followed by **Other Locations**. The NAS should be listed under the Networks section; click on it and on the resultant panel, enter the user's name and password as defined on the server and click **Connect** (the *Domain* field can be ignored). The shared folders on the server will be listed. To access one, double-click it. You may be prompted to provide the username and password again, in which case do so. The folder will then open and you can use the files in the standard manner.

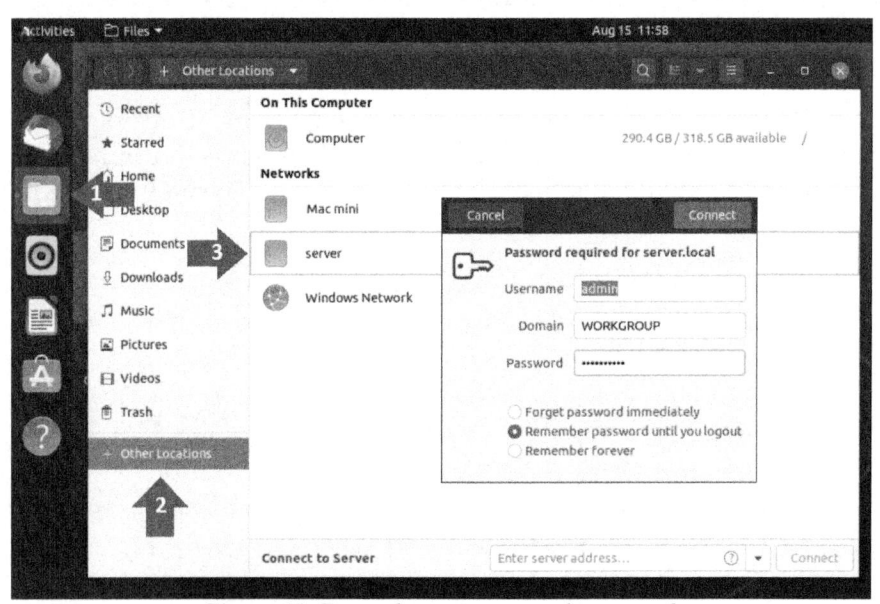

Figure 61: Enter the username and password

5.6 Connecting Smartphones and Tablets

Mobile devices such as smartphones and tablets are connected to QNAP servers using apps, available for download from the Apple and Google app stores. These are provided both by QNAP themselves, as well as from third parties. Many of the apps are specific to playing certain media types or have specialist purposes; the two discussed here are more generic apps for accessing the file system on the server.

Qfile

Qfile is from QNAP and is available for iOS and Android. It is used for browsing and managing files and shared folders; it can also play many popular media types, making it an ideal 'universal' app for many users.

When running Qfile for the first time it is necessary to enter the details of the server, username and password. If you want to use Qfile remotely you should enter the myQNAPcloud address that you registered; if you only want to connect locally, enter the IP address of the server instead. When viewing the contents of a shared folder there are small icons on the right-hand side of the screen that provide useful options, including the ability to upload files, add new folders, search etc.

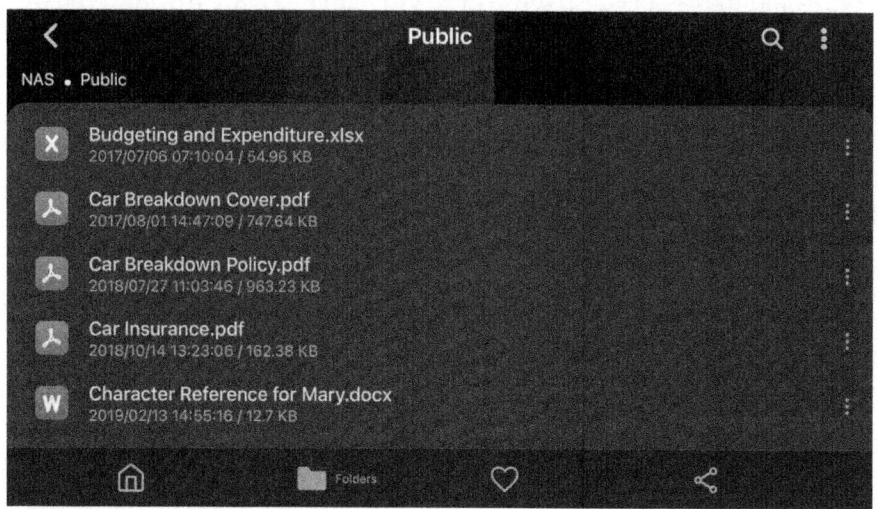

Figure 62: Qfile

Files App (iOS)

The Files App is an integral part of iOS and iPadOS. Having launched it, tap the three-dot menu at the top of the screen and tap **Connect to Server**:

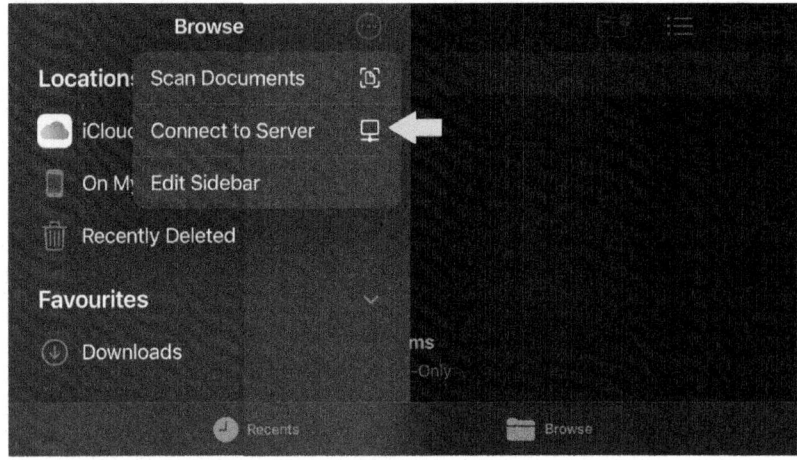

Figure 63: File App on iPhone/iOS

On the subsequent panels: enter the name of the server or its IP address and click **Connect**; choose the **Registered User** option; enter the name and password of a user that has previously been defined on the server and click **Next**. After a few seconds, you should be connected to the server, from where you can navigate through the file system to locate folders and files:

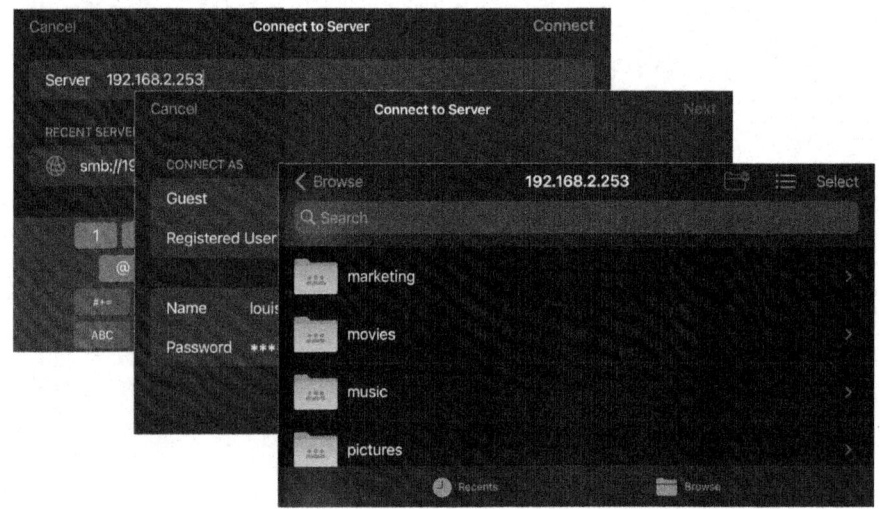

Figure 64: Connecting to and viewing files and folders on the server

5.7 Connecting Chromebooks

Chromebooks are a popular computing choice, particularly in education. In essence a Chromebook is a laptop that primarily runs Google's Chrome browser and the underlying operating system is minimalist compared to Windows or macOS. However, Chromebooks work well with NAS and can be used in the following ways:

Browser

Using the browser, as described earlier in section **5.2 Using a Browser and File Station**, for tasks such as working with File Station, playing back music using Music Station, downloading and uploading files and administering QTS.

Qfinder

QNAP have a limited version of *Qfinder* that can be downloaded from the (Chrome) Web Store. It scans the local network and identifies any NAS servers; clicking on a server will then take you to the logon page. There is no other functionality. There are no administrative tools, nor is it possible to map drives as the concept has no meaning on a Chromebook.

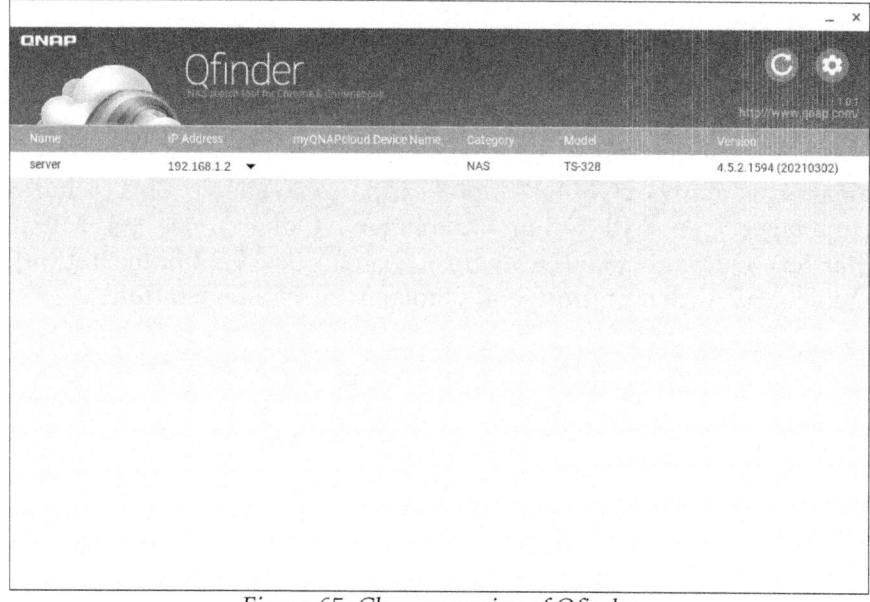

Figure 65: Chrome version of Qfinder

Files

To access the folders and files on the NAS, use the Chromebook *Files* utility. Click the three-dot 'snowman' icon in the top right-hand corner of the screen, followed by **Services > SMB file share**. On the resultant panel, enter the *File share URL* e.g. \\server\public, an optional *Display name*, plus the *Username* and *Password*. Optionally, tick the **Remember sign-in info** box. Click **Add**. The shared folder will now be added to the Chromebook's filing system.

Figure 66: Adding a file share

Android Apps

As Chromebooks can run Android Apps from the Play Store, this means that many of QNAP's mobile apps are available. This includes Qmanager (see **8.10 Using Qmanager**), Qmusic (see **9.4 Music Station**), QuMagie (**9.5 QuMagie**), Qphoto (see **9.6 Photo Station**), Qvideo (**9.7 Video Station**) and Qnotes3 (**10.5 Notes Station**).

6
SECURITY

6.1 Overview

Whilst the QTS software is a very secure platform, it is not and cannot be totally immune to the numerous security threats associated with running a sophisticated computer system. To help protect it, QNAP provide a variety of tools and mechanisms and it is recommended that you familiarize yourself with and make use of them.

6.2 Security Counselor

Security Counselor is a centralized management suite for the NAS and provides a 'one stop shop' for managing many aspects of security. It integrates several features, including a check-up of device security and automatic adjustment of suggested settings, plus provides a unified interface for the anti-malware and anti-virus tools discussed below. It is not essential to use Security Counselor, as several of the underlying functions can be accessed directly from the Control Panel, although it is convenient to have everything accessible from one place, with Security Counselor acting as a front-end portal.

Begin by downloading and installing Security Counselor from the App Center, then launch it by clicking the icon on the desktop. Upon running it for the first time, you are asked if you want to send the results of security check-ups to QNAP ('Security Analytics') – make a choice based upon your personal or organization's preferences. The initial screen is displayed after a short, optional overview.

By default, Security Counselor is pre-configured in ready-to-use mode: click **Scan now** to run an immediate scan, thereafter it will run automatically once a week, although this setting can be adjusted. You can choose your own *Security Policy*, meaning how protected or 'locked down' the NAS will be, and there are three choices:

Basic Security Policy – if you are setting up a QNAP NAS for the first time and are in a home setting, you may wish to start with this. Also, if you are in a test environment or the NAS is not directly connected to the outside world (a school setting, perhaps) then it may be appropriate.

Intermediate Security Policy – This provides additional security and is suitable if the server is being accessed from outside the premises.

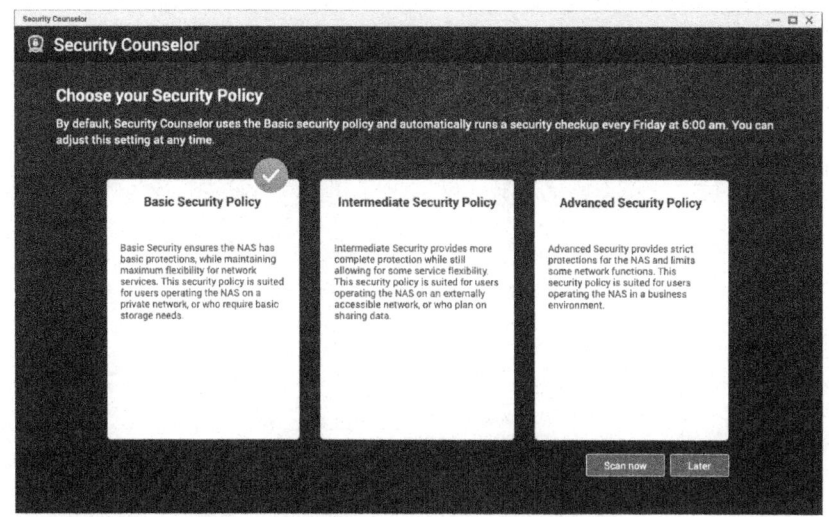

Figure 67: Choose your Security Policy

Advanced Security Policy - if you are operating in a business or enterprise environment, you should use this as it is optimized for such scenarios. One thing to note is that if you use the Advanced Security Policy, then secured http is enabled. So, the address of the server would become (for example) *https://192.168.1.2* rather than *http://192.168.1.2*, plus you may initially receive an SSL certificate warning.

Having made a choice, click **Scan Now** and the security check will run. The time taken to complete depends upon the policy chosen, the amount of data and the hardware performance of the NAS. When complete, the overview screen appears, showing the summary level results.

From the Overview screen you can run a security check-up, anti-virus scan, malware scan, manage the QuFirewall, or change the security policy. Some of the features need to be installed before they appear in the Security Counselor, for example QuFirewall has yet to be installed in the example below.

Listed down the left-hand side of the screen are links to various options, some of which duplicate links on the current page. Any security-related reports which have been generated can be viewed from this screen.

To view the current security policy in detail i.e. which settings are active, click the **Security Policy** option. The overall policy can be changed on that screen using the dropdown menu.

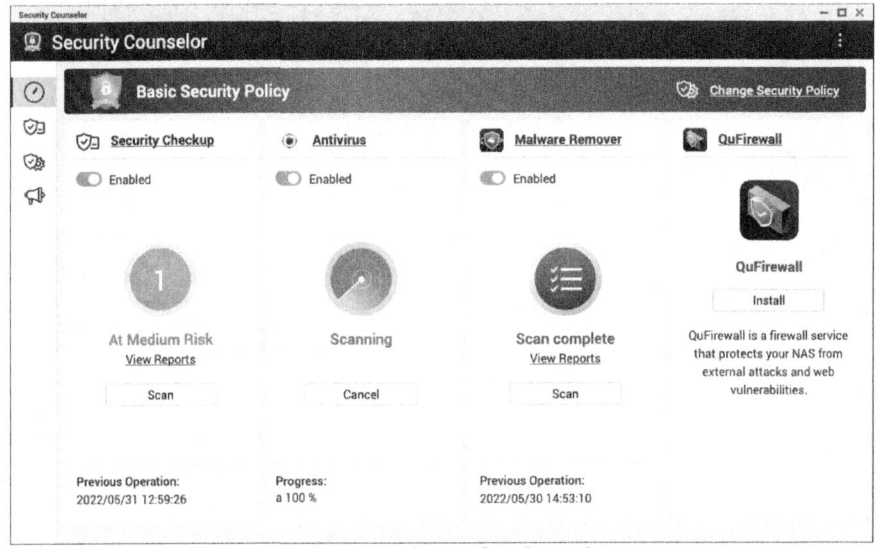

Figure 68: Security Counselor Overview screen

When logging into QTS, you will be advised of any security advisories i.e. security vulnerabilities affecting QNAP products and services. If you do not wish to see these, click **Security Advisory** and on the resultant panel set the *Notify me of new security advisories* switch to the off position.

6.3 Security Checkup

To run a security check-up and determine overall risks to the system, go into *Security Counselor* and click **Security Checkup** followed by the green **Scan** button. After it has finished running, a screen along the following lines is displayed, highlighting the risks using traffic light color coding:

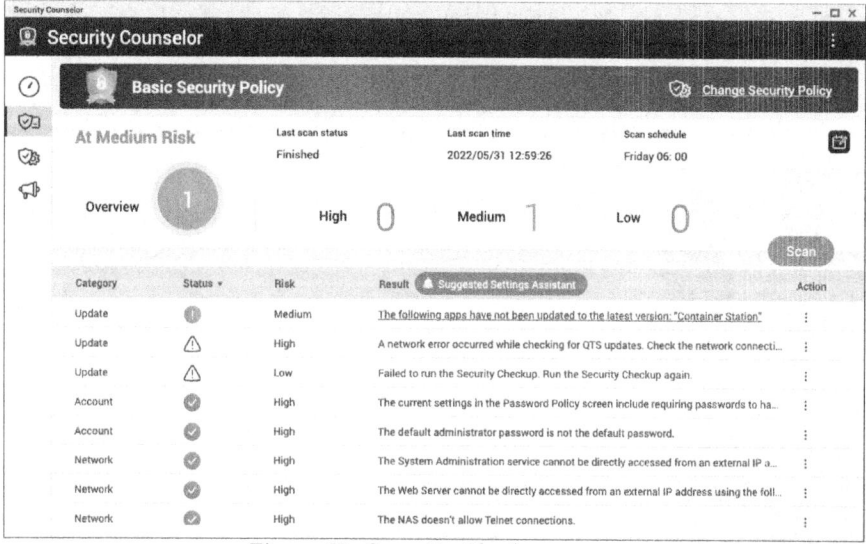

Figure 69: Security Checkup screen

The categories that are tested depend upon the security policy in use. If something is actionable, the result is displayed as a blue hyperlink and clicking it will take you to the appropriate section within Control Panel or elsewhere, from where it can be corrected. Alternatively, click the **Suggested Settings Assistant** button, which can resolve issues/potential issues for you (this button is present only if there are issues).

A scan can be performed at any point by clicking the green **Scan** button. To setup or modify an existing scheduled scan, click the **Scan Schedule** icon towards the top right-hand corner of the screen.

6.4 Antivirus Application

Files stored on the server by Windows computers and other clients may potentially become infected with viruses and hence need to be checked to prevent further distribution, and this can be checked using the built-in anti-virus application of QTS. It can be launched in two ways: if Security Counselor is being used, click the **Antivirus** link on the *Overview* screen; if Security Counselor is not being used, click the **Antivirus** icon within the **Control Panel**. The following screen is displayed:

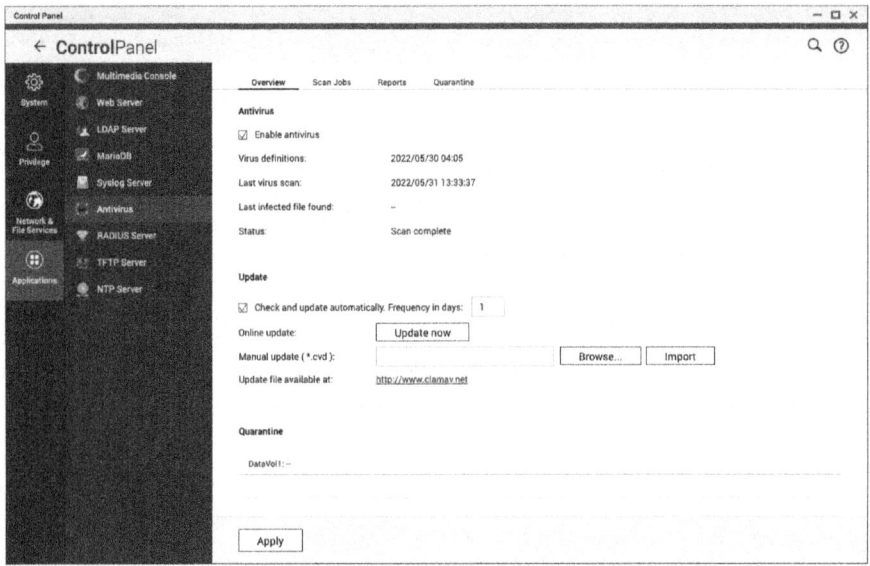

Figure 70: Configuring the anti-virus app

Tick the **Enable antivirus** box, along with the **Check and update automatically** box. The default update value is daily, but can be made less frequent if desired e.g. check every 7 days. Click the **Apply** button. You should also click the **Update now** button if this is the first time you have used Antivirus, to ensure it has the most recent definitions.

The antivirus program does not run constantly in the background in the way that an antivirus program on a Windows computer typically does; instead, scans are carried out on a scheduled basis. To setup a schedule, click the **Add a Scan Job** button on the **Scan Jobs** tab.

On the resultant panel, give the scan a Job Name (e.g. *weeklyAVscan*) and choose the default **All folders** option, followed by **Next**. On the subsequent panel specify the frequency e.g. Scan weekly. Scanning can result in high CPU and memory utilization and, depending on the amount of data stored on the server, can be time consuming. For this reason, it is best done out of hours, such as during the night or at weekends. In this example, the scan is set to start at 10.00pm/2200 on a Friday night. Keep clicking **Next** on the subsequent screens until the final one is reached, where you should choose the **Move infected files to quarantine** option. Click **Finish**.

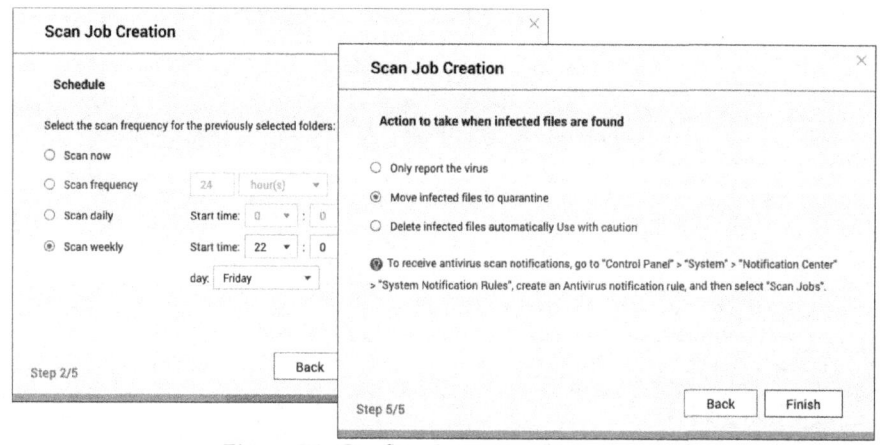

Figure 71: Configuring an anti-virus scan

Optionally, notifications for antivirus scans can be configured, although this has to be done elsewhere, using the Notification Center (see section **8.4 Notification Center**).

To run a scan manually at any time, go to the main Antivirus screen and click the small 'play' icon against a scheduled job in the Action column.

Running the antivirus application on the NAS does not remove the need to make separate provision for connected computers, which still need an anti-virus program installed on them e.g. Microsoft Defender Antivirus, AVG, McAfee etc.

6.5 Malware Remover

Whereas the antivirus application described above is for checking files stored on the NAS that originated from connected devices, the purpose of *Malware Remover* is to check for and remove any possible infections within QTS itself. Like the antivirus application, it is installed by default and is located on the Main Menu. It will be integrated within Security Counselor if that is installed and can be accessed from either. The first time it is run, there will be a message asking whether you are willing to share anonymized information with QNAP; reply *Yes* or *No* according to your preference. The screen then appears as follows:

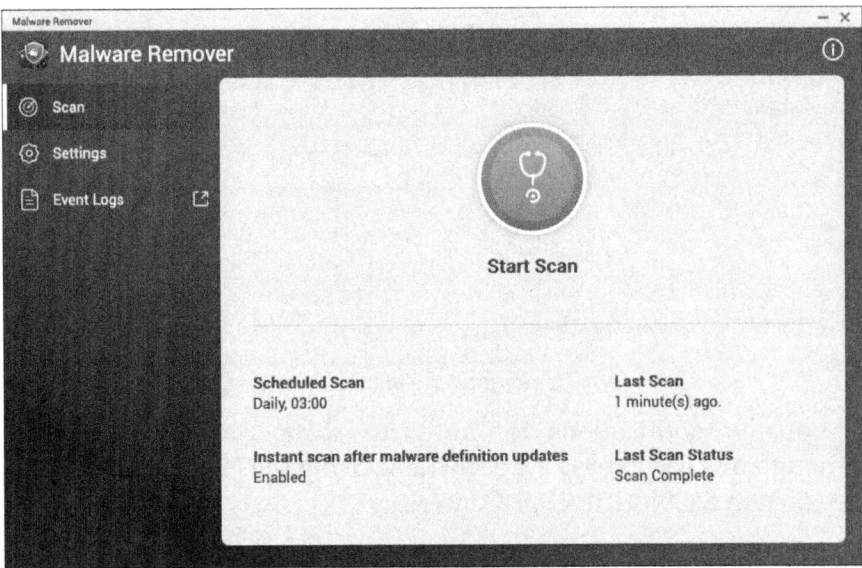

Figure 72: Malware Remover main screen

To initiate a scan, click the large blue button labelled **Start Scan**. To adjust the scheduling, click the **Settings** cogwheel on the left-hand side of the screen. To view the log file, click the **Event Logs** link to open it in QuLog Center (see **6.13 QuLog Center**).

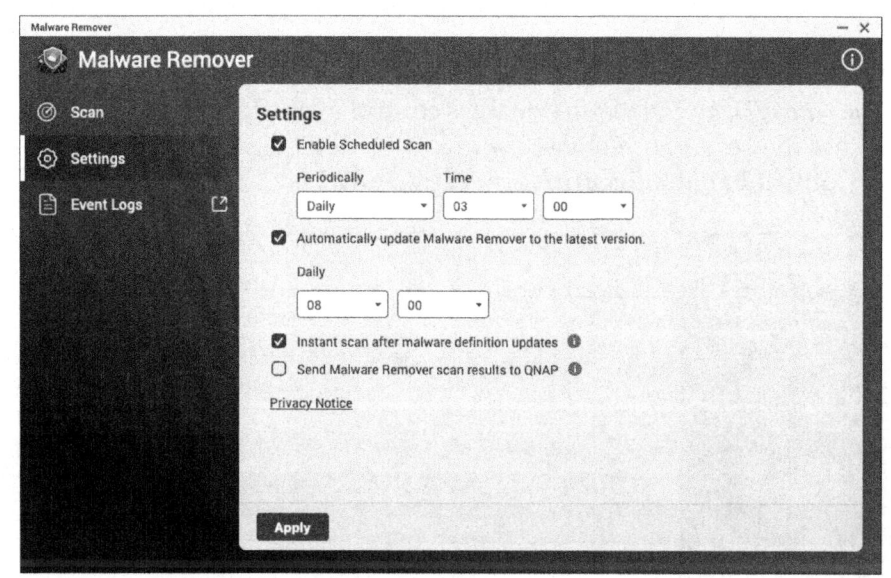

Figure 73: Malware Remover Setting & Scheduling

6.6 Allow/Deny List

The *Allow/Deny List* feature enables control over IP addresses that can access the server, or conversely are to be denied access. It is located at **Control Panel > Security > Access/Deny List**:

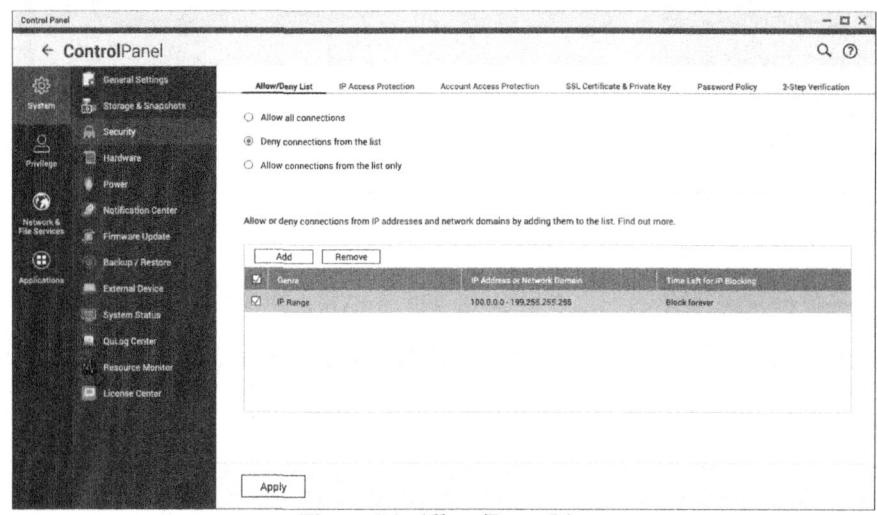

Figure 74: Allow/Deny List

By default, all connections are allowed, but there may be circumstances when this needs to be changed. Here are two examples:

Example 1: A specific external IP address is constantly trying to gain access, which may indicate a hacker or some other attempt to compromise the system. In such a case, click **Deny connections from the list**, click the **Add** button and specify the IP address(es).

Example 2: The server is being used in a managed office facility that contains other people who are unconnected with the business. A shared internet/network facility is provided and there is concern that they could intentionally or accidentally access the server. In such a case click **Allow connections from the list only**, click **Add** and specify the IP addresses of the computers in your organization.

Having made any changes, click **Apply** to implement them.

If QuFirewall has been installed (see **6.12 QuFirewall**), it will replace the Allow/Deny List and a link to it will appear on the tab instead.

6.7 IP Access Protection

The *IP Access Protection* feature is used in conjunction with the Allow/Deny List described above and enables access to be blocked based on the internet networking protocol being used by the clients. For instance, external hackers will frequently try to access computer systems using SSH and Telnet protocols. It can be accessed at **Control Panel > Security > IP Access Protection**:

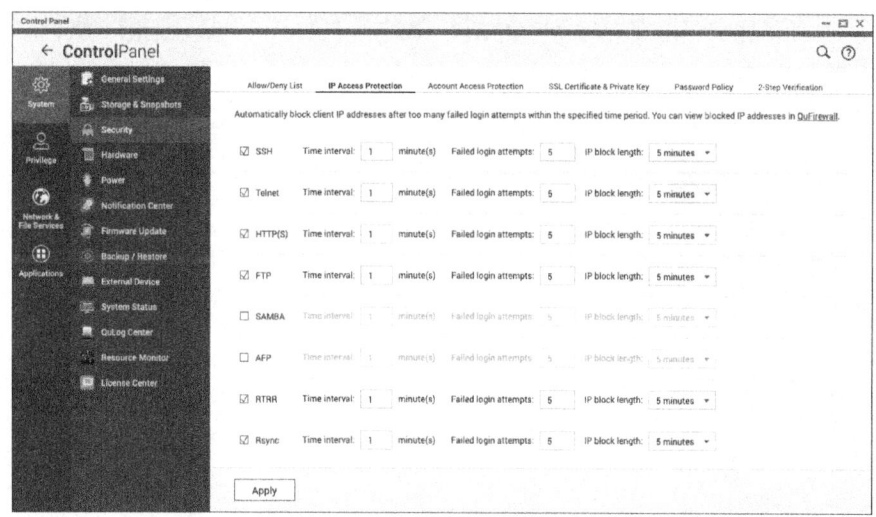

Figure 75: Access Protection

To protect against a particular type of network protocol access, place a tick in the appropriate box. The default values for SSH, Telnet, HTTP(s) and FTP are if there are 5 failed login attempts within one minute, then the IP address is blocked for 5 minutes. Most attempts at hacking are automated and these default values should be suitable to counter them, but you could tighten them by increasing the IP block length (the lockout period) to a higher value. Click **Apply** to make the changes.

To view IP addresses that have been blocked, use the Allow/Deny List tab or, if QuFirewall has been installed, click the link to that.

6.8 Account Access Protection

The *Account Access Protection* screen is used to automatically disable accounts if there are multiple failed login attempts within a specified time period. This security measure is partly aimed at users within the organization; for instance, imagine a scenario in which a curious or disgruntled employee is making systematic attempts to try and access a colleague's account.

It is located at **Control Panel > Security > Account Access Protection**:

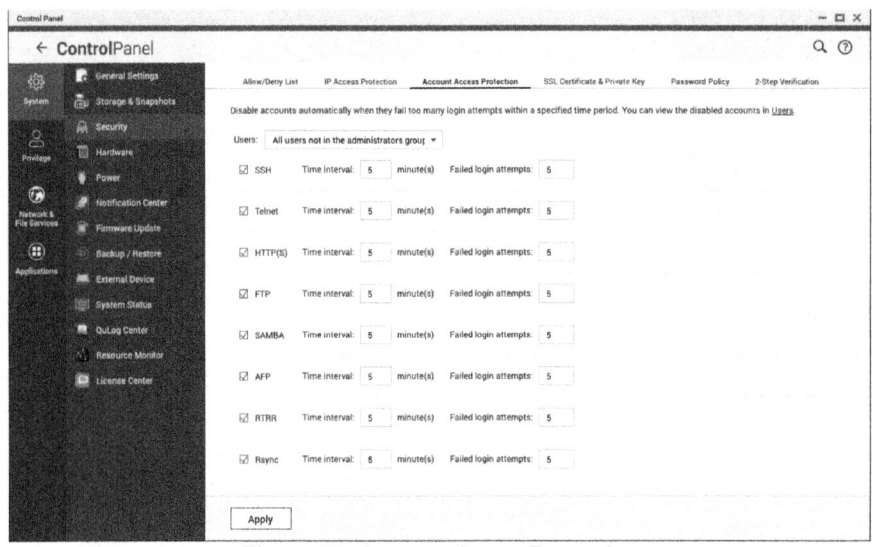

Figure 76: Account Access Protection

To protect against a particular type of network protocol access, place a tick in the appropriate box. The default values are that if there are 5 failed login attempts within one minute, after which the user account is disabled. Click **Apply** to make the changes.

To re-enable a blocked user, go to **Control Panel > Users**. Highlight the user, click the **Edit Account Profile** mini-icon and remove the tick from the **Disable this account** box.

6.9 SSL Certificate & Private Key

The *Certificate & Private Key* feature is an option within Security, used for managing SSL (Secure Socket Layer) certificates. The purpose of an SSL certificate is to validate the identify of a web server when using it and provide encryption when exchanging data, whether that is a conventional internet website or a QNAP NAS being accessed remotely. QNAP provide a default certificate; this will be sufficient for many home and small business users, but secure certificates can also be obtained from trusted (accredited) providers, both freely or on a commercial basis from QNAP and other sources. If secure TLS is to be used (not common in a home environment), custom root certificates can also be imported.

Going into **Control Panel > Security > SSL Certificate & Private Key** displays the following screen. It shows that the default certificate issued by QNAP is being used, along with its expiry date (certificates commonly have a maximum life of 24 months but this QNAP one applies for 10 years).

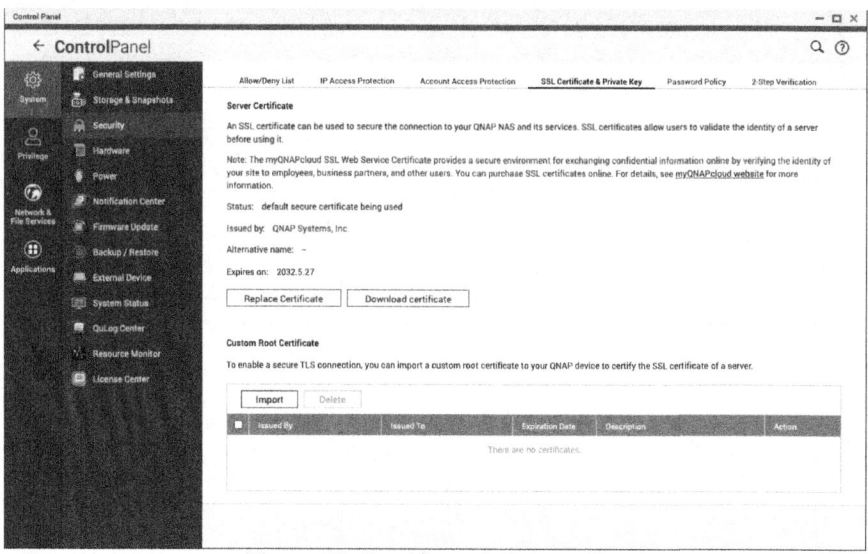

Figure 77: Certificate & Private Key

Two options are available:

Replace Certificate – This allows you to import a new certificate, for instance one obtained from QNAP or from the open certificate authority *Let's Encrypt*, which provides certificates free of charge (although they will accept donations). Or, you can 'roll your own' and create a self-signed certificate. Self-certified certificates should not be used for public facing websites but are considered fine for internal use.

Download Certificate – this allows you to download a copy of the certificate and private key from the NAS for safety and backup purposes.

More general information about using certificates can be located at the **https://letsencrypt.org/docs/** website.

6.10 Password Policy

The *Password Policy* security feature is for controlling the strength and characteristics of user passwords. Whenever a user account is created on the NAS, a password must be specified. By default, the password needs to be at least 8 characters and include letters and numbers. Passwords should be non-obvious – under no circumstances use words such as 'password', 'secret', 'NAS', 'QNAP', 'admin' or close variants. Nor is it a good idea to have the password the same as the user's name. The best passwords combine a mixture of upper and lower letters, numbers and punctuation and are not too short in length. For instance, a password such as *!N3y!YoRk!* would be quite difficult for someone to guess.

The settings are accessed from the **Control Panel > Security > Password Policy** tab:

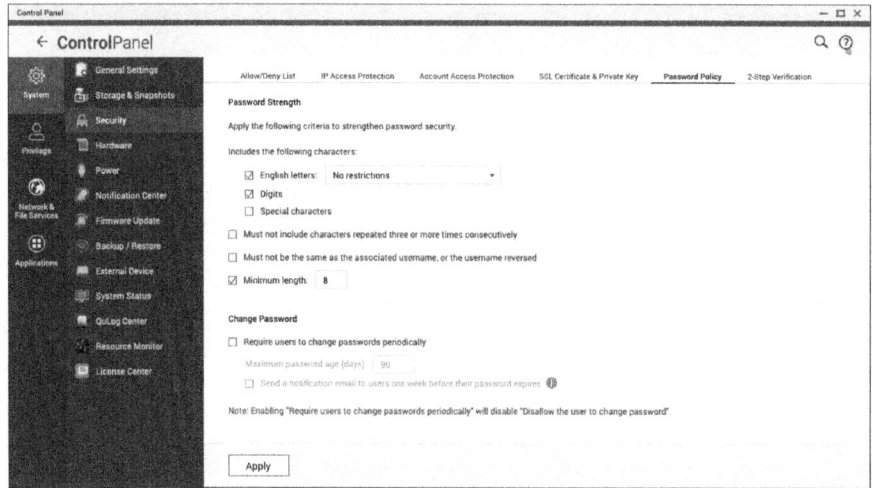

Figure 78: Password Policy

There are four options that can be specified:

The password has to contain a mixture of lower and upper case (English) letters, digits (numbers) and special characters e.g. *!N3y!YoRk!*

No character can be repeated more than 3 times consecutively e.g. *ssssecret* would not be allowed

The password cannot be the same as the username or the username spelled backwards e.g. a user called maria could not have a password of *maria* or *airam*.

Users can be forced to change their passwords on a regular basis e.g. every 90 days. Optionally, they can be sent a notification email a week in advance of when their password will expire. They can also see when their password will expire when logging out of QTS

Having made any changes click the **Apply** button.

These settings will apply to all users of the system.

6.11 2-Step Verification

When logging in to the NAS, a user provides a password to help verify their identity. With *2-Step Verification*, in addition to the password the user has to provide a unique, one-off code when they want to access the server. This is used in conjunction with a mobile device (tablet or phone) on which *Google Authenticator* or *Microsoft Authenticator* is installed. 2-Step Verification is enabled on a user-by-user basis; for instance, it could be used for administrators and users who work away from the office in a business environment.

The user should begin by installing the appropriate Authenticator app on their mobile device, which in this example is Google Authenticator. Then, they should login to the server from a standard computer and click **Options** (indicated by their user name in the top right-hand corner of the screen), click the **2-step Verification** tab, and on that click the **Get Started** button. Scan the QR code using the Authenticator app; alternatively, make a note of the account and security key to enter manually.

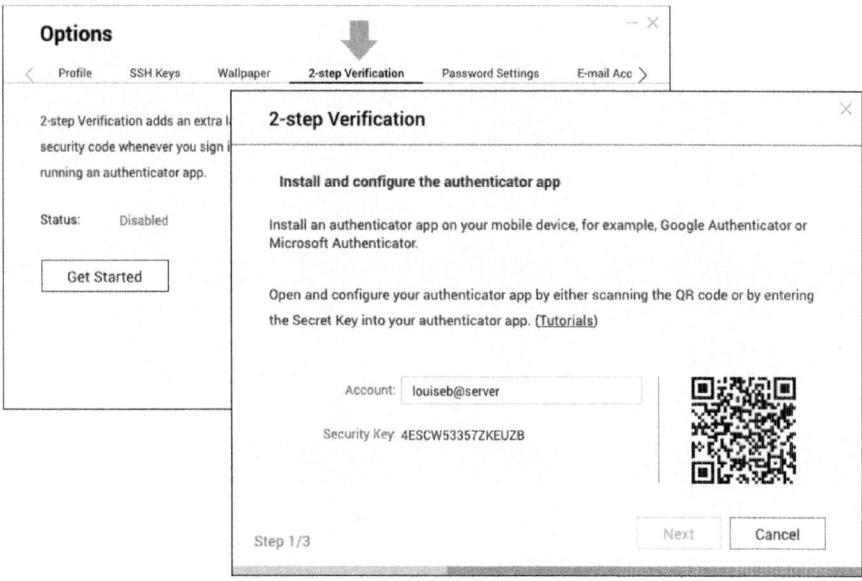

Figure 79: Setting up 2-step Verification

A security code will appear on the Authenticator app. On the computer, type in the code and click **Verify** and **Next**. Answer the security question and click **Finish** – after 5 seconds the user will be logged out. 2-Step Verification has now been setup.

To subsequently login, start the Authenticator app on the mobile device. Login to the computer in the standard manner by providing a username and password. There will then be a prompt for the security code generated by the Authenticator app, which has to be typed in to continue the login process. The code is time-limited, so has to be entered within 30 seconds or so.

Having setup 2-step Verification, the user can subsequently stop or reconfigure it. For example, a business user who is going on holiday might choose to use it temporarily to enhance security.

To enforce 2-Step Verification for a user, the administrator should go to **Control Panel > Security > 2-Step Verification** and tick the **Enforce 2SV** box against the user's name, followed by **Apply**.

If there are too many failed login attempts, the user account will be locked. It will then have to be reset by the administrator (**Control Panel > Users > Edit Account Profile**).

6.12 QuFirewall

A *firewall* allows the creation of rules which define access to a device, based upon various network criteria. It is almost certainly the case that your internet connection already has a firewall of some sort, either within the router itself or in the form of a separate appliance if you are a larger business user. QNAP offers an optional, second level firewall in the form of an app called *QuFirewall*, which can be used to enhance security on the NAS.

Download and install QuFirewall from the App Center. If Security Counselor has been installed, it will be integrated within it and can be launched from there, otherwise it can be accessed from the Main Menu. The first time it is used, a *Get Started* wizard will run – click **Start** to begin. As part of this process, the Allow/Deny List function (discussed in **6.6 Allow/Deny List**) will be migrated to QuFirewall. Work through the screens and choose a profile configuration i.e. settings and a collection of rules. In a home setting or very small business, you might want to choose **Basic protection** to start (the profile can always be changed subsequently). Click **Next**.

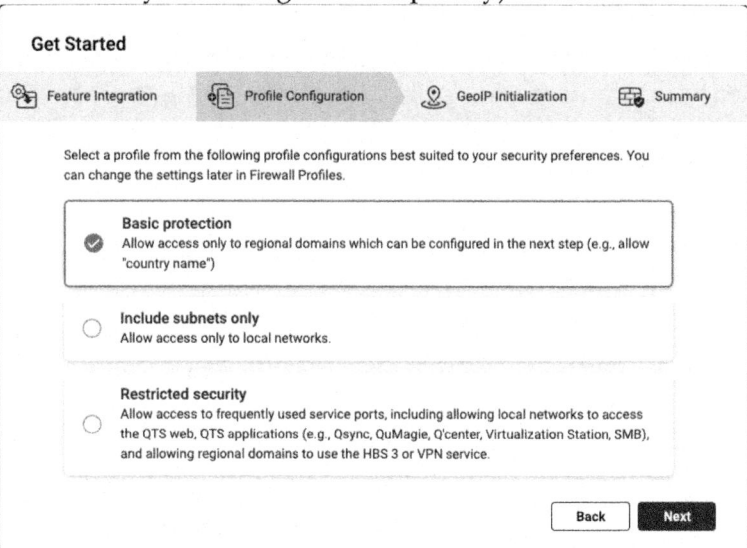

Figure 80: Choose a Profile Configuration

On the subsequent screen, choose your region/country from the dropdown and click **Next**. On the one after that, check that the **Enable firewall** box is ticked and click **Finish**. After a short delay, the standard QuFirewall screen is displayed:

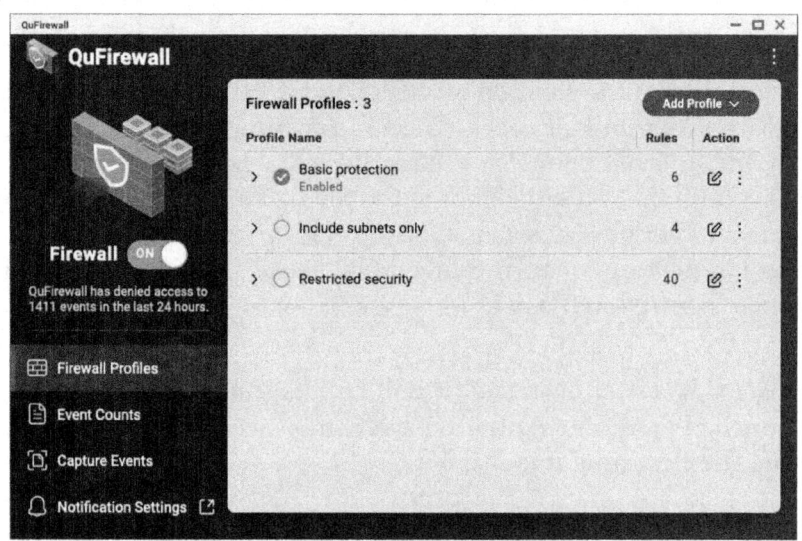

Figure 81: QuFirewall screen

Options are listed down the left-hand side of the screen:

Firewall Profiles – lists the profiles and enables new ones to be created. To manage an existing profile, click the **Edit** icon against it.

Event Counts – a record of the events (denied packets). The frequency and time period of events can be configured by clicking the vertical three-dot menu on the top-right hand corner of the screen and choosing **Settings > Firewall Event**.

Capture Events – enables packets to be captured for a specific time period. They can then be analyzed in greater detail to determine threats using third-party open-source software such as Wireshark, NetworkMiner or WinDump.

Notification Settings – links to Notification Center (see **8.4 Notification Center**).

One thing to be aware of is that unless the profile(s) used by QuFirewall are carefully tuned, it may record tens of thousands of events each day, creating the false impression that the system is under constant attack.

If you subsequently decide to disable QuFirewall, slide the Firewall switch to the 'OFF' position. This will require you to enter the server's admin password.

6.13 QuLog Center

QTS maintains a comprehensive audit trail of all significant activities, including when users login in to the system and which apps and system processes have been running. This information can be used to audit activity when there are suspected security violations, as well as more general access and other problems. This information is maintained in log files which can be viewed and analyzed using the *QuLog Center* app. *QuLog Center* is able to monitor not just the local device it is installed upon, but also other QNAP devices in the network. In this introduction we are concerned with local use only.

QuLog Center can be accessed from the **Main Menu** as well as the **Control Panel**. Running it for the first time will display a quick welcome tour, which can be worked through if required or skipped (if you do not want to see it on subsequent occasions then answer **No** to the displayed message). The *Overview* screen then appears as follows. There are two main panels that provide graphical summaries of the Event Log and the Access Log:

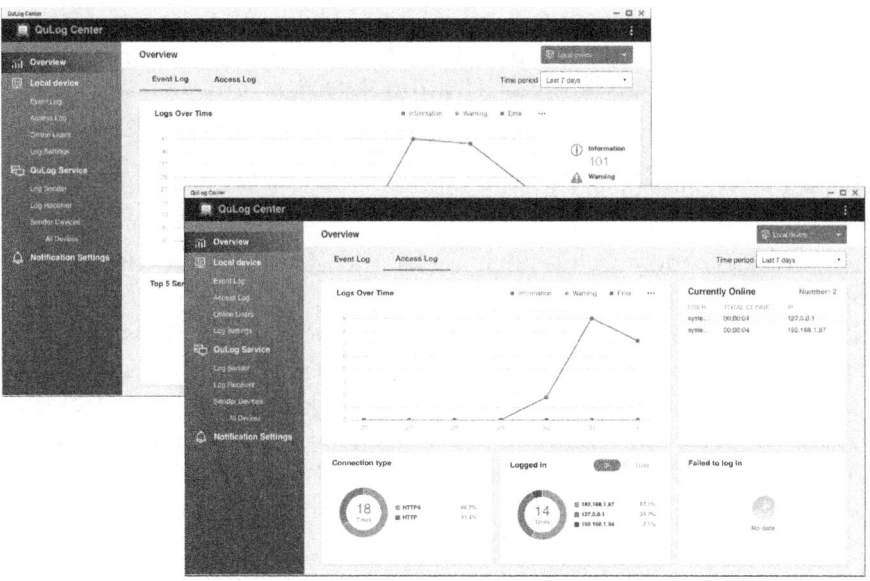

Figure 82: QuLog Center Overview screens

There are four tabbed sections in the Local device section:

Event Log – a record of all system activities. It can be filtered by severity level e.g. to only show errors rather than all categories. Entries can be sorted (e.g. by Date, Severity, Category etc) by clicking on the column headings. The log file can be exported into CSV or HTML formats for further analysis if required.

Access Log – a record of user activities, including when they logged on, logged off, created folders and so on. Entries can be sorted (e.g. by Date, Severity, Category etc) by clicking on the column headings. The log file can be exported into CSV or HTML formats for further analysis if required.

Online Users – gives a list of which users are currently connected to the NAS. By right-clicking a user, it is possible to disconnect them or add them to a block list on a temporary or permanent basis.

Log Settings – the maximum number of entries and how long they are retained is controlled from here. The Connection types that are logged e.g. HTTP/HTTPS, iSCSI, Telnet etc., can be specified. The log files can also be deleted from this section.

Optionally, QuLog Center can be linked to the Notification Center, which is discussed in section **8.4 Notification Center**. To define notification rules, go into **Notification Settings**.

6.14 Disallow USB Devices

USB devices, such as memory sticks and external hard drives, can pose a security threat since they enable data to be stolen; potentially, they could also be used to introduce malware onto the server. To protect against this, it is possible to disable USB devices. Go into **Control Panel > External Device** and click the **USB** tab. Tick the **Disallow USB devices** box. To disable all USB devices, click **Disallow all USB device types**. Alternatively, to disable storage devices but still permit keyboards, wireless dongles, mice and other peripherals, choose the **Disallow only USB storage devices** option.

If USB is disabled, the USB One Touch Copy feature (see section **7.5 USB One Touch Copy**) will not operate.

7
BACKUPS

7.1 Overview

It is important to backup data on a regular basis to cope with the problems that can arise with computers, which include deleting files by accident, malware infections, data corruption, computer failure and equipment being lost or stolen. Usually, the value of data far outweighs the value of the computers themselves; for instance, what price could be attached to the irreplaceable photos of a Wedding Day, graduation, children's first steps or other important occasion? In the case of businesses, around half that have a serious data loss subsequently cease trading within twelve months, plus there may be statutory requirements to retain certain data in some parts of the world. The assumption to follow is that it is more a question of *when* rather than *if* data will be lost at some point, which is when the backups will be needed.

The best strategy is to aim for a *3-2-1 solution*, meaning there are at least three copies of the data, they are held in at least two different formats, and at least one copy is held offsite, away from the premises. This approach of having multiple backups in multiple places ensures that there is always a fallback in the event of problems. For instance: The computers in the home or office are backed up to the NAS. The NAS in turn is backed up to an external USB drive. Optionally, the NAS or at least the most important data are backed up to a Cloud-based service. Additionally, the NAS can also be backed up to a second NAS located on or off the premises:

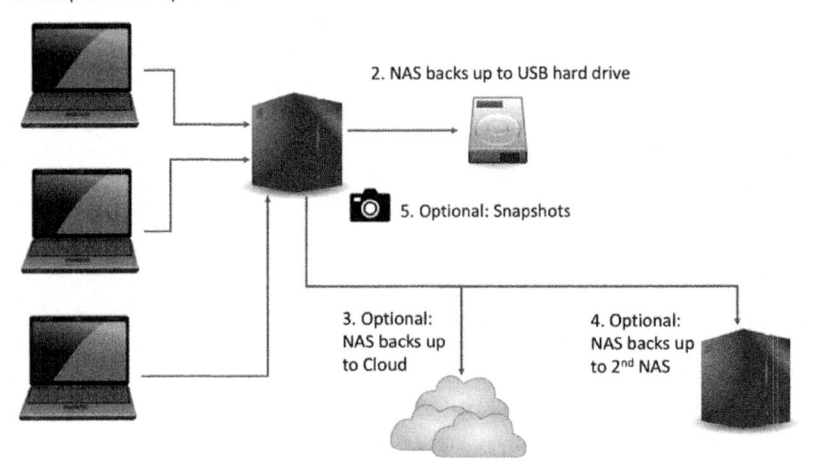

Figure 83: Example of multi-level backup approach

QTS has provision for all these types of backup and provides a single app – *Hybrid Backup Sync* – to handle them. The basic principle is 'any type of backup, to any destination' i.e. you can perform most types of backup operation with external drives, other NAS boxes and to a wide selection of popular cloud services. As mentioned above, the best approach to backups is to take a multi-tiered approach involving different types of backup technology and an important concept here is *off-site storage*, whereby a copy of data is held in a different location altogether. The extensive support for cloud services in Hybrid Backup Sync makes it very suitable for handling off-site backups.

Besides the comprehensive facilities available through Hybrid Backup Sync, QTS also features *Snapshots*, whereby data is effectively 'photographed' at moments in time. This is defined by QNAP as a storage-related rather than conventional backup mechanism and hence is discussed separately in section **12.4 Snapshots**.

7.2 Hybrid Backup Sync

Download and install Hybrid Backup Sync 3 from the App Center, then launch it by clicking its icon on the Desktop or choosing it from the Main Menu. The first time it is run, QNAP's privacy policy is displayed: take a decision and proceed. A short introductory tour is displayed; thereafter this overview screen is displayed:

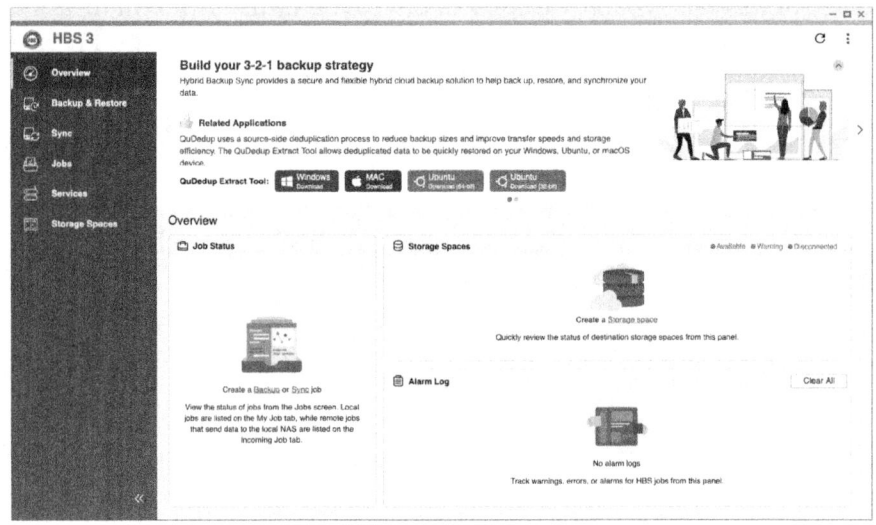

Figure 84: Hybrid Backup Sync Overview screen

On the left-hand side of the screen are links to the different sections, providing a choice of six main categories:

Overview – gives a high-level summary view of backup activities i.e. the above screen.

Backup & Restore – for creating and running backup and restore jobs e.g. a scheduled daily backup to an external drive.

Sync – enables data to be synced with external devices and cloud services, thereby providing offsite backups but also remote access to data.

Jobs – shows the status of the various backup tasks.

Services – used for enabling other backup options such as Time Machine, Rsync and One Touch Copy.

Storage Spaces – backup destinations, whether NAS or cloud-based, are called *Storage Spaces* by QNAP and their details can be checked from here.

What is QuDedup?

The top of the screen contains an advertisement for QNAP's *QuDedup* tool. De-duplication is a technique whereby duplicated data are identified prior to backup, to avoid backing up multiple copies of the same files and folders, thus saving time and space. The QuDedup tool is used for restoring such data onto Windows, macOS and Linux machines. It is optional and is not covered in this guide.

7.3 Backup to External Drive

This backup solution uses an external hard drive; in these examples we will assume the more common USB drive, although a small number of QNAP models can also use Thunderbolt drives. The drive should be USB 3.2. Gen1 specification or better (formerly known as USB 3.0); of sufficient capacity to hold all the data (for instance, if there is 4TB data then use at least a 4TB drive); portable if possible, as such drives do not require mains power and are more convenient to store, although there are capacity restrictions when compared to powered external drives.

To prepare a new drive for backup usage, plug it into a suitable USB socket on the NAS (it cannot be connected indirectly using a USB hub). A message may be displayed, confirming that an external device has been detected and asking how it should be used; the contents of this message can vary based upon whether or not the drive is pre-formatted. If this is the first time you are using the drive for backup purposes, it is suggested you tick the **Do not ask me again** box and choose **View external storage settings using Storage & Snapshots**, even if there is an option to '*Use this device for backup using Hybrid Backup Sync*'.

On the screen in Storage & Snapshots, highlight the drive, right-click it and choose the **Full Disk Format** option. A panel pops up, offering a choice of *File System*; choose *EXT4* from the dropdown, the only reason for choosing one of the others is that the drive can then be read by other computer types, thus potentially allowing more options for data recovery in the event of extreme circumstances. Give the drive a descriptive label (name) e.g. *Backup*. There is an option is to encrypt the drive; the reason for doing this is that if the backup was ever stolen or lost, then it would be very difficult for someone else to read its contents. One implication of using encryption is that it will slow down the backup process, but this may be a worthwhile trade-off if confidential data is being handled. Having chosen the formatting option, click the **Format** button and acknowledge the warning message by clicking **OK**. The time taken to format the drive depends on the capacity of the drive:

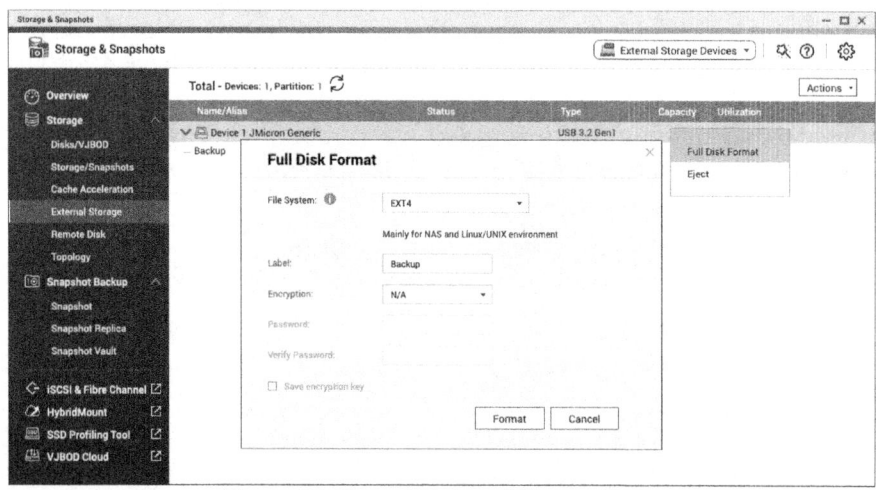

Figure 85: Format External Storage Drive

Once the drive is formatted, quit *Storage & Snapshots* and launch or return to *Hybrid Backup Sync*. Click **Backup & Restore** followed by the large blue **Backup Now** button, and from it choose **New Backup Job**:

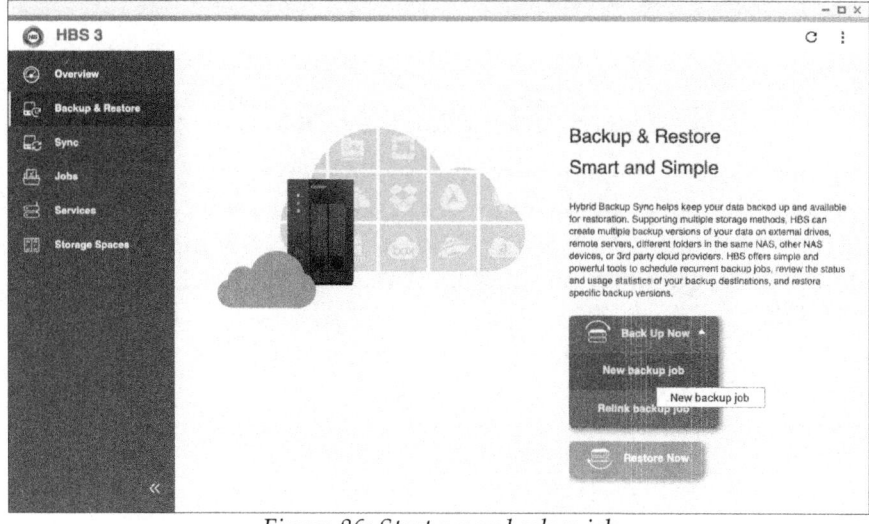

Figure 86: Start a new backup job

There is now a sequence of screens for defining and scheduling the backup. Regardless of whether the backup medium is an external hard drive, another NAS, or cloud service, they are handled in a consistent manner within HBS 3, so much of the information here is applicable to other backup methods described later in this chapter.

On the first screen, select the source folders to be backed up from the relevant volume(s) on the NAS, which in this example is called *DataVol1*. If folders contain sub-folders, they can be expanded and the sub-folders included/excluded as required. Do not include the backup drive itself, which is listed as an External Device, in the selection. Click **Next**.

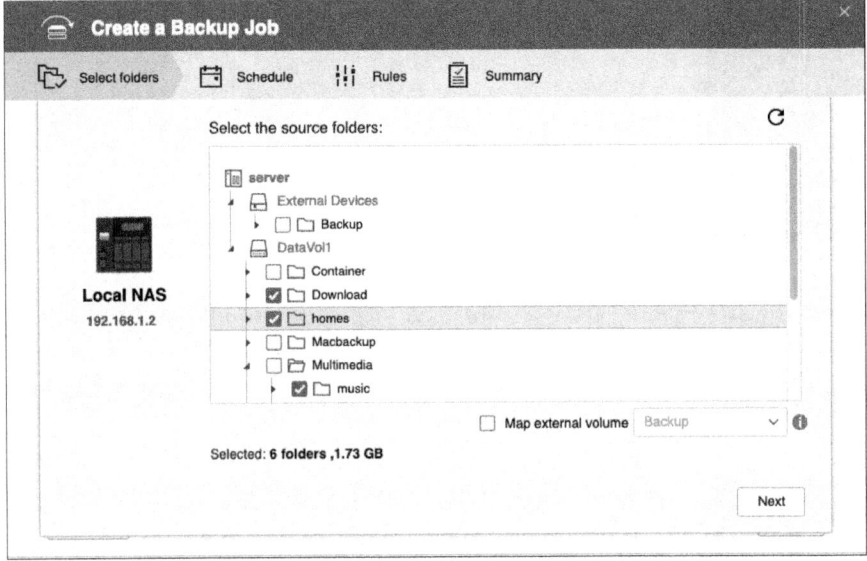

Figure 87: Select source folders for backup

On the following screen, select the destination storage space for the backup. The two categories are *NAS*, divided into *Local NAS* and *Remote NAS*, plus *Cloud Server*. Choose **Local NAS** and click **Select**. On the subsequent screen, highlight the external backup drive and click **OK**:

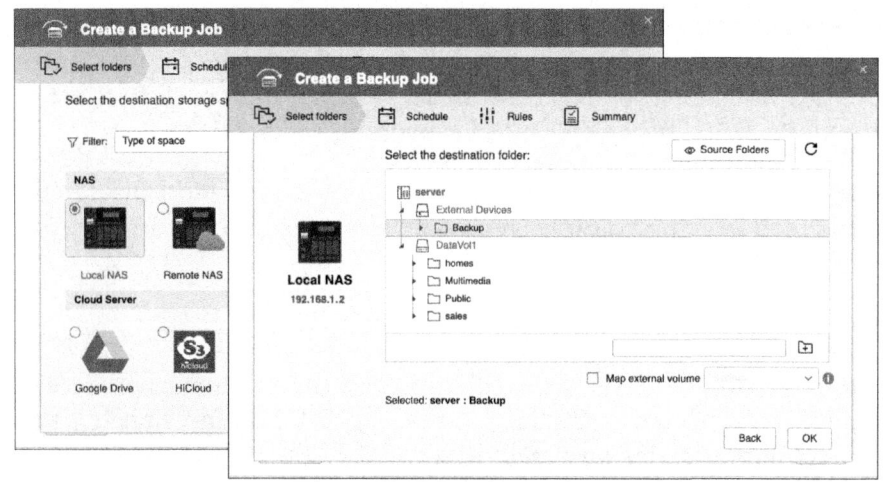

Figure 88: Select destination

A *Job Name* and optional *Description* can be specified. Click **Next**.

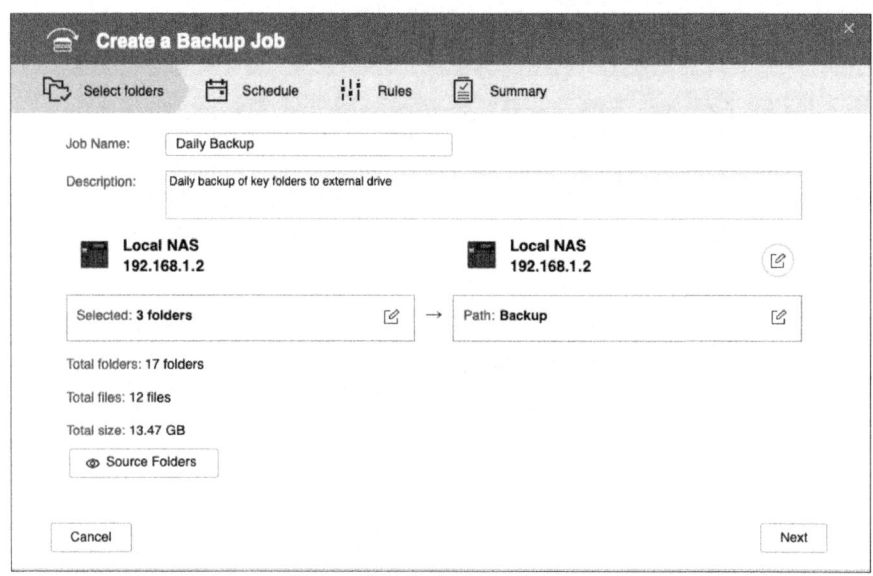

Figure 89: Specify a job name

The next screen is for setting a job schedule and there are four options:

Scheduler - enables the backup job to be scheduled to run on a regular basis e.g. daily, weekly, monthly. Up to 30 separate schedules can be defined. Click the **Scheduler** option, which will cause the panel to expand, then click the plus **(+)** button.

The backup should preferably run at a time when the server is not being used or is not busy, which will depend upon the circumstances of your household or business. In this example the backup is set to run daily at 10:00pm/22:00h in the evening. Click **OK**.

Run after job – the backup will run upon completion of another scheduled job. For example, you could schedule it to run after a virus check or disk check.

No schedule – no schedule will be defined.

Auto-backup – the backup will run each time an external storage device is connected to the NAS (also see **7.5 USB One Touch Copy** for an alternative backup method).

If the backup drive is to be subsequently removed and kept in a separate location until the next time it is used, tick the **Eject external volume after completion** box; if the backup drive is to be kept permanently attached, do not tick the box.

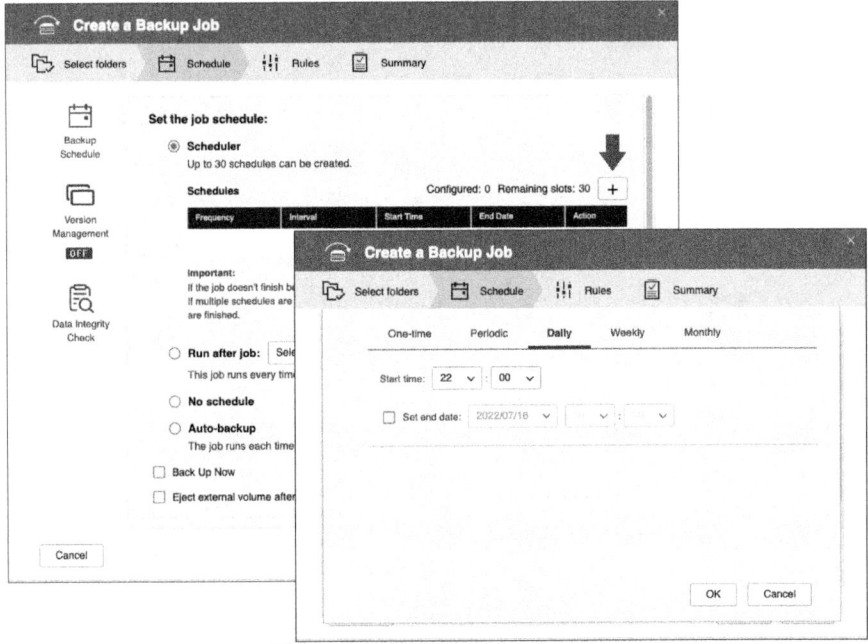

Figure 90: Create a job schedule

Version Management can be selected from the Schedule screen and it is suggested that you do so. With some computer backup systems, you can keep only one backup. But suppose you are performing daily backups, have a problem and need to revert to a copy of a file made, say, a week ago – then what? With Version Management, Hybrid Backup Sync will maintain multiple backups, enabling you to roll back in time to select a specific one. Click where it reads **Version Management** on the left-hand side of the screen, then tick the **Enable Version Management** box. There are two options:

Simple Versioning – retain a specific number of backups e.g. 100 (the maximum is 65536), or a set number of days e.g. 100 (the maximum number is 3650)

Smart Versioning – define the number of hourly, daily, weekly and monthly backups to be retained (if you are a macOS user you may be familiar with Time Machine, which operates in a similar manner, albeit without such granular control)

Regardless of the type of version management, when the backup disk is full the app will start to overwrite the oldest backups to recycle the space.

In this example we have selected Smart Versioning and opted to retain the last hourly, seven daily, eight weekly and ten monthly backups.

There is also an optional *Data Integrity Check* screen. This will cause the system to check the backup and ensure that it can be restored correctly should the need arise. The data integrity check can be run manually or scheduled. QNAP advise that this process uses a lot of resources and may be time consuming, and that an x86-based NAS using SSDs is recommended.

Having defined the schedule and other aspects, click **Next**.

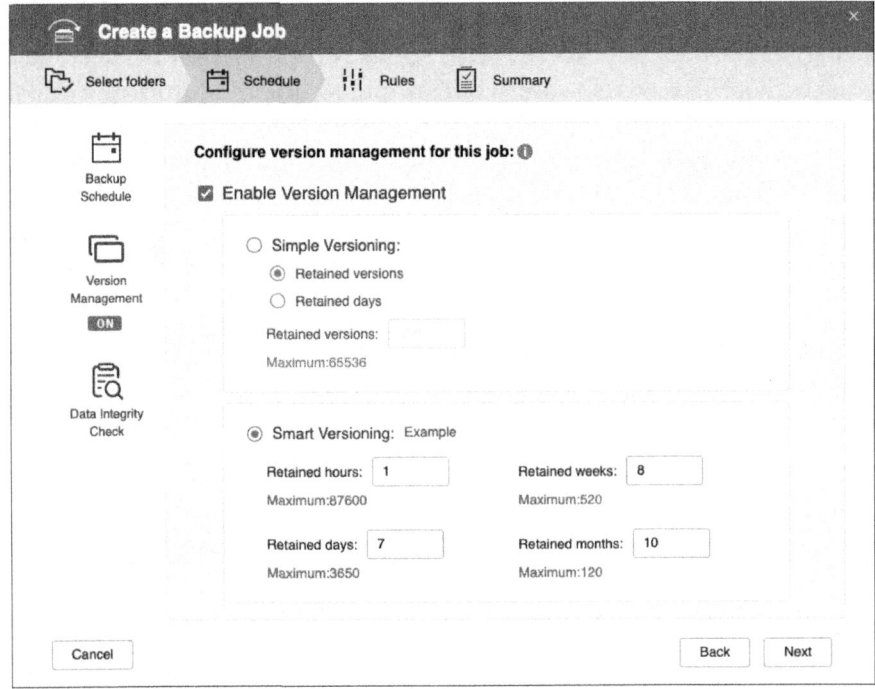

Figure 91: Version management

The next screen allows *Rules* to be applied: these consist of filters, defining the files to be included or excluded in the backup based on characteristics such as file type, size and date. Additional, more advanced options are also available by clicking on **Advanced Filters**, **Policies** and **Options**.

The optional **Advanced settings** is for use of *QuDedup*. This is QNAP's deduplication process, which prevents duplicate copies of data on client computers being backed up. It requires a utility to be installed on the clients and you may have seen references to it when launching Hybrid Backup Sync. For best results, QNAP recommend that the NAS is x86-based, with SSDs and that HBS is installed on an SSD volume. We will not be using it here.

Click **Next** when you have made your choices:

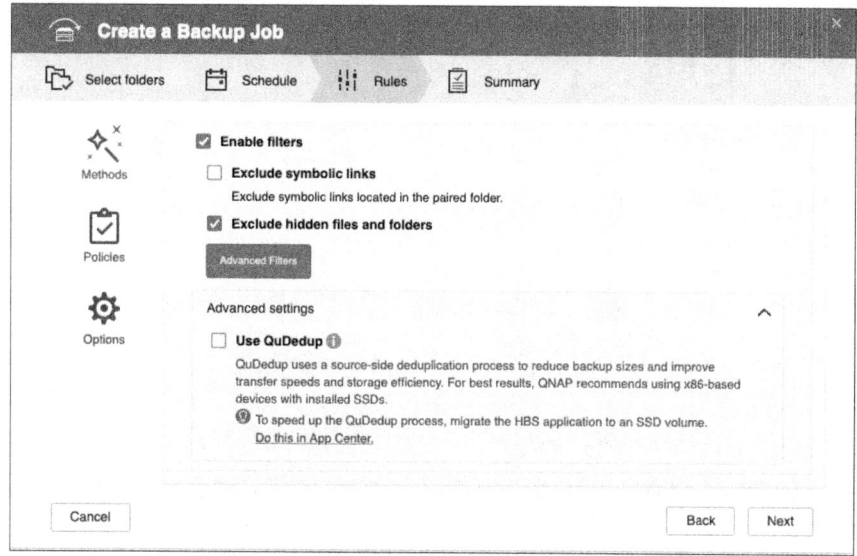

Figure 92: Rules (filters)

A screen to confirm the job settings is shown. The figure at the top of the screen – the estimated RPO or *Recovery Point Objective* – indicates the estimated age of data recoverable in the event of having to use the backup. It is only shown if scheduled backups are used. Assuming all is satisfactory and you wish to proceed, click **Create**:

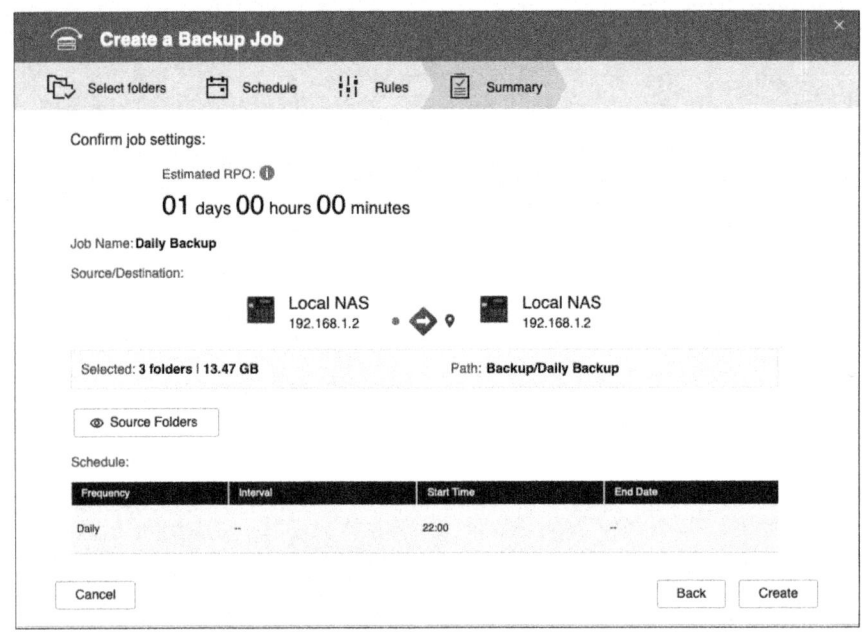

Figure 93: Summary screen for backup job

The backup job is listed in the main *Backup & Restore* section. To run it immediately, which is useful for testing purposes, or manually at any time, click the **Backup Now** button. There are also options to Edit and clone the job, plus view the backup reports.

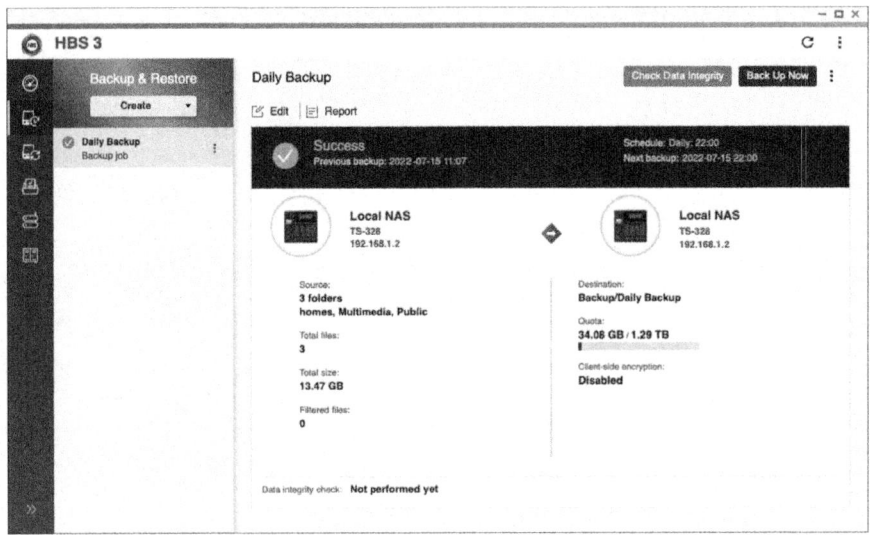

Figure 94: Job listed on main Backup & Restore screen

7.4 Restore Files from External Drive

In the **Backup & Restore** section in HBS 3, click **Create > Restore job** or click the three-dot 'snowman' menu in the right-hand corner and choose **Restore**. Choose the source storage space, which will be **Local NAS**, and click **Select**.

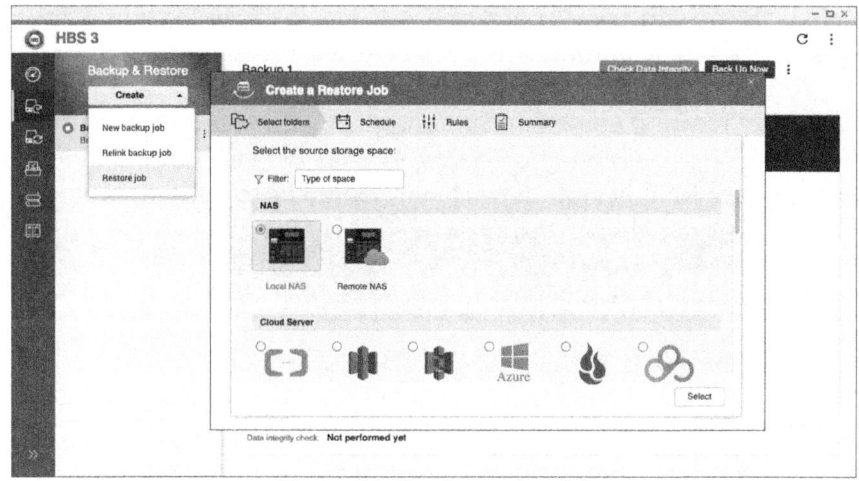

Figure 95: Create a restore job

On the next screen, optionally, specify a *Job Name* and *Description*. *Source* should be set to **Backup job**. Click the *Backup source* dropdown and choose the backup job that was used e.g. Daily Backup, Backup 1 etc.

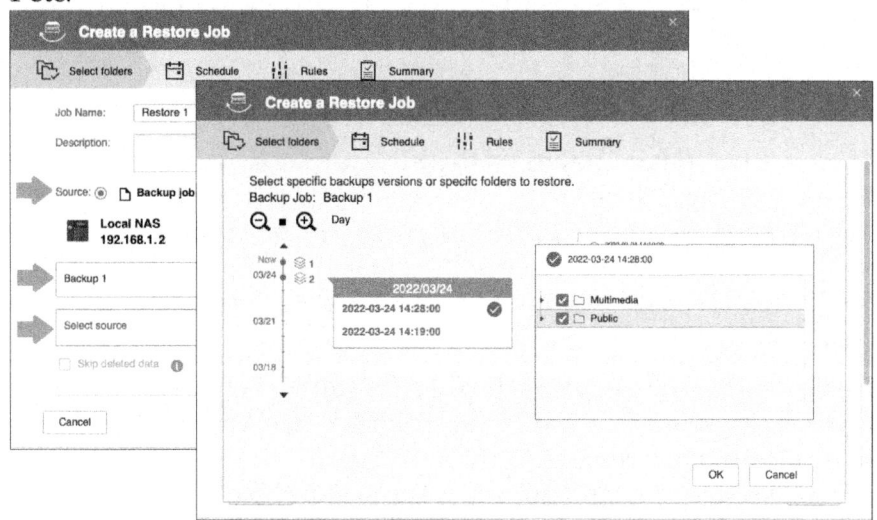

Figure 96: Choose the backup and folders

137

Click *Select source* and choose a backup from the left-hand side of the screen (if versioning is being used then multiple ones will be listed), and the folder(s) to be restored from the right-hand side. Click **OK**.

Returning to the previous panel, specify where the data will be restored to using the dropdown called *Selected location* on the right-hand side. If you choose **Original location**, the restored folder(s) will replace the existing one(s) on the NAS. Alternatively, if you want to check the restored folders and files before deciding to use them, do not restore them to the original location. Instead, create a new temporary location using File Station, specify that temporary location as the Selected location and restore to that, then subsequently copy them to their final destination when satisfied as to their suitability.

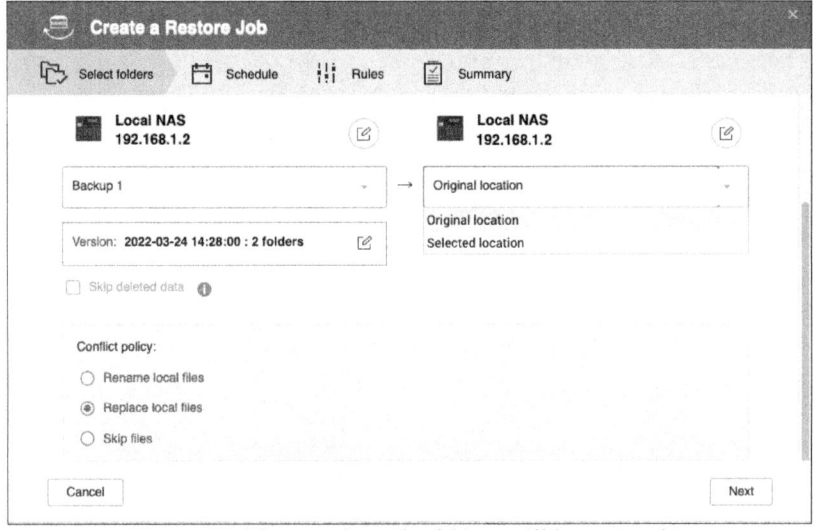

Figure 97: Choose where the folders will be restored to

There are two other options on this screen. First, if *Skip deleted data* is ticked, then files which were (intentionally) deleted from the NAS are not replaced. Second, the *Conflict policy* can be specified i.e. what happens when files and folders that are being restored already exist on the NAS. The choices are to rename, replace or skip them. Click **Next**.

On the *Schedule* tab, setup a schedule if required. For instance, if there was a large amount of data to be restored then you might want to schedule the job to run overnight. If you wish to restore immediately, choose **No schedule** and tick the **Restore Now** box. Click **Next**.

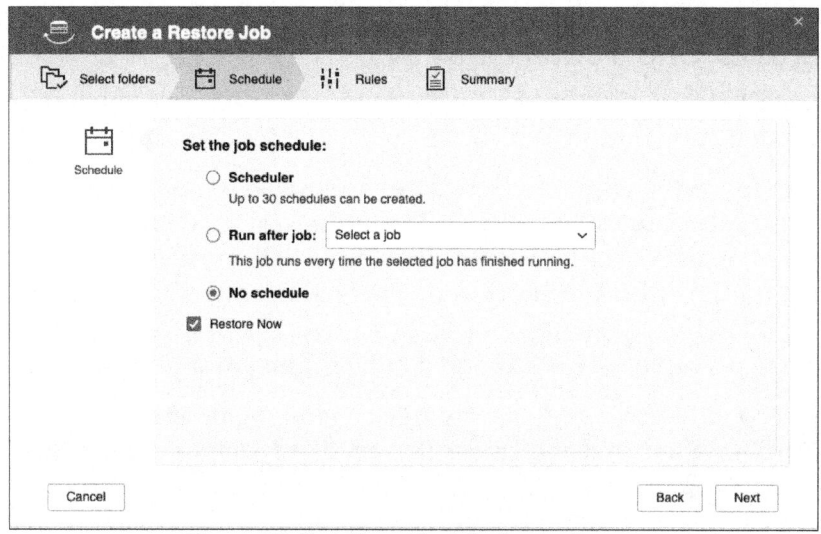

Figure 98: Specify a schedule for the Restore

The subsequent panel allows optional *Rules* to be defined. However, as there are only two - a policy of not taking a snapshot and an option of restarting the job if there is an abnormal termination – you might just click **Next**, which will lead to the *Summary* screen. From there, click the **Restore** button. If the *Restore Now* option was chosen the restore job will now run, else it will be scheduled according to the parameters that were supplied.

7.5 USB One Touch Copy

Many QNAP models have a front-mounted USB socket along with a dedicated copy button, which can be used in several different ways:

Smart Import – when a USB drive is plugged in, any photos and videos will be automatically copied to the server; **USB One Touch Copy** – copies the contents of the USB drive to the server or vice versa when the Copy button is pressed; **External Storage Drive** – Enables the USB drive to be shared and accessed over the network, effectively creating a simple way to expand a NAS running out of disk space.

The second of these options provides a simple and straightforward backup solution that will meet the needs of some people. Launch **Hybrid Backup Sync** from the **Desktop** or **Main Menu**, then click **Services** followed by **USB One Touch Copy**. Within that, select the **USB One Touch Copy** option. Insert a USB memory stick or external drive into the server's front mounted socket – wait a few seconds until a notification message pops up on the server confirming that the USB stick has been identified. The first time you may receive a message asking what to do with it: tick **Do not ask me again** and click **Close**.

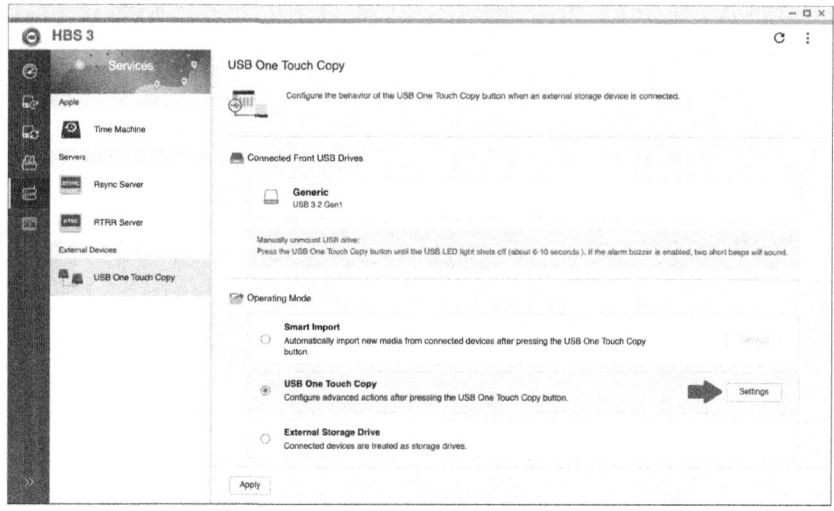

Figure 99: USB One Touch Copy screen

Click the **Settings** button. Set the *Backup mode* dropdown to **Back up to connected USB drive** and the *Backup action* to **Copy**. Underneath is an area for specifying the source and destination folders.

Click the plus sign (**+**) on the left-hand side and choose a source folder e.g. *Public* in our example. Click **OK**. Click the plus sign (**+**) next to *Add a paired folder* on the right-hand side and select the USB drive e.g. */FrontUSB1*. Click **OK**. The screen should now appear along the following lines. Click the **Apply** button at the bottom of the screen and then again on the main screen.

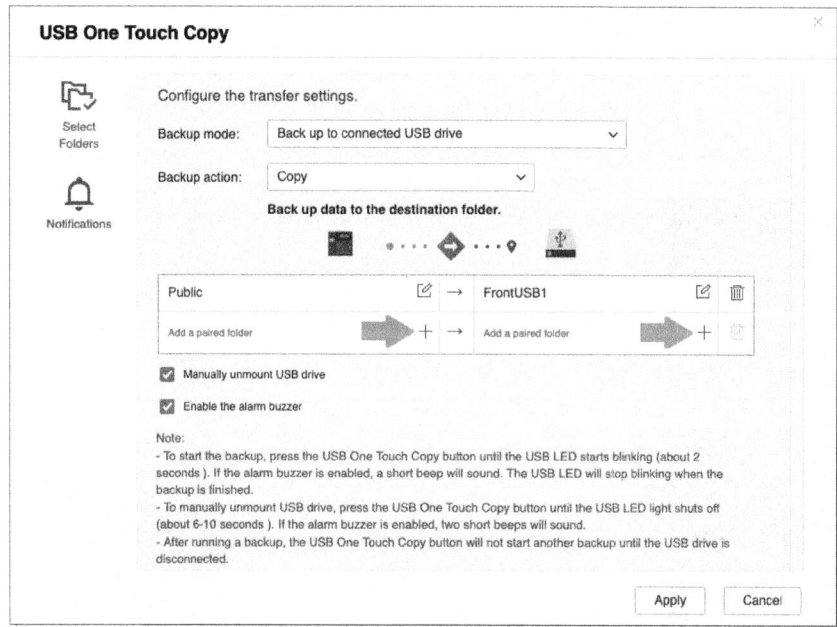

Figure 100: Configuring USB One Touch Copy

To take a backup, insert the USB drive. Wait until the USB indicator light stops flashing, meaning that the drive has been mounted. Hold down the server's USB One Touch Copy button for a couple of seconds until the USB indicator light starts flashing – this shows that the contents are being copied from the NAS. When the data has all been copied, the indicator light will stop flashing. The USB drive can now be unmounted and removed, which is done by holding down the USB One Touch Copy button until the USB LED shuts off, which takes around six seconds.

To restore files from a backup, reverse the process by changing the *Backup mode* dropdown to **Back up to NAS**.

Tip: On some models, the copy button is next to the server's on-off button. Make sure that you are holding down the correct button, else the server might power down unintentionally.

7.6 Sync to Cloud

Hybrid Backup Sync can be used to sync or backup data on the NAS with popular Cloud services such as *Microsoft OneDrive*, *Google Drive*, *Dropbox*, *Azure*, *Yandex.Disk* plus many others. This enables a simple and easily manageable off-site backup solution to be implemented.

Launch Hybrid Backup Sync and click the **Sync** tab followed by **Sync Now** > **One-way Sync Job** (if you already have some existing Sync jobs, click the **Create** button that will also be present instead).

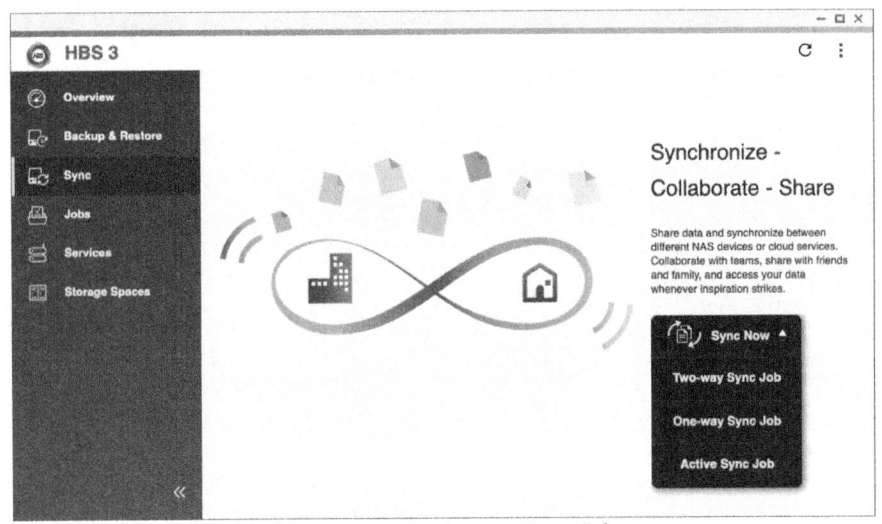

Figure 101: Begin new Sync Job

On the resultant screen, choose the destination storage space from the Cloud Server section; there are more than 30 supported services, both public and enterprise ones, although availability may vary by geographical location. Choose one that you have an account with and you will be prompted to login and authenticate with it, the details of which vary depending upon which one you are using. Having done so, you will be returned to HBS 3 and the *Create a Storage Space* panel, which is usually just a matter of clicking **Create**, although you could choose to give it a different name:

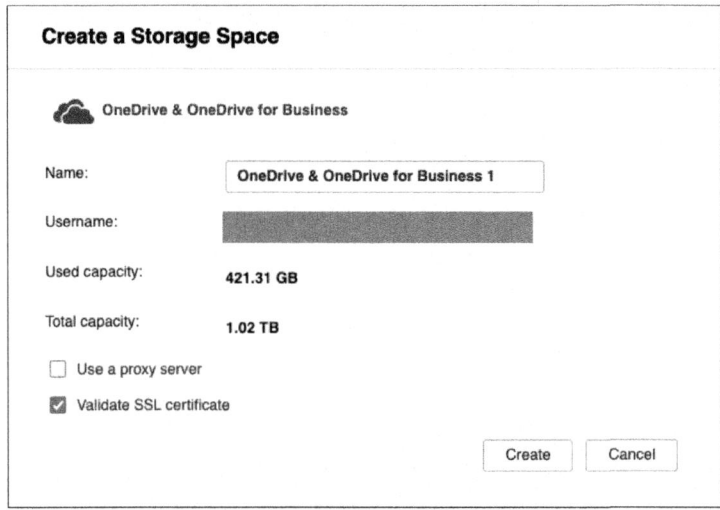

Figure 102: Create a Storage Space

Having done so, you will be returned to the previous screen, where you should highlight the account and click **Select**:

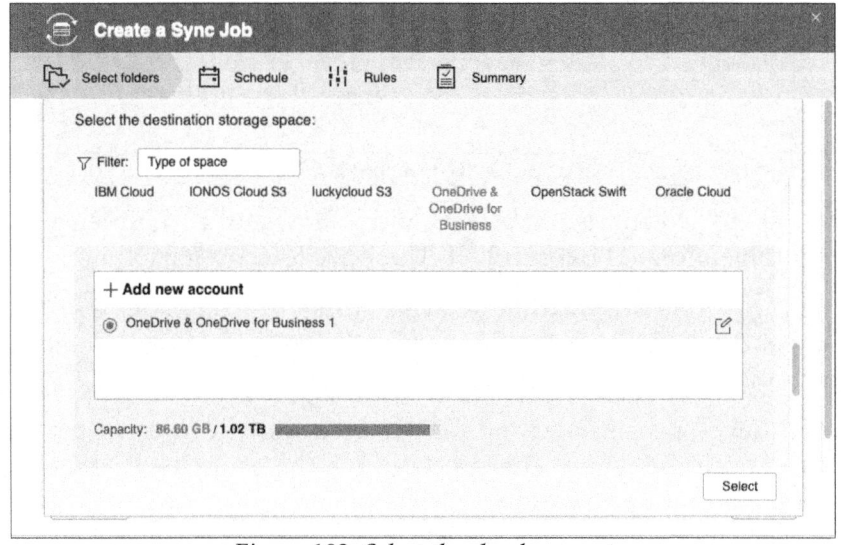

Figure 103: Select the cloud account

The subsequent screen is for setting up 'paired folders' for any folders that are to be synced to the cloud service. Click the plus sign (**+**) on the left-hand side and choose a folder e.g. *homes* in our example. Click **OK**. Click the plus sign (**+**) on the right-hand side next to *Add a paired folder* and select a folder on the cloud e.g. */OneDrive* in this example.

143

Click **OK**. Choose a *Conflict policy* i.e. what happens with duplicate files – we have chosen to replace them. Optionally, specify a descriptive **Job Name**. Click **Next**.

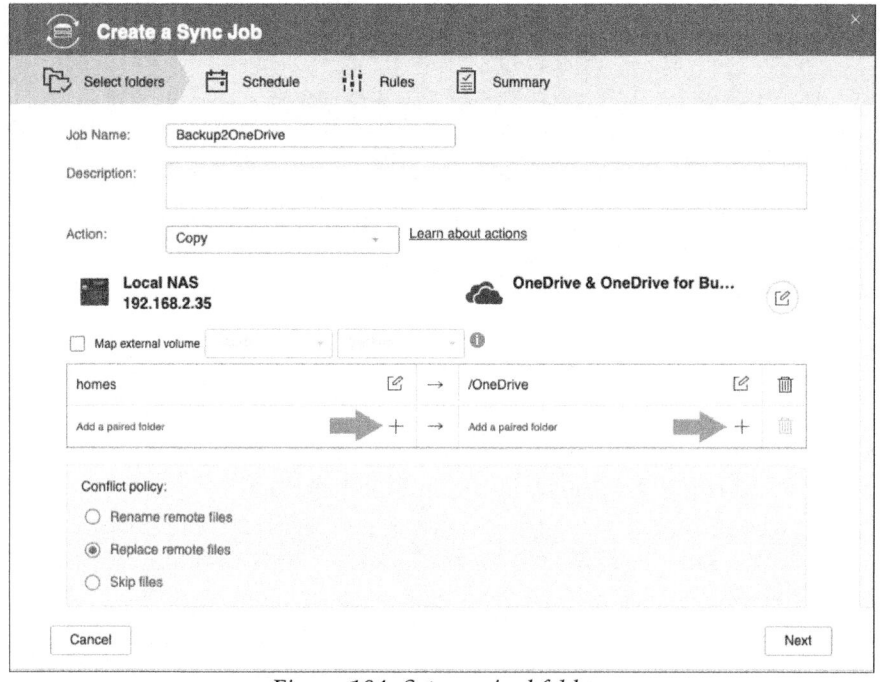

Figure 104: Setup paired folders

The next screen is *Schedule* and allows the frequency of synchronization to be controlled. There are four options:

Real-time Synchronization – every time the data on the NAS changes e.g. a file is updated or a new file created, it is immediately synchronized to the cloud.

Scheduler – synchronization occurs according to a schedule e.g. hourly, once a day etc. The procedure is the same as described in section **7.3 Backup to External Drive**.

Run after job – synchronization occurs after another previously defined job has taken place. For example, suppose there is already a backup job called *Daily Backup* which backs up the NAS to an external drive. Immediately afterwards, you may wish to automatically run a sync job that copies some or all of the data to a cloud service for additional security.

No schedule – choose this option if you always intend to run the synchronization manually.

Having made a choice, click **Next**:

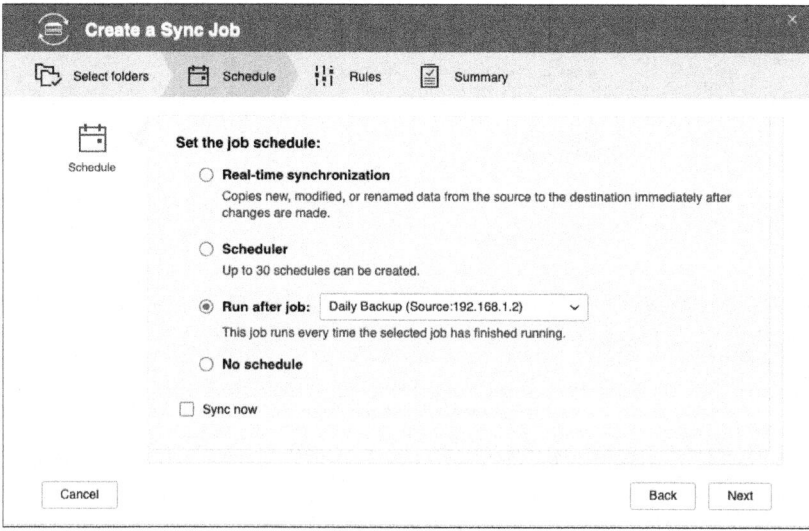

Figure 105: Scheduling options

The subsequent screen allows *Rules* to be applied; these are filters, defining the files to be included based upon characteristics such as file type, size and so on. For instance, when syncing to the cloud you might choose to exclude large files such as videos. If you wish to use filters, tick the **Enable filters** box, followed by the **Advanced Filters** button. If the **Use data compression** box is ticked, it will reduce backup sizes, improve transfer speeds and improve storage efficiency at the cloud end. However, files subsequently retrieved from cloud storage will have to be decompressed before they can be used:

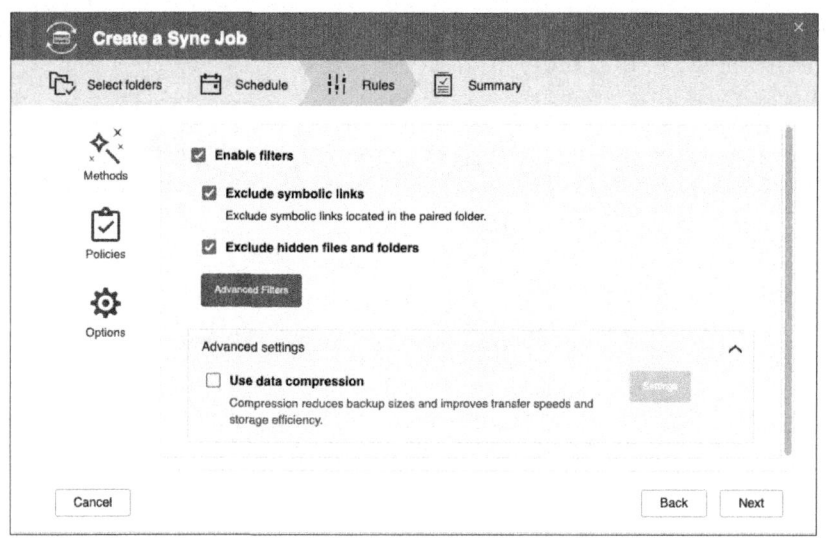

Figure 106: Rules/filters

Click **Next**. A *Summary* screen is displayed. Assuming everything is okay, click **Create**. The newly defined sync job is listed on the main *Sync* screen. To run it immediately, which is useful for testing purposes, or at any point manually, click the **Sync Now** button. There are also options to Edit (amend) the job, plus check the backup reports.

The speed of backup to a cloud service is dependent upon the speed of your internet connection but is typically many times slower than backup to a local drive. For instance, a backup of 1 terabyte of data that might take under an hour to a USB drive might take several days over the internet. For this reason, rather than use a cloud backup as the primary backup solution, it might be better to use it as a secondary backup for a limited selection of important data.

One common question is: as only one folder can be synced per job, what happens if there are multiple folders that need syncing? The answer is to define multiple sync jobs for different folders and schedule them accordingly.

7.7 NAS to NAS Backups Using Rysnc

One potential downside of using an external drive for backups is that it has to be physically located close to the server. In the event of a disaster – for instance, fire, flood or theft – not only might the server be lost but the backup drive might be as well. One way to mitigate against this is to use another NAS unit as a backup device. This gives a lot more flexibility as to where it is located; for instance, it could be in a totally different part of the building or another building altogether. The second NAS can be in addition to or in place of the USB backup drive.

Note that we have used the term NAS rather than QNAP, as it is possible to use just about any brand of network attached storage and you are not restricted to QNAP, although this would be the obvious choice for most people. For example, consider a scenario where you are upgrading from another vendor to QNAP, in which case you might be able to re-designate the old NAS as a backup unit. This is possible because most NAS operating systems, including QTS, are based on or derived from Linux. Linux itself is a derivative of UNIX, and in the UNIX world a program called *rsync* ('remote sync') gives the capability to backup one computer to another. When doing so, the one containing the original data is referred to as the *source* and the one that will hold the backup is the *destination*. QNAP also refer to destinations as storage spaces, but the term destination is more obvious and will be used here.

Start off by enabling the network backup capability of the destination NAS. The method for doing so with QNAP is as follows; if you are backing up to a different brand of NAS these instructions will not apply, but there should be something analogous (specifically you want SSH and encryption on port 22 enabled).

- As administrator, install and run Hybrid Backup Sync 3.
- In the **Services** section, click **Rsync Server** and click the **Enable Rsync Server** button.
- Tick the **Shared rsync server account** box.
- The default **Username** is *rsync* but it is not essential to use it and sometimes it is problematic, so you may wish to use your administrator credentials instead. The Local NAS accounts

option can only be used if both source and destination are QNAP units, but even then it is not essential to do so.
- Optionally, you can limit the Download limit speed. You might choose to do this if the servers are connected remotely over the internet in order to preserve bandwidth and reduce disruption to other activities. It is not necessary if the devices are on the same LAN.
- Click **Apply** - there will be a message about the NAS being disrupted for a few seconds whilst the changes are applied.

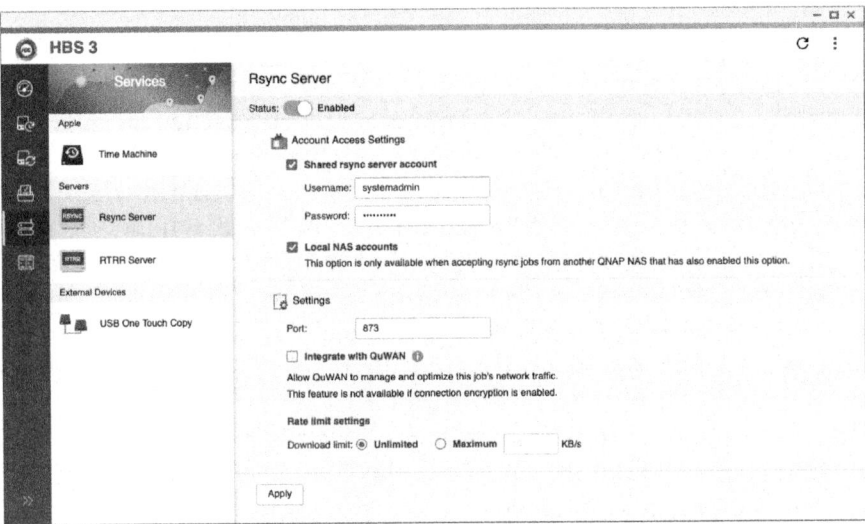

Figure 107: Enable Rsync on destination server

Next, create a shared folder on the destination server (creating shared folders is described in section **3.2 Creating a Shared Folder**). Call it *NetBackup* and give full rights to the *administrative* user. Finally, go into **Control Panel > Telnet/SSH** and tick the **Allow SSH connection** box. The Port number should be 22. Click the **Edit Access Permission** button and confirm that the administrators have access on the resultant popup panel. Click **Apply**.

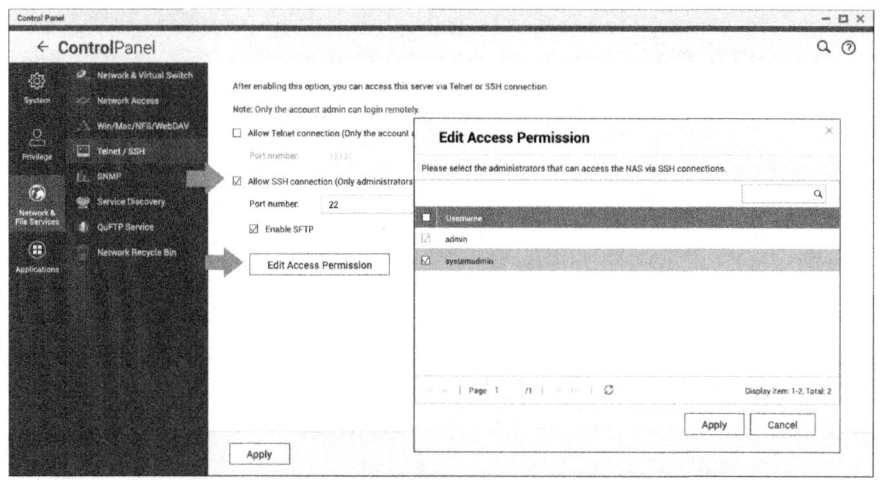

Figure 108: Enable SSH on destination server

The NAS that is being backed up - the *source* – now needs to be configured. Begin by enabling SSH on it as described above. Then, launch **Hybrid Backup Server** and click **Sync > Sync Now > One-way Sync Job**. Choose **Remote Rsync Server** and a pop-up form will appear.

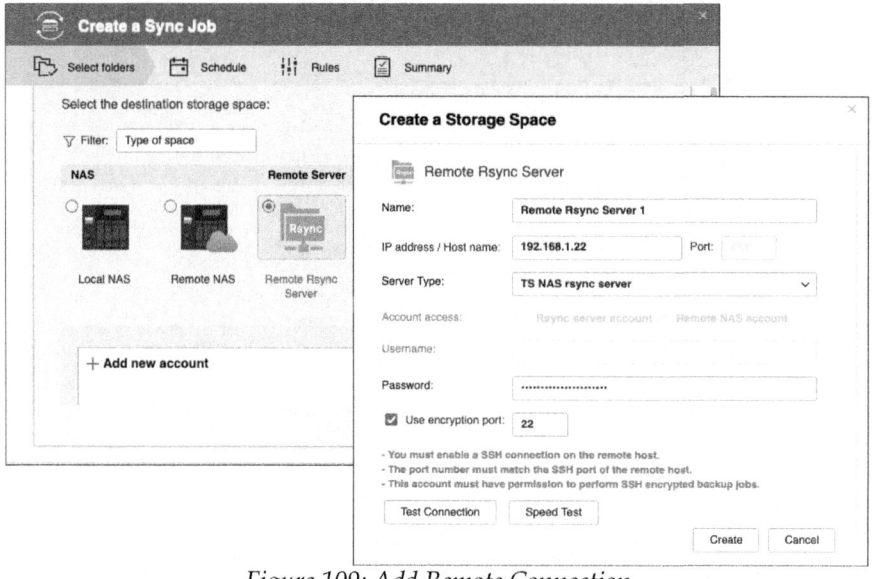

Figure 109: Add Remote Connection

Enter the *IP Address/Host Name* of the destination server, which can be an internal or external address. Ignore the *Port*.

Choose the *Server Type* from the dropdown – for another QNAP this would be **TS NAS rsync server**. The *Account Type* is **Rsync server account**. Enter the details for an administrative user on the destination server i.e. Username and Password. Tick the **Enable encryption** box, leaving the port encryption number as 22. There are helpful **Test Connection** and **Speed Test** buttons so you can check the two servers are communicating and the speed of the connection. Click **Create** and you will be returned to the previous screen.

What you have just done is create what Hybrid Backup Sync refers to as an *account* - make sure it is highlighted and click **Select**. On the subsequent screen it is necessary setup 'paired folders' for any folders that are to be synced to the destination server. For the *Local NAS*, click the plus sign (+) and choose a folder e.g. *homes* in our example. Click **OK**. Click the plus sign (+) on the right-hand side for the *Remote Rsync Server*, next to *Add a paired folder*, and select the *NetBackup* folder on the rsync server. Click **OK**. Optionally, specify a descriptive **Job Name**. Click **Next**.

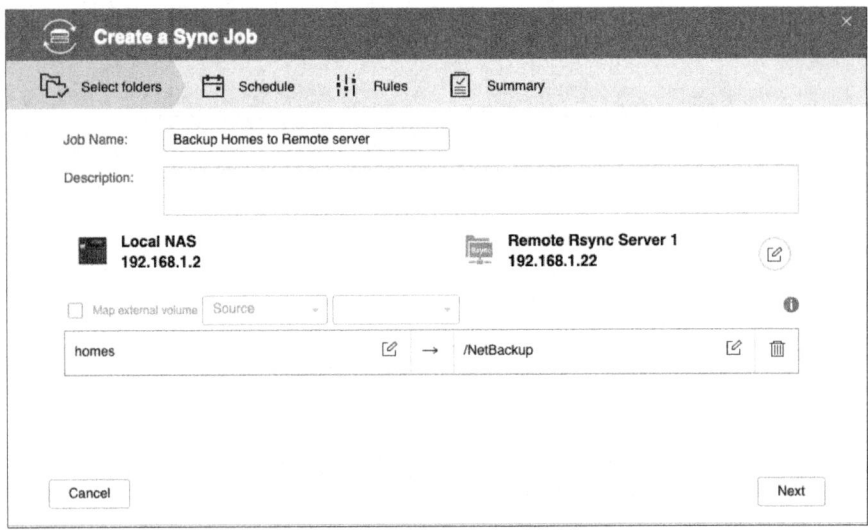

Figure 110: Setup paired folders

The next screen is *Schedule* and allows the frequency of synchronization to be controlled. There are three options:

Scheduler – synchronization occurs according to a schedule e.g. hourly, once a day etc. The procedure is the same as described in section **7.3 Backup to External Drive**.

Run after job – synchronization takes place after another previously defined job has taken place. For example, suppose there is already a backup job called *Backup 1* which backs up the NAS to an external drive. Immediately afterwards, you may wish to run a sync job that copies some or all of the data to a remote server for additional security.

No schedule – choose this option if you always intend to run the synchronization manually.

Having made a choice, click **Next**:

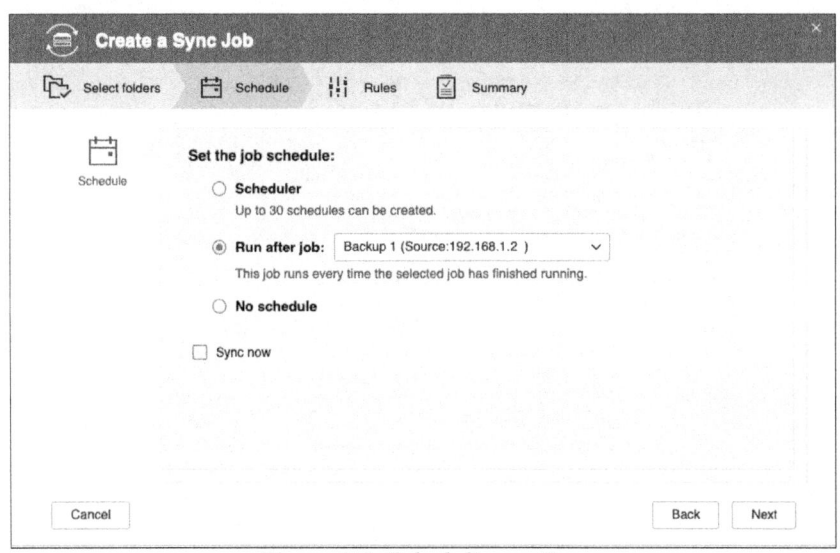

Figure 111: Scheduling options

The subsequent screen is for fine tuning the backup using *Rules* (Policies, Options, Network). In many cases the default values will be suitable; however, if you are using a physically remote rsync server over an internet connection, you may wish to tick the **Use rate limits** box and click **Settings**. This will limit the transmission speed to avoid saturating it and slowing down general internet usage for your users and other processes. It is also possible to specify a particular network adapter by clicking the **Network** icon, which allows for greater control in larger configurations. Click **Next**:

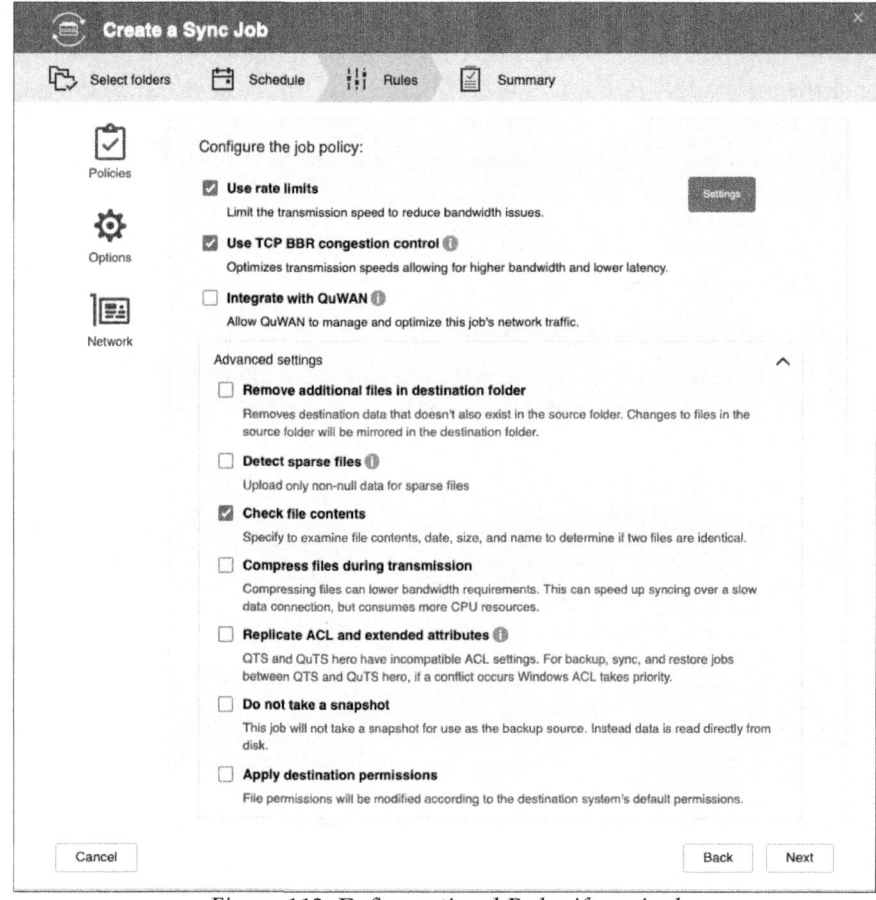

Figure 112: Define optional Rules if required

On the Confirm job settings screen, click **Create** and the newly defined sync job will be listed on the main *Sync* screen. To run it immediately, which is useful for testing purposes, or at any point manually, click the **Sync now** button. There are also options to Edit (amend) the job, Clone it (click the three-dot menu next to the **Sync now** button), plus review the backup reports.

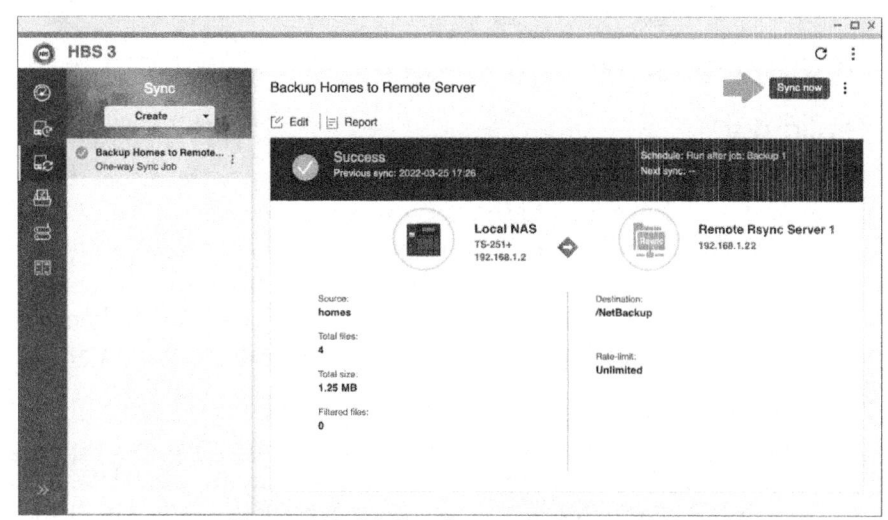

Figure 113: Job listed on main Sync screen

On the destination server, assuming it is another QNAP, the status of the job can be checked within Hybrid Backup Sync by clicking **Jobs > Incoming Jobs**.

One frequent question is: as only one folder can be synced at a time, what happens if there are multiple folders that need syncing? The answer is to define multiple Rsync backup jobs for individual folders and schedule them.

7.8 Backing up Windows PCs using QNAP NetBak Replicator

QNAP NetBak Replicator is a comprehensive program used for backing up Windows PCs to the server. It is especially useful where laptops are in use and being taken outside the business or home, as they may have data stored on them locally that is not otherwise being backed up. Although all versions of Windows have a built-in backup program of some sort, *NetBak Replicator* has three key advantages:

- It is more flexible and capable than the Microsoft offerings
- Only Professional editions of Windows can backup to network drives, with Home editions being restricted to external USB drives only. In contrast, *NetBak Replicator* allows any Windows PC to back up to a network
- Different versions of Windows have different backup programs e.g. Backup & Restore in Windows 7, File History in Windows 10 and 11. *NetBak Replicator* runs on all versions of Windows, including some older versions, making it a universal solution

It is not required to install any additional components on the server to use NetBak Replicator, as everything is done by the Windows client program.

An alternative approach to *NetBak Replicator* might be to use *Qsync* as discussed in section **11.4 Qsync**.

Installation and Getting Started

Download NetBak Replicator from the QNAP website and accept all the defaults during installation. When run for the first time it will ask whether the setup Wizard should be shown again in the future – tick the **Don't show this wizard again** box then click the large **Start** button. If a message about allowing access through the firewall appears, grant access.

The first significant screen is the *Network Location Wizard*, which allows the server to be selected (if multiple servers are available, they will be listed). Click **Next**:

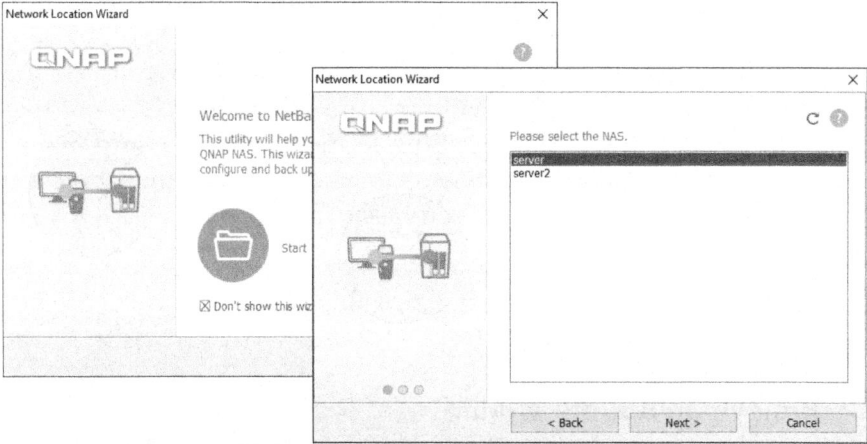

Figure 114: Network Location Wizard

On the second screen it is necessary to 'select the shared folder'. This is misleading as it actually means the destination for the backup. The best choice is usually the *Home* folder, as this is unique to each user. If it is not listed, tick the **Show all folders** box, although in most instances only the *Home* folder will be shown anyway. Click **Next**. A panel will appear requesting the login details of the person who uses the computer. If they are the sole user of the computer, the **Remember user name and password** box can be clicked. Click **OK**:

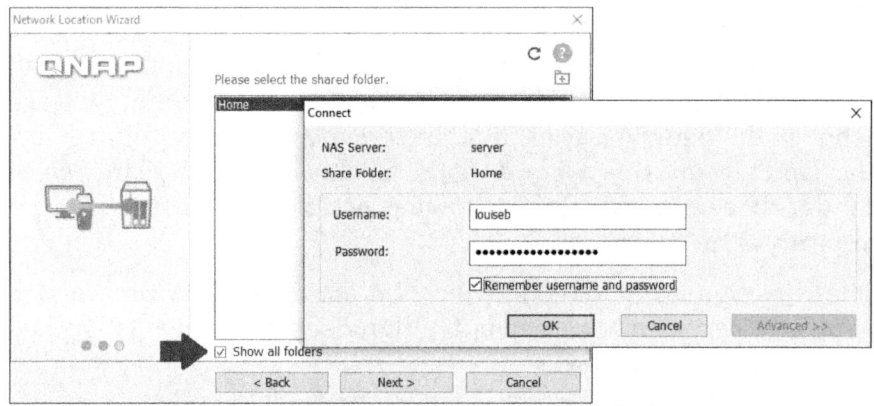

Figure 115: Choose the folder to hold the backups

A congratulations message is displayed – click **Finish** to complete the installation. *NetBak Replicator* will now run. There is a choice of two modes: *Simple* and *Advanced*. In Simple mode, the software makes some assumptions about what needs to be done and hence there are just two options, *Instant Backup* and *Instant Restore*.

In Advanced mode, which is selected by clicking the icon in the bottom left-hand of the screen, it is possible to exercise much greater control and schedule the backups.

Backing Up in Simple Mode

Click the **Instant Backup** button and the screen to select the source files is shown. By default, the program will backup all the local files of the current user i.e. their *Documents*, *Photos*, *Music* and so on. This is the requirement for most people so just click **Next**, although the entry can be expanded to customize it if required (for instance, *AppData* is a candidate folder within the User folder that can be removed from the backup). If the Microsoft Outlook email client is installed on the computer, it will be detected and the PST file can be included in the backup. Click **Next**. A reminder about the backup destination is shown. There is no need to change this so just click **Start**:

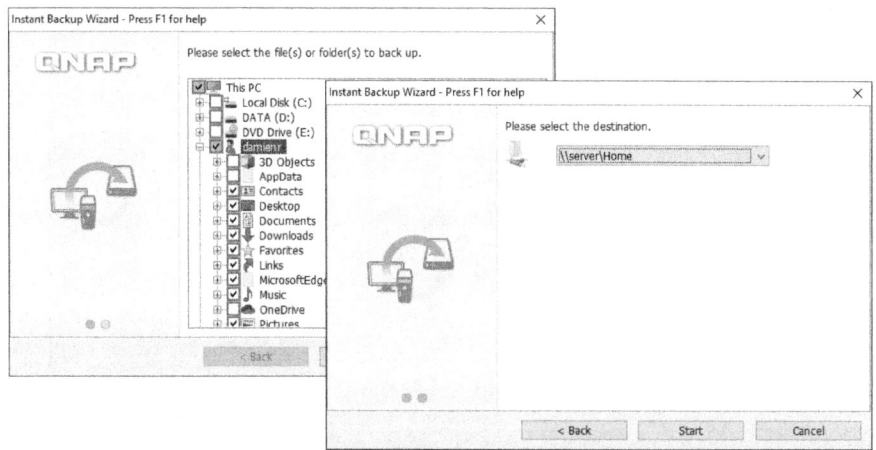

Figure 116: Specify what is to be backed up

The time taken for the backup depends upon the amount of data, how many files have changed since the last backup and the speed of the local network connection. Whilst the backup is running a status screen is displayed. When the backup is complete, click **Finish**.

The first backup may take some time, depending on the amount of data. However, note that subsequent backups should be quicker as NetBak Replicator only backs up the files that have changed since the last backup, rather than all of the files i.e. it performs incremental backups.

Restoring in Simple Mode
One great benefit of NetBak Replicator is that users can restore their own files from the server in the event of problems. Suppose, for instance, a user has accidentally deleted files from the *Documents* folder on their computer and needs to restore them. To do so, he or she should run NetBak Replicator and, whilst in Simple Mode, click the **Instant Restore** button to display the following screen. Expand the tree until it shows the desired folders and select them. Click **Next**:

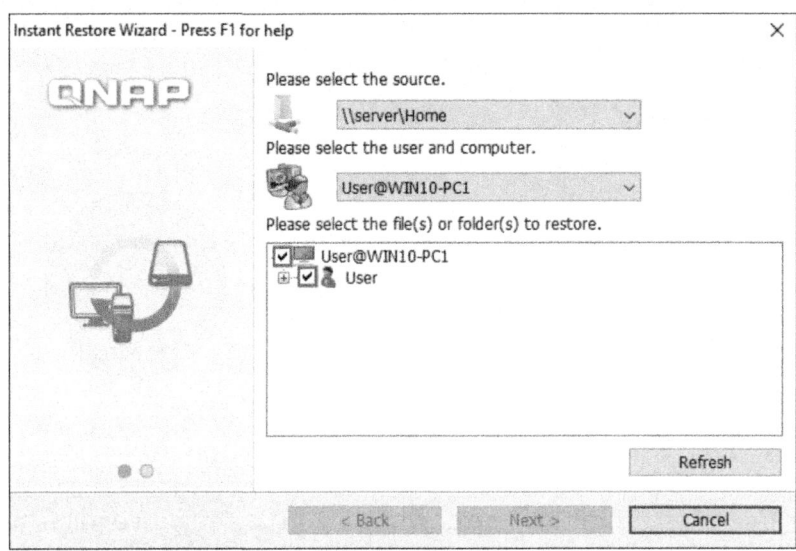

Figure 117: Specify the folder(s) to be restored

On the subsequent screen there are several options. Firstly, decide if the restored files are to be placed in the original location(s) or somewhere else. Secondly, decide on what to do if there is already a file or folder of that name. The choices are: *Skip the file and continue; Display a warning dialog; Restore all files*. Then click **Start**:

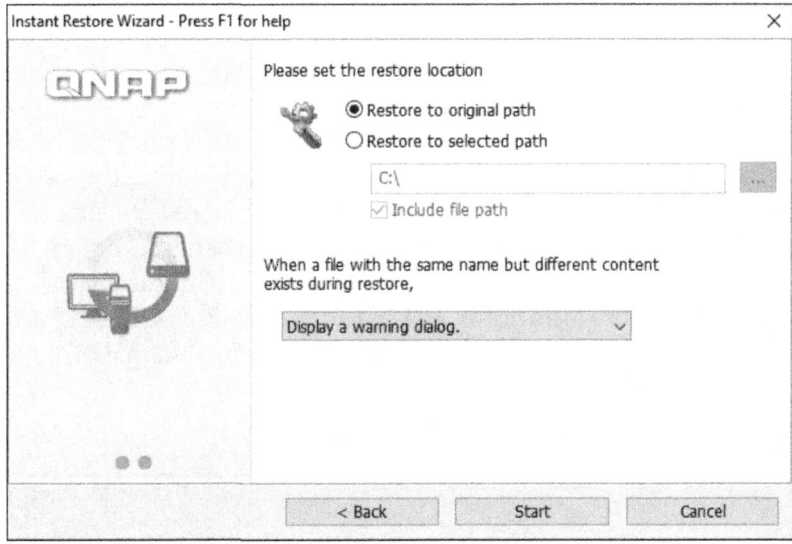

Figure 118: Additional restoration settings

When the restoration is complete, click **Finish**.

NetBak Replicator Advanced Mode

The Advanced Mode of NetBak Replicator allows more control over the backup process. It is potentially of use in more demanding and specialist situations and is a useful tool for those charged with looking after and supporting such environments, for example in a business setting. A full discussion is outside the scope of this book but some of the additions over Simple Mode include: The ability to schedule backups e.g. so they run hourly, daily, weekly or monthly; Auto-Backup, whereby any changes on the computer are automatically backed up to the server; Control over whether NetBak Replicator starts up automatically when the PC starts; Email notifications; Access the log files generated by backup and restore operations.

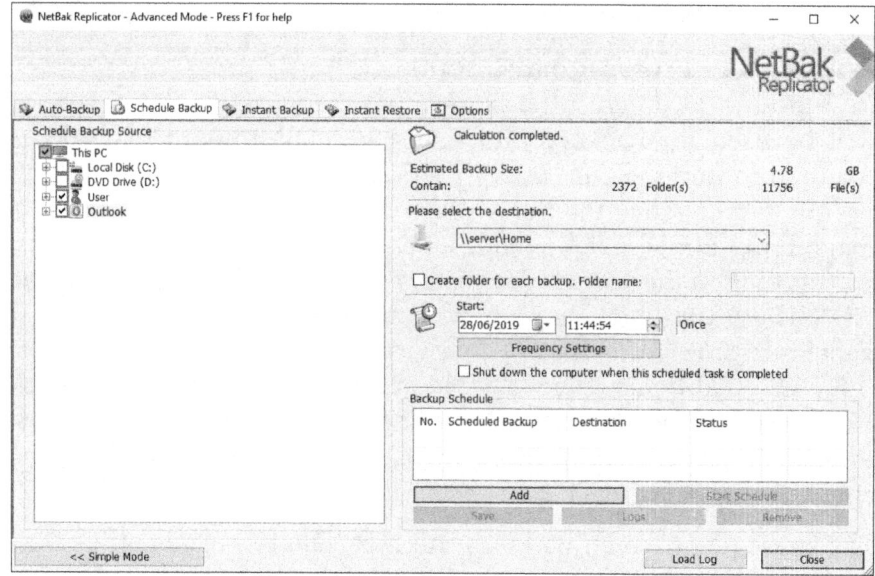

Figure 119: NetBak Advanced mode

7.9 Backing up Computers using built-in Windows Backup Programs

Although QNAP's NetBak is a capable program, all versions of Windows include a built-in backup program that some people may prefer to use and this might be a simple matter of preference or because of familiarity. However, only Professional (not Home) editions are able to use network drives. In Windows 7 the program is called *Backup and Restore*, in Windows 10 and 11 is called *File History*. The Windows backup program assumes that you will be using an external USB drive and all that is necessary is to change the backup location so that it points to the user's home folder on the server; thereafter it can be used in the normal fashion.

Windows 11 Professional Clients

In Windows 11, Microsoft assumes that the *OneDrive* cloud service will be used for backups and hence a small amount of effort is required to find the *File History* program that is needed for backing up to a server. Click the **Search** icon on the Taskbar (it looks like a magnifying glass). Click where it reads **More** and select **Settings**. Start typing in the words 'File history' and it will quickly locate the File History utility on the Control Panel – click to open it. The first panel is to *Select a File History drive* i.e. a destination for the backups. If the mapped home drive (e.g. H:) is not displayed in the list, click **Add network location**. If still not shown, click **Show all network locations**. If necessary, the search path to the user's folder can be entered in UNC format e.g. *server**home*.

The subsequent screen will indicate that 'File History is off' – click the **Turn on** button. The screen will update to show that 'File History is on' – click the **Run now** link to start a backup.

To adjust the parameters of the backup, click **Exclude folders** to modify the folders and libraries which are/are not backed up, and **Advanced settings** to adjust the frequency of the backups and their retention period.

Windows 10 Professional Clients

Begin by mapping the user's home drive on the server using one of the techniques described in section **5 ACCESSING THE SERVER** if not already mapped.

Click **Start** > **Settings** > **Update & security** > **Backup**. Click **Add a drive** and after a few seconds the list of mapped drives will be displayed – click on the user's home drive. Having done so you will be returned to the main Backup panel, where an option to *Automatically back up my files* will have appeared and been set to *On*. That is it – a backup will now run on an hourly basis, copying the user's files from the computer to their home drive on the server.

For greater control over the process, such as controlling the frequency at which the backup runs, click **More options**. From here you can: review the backup status; make the backup run immediately; change the backup frequency (anything from every 10 minutes through to 1 day); change the retention period for the backed-up data.

Windows 7 Professional Clients

Click **Start**, followed by **All Programs**, **Maintenance** then **Backup and Restore**.

Click on **Set up Backup**.

Click the **Save on a network** button. On the next panel, enter the **Network Location**. Specify the user's home folder, using the format *server**username* or click the **Browse** button to navigate to it. Enter the user name and password as defined on the server then click **OK**. The subsequent screen is for choosing what data files are backed up. The default option of **Let Windows choose (recommended)** is suitable in many cases so just click **Next**.

The follow-on screen is a summary of settings; click **Save settings and run backup**.

The backup will run for the first time, during which the status is displayed. Windows will have defined a schedule to subsequently run backups automatically on a regular basis, in this example every Sunday at 7:00pm. If this setting is not suitable it can be altered by clicking **Change settings**.

7.10 Backing Up Macs

Time Machine is the standard backup solution for Mac users and an integral part of macOS. Typically used with an external drive connected to a Mac, support is provided in QTS, thus enabling the server to be specified as a backup destination for Time Machine.

Begin by creating a shared folder on the server, which will be used to hold the backups. Creating shared folders is described in section **3.2 Creating a Shared Folder**, but in essence is done using **Control Panel > Shared Folders > Create > Shared folder**. Give the folder a meaningful name e.g. *Macbackup*. Specify the *Disk Volume* if there is more than one to choose from; if the network has many Mac users, consider having a dedicated volume for storing the Time Machine backups. On the *Configure access privileges for users* panel, assign RW (Read Write) privileges to the Mac users who will have access to the facility. On the *Properties* panel, scroll down to the bottom and tick the **Set this folder as the Time Machine backup folder (macOS)** box. Click **Finish**.

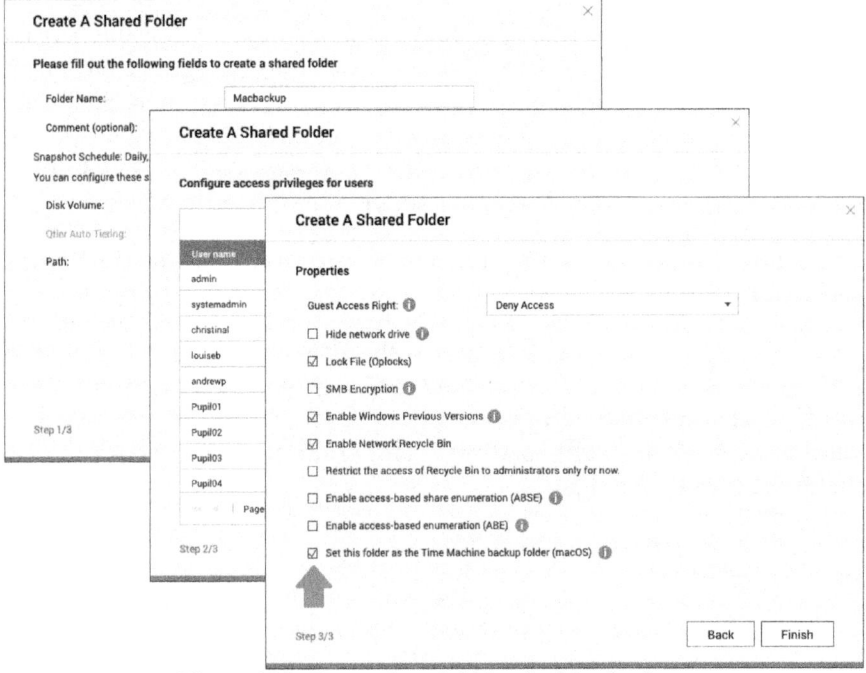

Figure 120: Create shared folder for Mac backups

Launch Hybrid Backup Sync and choose **Services > Time Machine**. Tick the **Local NAS accounts** box and make sure that the *Shared Time Machine account* box is **not** ticked. Click **Apply**. A message may be displayed, advising that the 'Highest SMB version' will be set to SMB 3.0, if so click **OK**. There will then be a short delay.

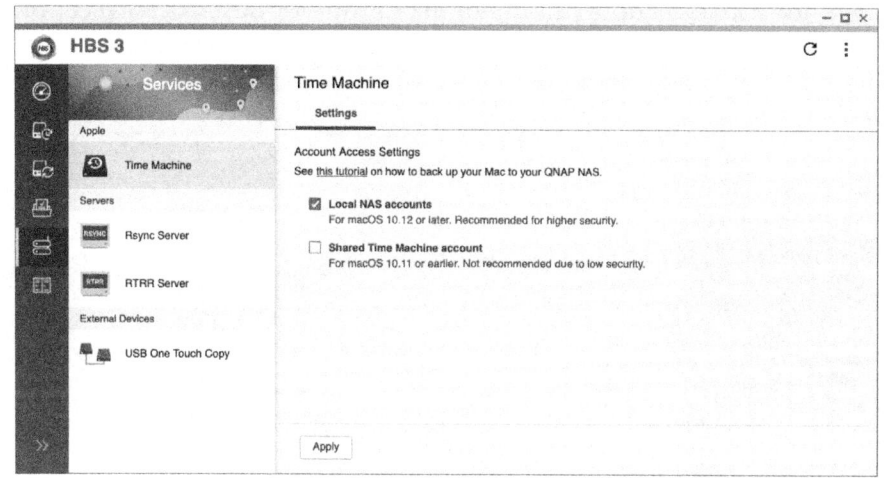

Figure 121: Enable Time Machine multi-user support

To perform a backup, go to a Mac. From Finder, choose **Go > Connect to Server** and enter the name or IP address of the NAS with a prefix of *smb://* e.g. *smb://server* or *smb://192.168.1.2*. Click **Connect**. When prompted to login to the server, choose the **Registered User** option and enter the name and password of a user (as defined on the server, not on the Mac). From the list of volumes (i.e. folders), choose *Macbackup* and click **OK**.

Go into **System Preferences** and click **Time Machine**. Click **Select Disk**, choose *macbackup* from the list and click **Select Disk**. Thereafter, Time Machine will operate in the standard manner. The first time the backup is run it will take some time, but subsequent backups will be quicker as they are incremental in nature.

Setting Backup Quotas for Users

To prevent the server filling up with Time Machine backups, set a maximum quota for each user. Go to **Control Panel > Quota** and tick the **Enable quota for all users** box. For the **Quota size on the disk**, specify a value e.g. 1000 GB and click **Apply**. The lower half of the screen will then be populated with the list of users; highlight a Mac user and click **Edit**.

On the resultant panel, adjust their personal quota to an appropriate amount; this can usefully be set as twice the amount of storage that they have on their Mac e.g. if the Mac has a 128GB drive, then set the quota to 256GB and click **OK**. Repeat for each Mac user. Alternatively, consider setting up a specific group for Mac users and applying a group quota (the creation of groups is described in section **4.5 User Groups**). For the users who do not require Time Machine, they can have their quota reset to **No Limit**.

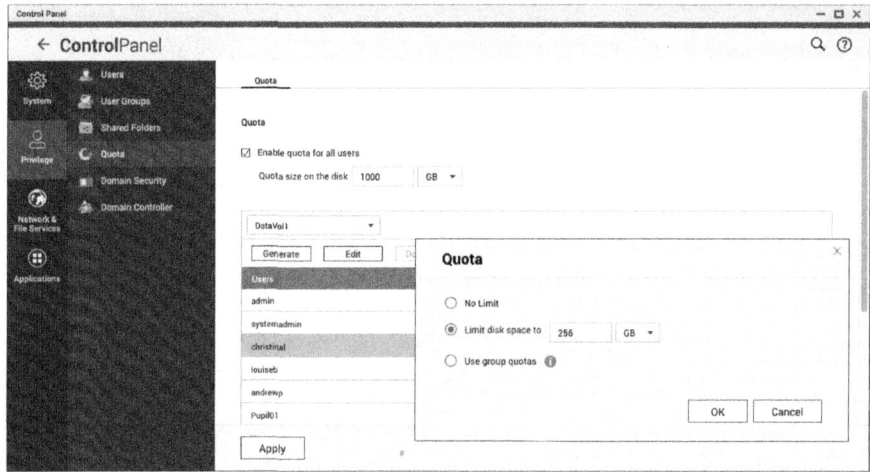

Figure 122: Setting storage quotas

7.11 Backing up System Settings

Although we have discussed how to backup data from the server, there is another type of backup that should be carried out on an occasional basis. A lot of customization may have gone into the server in terms of defining users, shares, permissions and other settings. In the event of serious problems with the server - for example, of the sort necessitating a complete re-installation - all this configuration information would have to be re-entered. This is likely to be both difficult and time consuming on all but the simplest of systems. Fortunately, there is a facility to quickly backup and restore the configuration.

Choose **Backup/Restore** from **Control Panel** and click the **Backup/Restore Settings** tab. Click the **Backup** button. A system backup file will be generated and saved in the local computer's download folder, with a name in the format *backupdata_[yyyy-mm-dd].bin*. Keep the file in a safe place (you might want to consider putting a copy on a USB memory stick, for instance).

Should it ever prove necessary to use this configuration file, choose **Backup/Restore** from the **Control Panel** and click on the **Backup/Restore Settings** tab. In the **Restore System Settings** area, click the **Browse** button and navigate to the location of the configuration file. Then click the **Restore** button.

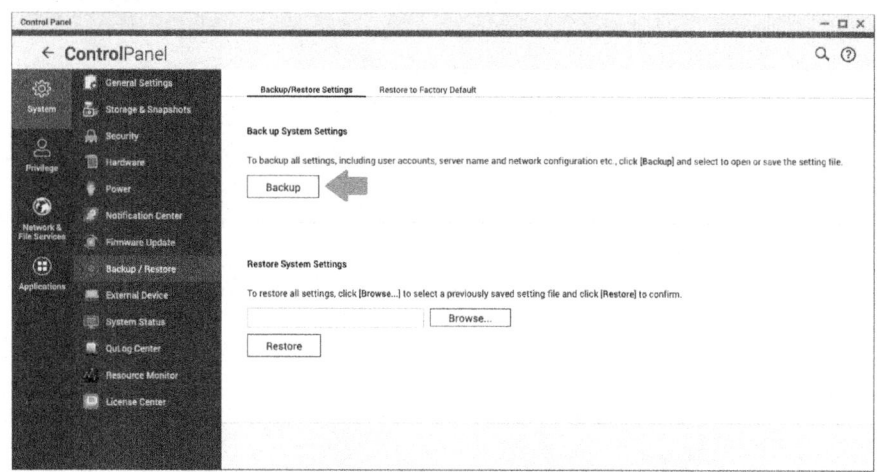

Figure 123: Backing up the server configuration

8

HOUSEKEEPING & MAINTENANCE

8.1 Overview

The server should be checked on a regular basis to ensure there are no problems. In the case of a home system this only needs doing occasionally, but in a business environment a more systematic approach is preferable, perhaps once a week at least or maybe even a daily check. Things that can be usefully looked at include checking for QTS Updates; storage space; health of disk drives; confirmation that the backup has completed successfully; log files generated by anti-virus and malware scans; security issues and violations. Monitoring can be done in a variety of ways: with the Dashboard; the Desktop Notice Board; using the QNAP Assistant software; using Qmanager on a portable device such as a tablet or smartphone; setting up automatic notifications.

8.2 Checking for QTS Updates

The QTS software is updated on a regular basis by QNAP. Updates may be major e.g. from QTS 4 to QTS 5, although typically these only occur every couple of years, whereas significant updates e.g. from QTS 5.0 to QTS 5.1 are more frequent, typically once a year. Additionally, there are more regular updates to fix specific problems, such as security threats and these are made available by QNAP as required, typically every couple of months.

If an update is available, it will be indicated by the appearance of a notification within the Desktop and by checking **Control Panel > Firmware Update**:

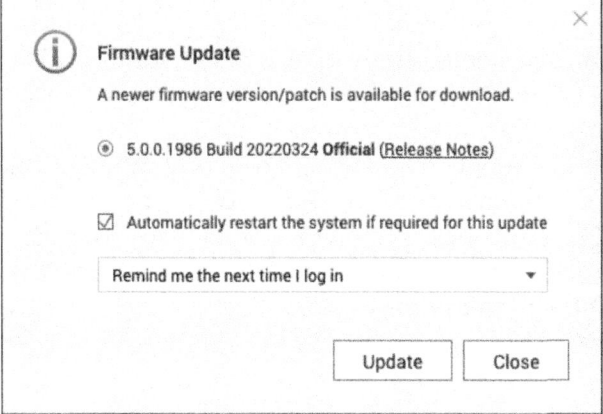

Figure 124: Firmware Update available

Alternatively, to check for updates at any point, launch **Control Panel** and click **Firmware Update**. There are two tabs: *Firmware Update* and *Manual Installation*. On the first tab, click the **Check for Updates** button:

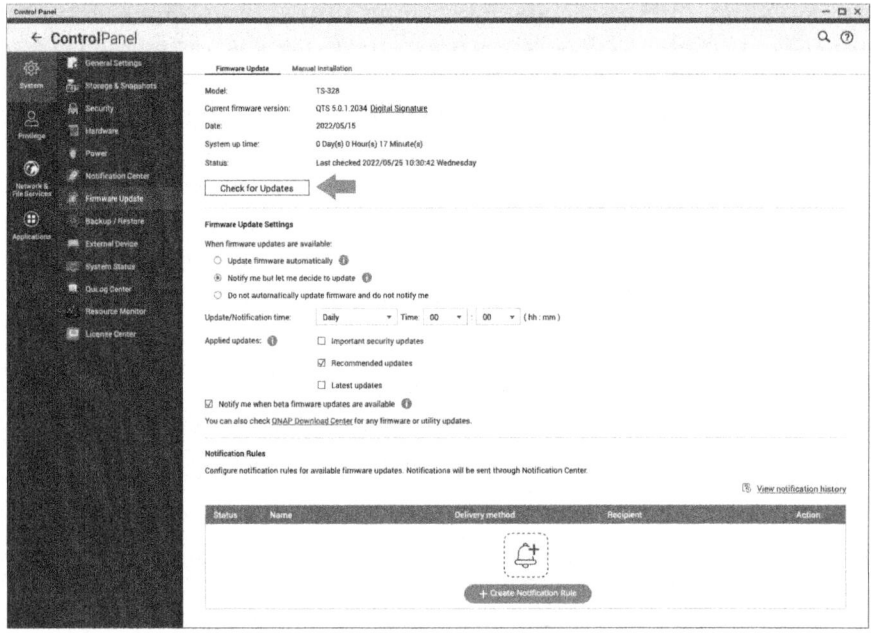

Figure 125: Firmware Update screen

Underneath is a *Firmware Update Settings section*, listing the options when updates are available. Firmware updates necessitate a reboot of the system and it is therefore suggested that they are performed at a time when nobody needs to use the system, so as to minimize disruption. It is advised that before updating QTS, a complete backup of the data and server configuration is made. It might also be the case that some Apps will need to be upgraded follow a firmware update. Also, it can take an hour or more to update the system, plus in a business environment it would be prudent to allow additional time for testing. It is not necessary to always be on the 'latest and greatest' version of QTS and some people prefer a more cautious approach to updating. For these reasons, you might wish to choose the **Notify me but let me decide to update** option.

Updates may resolve potential security issues and/or provide bug fixes and improve functionality. There is a choice as to what type of updates will be applied and QNAP suggest that most users choose the **Recommended updates** option. For maximum stability, it is recommended that you do not tick the *Notify me when beta firmware updates are available* box, particularly if you are in a business environment.

Notification Rules for firmware updates can be configured. These will then be sent through the Notification Center (for information on the Notification Center, see section **8.4 Notification Center**).

Having made any changes to the settings, click **Apply**.

Manual Installation

Alternatively, firmware can be installed from a location to which it has previously been downloaded. This method allows for greater control over the process and special circumstances, such as having to load a different version of the firmware or being able to update when there is no live internet connection. Note that you cannot 'downgrade' an existing installation and revert, for example, from QTS 5.1 to QTS 5.0. To do this: click on the **Manual Installation** tab: click **Browse** and navigate to where the downloaded copy of QTS is located on your computer and select it; click **Update System**.

Using Qfinder Pro

Firmware can also be updated using the Qfinder Pro utility. Highlight the server and from the menu bar in the utility, click **Tools > Update Firmware**. Login as an administrator. The resultant panel will show the firmware status of the server(s). If the latest version is not in use, choose the **Automatically update the firmware to the latest version** option, or browse to a downloaded image file. If there are multiple servers in the network and they are all the same model number, you can choose to upgrade all of them at the same time.

8.3 Dashboard

In the top right-hand corner of the server's Desktop screen is an icon which looks like a dial or speedometer. Clicking it will show the *Dashboard*, which provides an 'at a glance' overview of the health and status of the server. The Dashboard is made up of several smaller panels and these panels can be dragged onto the Desktop on an individual basis if desired. All of the panels are clickable and doing so will take you to the corresponding utility within the Control Panel:

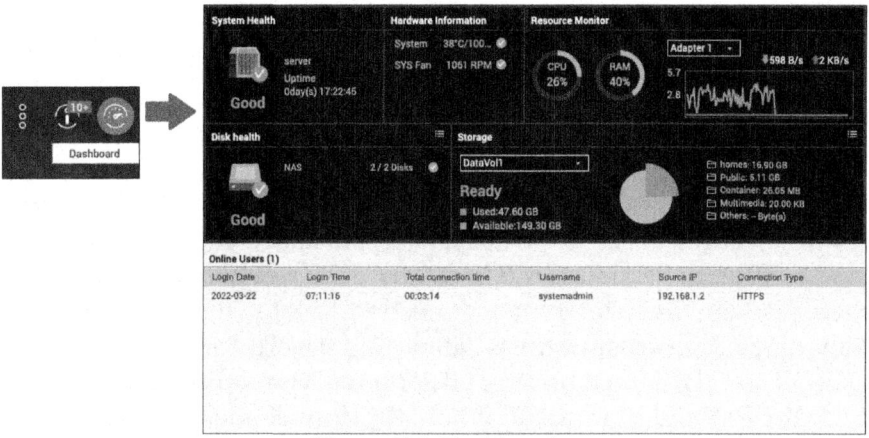

Figure 126: Dashboard

The items monitored by the Dashboard include Overall System Health, including uptime and server temperature; Status of the hard drives(s); Memory, CPU and network adapter utilization; Details of online users and their IP addresses.

To close the Dashboard, click on an empty area of the Desktop.

8.4 Notification Center

Whilst it is important to check the server on a regular basis, it may not always be possible to do so in person. For instance, the person responsible – you, presumably - may not be located on the premises. Plus it is better to deal with some problems as soon as they arise, rather than learn about them later. For these reasons, QTS can pro-actively advise when issues occur, using automatic notifications sent by email, SMS, instant message or push notification from the *Notification Center* app. These notifications can be controlled with user-defined rules.

Launch Notification Center by clicking its icon in the **Main Menu** or **Control Panel**. The first time it is accessed, a short tour is presented, which can be worked through or skipped as required. The main screen is then presented but overlaid with a message is stating that no notification rules have been defined. It can be closed by clicking the cross in the top right-hand corner of the panel, but will continue to be displayed upon launching Notification Center until at least one rule is defined, as described shortly:

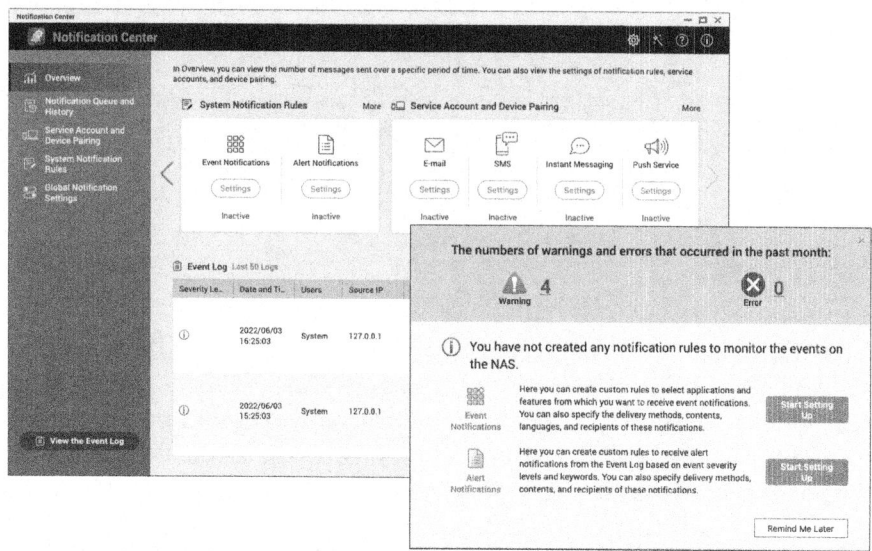

Figure 127: Notification Center, Overview screen and warnings

The *Overview* screen provides summary information and gives links to other sections, listed along the top of the screen and down the left-hand side.

All significant events are recorded in the *System Logs*; these are summarized on the Overview screen but to obtain a longer and searchable list click **View the Event Log**, from where the logs can be sorted by severity level and searched.

As mentioned above, notifications can be sent to a variety of devices and using a variety of methods and the two most widely used ones are detailed below.

Setting Up Email Notifications

Click **Service Account and Device Pairing** followed by the **E-Mail** icon, then the **Add SMTP Service** button:

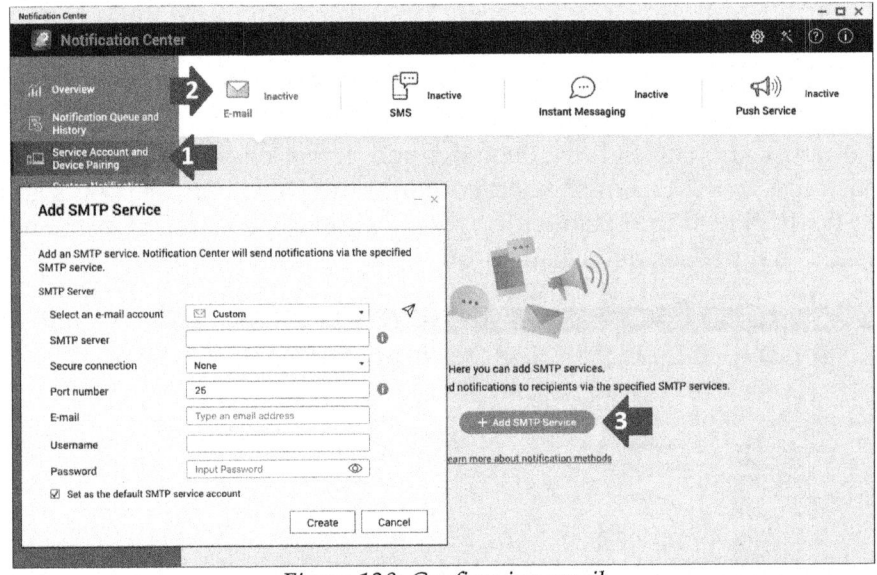

Figure 128: Configuring email

Click the *Select an e-mail account* dropdown – there is built-in support for several popular email services, such as *Gmail, Yahoo, Outlook* and *QQ*. Once you start typing the email address, you will be prompted to login to the email provider's website for login details and authorization. To add a private email system, such as a business or other email address, choose **Custom** and enter the name of your SMTP server; the SMTP port number (usually 25, but check first); an email address, user name and password - this should be for an existing account, such as your own. If a secure connection is used i.e. SSL or TLS, the port number should be 465 or 587 respectively.

Click **Create** and the email account will be added to the underlying screen. To send a test mail, click the mini icon that looks like a paper aeroplane. To change the account details, click the mini icon that looks like a notepad. To delete the account, click the trashcan mini icon. It is possible to use more than one email account.

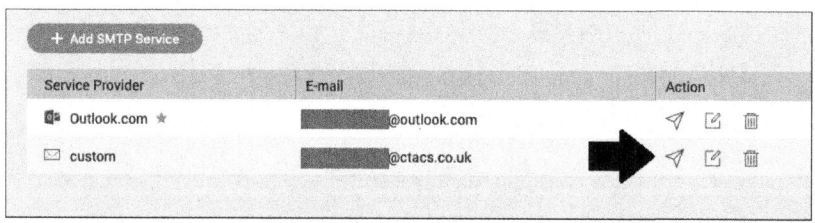

Figure 129: Email accounts

Setting Up Push Service Notifications

The Push Service allows notifications to be sent directly to mobile devices running the *Qmanager* application and to supported browsers such as Chrome, Firefox, Safari and Edge. The Push Service uses the myQNAPcloud service, so this needs to have been setup; this may have been done during the installation of QTS or subsequently as described in section **11.2 myQNAPcloud**.

To send notifications to a browser, it is necessary to 'pair' it. Go to the computer which is to receive notifications and login to the server as the administrative user. Launch Notification Center and click **Service Account and Device Pairing** followed by the **Push Service** icon. Click the **Pair** button, a new browser window will open and after a few seconds the browser will be listed as a paired device. Note: in practice this process is often problematic as frequent changes in version numbers mean that supposedly supported browsers may not be recognized.

To use Qmanager for receiving notification, install it on a suitable device. During installation or when running it for the first time, you may receive a prompt asking if you wish to receive notifications. If you reply in the affirmative, your device will be 'paired' and receive messages sent from the *Notification Center* app. The wider use of Qmanager is discussed in section **8.10 Using Qmanager**.

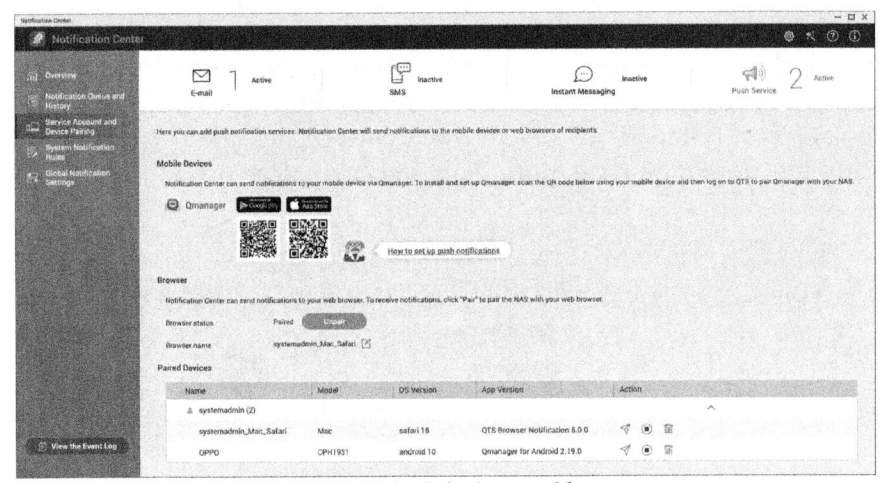

Figure 130: Paired devices and browsers

Other Notification Methods

In addition to email and push service notifications, Notification Center can use SMS (text messaging) and Instant Messaging using *Skype*, which will require authentication with the corresponding service providers. The SMS option requires a subscription to a commercial operator such as *Clickatell*, *Nexmo* or *Twilio*.

Global Notification Settings

The QTS features reported upon and the notification methods used are controlled from the **Global Notification Settings** screen by adding or removing ticks in the appropriate columns and boxes. In the example below, some notifications are sent by Email only, some by Push Service only, whereas some are sent using both methods. SMS and Instant Messaging are not used here, so no features have been selected.

Having made any changes, click the **Apply** button.

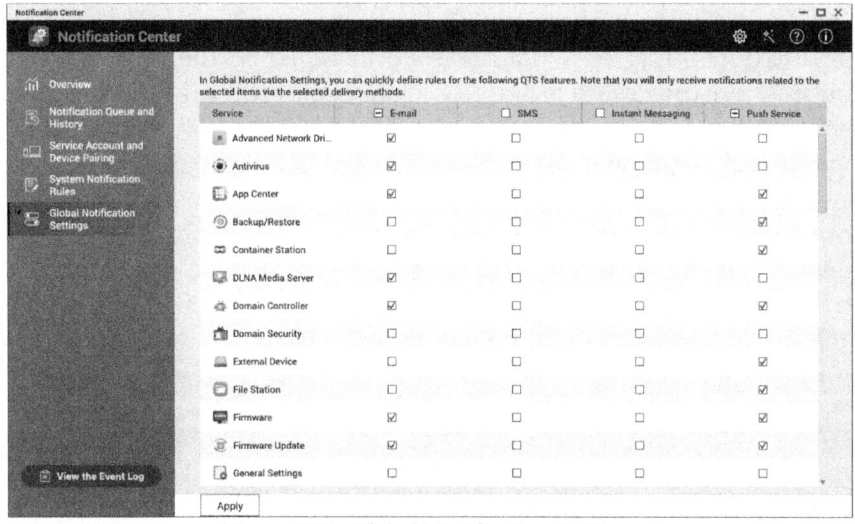

Figure 131: Global Notification Settings

System Notification Rules

A rule comprises a set of events of interest, notification criteria, notification methods and recipients. The *Global Notification Settings* screen defines some basic rules regarding notifications, but it is possible to create additional custom rules. To do this, click **System Notification Rules**, followed by the **Create Rule** button on the resultant panel.

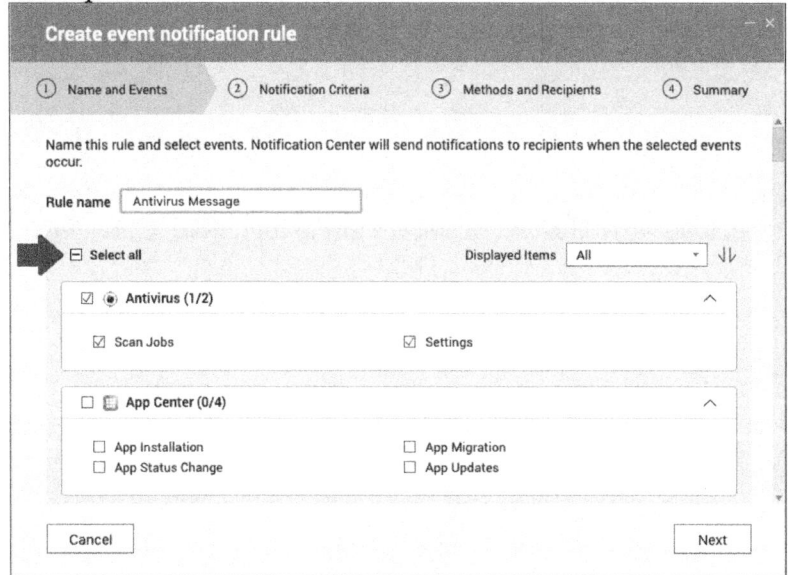

Figure 132: Create event notification rule – Name and Events

By default, all the applications and features are selected, with the list varying depending on what has been installed on the NAS, though you may wish to remove the tick from the **Select all** box and then choose only the item(s) you are interested in. Give the rule a meaningful name and click **Next**. On the second panel, select the severity levels; you can also restrict the time during which notifications are sent, so as not to disturb people overnight, for instance. In this example, we are only interested in warnings and errors and want to receive notifications from 0800 to 1800 (8.00am to 6.00pm). Having specified the details, click **Next**.

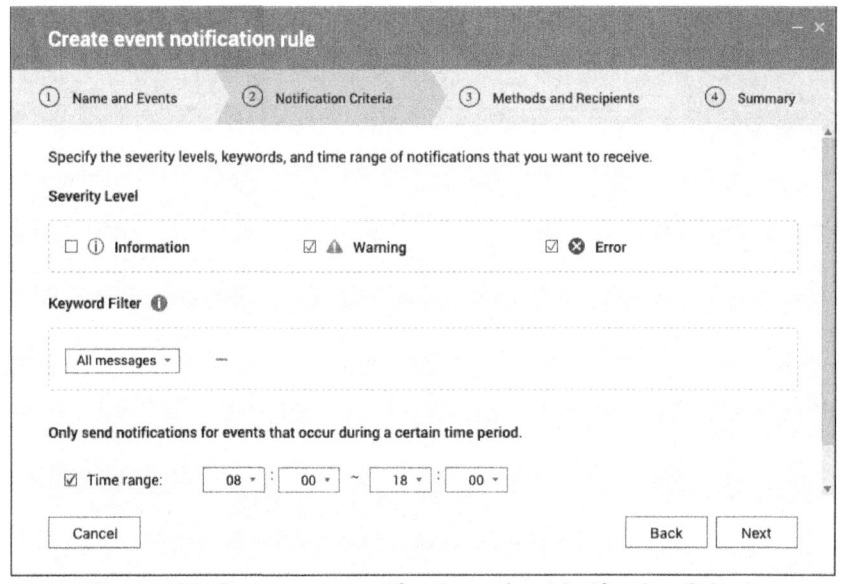

Figure 133: Create event notification rule – Notification Criteria

On the third panel, specify the method for sending the notifications to the recipients; in this example, we are using email. Click **Next**:

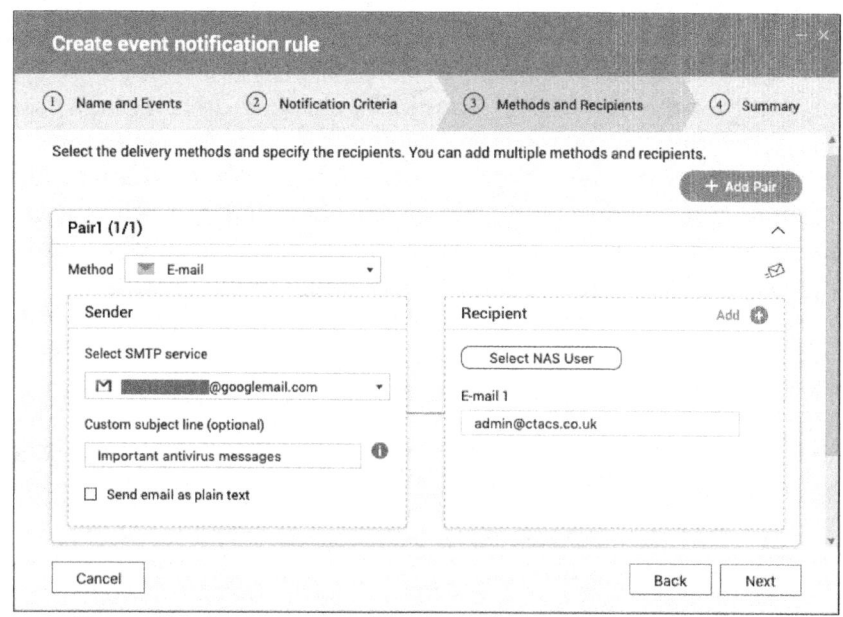

Figure 134: Create event notification rule – Methods and Recipients

The fourth and final panel is a summary screen; assuming everything is correct, click **Finish**. The rule will now be processed and added to the System Notification Rules screen, from where it can subsequently be enabled/disabled, edited or deleted.

8.5 Checking the Health of the Disks

The health of the disk drives should be checked on a regular basis, especially if there appear to be problems or if the NAS has shut down unexpectedly for any reason, as this can result in damage and potential data loss. Checking can be done manually or scheduled to take place automatically. The server will also provide notifications of any problems, with messages such as the following:

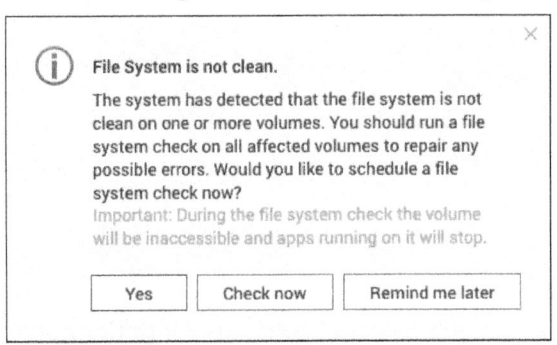

Figure 135: Warning message about File System

If the message is received, then you should immediately run a check by clicking the **Check now** or **Yes** buttons, which will invoke the *Storage & Snapshots* app. A further warning message is displayed, advising that services will be disrupted and that the checking and repairing may take a considerable amount of time; click **OK** to proceed and the process will begin.

To manually check the health of the disks anytime, go to **Control Panel** or **Main Menu** and launch **Storage & Snapshots**. Click **Disks** on the left-hand side to show the following screen:

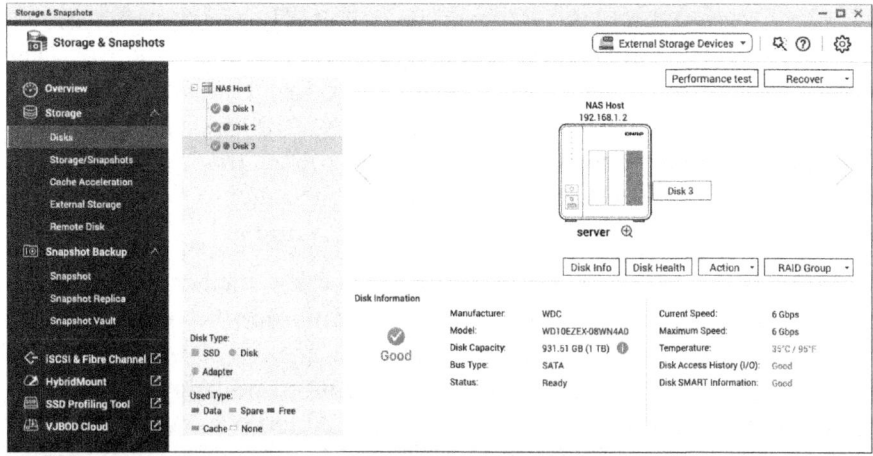

Figure 136: Checking the health of the hard drive(s)

Under normal circumstances the status of the disk(s) will be 'Good', meaning no further action is required. If there are any concerns, click the **Disk Health** button; if you have more than one drive in the system you will first need to select the drive, which you can do by clicking on the appropriate drive bay in the pictorial representation of the server, or from the dropdown in the resultant panel:

Figure 137: Disk Health panel

There are a minimum of four sections within the Disk Health panel and if a Seagate IronWolf drive or an SSD is being used there will be additional entries for their specific features. The first section – *Summary* – largely duplicates what we have already seen whilst the *SMART Information* section provides more detailed technical information about drive's S.M.A.R.T. status.

179

The *Test* section enables a drive to be tested. There are two options: *Rapid test* and *Complete test*. Select **Rapid test** and click the **Test** button. A message advising how long the test will take is shown, which can be acknowledged by clicking **OK**. After the test completes the status on the screen is updated, ideally stating that no errors were found. The **Complete test** option takes much longer to run and is best performed during a time when the system is unused.

Best practice is to automate the testing process, which can be done by going into the *Settings* section. In this example, a rapid test for Disk 1 has been scheduled to run weekly on Saturdays at 6.00am/06:00, with a complete test on the 1st of each month at midnight. Also note that the temperature alarm has been enabled to check that the drive(s) are not running too hot; for guidance, mechanical drives should be running at less than 55C/131F. After setting up a schedule click the **Apply to All Disks** button, or the **Apply To All HDD** or **Apply To All SDD** buttons which are displayed if there are a mixture of disk types:

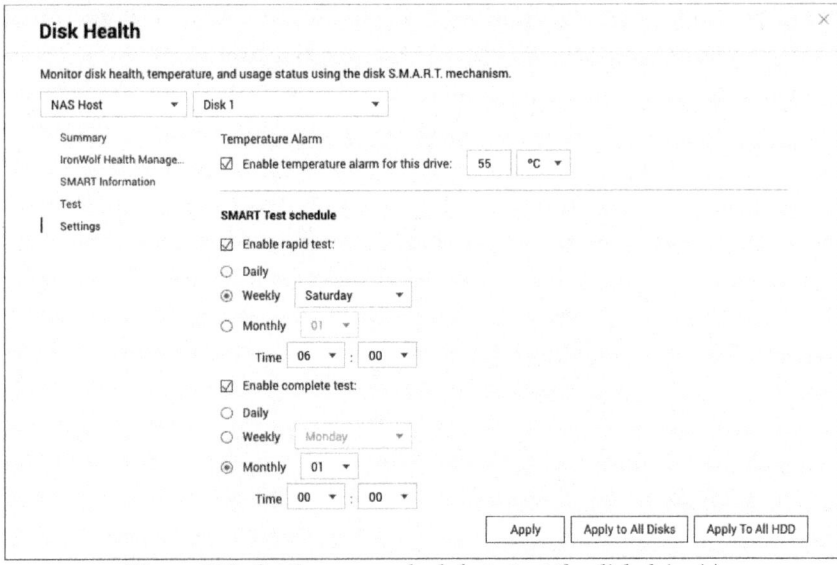

Figure 138: Setting up a schedule to test the disk drive(s)

If a drive fails the S.M.A.R.T. test, it should be replaced at the earliest opportunity to reduce the risk of data loss.

8.6 RAID Data Scrubbing

Due to the nature of computer systems and disk drives, there is always a risk of potential data corruption. Inevitably, corrupt data is not detected until an attempt is made to access it, by which time it is too late. To try and prevent this problem, a technique called *RAID Data Scrubbing* can be used. This is an error detection process whereby data stored in a RAID array is systematically checked for any errors on a scheduled basis, which are then corrected using checksums or copies of data. It is managed from within Storage & Snapshots and is available for use on RAID 5 and RAID 6 volumes.

To enable scrubbing and setup a schedule, go to **Storage & Snapshots** and click the **Global Settings** cogwheel in the top-right corner of the screen. Within the **Storage** section, against **RAID Scrubbing Schedule**, slide the switch to the 'On' position.

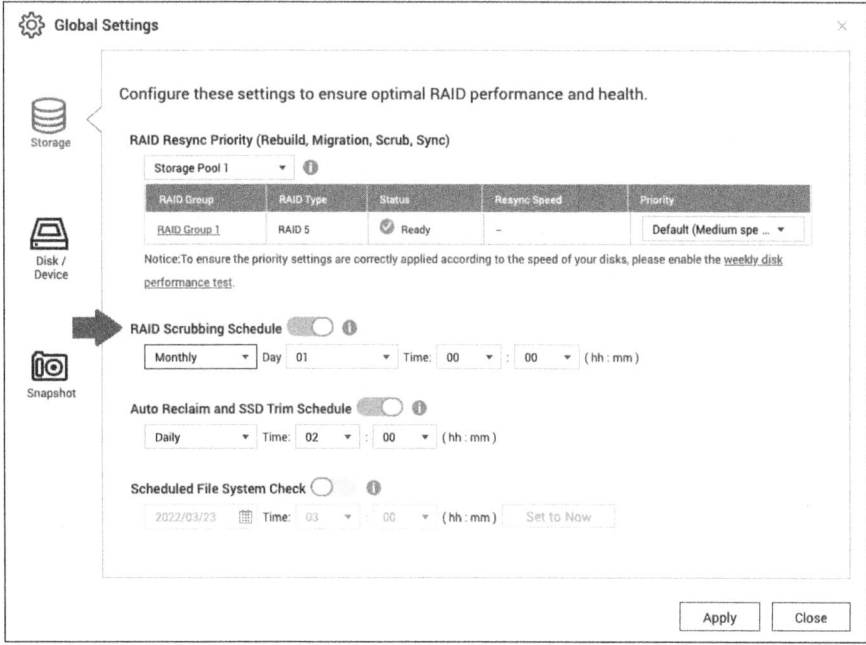

Figure 139: RAID Data Scrubbing

Use the dropdowns to set a frequency, day and time. There is a choice of daily, weekly or monthly, with the latter being sufficient in most cases.

The amount of time taken for data scrubbing is dependent on the amount of storage and specification of the server, but could potentially take a long time and impact the performance of the system. For this reason, it is suggested that it is done out-of-hours or at other times when the server is not being heavily used; in this example the scrubbing will take place on the first of each month at midnight / 00:00. Having made change, click **Apply**.

8.7 System Status

System Status can be viewed by clicking its icon within the Control Panel. It is a more technical and detailed alternative to the Dashboard, possibly more of interest to IT technicians. Nothing can be changed from this screen and it is for information purposes only. There are four separate tabs that provide summary information about various operational aspects of the NAS:

System Information – Summary of some basic settings

Network Status – Detailed information on the network settings and activity

System Service – Listing of the various services and ports in use

Hardware Information – Information about the processor, memory and disks

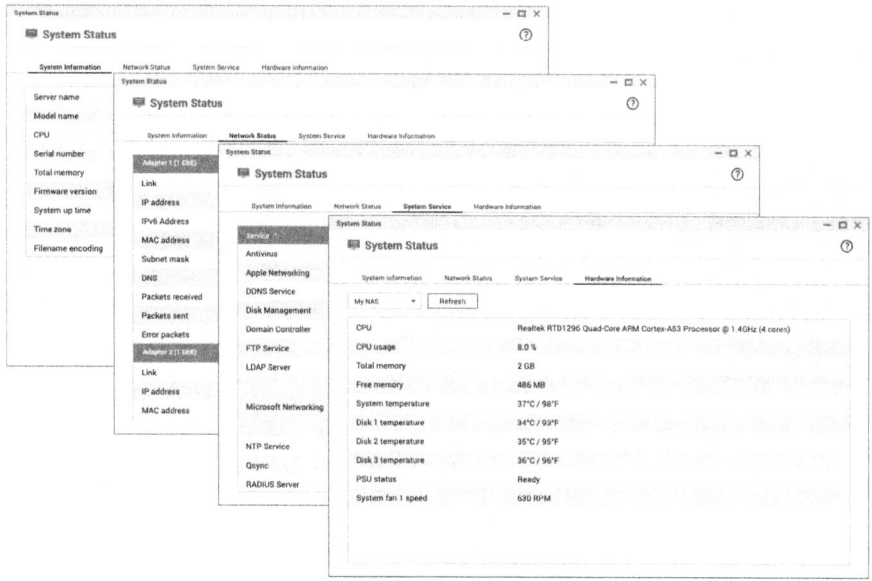

Figure 140: System Status

8.8 Resource Monitor

Resource Monitor, located in the Control Panel, generates charts that provide real-time information about CPU usage, memory usage, disk usage, bandwidth usage, processes and disk performance. This information can be useful when trying to identify performance problems and bottlenecks in a system. For instance, if the server is short on memory then it might be a matter of stopping unused applications, rebooting the NAS or running Qboost (see **8.9 Qboost**). If it is frequently short of memory, then one option is to upgrade the RAM, should that be an option on that particular model. Or, if network utilization is high, then one option might be to add an additional network adapter (again, assuming that is an option for the model in question).

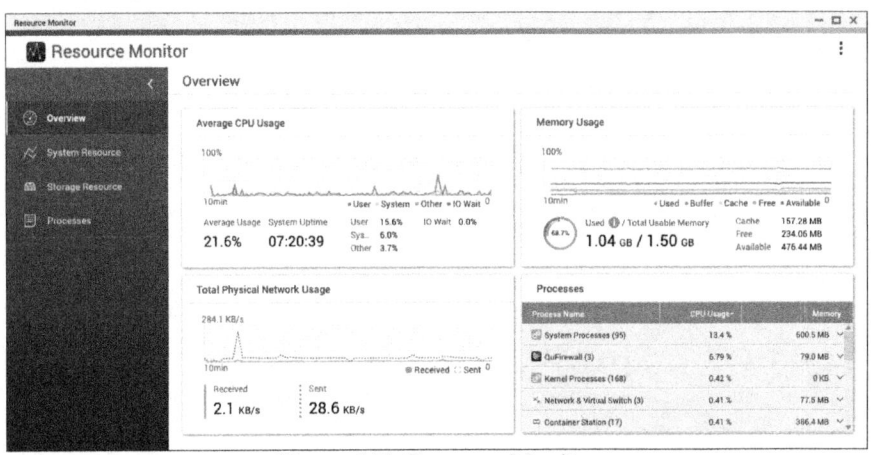

Figure 141: Resource Monitor

A version of Resource Monitor can be invoked from the QNAP *Qfinder Pro* utility. For this reason, you may wish to leave a copy on your own computer specifically for this purpose, particularly if you are working in a business and responsible for the server. Launch *Qfinder Pro*. Click the **Resource Monitor** icon and login as the server administrator when prompted. The following panel is displayed and it remains running even if the main *Qfinder Pro* screen is subsequently closed. The panel can be dragged to any convenient location on the screen. It monitors status, disk space, CPU and memory utilization, plus network activity.

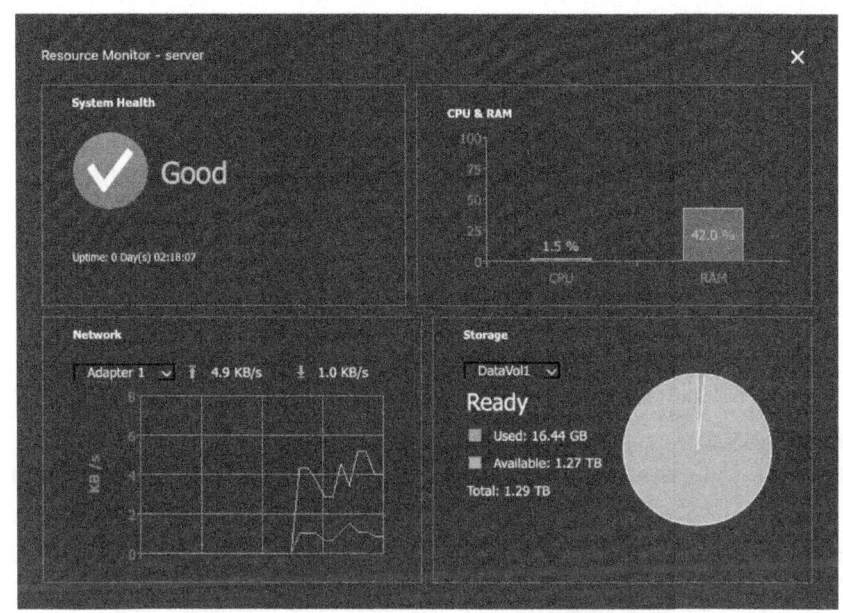

Figure 142: Resource Monitor, as invoked from Qfinder Pro

8.9 Qboost

Qboost is an optional app, downloadable from the App Center, which aims to improve the performance of the NAS by cleaning up unused memory and deleting the temporary files that accumulate during the normal operation of QTS. It can also be scheduled to automatically enable and disable apps, so that system resources can be allocated more efficiently. If you have an Android-based smartphone or tablet, you may have an app on it that does something similar.

Qboost runs continuously and normally appears in the bottom left-hand corner of the screen when you are logged in as admin. Hovering the mouse cursor over the Qboost character will cause it to display a message; for instance, in the above example it indicates that there is currently 'Sufficient memory' i.e. RAM. Clicking the character will result in a display showing the status of Memory, Junk Files and Applications:

Figure 143: Qboost character and main panel

To maximize the amount of available memory, click the blue **Optimize** button. This will typically take around 15 seconds, after which a status panel is displayed, advising how much RAM has been released and what is now available to QTS. To remove unwanted junk files, click the green **Clear** button. When the process is complete, a status message is shown. To control whether the Recycle bin is emptied, click the menu dots to expand the panel and tick or untick the **Recycle Bin files** option before clicking the **Clear** button:

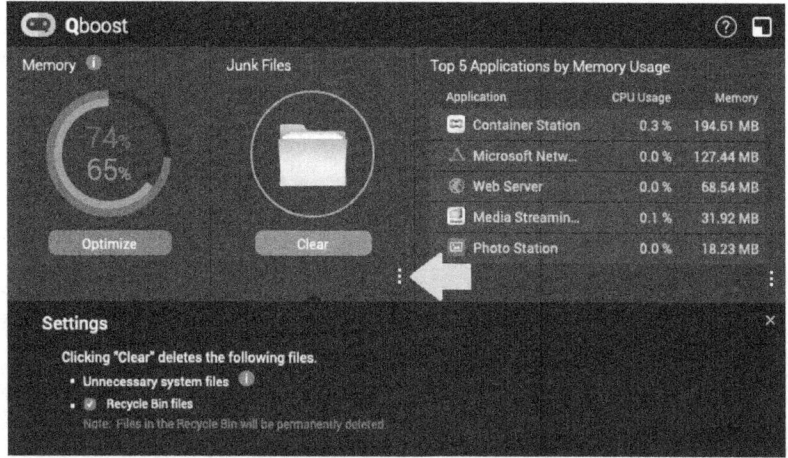

Figure 144: Recycle Bin Settings

To manage Applications, click the menu dots to expand the panel on the right-hand side of Qboost. The screen lists the running applications. They can be sorted by *Application* name, *CPU Usage*, *Memory* usage, *CPU Time* and *Status* (click on the headings to sort). Against each application is a selection of actions, represented by mini icons. Specifically, applications and services can be stopped (disabled), started (enabled), and in some instances deleted.

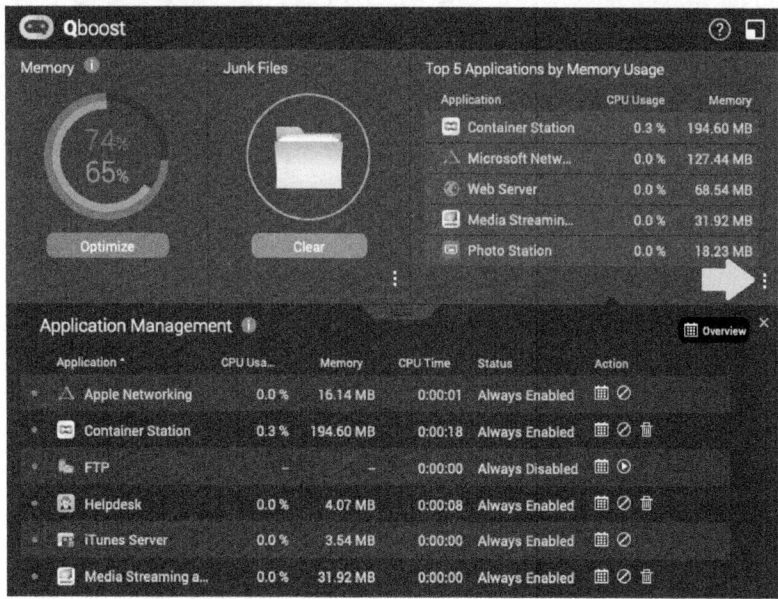

Figure 145: Application Management Settings

Individual applications can also be scheduled, so they are only active at particular times. Against each application is a small calendar mini-icon; clicking it will expand it to show a time-grid for the week. Tick the **Enable Schedule** box, 'paint' the schedule using the mouse cursor and click **Apply**. If a power schedule has been set for the NAS (see **2.6 Hardware & Power Options**), then this will override the settings for scheduled applications.

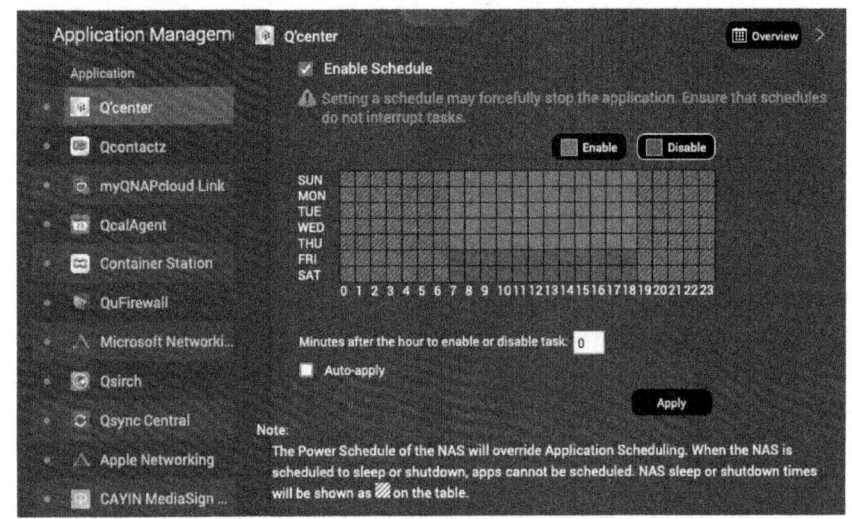

Figure 146: Scheduling an application

The animations associated with Qboost may be distracting. To stop Qboost, right-click the character and choose **Stop,** or you can choose to **Hide** it. To restore it, find it in the My Apps section of App Center and click **Open**.

8.10 Using Qmanager

Available for iOS and Android from the respective app stores, *Qmanager* is a comprehensive utility for managing and monitoring the status of servers from smartphones and tablets. It can be used for creating users, groups, shared folders and installing apps. It can monitor storage, technical and network information, as well as monitor server events (for instance the backup status and who is using the server). It can also be used for updating the firmware, as well as restarting and shutting down the server. If you are responsible for supporting QNAP servers and may not be at the location all the time, it is an indispensable toolbox.

When installing Qmanager and/or running it for the first time, you may receive a prompt asking if you wish to receive notifications. If you reply 'yes', your device will receive messages sent from the *Notification Center* app.

Figure 147: Qmanager running on iPad

The following is a summary of the menu options for some common maintenance tasks, along with corresponding links for doing the same within QTS:

Resource Monitor – **Resource Monitor** with various options listed at bottom of screen (also see **8.8 Resource Monitor**)

Locating the NAS – **System Tools > System > Locate my NAS** (also see **8.11 Locating the NAS**)

Check for Firmware Update - **System Tools > System > Check for Firmware Update** (also see **8.2 Checking for QTS Updates**)

System Logs – **System Logs** (also see **6.13 QuLog Center**)

Creating Shared Folders – **Privilege Settings > Shared Folders**. Tap 3-dot menu in top-right corner of screen, then tap **Create A Shared Folder** (also see **3.2 Creating a Shared Folder**)

Creating Users – **Privilege Settings > Users**. Tap 3-dot menu in top-right corner of screen, then tap **Create A User** (also see **4.2 Creating Users**)

8.11 Locating the NAS

QTS can locate a NAS by beeping the buzzer and making the LEDs on the front of the unit flash. You might consider it unlikely that you would 'lose' a NAS and need such a facility, but there are several scenarios in which it can be useful. For instance, you may be unfamiliar with the location of the NAS in someone else's home or office. Or you might be in an environment where there are multiple units, maybe even dozens or hundreds of them in racks and finding the one you want could be a challenge.

From QTS

To locate a NAS, login as an administrator. Click the username in the top-right corner of the screen and from the drop-down menu choose **Locate my NAS** to display the following:

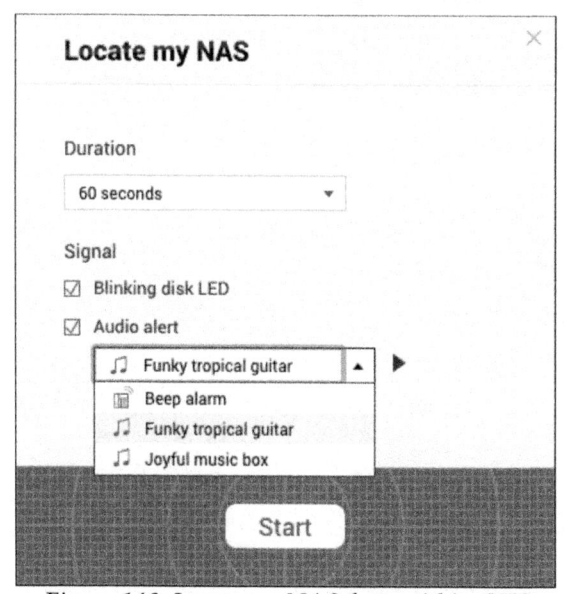

Figure 148: Locate my NAS from within QTS

Use the drop-down for the duration, which can be 5 seconds, 60 seconds or continuous. Select the blinking disk LED and audio alert required (if the NAS has a built-in speaker, it can play a tune rather than just buzz). Click the **Start** button.

Using Qfinder Pro

A NAS can also be located using Qfinder Pro. Click the **Locate This Device** icon, login as the *administrator* and click the **Start** button.

Figure 149: Locate my NAS with Qfinder Pro

8.12 Managing Multiple Servers

Most home and small business installations consist of a single NAS, maybe two or three. As such, monitoring and management is not usually a difficult or time-consuming matter. But in a larger environment there may be many, maybe dozens or hundreds of servers, plus they may be dispersed across different physical locations. To enable management of such environments, QNAP offer an app called *Q'center*, whereby all servers can be monitored from a central location. The tool is aimed at organizations running x86-based and 64-bit ARM servers and/or virtualized environments, and includes many sophisticated reporting and management tools, presented within a dashboard and with numerous reporting options available. There are features to update the firmware and install apps on remote servers. A powerful capability is the ability to define rules or policies that control the behavior of individual servers or groups of servers (analogous to Group Policy in Windows Server environments).

Q'center is downloaded and installed from the App Center onto a designated centralized server, from where the other ones will be monitored and controlled; in a very large environment, it is possible to run multiple Q'center servers. The server(s) to be monitored need to have the *Connect to Q'center* app installed, downloadable from the App Center or deployed from an existing Q'center server.

Once loaded, Q'Center runs in a separate browser window. Upon first run, there is the choice of Initializing Q'center or importing settings from an existing or previous installation and we will assume the former. Servers have to be added to it and there are several ways of doing so: by IP address; by hostname subnet; using a list from a CSV file and so on. One useful option is to add using the myQNAPcloud address, as this enables remote servers to be easily managed. As part of adding a server, SMTP can optionally be configured so that Q'center will send email notifications.

If you have multiple servers that need managing, then this tool may prove very useful.

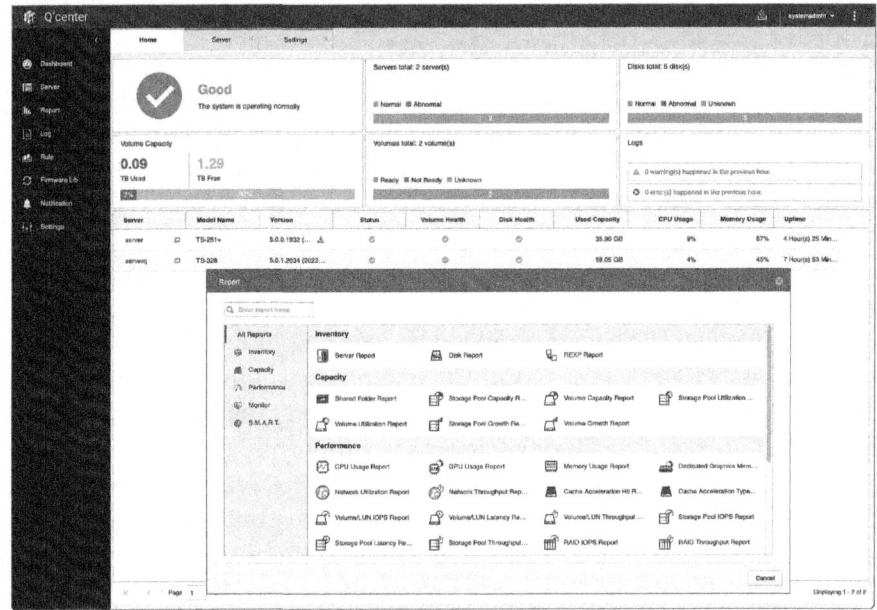

Figure 150: Reporting options in Q'Center

9

MULTIMEDIA & STREAMING

9.1 Overview

One of the most popular uses of a home network is for the storage and playback of media such as music and videos and the viewing of photographs. The NAS can playback the stored media onto a variety of devices including computers, gaming consoles, tablets, smartphones, smart TVs and streaming devices. Some QNAP models are equipped with a HDMI port, enabling them to be connected directly to a suitable television set and to act as a home theater media player, using an app called *HybridDesk Station* and which is described in section **9.10 HybridDesk Station**.

QNAP offer a wide range of multimedia apps, including:

DLNA Media Server – a universal system for media playback to many types of devices
MusicStation – for playback of music and audio files
VideoStation – for playing back videos and movies
PhotoStation – for managing and displaying photographs and other images
QuMagie – a 'next generation' photo application with AI-based image recognition
Cinema28 – enables media to be centrally streamed to devices
CAYIN MediaSign Player – alternative video player, promoted by QNAP

Begin by doing some basic preparation work. In section **3.2 Creating a Shared Folder** we created a folder for *Multimedia*, but to better help organize your files you may wish to create three sub-folders within it called *photo, video* and *music*. These are standard folders, not shared folders, and can be created as follows:

Launch **File Station** and highlight the *Multimedia* folder. Click the **New Folder** mini icon towards the top of the screen and choose **Folder** (this is a regular folder, not a shared folder). Name the folder *photo* and click **OK**. Repeat, creating folders called *video* and *music*.

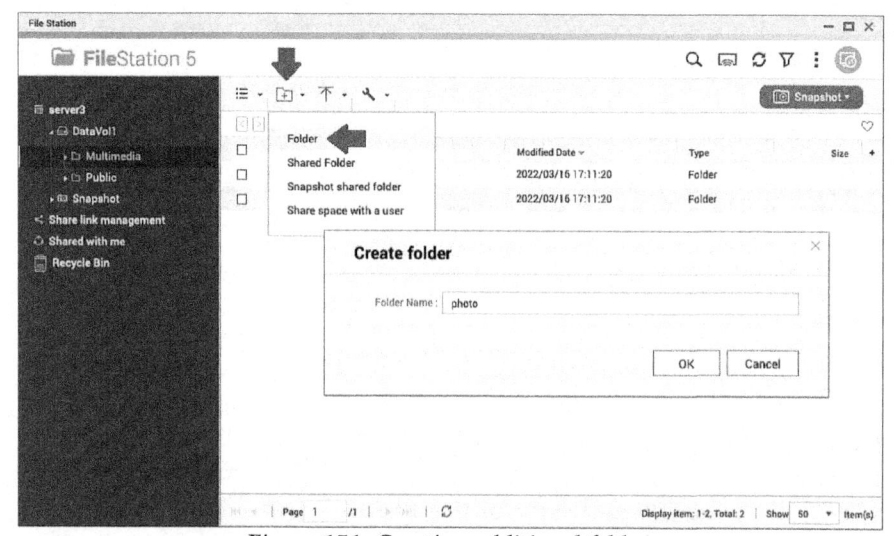

Figure 151: Creating additional folders

You do not have to do this and you can call the multimedia folders whatever you wish and put them wherever you want, but it is a sensible starting point. Having created the folders, populate them by copying your photos, videos and music into them using the techniques described in section **3.5 Loading Existing Data into Shared Folders**, directly from File Station if you are using the Chrome browser, or using the Media Upload feature in Qfinder Pro (see **9.11 Media Upload from Qfinder Pro**).

9.2 Multimedia Console

The *Multimedia Console* is a portal to the multimedia apps, enabling them to be managed and controlled from a single place. There is an entry for it in the Control Panel, but initially it is just a link to the App Center, from where it needs to be downloaded and installed; thereafter it can be launched from the Main Menu, Control Panel and Desktop. The first time it is run, a short tour is given to explain its purpose.

It is important to understand the different functions of the Multimedia Console, as it is key to successfully using multimedia on a QNAP NAS. There are initially six sections, discussed below: *Overview; Content Management; Indexing; Thumbnail Generation; Transcoding; Multimedia App Suite*. Installing *QuMagie* (and some other applications) will add a seventh section, *AI Engines*, plus update the Overview screen with entries for *Facial Recognition, Object Recognition* and *Similar Photo Recognition*. This is shown in the screenshots below but may not initially be present on your system.

Overview

The Overview screen gives a summary of the media files on the NAS.

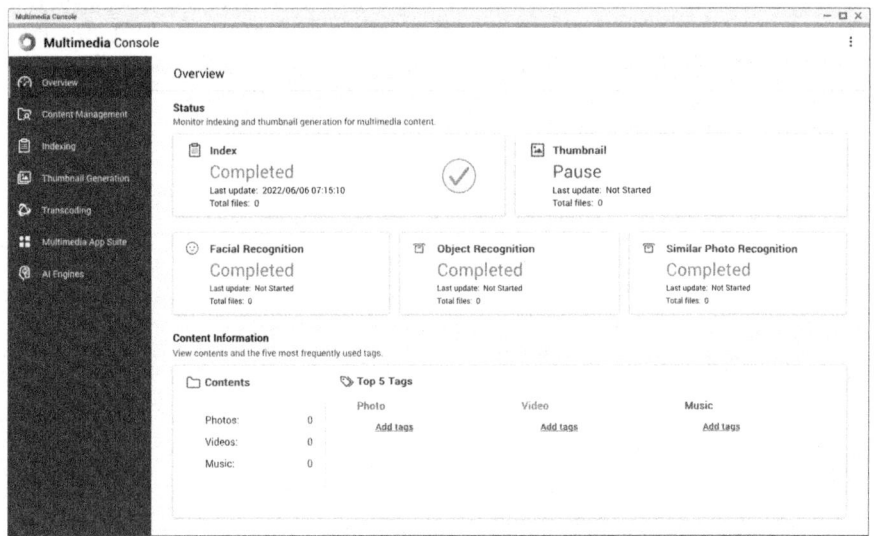

Figure 152: Multimedia Console Overview Screen

There are several areas, advising on the status of indexing, thumbnail generation, the number and type of media files, along with image recognition (if *AI Engines* have been installed). These sections are clickable and link to other parts of Multimedia Console or to the multimedia apps themselves as appropriate.

Content Management

The Content Management screen is for defining the folders used by the various multimedia apps that have been installed and which will be listed along the top of the screen. Initially, there will only be an entry for DLNA, which is built-in to QTS, but the screen will become populated as the multimedia apps are installed. In this example we have installed Photo Station, Video Station and Music Station.

In section **9.1 Overview** we placed our photos in the *multimedia/photo* folder, videos in *multimedia/video* and music in *multimedia/music*; we now need to configure the apps to use them.

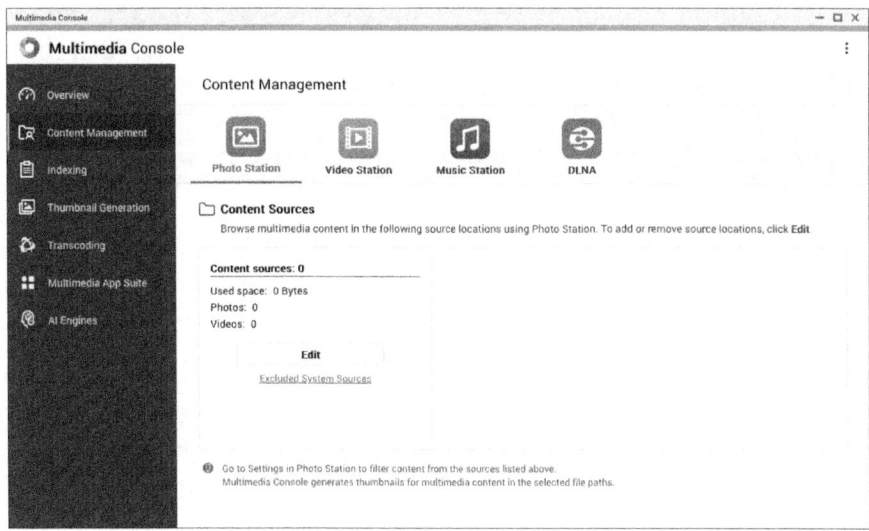

Figure 153: Content Management screen

We will commence with Photo Station in this example. Click its icon, then click the **Edit** button in the *Content Sources* section. Browse to where the photos are located (i.e. *multimedia/photo*), tick the box and click **Apply**. If you have already loaded some photographs into the *photo* folder, this may potentially cause activity as the system generates thumbnail pictures in the background:

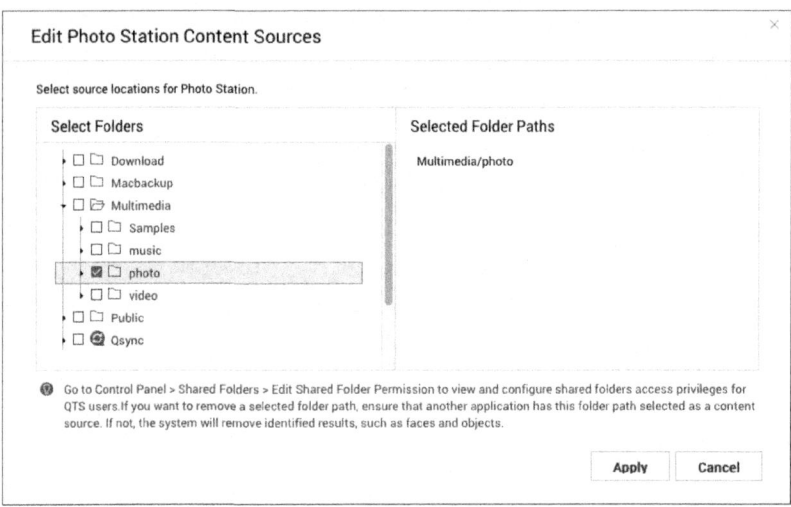

Figure 154: Specify the Content Sources

Returning to the previous screen, click the **Video Station** tab. Click the **Edit** button in *Content Sources*. Browse to where the videos are located (i.e. *multimedia/video*), tick the box and click **Apply**. Next, click the **Music Station** tab and click the **Edit** button in *Content Sources*. Again, browse to where the music is located (i.e. *multimedia/music*) and tick the box, followed by **Apply**. This process should be repeated for any other multimedia apps which are being used.

Suggestion: if you only intend using the DLNA application, you could set the folder to the shared *multimedia* folder.

Indexing

Indexing is the process where multimedia files are catalogued on the NAS. This makes it easier for you (and the NAS) to locate them, plus enables Multimedia Console to generate thumbnails for pictures and to transcode videos for more efficient playback (transcoding is discussed shortly).

When multimedia files are added to the designated folders, the NAS will index them. If you have already copied some media files to the designated folders, you may need to click the **Re-index** button. Media indexing can use considerable processing resources and, depending on the number, size and type of files and the hardware capabilities of your NAS, could take a relatively long time to complete.

The priority or resources assigned to indexing can be set to *Low* or *Normal*. With Low, system impact is reduced but indexing will take longer. With Normal, indexing is faster, but system impact is higher.

The Text encoding dropdown is for changing the language (code page) used in indexing and would usually be left as the default.

Having made any changes, click the **Apply** button.

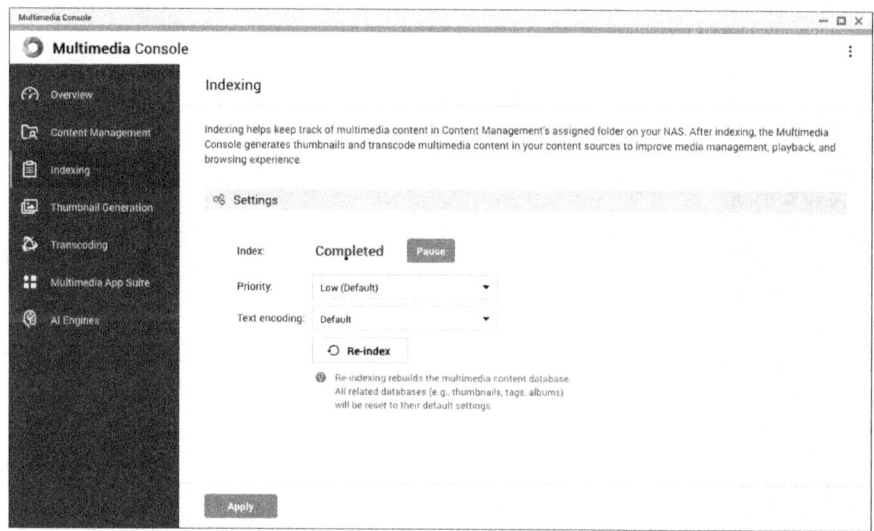

Figure 155: Indexing screen

Thumbnail Generation

Thumbnails are miniature preview pictures of media files that enable you to visually identify items (e.g. photographs) when browsing. Because generating thumbnails can be resource intensive, there are options to manage the process, which are accessed by clicking **Thumbnail Generation** within the Multimedia Console. The switch in the top right-hand corner of the screen needs to be in the **Enabled** position.

Thumbnails can be generated in real time i.e. when files are added to the NAS, manually, or according to a schedule. On a powerful model you might choose to use real time, whereas on a less powerful model you might want to generate them manually or according to a schedule. To do so, set the *Schedule* dropdown to *Generate using schedule*, which will result in additional options becoming available.

Specify the frequency and times: in the example below, thumbnail generation will take place every day between 0100 and 0200, when it should not impact users.

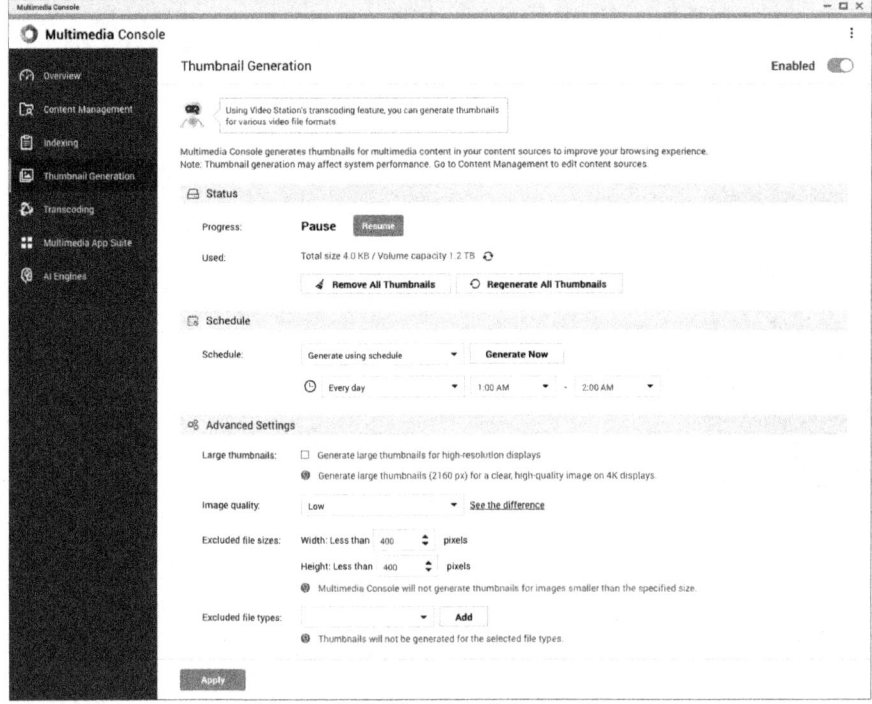

Figure 156: Thumbnail Generation

Within the *Advanced Settings* section are some additional options:

Large thumbnails – if you are working with a 4K monitor screen, you may wish to generate larger thumbnails. Otherwise, do not tick this box as it uses additional resources.

Image quality – thumbnails can be generated in high or low quality. Low quality thumbnails use less resources and are often sufficient for most purposes.

Excluded file sizes – you can choose not to generate thumbnails for images which are below a certain size e.g. those below 400 x 400 pixels.

Excluded file types – you can choose not to generate thumbnails for certain type of files. For example, you could exclude m4a, mp4 and mov files if you did not want thumbnails for videos.

Having made any changes, click the **Apply** button.

Transcoding

The purpose of transcoding is to change or convert the format or resolution of video files to render them more suitable for playing on different devices. For instance, the current standard for high-resolution home video is 4K, known as Ultra High Definition or UHD; however, such large files may be sub-optimal for playback on, say, smartphones, where screen resolution might be 720p or 1080p. With transcoding, the file is rendered at a lower resolution, and this can be done 'on the fly' when required, or in advance on a scheduled or batch basis. Transcoded videos will always be in MPEG-4 format. Transcoding, especially real-time video transcoding, uses a lot of processing power and may be beyond the capabilities of some low-end NAS models. In practical terms, real-time transcoding requires x86-based models with a reasonable amount of RAM; some QNAP models feature a GPU (Graphics Processing Unit), in which case this can be used for transcoding.

Transcoding is provided in conjunction with the *CAYIN Media Sign Player*, so this needs to be installed and enabled (see section **9.8 CAYIN MediaSign Player**). Until this is done, the Transcoding section will be blank.

To access the options, go into the **Multimedia Console** and click **Transcoding**. There are two tabs on the resultant screen: *Overview* and *Settings*. The first one shows the status of transcoding tasks, whilst the second one controls the process. Click **Settings** to display the screen below.

An important decision is when transcoding should take place and there are three choices. If you have a reasonably powerful QNAP model you can use the *Scan in real time* option, particularly if GPU-accelerated transcoding is available, otherwise you should consider *Scan by schedule* or *Manual scans*.

In the *Background Transcoding Folders* section, specify where the video files are located by clicking the **Add** button; in this example, we are using the *multimedia/video* folder. Specify the resolution(s) of the resultant transcoded files; here we have chosen for the system to create transcoded copies in both 360p and 720p resolutions.

Having specified all the parameters, click **Apply**, followed by **Apply** again upon returning to the previous screen.

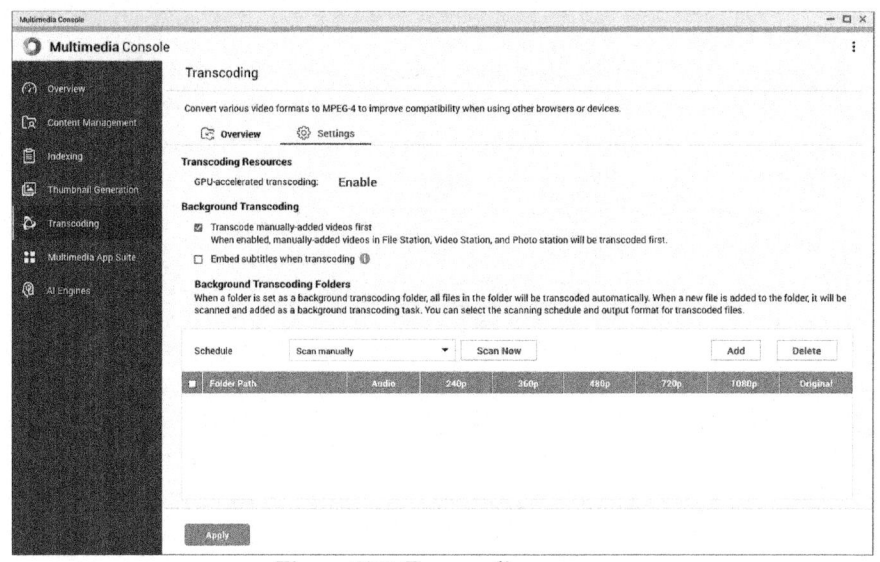

Figure 157: Transcoding screen

Multimedia App Suite

The *Multimedia App Suite* tab provides easy access for configuring and managing the individual media apps: in effect, it is a portal or menu for accessing them. Clicking an icon will take you to the appropriate management screen for that app; if the app has not yet been installed it will take you to the App Center for download and installation.

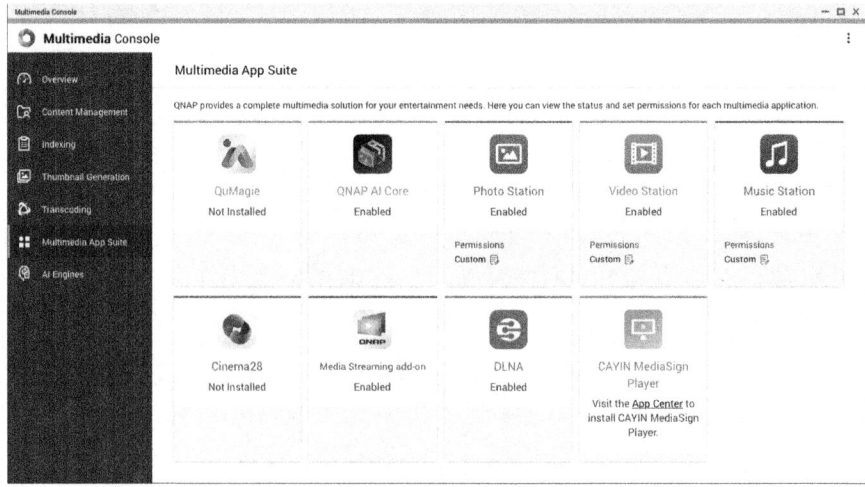

Figure 158: Multimedia App Suite

AI Engines

The installation of some applications e.g. *QuMagie,* adds a further section to the Multimedia Console, called *AI Engines*. This shows the status of the facial, object and similar photo recognition processes, similar to how the Overview screen shows the status of the indexing and thumbnail processes. These processes run in the background because they are processor intensive and can affect overall system performance, so there is an option to pause them at any point. In NAS models equipped with a GPU – *Graphics Processing Unit* – this will be used for object recognition processing, as it is more efficient than using the server's CPU.

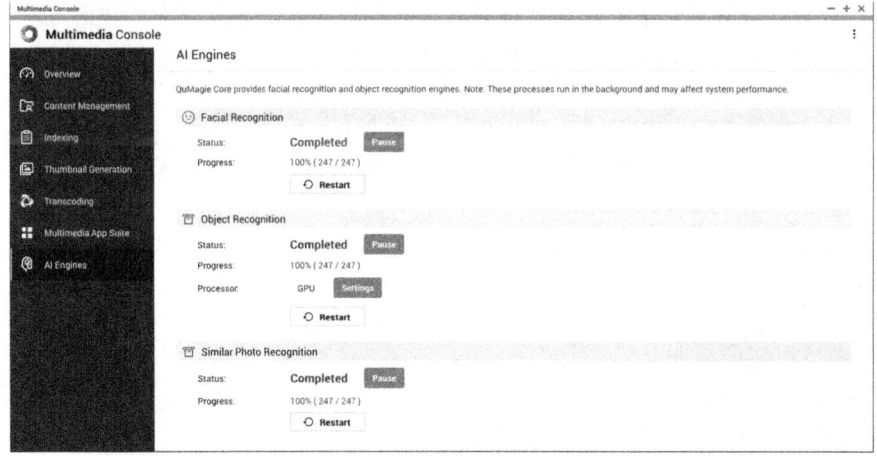

Figure 159: AI Engines tab within Multimedia Console

9.3 DLNA Media Server

DLNA is the abbreviation for *Digital Living Network Alliance*. It is a standard for interconnecting home network devices so they can stream and play multimedia, without worrying about passwords, network protocols and other technical issues. Many devices are DLNA-compliant including computers, smart televisions, media streamers such as Roku and Chromecast, gaming boxes such as the Xbox and PlayStation smartphones, Blu-ray players and more. DLNA Media Server is an integral part of QTS.

To access the DLNA Media Server controls, go to **Control Panel > Applications > DLNA Media Server**. Alternatively, click on **Multimedia Console > Multimedia App Suite** and click the **DLNA** icon. Confirm that the **Enable DLNA Media Server** box is ticked. Using the dropdown, change the *Select default user account* to your administrative account if it is not already set. Click **Apply**. When control is returned, click the **Scan now** button.

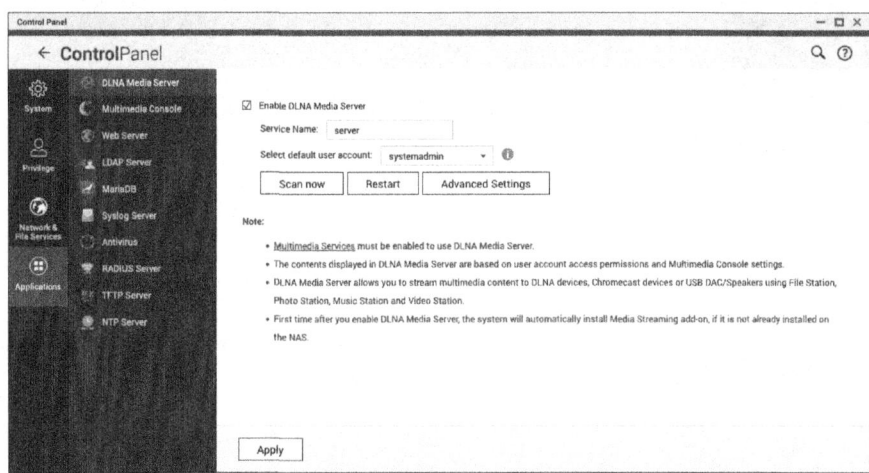

Figure 160: Enabling DLNA Media Server

You should now be able to connect your DLNA client to the server. As DLNA devices vary considerably, there is no single method for doing so. Some clients, for instance Windows PCs, will see the media server within File Explorer/Windows Explorer. Double-click the server entry and the computer's default media player should open – you should then be able to access photo, music and videos (in the case of Windows Media Player, the server will be listed underneath the *Other Libraries* section).

On other devices, such as smart TVs and set-top boxes, it may be necessary to explicitly go into network settings or there may be an option to search for media servers - refer to the manufacturer's instructions or website for details.

Closely associated with the DLNA Media Server is the *Media Streaming add-on*, used for managing streaming devices. This has probably been installed automatically by QTS, otherwise it can be downloaded and installed from the App Center. It can be accessed by clicking the **Advanced Settings** button on the DLNA Media Server screen and doing so will display the following screen in a new browser tab:

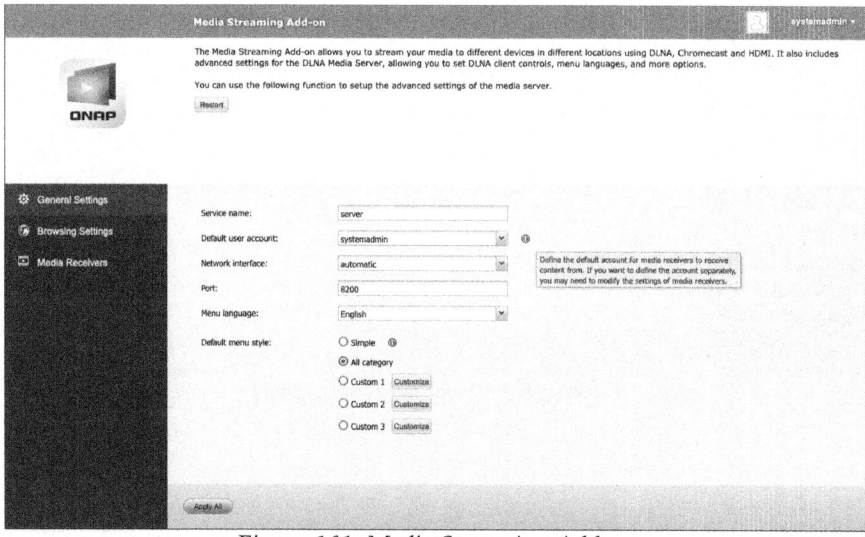

Figure 161: Media Streaming Add-on

There are three main sections, listed down the left-hand side of the screen. Within *General Settings*, change the *Default user account* to your administrative user if it has not already found it. The other settings on this tab, plus those on *Browsing Settings* will be suitable in most instances and do not need adjusting. However, there is the option to assign a dedicated network interface to maximize throughput in an installation where streaming is used extensively.

To check that your streaming devices are being identified, make sure they are powered on then click **Media Receivers**, where they should be listed. In this example, three devices have been found; the *Device Names* may be missing or incorrect, although this will not affect matters. The *Menu Style* and *User Profile* for each device can be changed if required, by clicking in the appropriate area to cause a dropdown selection to appear.

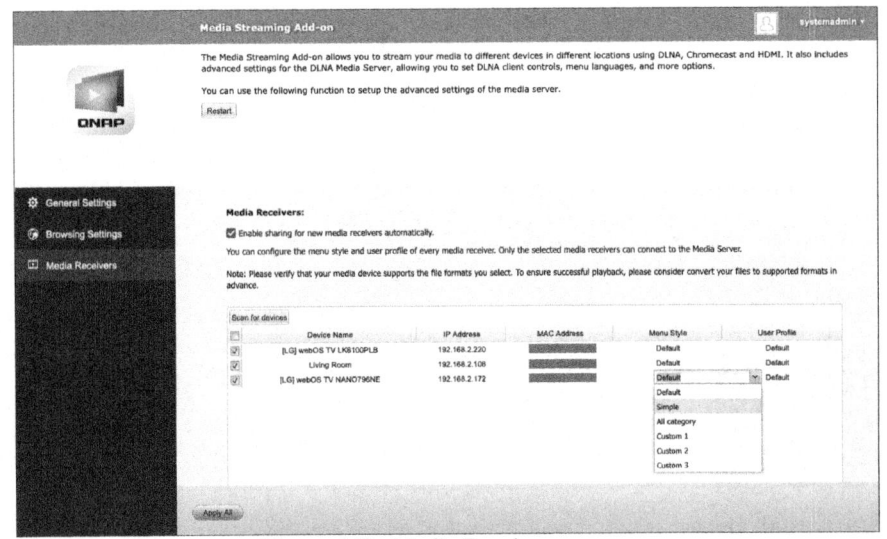

Figure 162: Media Receivers screen

9.4 Music Station

Music Station is a downloadable application from the App Center (see **15.2 App Center**) that enables a music collection to be held and managed on the NAS and played back through a browser or streamed to other devices. All browsers will play back MP3-format audio files, although might not support other audio formats.

Start off by placing your music in the shared *Multimedia* folder – you may wish to create a sub-folder within it called *music* to make it easier to organize your collection as described in section **9.1 Overview**. Having done so, go into the *Content Management* section of **Multimedia Console** and specify the *Content Sources* for Music Station, as described in section **9.2 Multimedia Console**.

Click the **Music Station** icon, which will be on the desktop and in the **Main Menu**. The first time it is run there may be a message about thumbnails – click **OK**. You are then presented with a short tutorial, explaining how the app works. The app itself has two modes: *Spotlight* and *Manage*. The former provides quick and convenient access to playing music, whereas the latter is more flexible in organizing and selecting it. The music can be viewed and sorted in various ways such as by album, by artist, genre and other categories, and can be displayed as a text list, as icons or as album covers.

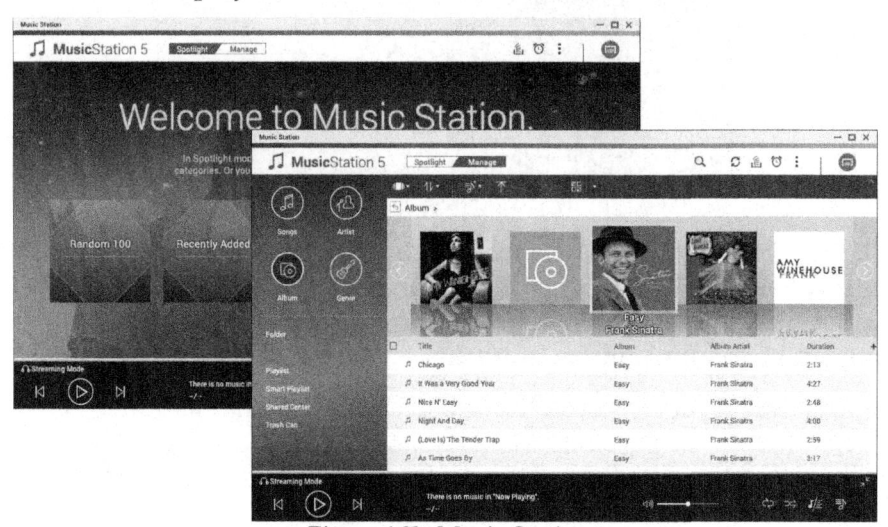

Figure 163: Music Station

There are several options for playing back music:

Double-click a track and it will play on the computer you are using via Music Station and through the browser.

If the Multimedia folder is being accessed on a computer, double-click a track and it should playback via the computer's default audio application e.g. Windows Media Player, Groove Music, QuickTime etc.

If the NAS has a built-in speaker, it can be played through that.

If the NAS has a HDMI connection, it can be played through that.

If there is a connected network media player (DLNA – see section **9.3 DLNA Media Server**), it can be sent to that by clicking on the icon in the top-right corner of the Music Station screen:

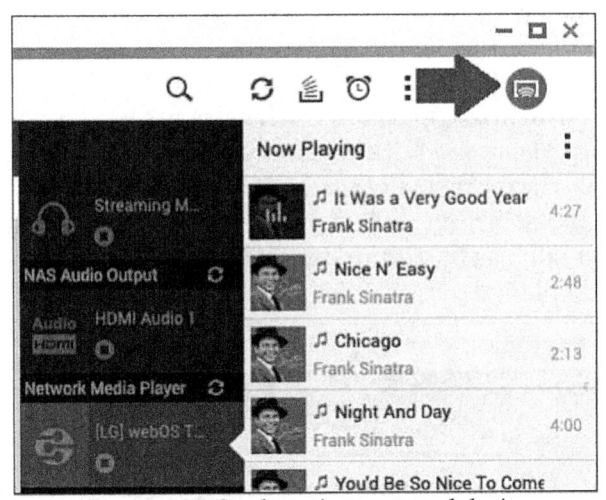

Figure 164: Send music to external device

If music tracks are not appearing in Music Station, launch **Multimedia Console** and click the **Indexing** tab, followed by the **Re-index** button. This will re-index the music, which may take some time depending on the number of tracks.

The album cover art should have been retrieved automatically. If the artwork is missing, go into Manage mode and choose **Show items in a list** or **Show items as icons**. Right-click an album and click **Information** from the pop-up menu. On the resultant panel, click **Search** and then select the most suitable artwork when (if) it is located. Click **Save**.

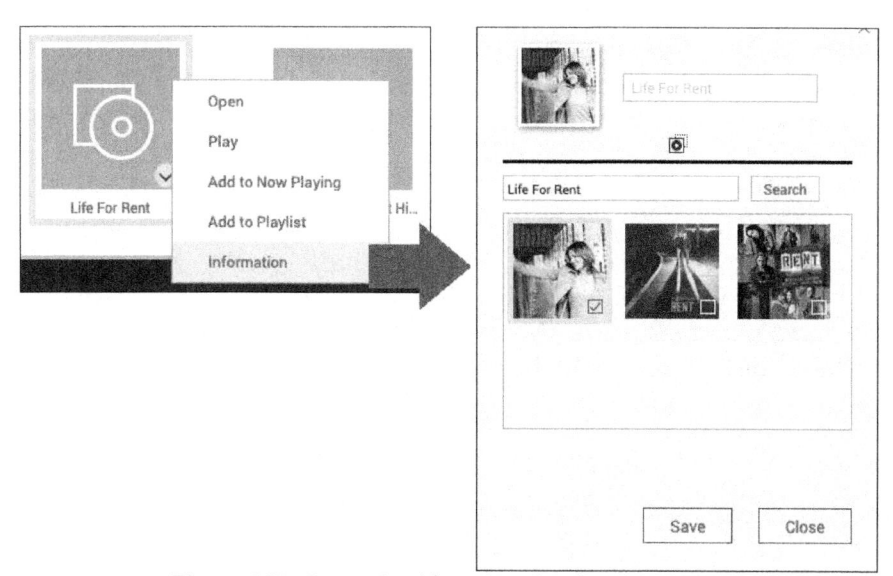

Figure 165: Correcting/changing the album cover art

Access to Music Station can be controlled on an individual user basis. There are several ways of doing so, but the most flexible method is from within Music Station itself, as this allows access to be controlled on a user-by-user, feature-by-feature basis. Click the three-dot snowman menu icon at the top of the screen and choose **Settings > Access Permissions**. Tick the boxes against each user to define what is available. When finished, click **Save**.

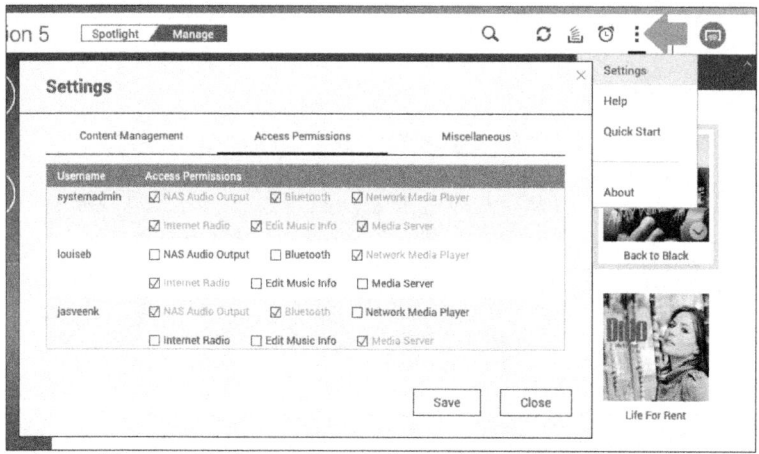

Figure 166: Access Permissions within Music Station

211

Qmusic

The *Qmusic* app is for playing back music from the server on smartphones and tablets. It is a free download from QNAP and available for iOS and Android tablets and smartphones. When running Qmusic for the first time, it is necessary to specify the details of the server. If you are connected locally you can let the app find your server on the network, else manually specify the name or address. If you are using Qmusic remotely you can enter the myQNAPcloud address. Music can also be downloaded to the portable device so it can be played back when there may be no network connection, such as when travelling.

9.5 QuMagie

QuMagie is a next-generation photo management app application from QNAP. It is one of two such applications available from QNAP, the other being *Photo Station* (see **9.6 Photo Station**). The main difference between them is that QuMagie features AI (Artificial Intelligence) technology, enabling it to perform improved facial and object recognition. However, although this feature is available to all current QNAP models which have x86 or 64-bit ARM CPUs, it is not available on older 32-bit ARM models. QuMagie is downloaded from the App Center; during the installation process you may be prompted to install some dependent applications - *Container Station* and *QNAP AI Core* - which you should do by answering **OK** to the prompt. Installation will take several minutes, after which it can be run from the Main Menu, the Desktop or from the Multimedia Console.

The main screen opens in its own browser window. As the app needs to generate thumbnails, the photos may take a while to appear the first time it is used, with the time taken depending on their number, size, resolution and the hardware capabilities of the NAS.

Figure 167: QuMagie Timeline view

The layout of the main screen can be changed by clicking on the **View** dropdown in the right-hand corner of the screen, giving a choice of timeline or thumbnail views, along with a choice of thumbnail size and the option to sort the photos using different criteria.

To view an individual photo in full screen mode, click it. By clicking the **Info** icon, you can edit the timestamp and tag information. There are back and forward icons for moving through the photos, or you can return to the main screen:

Figure 168: Viewing an individual photograph

Searching for People and Things

QuMagie automatically identifies faces and common objects, using *tags*. In the case of objects, tags are applied automatically; for people, the tags (names) must be applied manually and thereafter the program will be able to recognize them. The tags can then be used to search for people or object types amongst the photo collection.

To search, click the **Albums** option in the top left-hand corner of the screen. At the top of the screen, the results will include *People, Things, Similar Photos* and other categories:

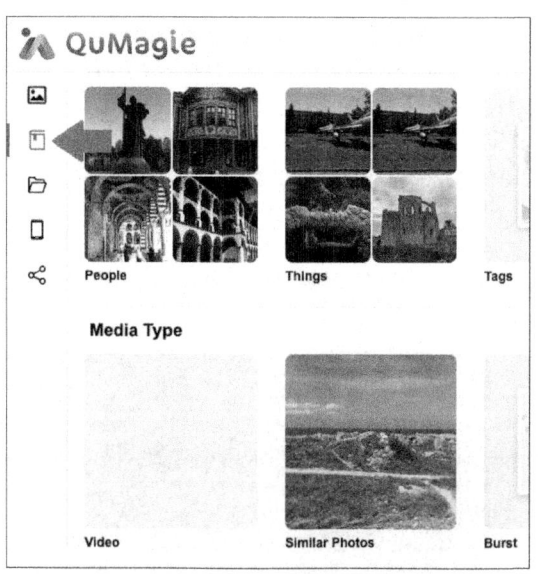

Figure 169: Switch from Photos to Albums mode

Click **Things**, which will then expand into multiple categories, depending on what was found in your collection of photographs. In this example, it has identified categories such as animals, food, greenery, sports and so on, although different categories may be identified on your system. Clicking one of them will then display all of the photographs within that category, which may in turn identify further sub-categories.

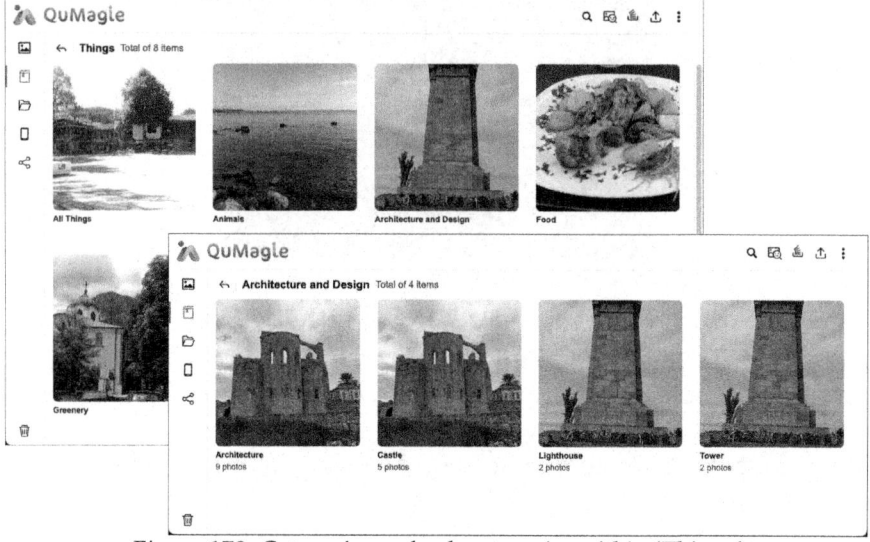

Figure 170: Categories and sub-categories within 'Things'

QuMagie Mobile App

The *QuMagie Mobile* app is available for iOS and Android devices, downloadable from the appropriate App Store. When running it for the first time, it will offer to search the local network for any QNAP server(s) – click **OK**. If it fails to find the server, click the **Add NAS manually** or **Sign in QNAP ID** option and enter the server's details. If you receive a message about granting access to local photos on the device, do so. The app operates as expected, enabling photos to be viewed as thumbnails or full screen, and searched using Tags.

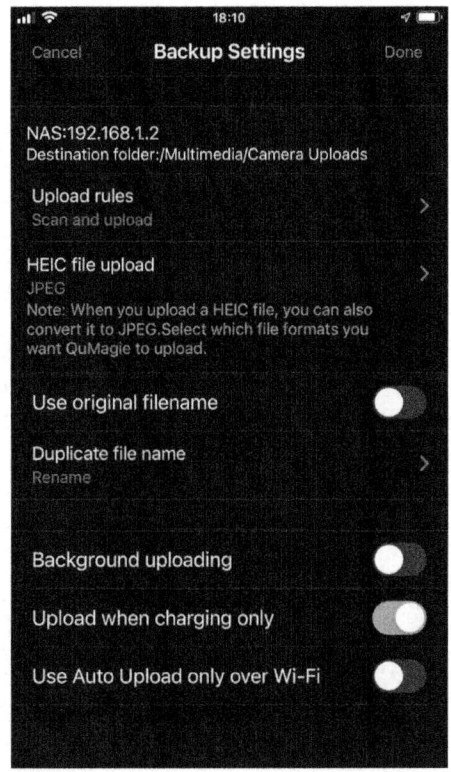

Figure 171: Backup Settings in QuMagie Mobile app

To configure the mobile app to upload/backup photos from the mobile device, tap the three line 'burger' menu in the top-left hand corner of the screen, then tap **Settings > Backup**. Tap the **Set up now** button and slide the switch to the 'On' position. Choose the server as the backup destination and specify the folder which will be used to hold the backups. Additional options can be specified, for example to restrict uploading to when the device is being charged and to restrict auto uploading to Wi-Fi connections only.

9.6 Photo Station

Photo Station is an application from QNAP, downloadable from the App Center, that allows photo collections to be managed on the NAS and viewed through an internet browser or on a mobile device. It is one of two such applications available from QNAP, the other being *QuMagie* (see **9.5 QuMagie**).

Begin by placing your photos in the shared *Multimedia* folder – you may wish to create a sub-folder within it called *photo* to make it easier to organize your collection as described in section **9.1 Overview**. Having done so, go into the *Content Management* section of **Multimedia Console** and specify the *Content Sources* for Photo Station, as described in section **9.2 Multimedia Console**.

The first time Photo Station is run it will display a short tour. You might also receive a message about support for 360-degree photos and videos in panorama mode – if this is important to you, click **Yes**. A panel is displayed, giving the opportunity to import a folder of photos. This is optional.

Eventually the main gallery screen is displayed, although depending on the number of photos and the performance of the NAS it may be a short while before the screen is fully populated:

Figure 172: Photo Station Gallery view

The collection of photos can be viewed in several ways: as a list, as icons, as folders or as a timeline. To quickly change the gallery view, click the **Display Settings** button towards the top of the screen. For a wider range of viewing options click the **Manage** button, which will result in the following display (following a quick tour the first time you do so):

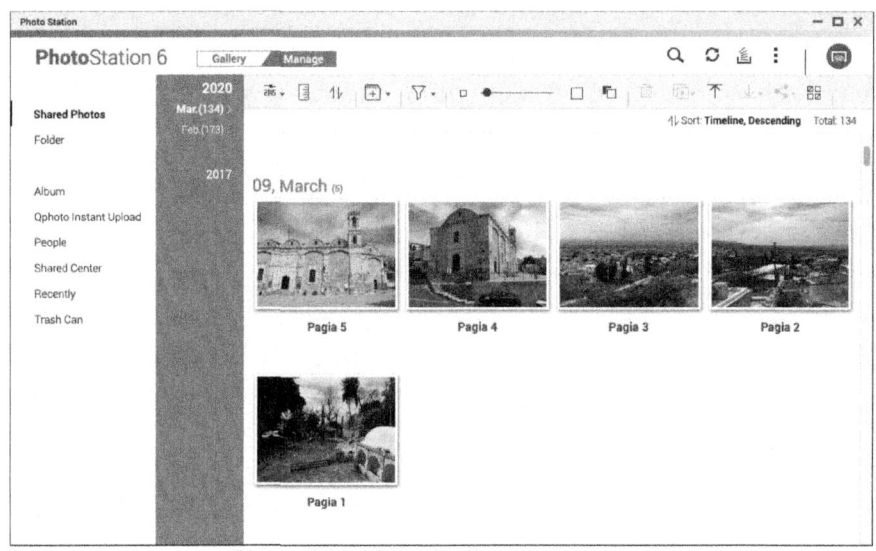

Figure 173: Photo Station Manage view

To view a specific photo, double-click it. Photos can be made full screen, downloaded to the local computer, shared via social media, or set as the user's wallpaper. They can also be played as a slideshow, or streamed to a network media player:

Figure 174: Working with an individual photo

When finished viewing photos, close Photo Station by clicking on the cross icon in the top right-hand corner of the app.

Access to Photo Station can be controlled on an individual user basis. Go into **Control Panel**, click **Users**, select the user's name and then click the small **Edit Application Privilege** icon on the right-hand side. Place or remove a tick against **Photo Station** then click **Apply**.
If your photos are not being listed in Photo Station, launch **Multimedia Console** and click the **Indexing** tab, followed by the **Re-index** button. This will cause the media to be re-indexed (this may take some time).

Tagging People

Photo Station can recognize people using face recognition, in a process called *Tagging*. To configure it, switch to *Manage* mode and click **People** on the left-hand side of the screen. Tagging requires that an additional component called *QuMagie AI Core* has been installed, along with its dependent application Container Station, and there will be a link to do so if it is not already in place. Once this this has been done, which may take some time, the People screen will advise that no people have currently been tagged; click **Suggested**, which will search through the photographs and generate a display of faces. Choose a person, click **+Add a name** and enter their name. They will then be added to the list of tags.

To subsequently search for photos containing that person, go to *Manage* mode and click **People > Tagged**. Double-click the person and all images in which they feature will be displayed.

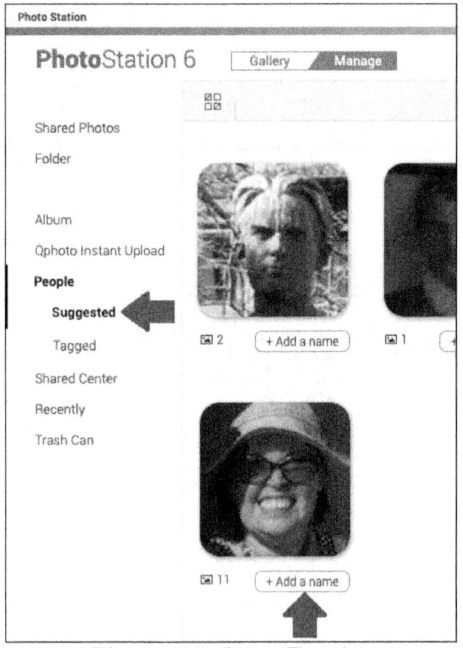

Figure 175: Setup Tagging

Qphoto

Qphoto is available for iOS and Android and can be downloaded from the respective App Stores. When running it for the first time, it is necessary to specify the details of the server. If you are connected locally you can let the app find your server on the network, else manually specify the name or address. If you are using Qphoto remotely you can enter the myQNAPcloud address. For maximum capabilities, Qphoto requires access to local photos on the mobile device, so grant this.

Qphoto has a comprehensive range of features for viewing photos stored on the NAS. These include Customizable view modes with timeline, thumbnail, list and folder; Share photos using email and social media; View albums from Photo Station; Slideshows; Upload photos taken on the Smartphone or tablet to the NAS; Download photos from the NAS to the Smartphone or tablet.

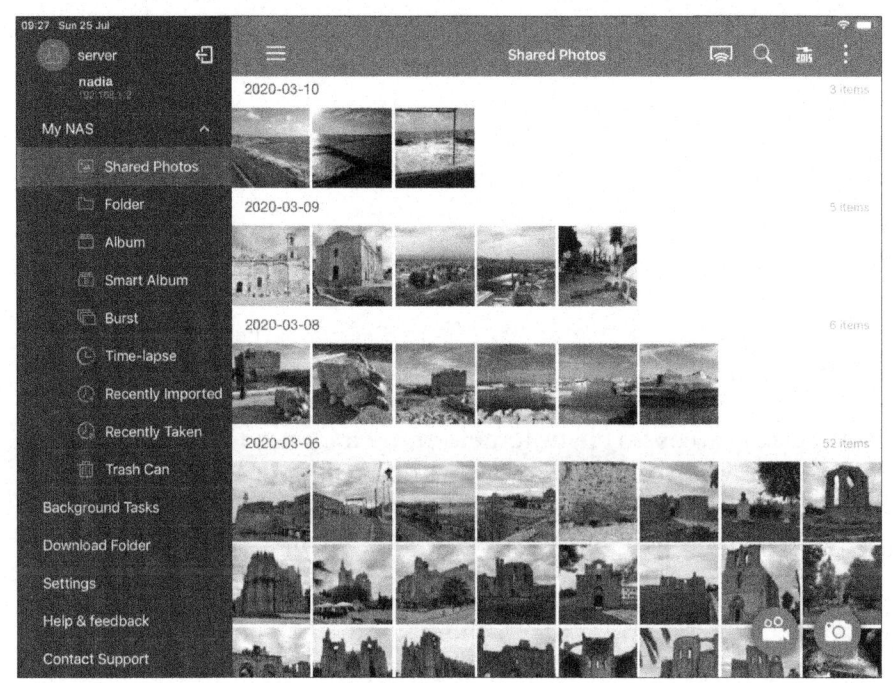

Figure 176: Qphoto running on iPad

Photographs taken on modern Smartphones are often high resolution and the file sizes may be large. If your data plan has restrictions, you may wish to configure Qphoto such that it will only upload and download when connected to Wi-Fi. To do this, click on **Settings**, scroll down to the relevant section and slide the Wi-Fi only switch to the 'On' position.

9.7 Video Station

Video Station is QNAP's web-based application for watching videos, played back within an internet browser. It is downloaded from the App Center (see section **15.2 App Center**).

On a suitable computer, DVDs can be 'ripped' into a format such as MP4 and these copies can be played back from the NAS, thus enabling more convenient access and streaming, plus protecting the originals against wear and tear. The NAS can playback the stored media onto a variety of devices including smart TVs, computers, gaming consoles, tablets, smartphones and streaming devices. It may be necessary to experiment to determine the video format that gives best results, but some people report that MP4 format videos created by tools such as *Handbrake* and *DVDFab* work well. Be aware that the copying of commercial DVDs is prohibited in some countries and local copyright and other legal restrictions should be observed.

Begin by placing your ripped videos into the shared folder called *Multimedia* – you may wish to create a sub-folder within it called *video* to make it easier to organize things as suggested in section **9.1 Overview**. Having done so, go into the *Content Management* section of **Multimedia Console** and specify the *Content Sources* for Video Station, as described in section **9.2 Multimedia Console**.

The first time Video Station is run it will run a Quick Start guide, which provides a brief introduction to the app. The main screen is then displayed:

Figure 177: Main Video Station screen

The list of titles can be viewed and sorted in several ways. You can specify additional information or change the artwork for a title by highlighting it and clicking the small Information button in the lower right-hand corner.

To play a video, click the small play button icon against the video. Or, right-click a video and choose **Open with Browser**; this will play it full screen in a new browser tab.

QNAP also have an app called *Qmedia* for video playback on Apple TV, Amazon Fire Stick and selected Android-based TVs and set-top boxes.

Access to Video Station can be controlled on an individual user basis. There are several ways of doing so, but the most flexible method is from within Video Station itself, as this allows granularity e.g. controlled access on a user-by-user, feature-by-feature basis. Click the three-dot snowman menu icon at the top of the screen and choose **Settings > Privilege**. Tick the boxes against each user to define what is available. When finished, click **Save**.

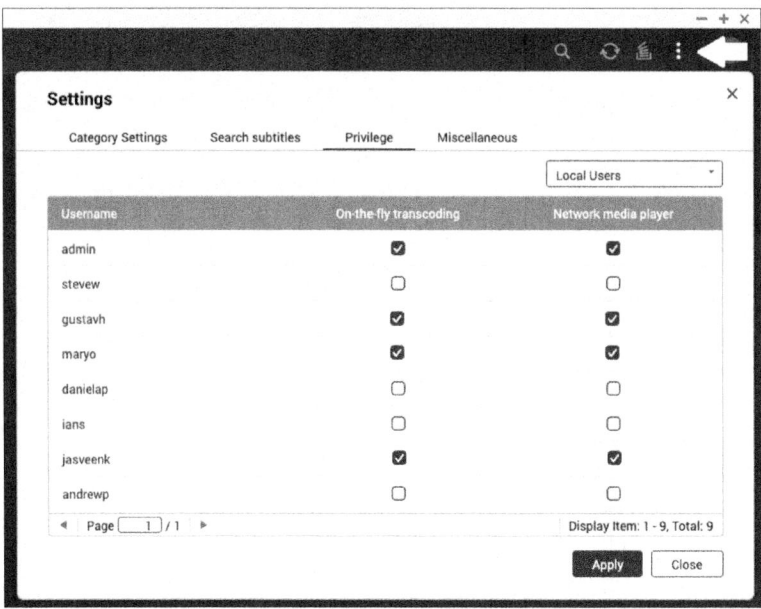

Figure 178: Privilege settings within Video Station

Qvideo

Qvideo is an app for watching videos on smartphones and tablets. It is available as a free download for iOS and Android from the respective app stores. When running Qvideo for the first time, it is necessary to specify the details of the server. If you are connected locally you can let the app find your server on the network, else manually specify the name or address; if you are using Qvideo remotely you can enter the myQNAPcloud address. Videos can also be downloaded to the portable device so they can be played back when there is no network connection, for example whilst travelling.

9.8 CAYIN MediaSign Player

CAYIN MediaSign Player is a web-based app for playback of videos from a QNAP NAS and as such can be considered an alternative to the more widely used Video Station discussed previously. Although a third-party product, it is promoted by QNAP and may possibly be a longer-term replacement for Video Station.

CAYIN MediaSign Player is downloaded and installed from the App Center. However, before it can be used it is necessary to activate a license for it and a message about it this is displayed when running it for the first time. Click the link to the Software Store and choose a license; there is a choice of a 'Basic' edition, which is free, or a 'Plus' version with additional features and which has to be paid for. We will assume the Basic version. To use the Software Store, it is necessary to have a QNAP ID. For more general information about licenses, see section **15.4 License Center**.

Having obtained and activated a license, go into CAYIN MediaSign Player. It may have detected the shared Multimedia folder we created earlier but to check/confirm/change this, click the three-dot snowman menu in the top-left hand corner of the screen and click **Manage Folders**. On the resultant panel make sure that the *Multimedia/video* folder is selected and click **Apply**.

Figure 179: Manage folders in CAYIN MediaSign Player

Returning to the main screen, expand the *Multimedia* folder in the left-hand panel and click the *video* sub-folder.

A list of videos will be displayed (if they are not listed click the **Refresh** icon):

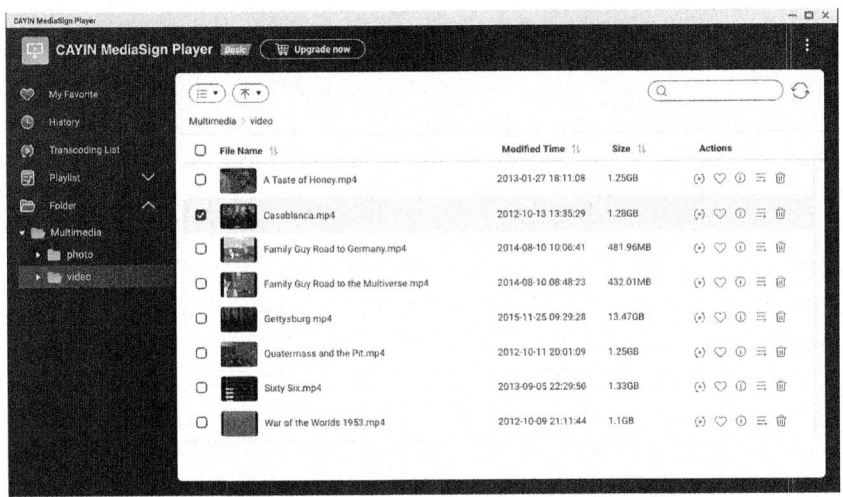

Figure 180: List of videos in CAYIN MediaSign Player

To play a video, highlight it and click the **Play** icon. The video will play in a re-sizeable window. Hovering the cursor will cause a selection of controls to be displayed; from here you can pause/play, rewind 10 seconds, fast forward 10 seconds, change the playback speed and adjust the volume. To change the resolution, click the settings cogwheel. Clicking the icon to the left of the cogwheel will cause the video to play full screen. One thing which may not be obvious is that multiple videos can be clicked whilst selecting them for playback, which will build-up a playlist:

Figure 181: Video playback and controls

9.9 Cinema28

Cinema28 is a media playback/management app that can send music and video files to a wide range of devices, controlled from a single location. It is useful in a household with multiple smart televisions and streaming devices; for instance, you might choose to send different music playlists to different rooms to help establish a certain mood. Another use would be to send a list of videos to a home theater system.

It can be downloaded from the App Center. It requires the Media Streaming add-on, so this must also be installed if not already in place. Upon running it for the first time, a quick overview is given, then the main screen is displayed:

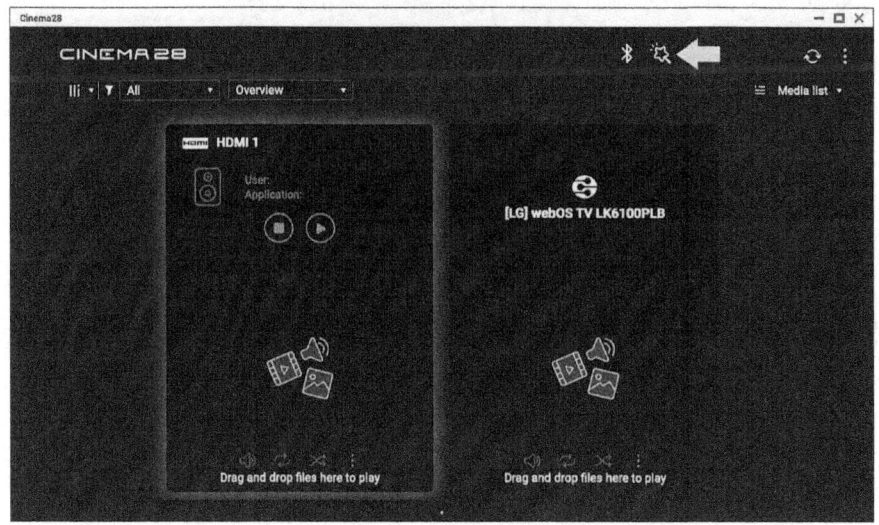

Figure 182: Cinema28

Eight different types of media device are supported: AirPlay (such as Apple TV); Chromecast; DLNA clients, such as smart TVs and streamers; USB (speaker or DAC); HDMI (on suitably equipped QNAP models); HD Player (requires HybridDesk Station and HD Player); Bluetooth (adapter needs to be added to NAS); Audio output or speaker on suitably equipped NAS. Cinema28 should automatically identify any suitable multimedia devices, otherwise click the Device Wizard (indicated in screenshot above) to add them.

In this example, we are running Cinema28 on a NAS with a HDMI port and with a DLNA-compatible smart TV connected to the network.

To playback media, click the **Media list** dropdown and choose the source, which we will assume to be the server. Navigate to where the media are stored, highlight the file(s) and drag onto the chosen playback device: a few seconds later, the files will begin playback. Photos, music and videos can all be streamed.

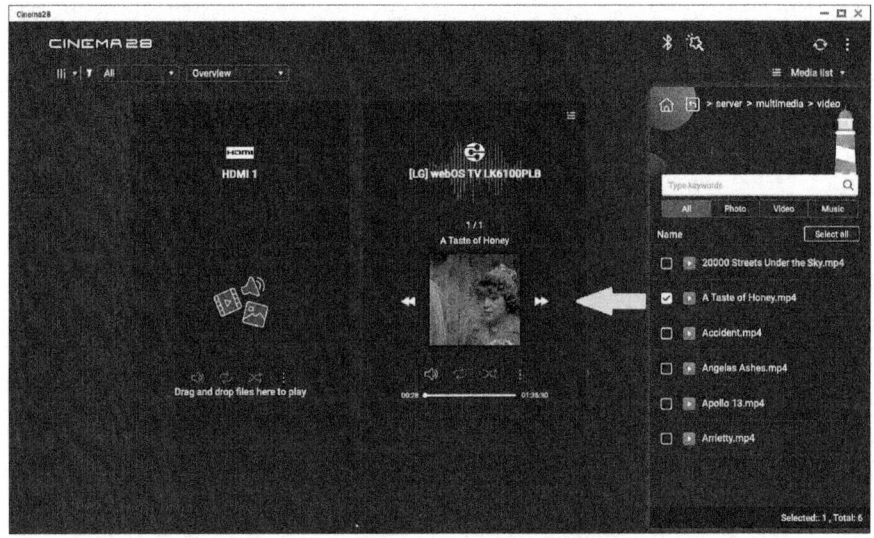

Figure 183: Choosing a file and device

9.10 HybridDesk Station

Whilst all QNAP models provide multimedia features, some are optimized for this purpose and have HDMI output, enabling them to be connected directly to a HDMI-equipped television or screen. The NAS can then be used as though it was a regular PC in conjunction with a keyboard and mouse, or as a home theater system in conjunction with a remote-control handset. All of this is managed using the *HybridDesk Station* feature and if you have a HDMI model it will have been installed automatically as part of QTS. When it is used, the output from QTS is displayed, suitably formatted, on the external screen and the usual browser display is disabled. There are special HybridDesk Station apps available, such as the Chrome and Firefox browsers, Spotify, LibreOffice, Facebook, YouTube and many others.

Whilst logged-in to QTS from a browser on a computer, launch **HDMI Display Applications**, which is located in the *Applications* section of **Control Panel** and click the **Get Started Now** button. Acknowledge the warning message and on the next panel, choose the apps you want to load and click **Apply**. Note that some of the apps are required for correct operation of HybridDesk Station and cannot be deselected.

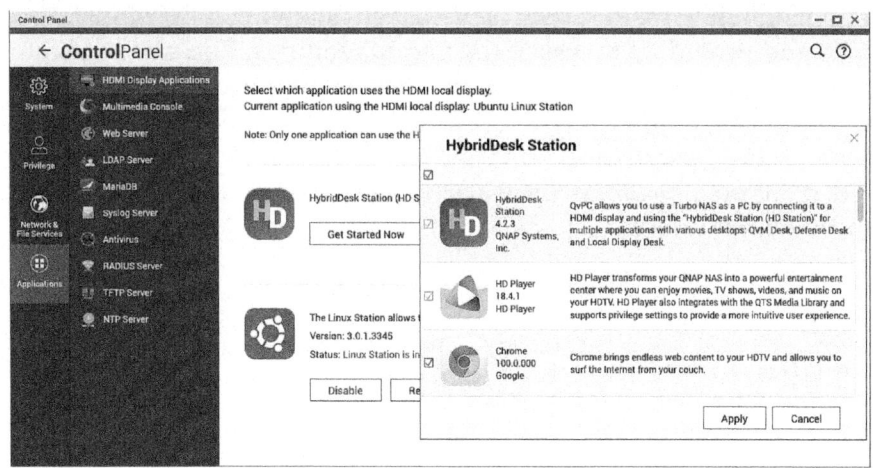

Figure 184: Setting up HybridDesk Station

Depending on the number and type of applications selected, installation may take some time. When complete, close down the App Center if it is open and restart HybridDesk Station, which can be done by click the **Restart** button. Or, on models with a One Touch Copy button, hold it down for six seconds. Wait a minute or so, then switch to the HDMI screen. Using the mouse or remote control, click the large admin user icon and login:

Figure 185: Login to the NAS

Upon login, the main screen is displayed, showing a list of installed apps and providing access to the various settings. You can switch to 'regular' QTS from here, as well as launch Chrome or Firefox for full access to the internet. Many of the applications are for multimedia, both native QNAP ones such as PhotoStation, MusicStation and VideoStation, as well as third party ones such as Spotify, YouTube and TuneInRadio.

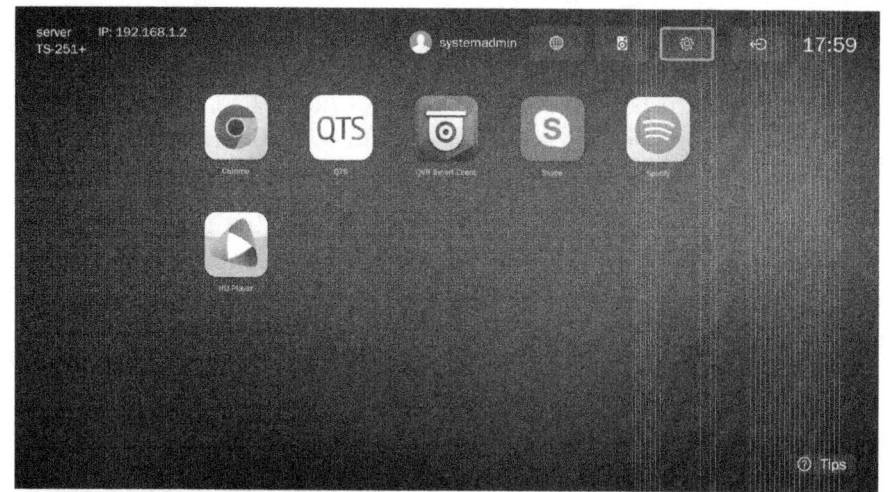

Figure 186: The Desktop, as viewed on a television screen

At the top of the Desktop is a Settings icon (it looks like a small cogwheel). Many aspects of HybridDesk Station can be customized from here, plus further apps can be installed.

9.11 Media Upload from Qfinder Pro

Media files can be uploaded from Qfinder Pro, provided the Multimedia Console described in section **9.2 Multimedia Console** has already been installed.

On a computer, highlight the server in Qfinder Pro, click the **Media Upload** icon and login to the server. Click the **Upload Files** icon, then check that the *Destination* (folder) is set correctly. Click the **Add Folder** icon and navigate to where the media files (photos, videos or music) are stored on your computer. Click the large **Start Upload** button.

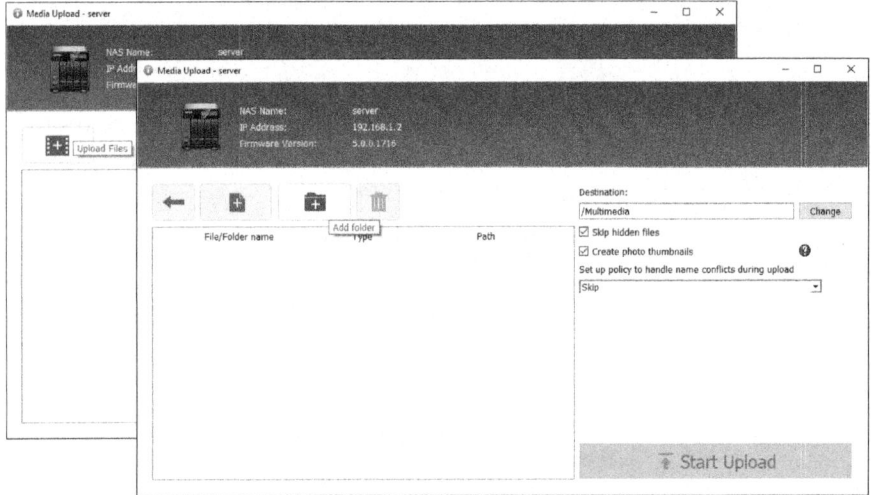

Figure 187: Media Upload feature in Qfinder Pro

9.12 Other Multimedia Apps

QNAP provide a wide range of multimedia applications and additional ones are available from third parties. These apps may provide additional and improved capabilities, interface to a wider variety of devices for playback, or may just be more familiar or preferable to some people. Some of these are cross-platform systems which, although they run on QNAP, were not specifically designed with it in mind and may not be as user-friendly as native QTS apps.

A good example of this is the highly popular *Plex Media Server*; in fact, may people specifically invest in a NAS system just in order to run this widely regarded piece of software. Some of its features include:

- Ability to consolidate all your media – videos, music, photos – in one place
- Support for virtually all media types and file formats
- Access to your media from any location worldwide
- Mobile Sync, enabling media to be viewed offline on tablets and smartphones
- Share media with friends and family
- Parental controls
- Customizable playlists
- Access to live TV, with recording (DVR) capabilities

An official Plex Media Server can be downloaded and installed from the App Center. In order to use Plex Media Server, it is necessary to have an account with Plex. Also, some features require a paid subscription.

Most QNAP models can run the Plex Media Server. However, entry level and less powerful models may not support hardware transcoding, which enables Plex to reformat videos into formats and resolutions which are better suited to playing on portable devices.

Plex clients, for connecting devices to the Plex Media Server, are available for Windows, Internet Browsers, Android, iOS, Apple TV, Roku, Amazon Fire TV, Chromecast, Xbox, PlayStation, Nvidia Shield and selected Smart TVs.

10
PRODUCTIVITY & PERSONAL APPS

10.1 Overview

QNAP have a range of productivity applications, designed for both personal and team use. All are downloadable from the App Center and are free of charge. The ones discussed in this chapter are:

Qsirch – a search engine for the NAS (think 'personal local version of Google')

QContactz – for managing contacts for a team or organization

QcalAgent – connects the NAS to popular online calendar services

Notes Station– for creating and managing personal notes (similar to Evernote or Microsoft OneNote)

Download Station – used for downloading files from BitTorrent and other services

Text Editor – basic text editing/word processing app for creating simple documents and editing code

Web Server – allows the NAS to host internal and external websites

10.2 Qsirch

A NAS system may contain thousands or even millions of files. Consequently, locating a particular file can sometimes be time-consuming and difficult. To address this problem, QNAP have developed a powerful search engine in the form of *Qsirch*. In simple terms, this can be thought of as analogous to Google, but a local version for use with the data stored on your NAS.

Qsirch is downloaded and installed from the App Center; doing so may result in other supporting and related components being installed. Launch it by clicking on the icon on the Desktop or from the Main Menu. Upon first run, there is a privacy statement asking if you wish to join the user experience program and share information with Google Analytics. Qsirch will work regardless of the decision, so make a choice and click **OK**. There follows a panel to enable OCR Setup, for Qsirch to search for images containing specific text. This is optional and QNAP advise that it should only be enable on devices with at least 4GB RAM. A short tour is then given, which you can work through or skip, before the main screen is displayed.

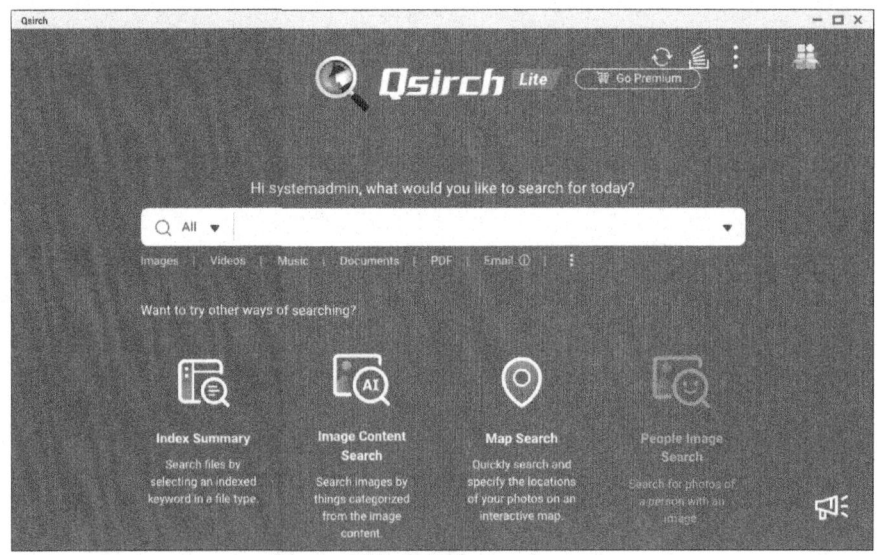

Figure 188: Qsirch search screen

Qsirch installs as *Qsirch Lite*, which is usually sufficient for many home users and small organizations. It can optionally be upgraded at cost, for a more comprehensive version called *Qsirch Premium*.

To search for an item, type in its name or part of its name. If desired, searches can be limited to a particular file type such as images, videos, music, documents, PDFs, emails and specific Microsoft Office formats. If the downward-pointing chevron on the search box is clicked, it switches to an Advanced Search mode that allows the terms to be fine-tuned e.g. exact words only, file size, date range and so on:

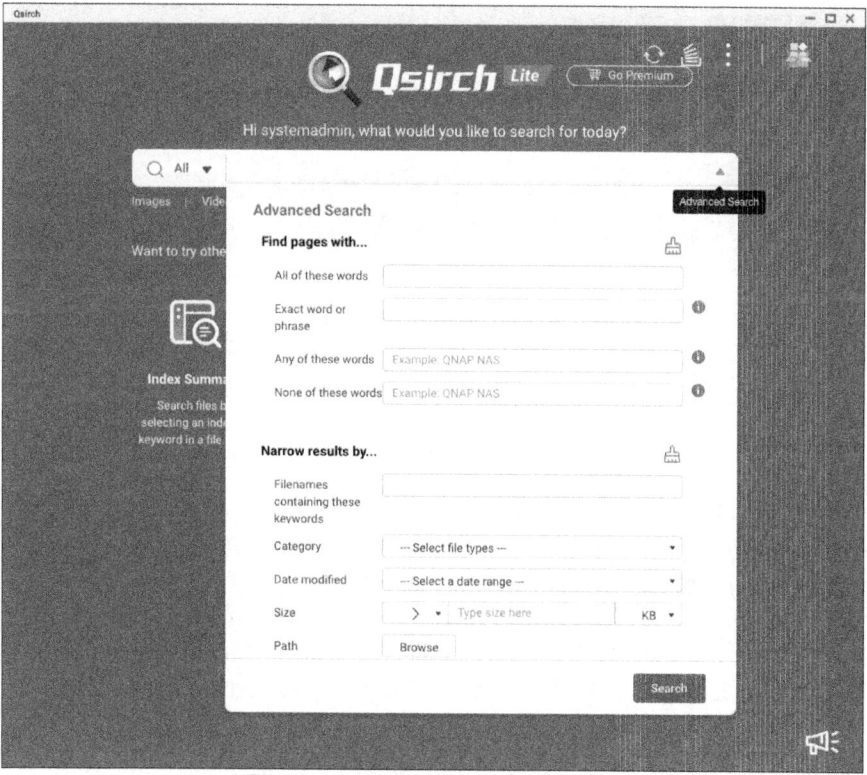

Figure 189: Advanced search screen

More detailed searches can be performed. If photographs have been geo-tagged with GPS co-ordinates, which most smartphone cameras do, then a *Map Search* can be performed to find photos taken at a specific location. Or, tags and other parameters can be specified; for instance, in this example we are searching for photos taken in 2022. Additional filters of Date Modified and Size can also be specified, with even more filters are available in the premium edition:

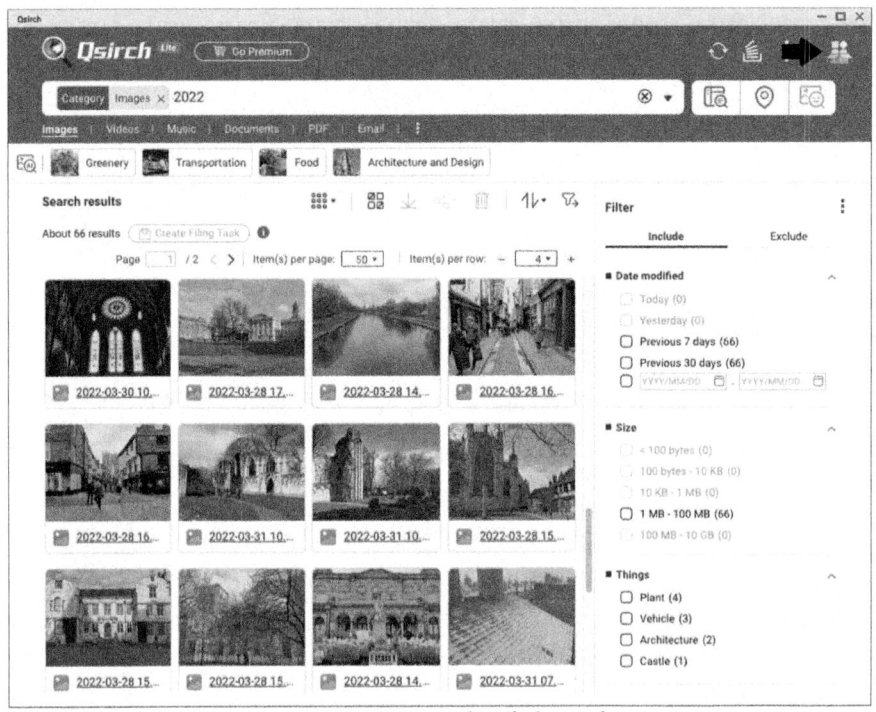

Figure 190: More detailed search

Additional Qsirch Solutions

QNAP offer several apps/utilities which can be used in conjunction with Qsirch. They can be downloaded by clicking on the icon in the top right-hand corner of the Qsirch screen (indicated by an arrow in the above screenshot): Qsirch PC Edition; Qsirch Mobile Apps for iOS and Android; Qsirch Helpers, for Chrome and Firefox browsers.

10.3 QContactz

QContactz enables the centralized management of contact information, for use by individuals as well as organizations. It is downloaded and installed from the App Center and requires Container Station, which will be installed as well if not already in place.

Launching QContactz will open it in a new browser window. The first time it is run, a quick overview is given. The application initially appears as follows; once contacts are added, they are listed on this screen in a tabular format.

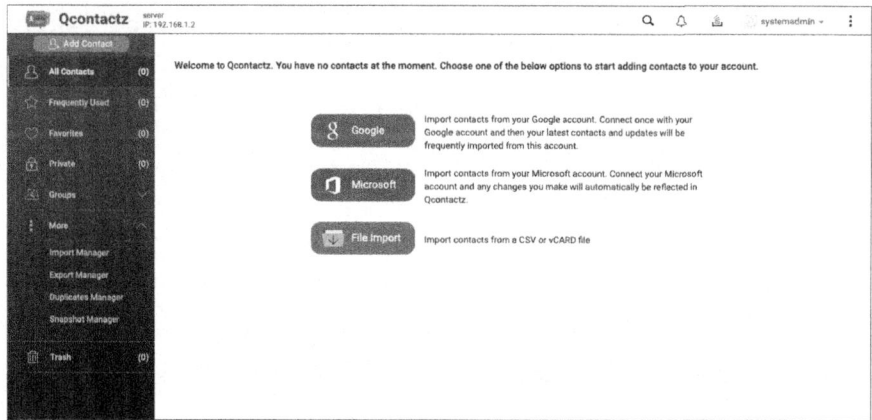

Figure 191: QContactz initial screen

Existing contacts can be imported into QContactz and there are options to do so from Google and Microsoft accounts, or from CSV or vCard 3.0 files (many contact applications use or can export vCards). If Google or Microsoft are chosen, it is necessary to login to the appropriate account and grant permissions for QContactz to access the data. These links to Google and Microsoft are 'live', so any new contacts to them will be imported to QContactz; to manage this and change the import schedule, click **More > Import Manager > Manage Accounts**.

To manually add a new contact, click the large blue **Add Contact** button from the main screen, which will display the following form. The form contains all the expected fields (name, email, phone number and so on), plus additional ones can be added.

A photograph of the contact can optionally be uploaded; this should be in JPG format and no more than a few 100 KB in size. When the form is complete, click **Save** to add the new contact.

Figure 192: Add New Contact form

The list of contacts can be sorted by first name or last name, plus columns can be added or removed. When contacts are selected, a series of icons become available at the top of the screen, enabling them to be deleted, added to favorites, exported or added to a group:

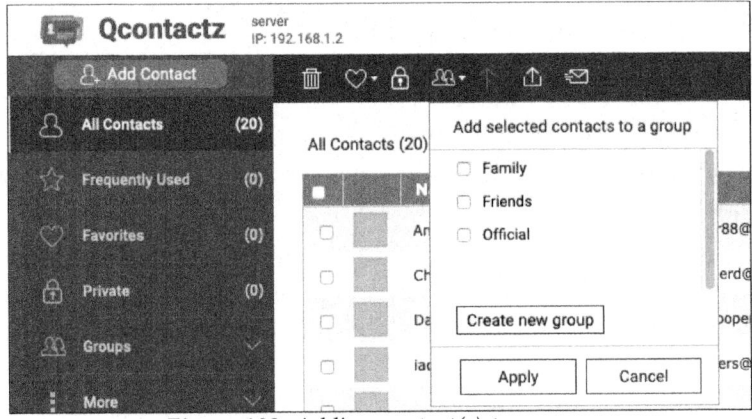

Figure 193: Adding contact(s) to a group

Qcontactz enables individual entries to be made private. To do this, first click **Private** and set a password on the resultant form. Then, highlight a contact and click the padlock icon on the list of icons at the top of the screen.

Contacts can be exported in CSV format for uploading into another copy of QContactz or into Google. They can also be exported into vCard format; many applications, including desktop Outlook and Contacts (macOS) will open vCards and will then sync them to any linked devices.

10.4 QcalAgent

QcalAgent enables you to access an online calendar from the NAS, plus help synchronize it across multiple devices. Because it supports Snapshots, it is also possible to roll-back in time and view the calendar as it was on an earlier occasion.

Download and install QcalAgent from the App Center. It is implemented as a container, so Container Station will need to be installed if it is not already in place.

When launched, it will open in a new browser tab. To add a calendar, click the **Add Calendar** button and choose from Google, Outlook or Yahoo; you will be taken to the corresponding website, where it is necessary to login to the appropriate account and grant permissions for QcalAgent to access the data. Having done so, the data will be synced and after a short while the calendar will be displayed on the NAS. You are not restricted to a single calendar and could, if required, have several.

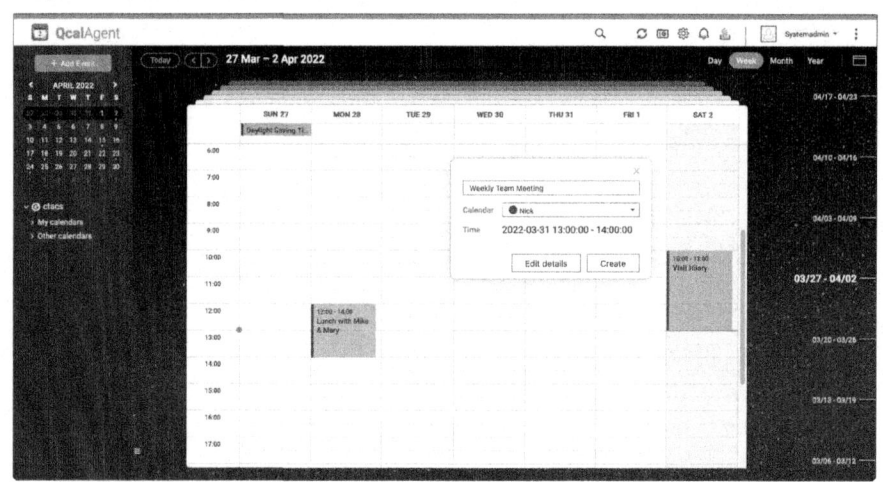

Figure 194: Calendar as viewed from NAS

The calendar can be viewed in several different ways: by day, week, month and year. Navigation is facilitated by a clickable timeline down the right-hand side of the screen (if you have used Apple's Time Machine, the interface will seem similar).

To make a new entry, click on the calendar at the appropriate day and time, then click **Create**. Or, for a more comprehensive entry that requires additional details, click the **Add Event** in the top left-hand corner of the screen.

At the top-right hand side of the screen are multiple icons. These include *Search*, *Refresh* (click if events are not synchronizing across devices), *Snapshot* and *Settings*. You can also logout from QcalAgent here.

If QcalAgent is opened but not used for a length of time, you will be logged out as a security measure. It is possible to login in again from the screen, rather than having to relaunch the app from QTS.

10.5 Notes Station

Similar to applications such as Evernote and Microsoft OneNote, *Notes Station* is a sophisticated personal information management app or PIM running on the NAS that allows notes to be created, viewed, managed and shared. Notes can be content-rich, with fonts, formatting, attachments and embedded media.

Begin by downloading and installing Notes Station 3 from the App Center. It may download and install other components, so installation might take a short while, after which an icon appears in the Main Menu and on the desktop. Upon launching Note Station, it will open in its own browser window. First time around, it will offer to show a quick guide, which you might want to read to gain familiarity. Thereafter the main screen is along the following lines:

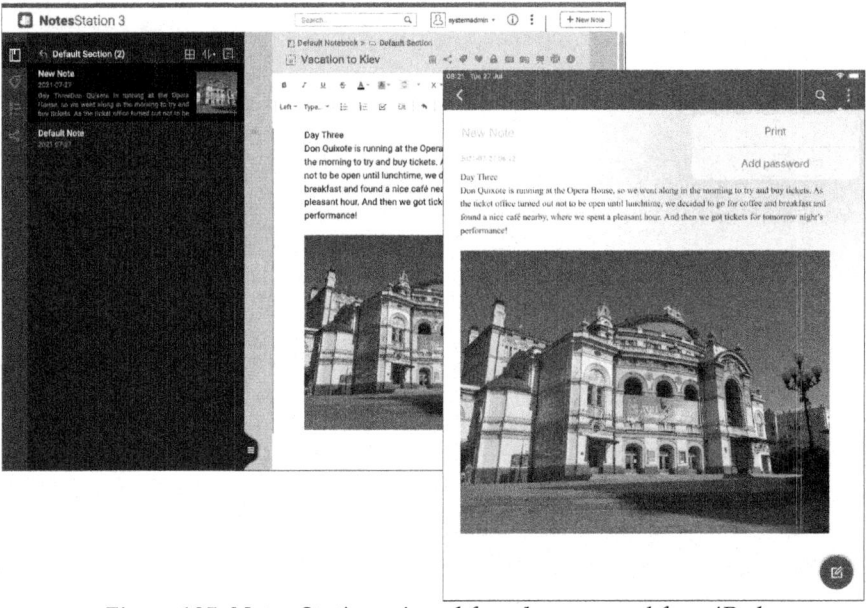

Figure 195: Notes Station, viewed from browser and from iPad

There is also an app for portable devices which enables Notes to be used on iOS and Android smartphones and tablets, in the form of *Qnotes3*, which is a free download from the respective app stores. When run, it gives the option of local operation or connecting to and syncing with Notes Station on the server and most people will choose the latter. Besides the standard features for adding and editing notes, it is possible to use photos and sound recordings in notes.

10.6 Download Station

Download Station is one of the most popular applications for QNAP NAS and allows you to download files from Internet-based services such as BitTorrent, FTP, HTTP, plus subscribe to RSS feeds. Many thousands of free and public domain movies and other items are available.

Begin by downloading and installing Download Station from the App Center. Its icon will be placed in the Main Menu; upon running it for the first-time term you must agree to the terms and conditions (basically that you will not use it with illegal or copyrighted content). The main screen appears as follows:

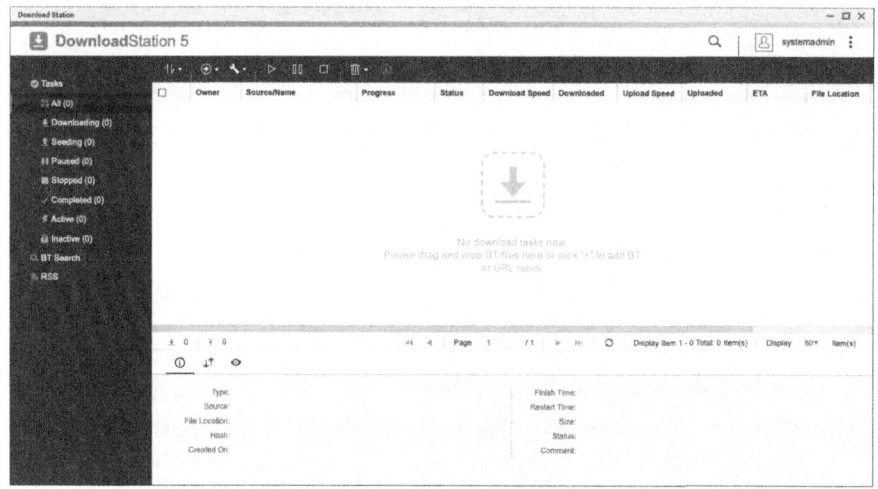

Figure 196: Download Station

If you are familiar with BitTorrent, you will find that Download Station is an effective client with all the features that you might expect. If you are new to the topic, it has already been programmed with defaults and features to make it immediately useful and not require any additional knowledge.

To search for content, click **BT Search** on the left-hand of the screen, then click the magnifying glass in the top-right corner. The first time this is done, you will be taken to the global search settings – read the message and if you agree tick the two boxes and click **Apply** and **Close**. Thereafter, clicking the magnifying glass will display the 'BT Search' box.

Type in the topic of interest and Download Station will search using several pre-defined search engines and return a list of suitable titles; depending on the search criteria, this may return none, several or many candidates. In this example we are searching on 'NASA':

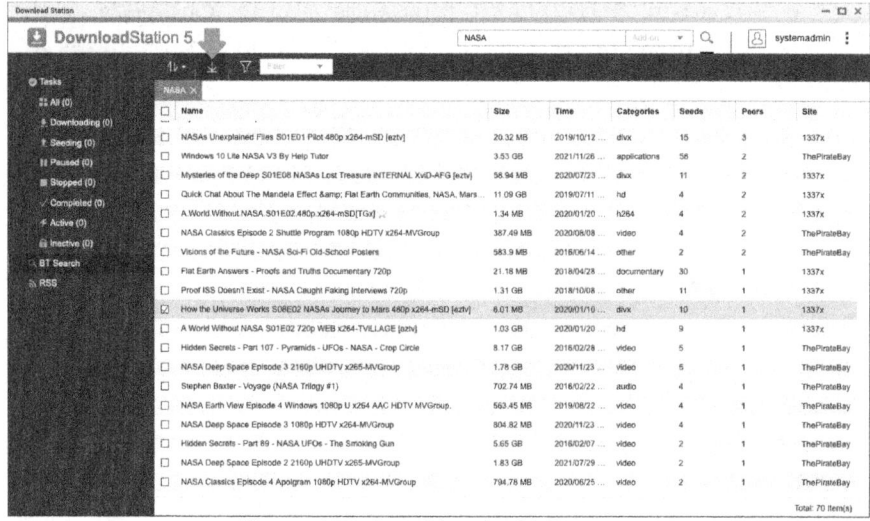

Figure 197: Searching for BitTorrents

Tick the desired file(s) and click the download icon at the top of the screen. On the first panel that appears, click **Next**. On the second, specify a location for the temporary files that are generated, plus a location as to where the completed downloads will be placed, and click **Apply**. In this instance we have specified *Public* and *Multimedia* respectively, but an alternative could be to create dedicated shared folders for use with Download Station.

The status of the downloads can be monitored by clicking the options on the left-hand of the main screen, such as Downloading, Active, Completed and so on.

The parameters involved with downloading can be controlled by clicking the three-dot menu in the top-right hand corner of the main screen and choosing **Settings**. Some of the items that can be controlled include:

Global – specify a download schedule and setup notifications

HTTP and **FTP** – specify the maximum number of concurrent downloads and the bandwidth limit

BT – connection settings (ports) and bandwidth limits for uploading and downloading

RSS – adjust update checks

Add-on – manage search engines (already pre-populated with several popular ones for BitTorrent

Download Manager can also be accessed using the Qmanager app on iOS and Android devices.

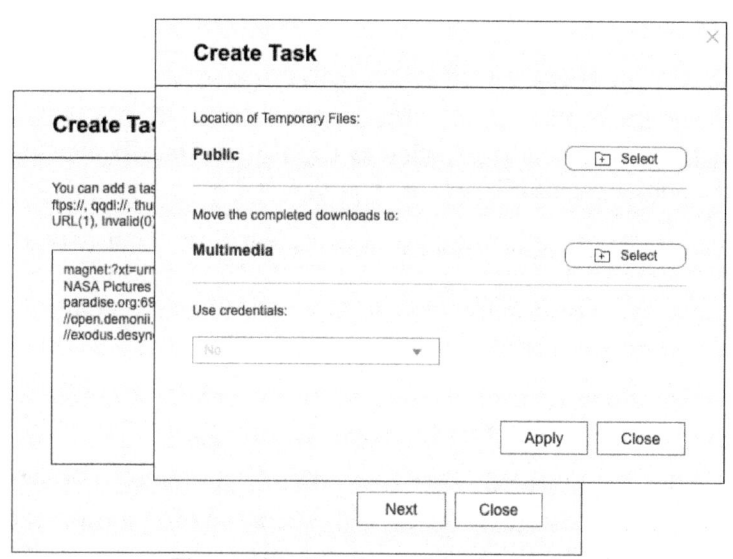

Figure 198: Creating a download task

10.7 Text Editor

Text Editor is a basic text-editing/word processing application, analogous to *WordPad* in Windows or *TextEdit* on the Mac. It can be used for creating simple documents or editing code, and can operate in a variety of different languages. The benefit is that documents and file can be edited directly on the NAS, rather than have to work on a separate computer and then upload or download files.

Text Editor is downloaded from the App Center. Upon installation, an icon is placed on the desktop, from where it can be run as a standalone application. It also integrates itself with File Station and when a suitable file is right-clicked the option to edit it using Text Editor becomes available.

The *View mode* can be changed to optimize for different usages, such as working with HTML, JavaScript, Ruby and many others. The workspace can optionally be split into multiple panels, split horizontally or vertically.

Files can be made read-only by clicking the small padlock icon that appears on the right-hand side above the first line.

Clicking the cogwheel in the top-right hand corner of the screen enables several settings to be altered, such as word wrap, font size, background color and display of line numbers.

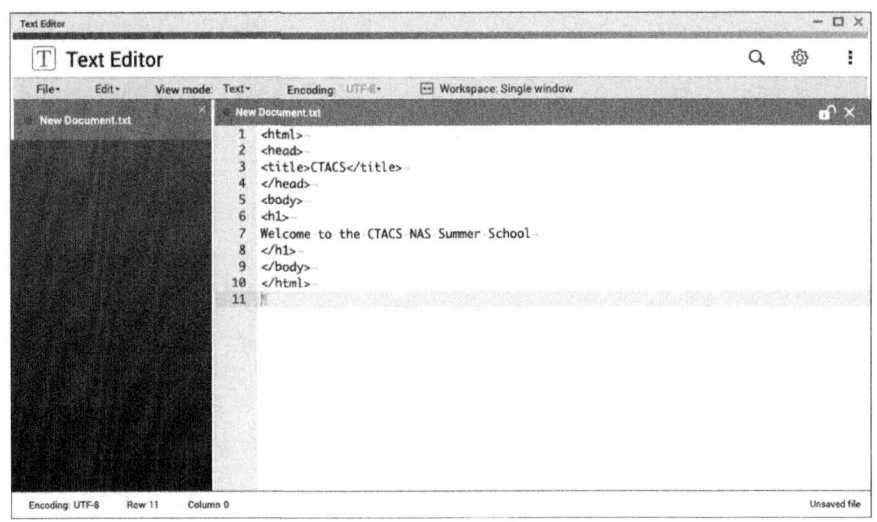

Figure 199: Text Editor

10.8 Web Server

QTS can host websites on the internet. Because of security and capacity implications and, given that dedicated web hosting services are readily available for free or low cost elsewhere, it may not be of interest to everyone. However, it may appeal to organizations that develop websites and wish to work on them in-house i.e. not accessible from outside the organization, as well as individuals wanting to learn about website and applications development. In this introduction, we will consider this to be the requirement.

The QTS interface is browser-based, meaning that it is already using a web server. To enable the facility for wider usage, go to **Control Panel > Web Server** and tick the **Enable Web Server** box, followed by **Apply** (depending on what apps have been installed, you may find that it is already enabled).

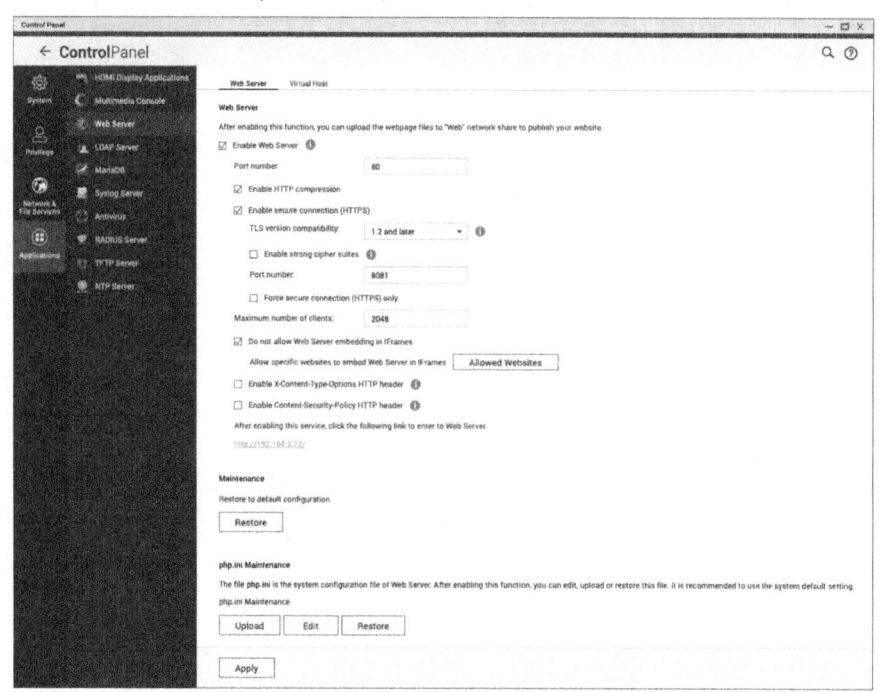

Figure 200: Enabling Web Server

The HTML, PHP and other files for the website should now be placed in the shared *Web* folder, which is created automatically when Web Server is enabled.

To confirm that Web Station is running correctly, use a browser to navigate to the IP address of the server. Rather than seeing the regular QTS screen, you should now be presented with your own website. Usually, QTS redirects the IP address to port 8080, but now it is displaying via the standard HTTP port 80. To view the standard QTS screen, explicitly type the address of the server followed by *:8080*, for example 192.168.1.2:8080. Alternatively, you can also setup a HTTPS page on port 8081.

In the event of difficulties, the original configuration can be restored by clicking the **Restore** button in the *Maintenance* section.

11

REMOTE ACCESS & CLOUD

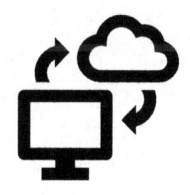

11.1 Overview

Being able to access data remotely is an important requirement for many people and there are multiple ways of doing so with a QNAP NAS. Firstly, the NAS can be accessed using nothing more than a browser from any internet-connected device. Secondly, there is *Qsync*, which is like a private version of *Dropbox*. Thirdly, there is *HybridMount*, which integrates the NAS with popular cloud-based file sharing services such as *Google Drive*, *OneDrive*, *Dropbox* and others. Finally, it is possible to setup a *Virtual Private Network* (VPN), which may be of particular interest to business users. Computers and portable devices such as tablets and smartphones can be used with these connection methods.

To access the NAS remotely, it first needs to be connected securely to the internet and configured in such a manner that it can be 'seen' from outside the home or office. There are two ways of doing so, one of which is a simple and straightforward method that will suit most home and many small business users, plus there is a more advanced method for more demanding requirements and which requires a certain amount of technical knowledge.

11.2 myQNAPcloud

myQNAPcloud provides an easy, straightforward mechanism for remotely accessing the NAS and works as a relay service, passing data to and from computers and the NAS over the internet via QNAP. No data is stored at QNAP itself and it remains your data on your computers. Because the service uses standard web protocols it removes the need for techniques such as port forwarding, router configuration and domain services in most instances. This also means remote access is often available in many places where there may be no opportunity to make technical changes to the underlying environment, such as in schools, colleges, corporate workplaces and so on. *myQNAPcloud* is suitable for most home and small business users.

To access the NAS remotely you need a *myQNAPcloud* account. When you installed QTS, you may have set one up at that point, else you can do so subsequently by clicking on **myQNAPcloud** in the **Main Menu**. Click the green **Get Started** button that initially appears on the screen to run a wizard that takes you through the sign-up process. On the third panel, a decision has to be taken about the *Auto Router Configuration* option: if the box is ticked, the wizard will automatically configure port forwarding rules on the router. This is the easiest option if you are a non-technical person, but means the router is potentially less secure. If you are a technical person, you might want to leave it unticked and manually configure the router yourself. Either way, change the *Access Control* from Public to **Private** so as to make your NAS invisible to internet search engines. Click **Next**.

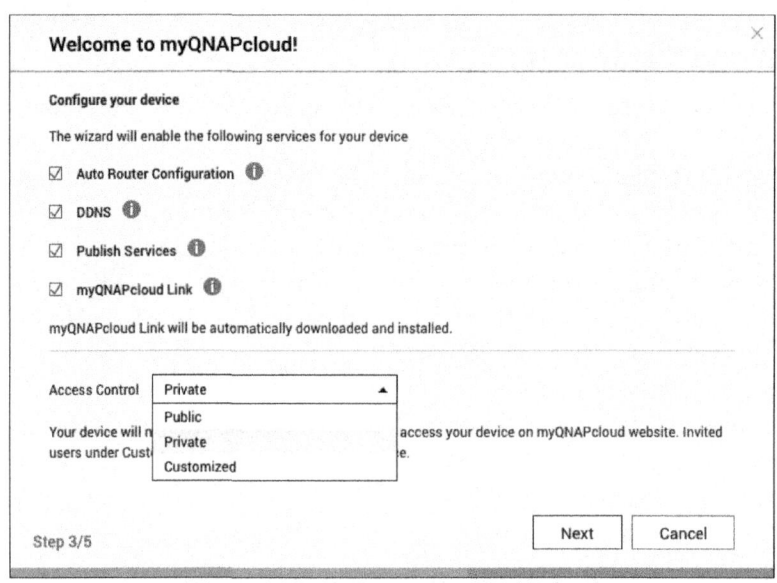

Figure 201: Setting up myQNAPcloud

You need to register a name for the NAS when signing up with myQNAPcloud. Most models have a sticker on them specifying the unique Cloud Key and this will be many people's choice for the device name. However, it can be changed to something more meaningful or memorable, with the proviso that all the obvious names have long since been taken. A confirmation email will be sent to the email address you specified and which may have to be acknowledged before things will work. The process of setting up myQNAPcloud downloads and installs the supporting app, makes a number of configuration changes to the server and configures your router. Upon completion of the wizard, the main screen will update along the following lines (some fields have been grayed out for reasons of confidentiality). Make a note of the Smart URL address, as this is used for accessing the server. It is in the format *https://qlink.to/device*, where *device* is the name you specified. For instance, *https//qlink.to/Q9999999*. You can also refer to it as *device.myqnapcloud.com* e.g. *Q9999999.myqnapcloud.com*.

Figure 202: Configuration for remote access complete

If the screen looks like this, then you are ready to go and can skip to section **11.3 Accessing with an Internet Browser**. You can ignore the SSL Certificate message for now. However, if the *Auto Router Configuration* section shows this error...

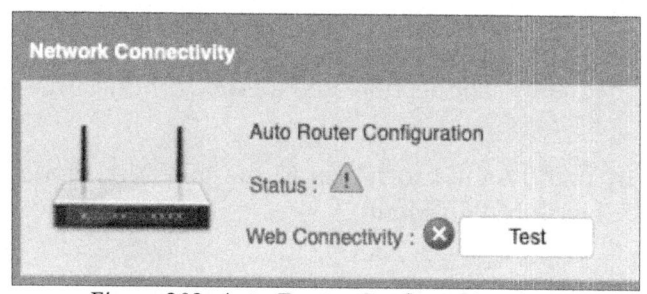

Figure 203: Auto Router Configuration error

...then you will probably need to act as the router has a cross against it, meaning that auto configuration failed. This issue is relatively common and usually relates to *UPnP port forwarding* problems on the router. Here's what to try:

Click **Auto Router Configuration**. On the resultant screen, check that the **Enable UPnP Port forwarding** box is ticked and that the green status message reads *'Found UPnP router on the network'*. You may have to wait 30 seconds or so.

Tick the boxes for the required services, which at a minimum is *NAS Web, Secure NAS Web* and *Secure Web Server*. Click **Apply to Router**. Wait a further 30 seconds, then return to the main **Overview** screen. Hopefully, you will now find that everything is now okay. Otherwise the router will have to be configured manually. How to do so is outside the scope of this guide as it depends upon the model of router and there are thousands of different ones, but instructions for configuring most routers can be found at the *www.portforward.com* website. From a technical perspective, the requirement is to forward external traffic on ports 8080, 80, 443 and 8081 to the internal IP address of the server. Note that despite having then configured the router manually and got it into a 100% working state, it may still be showing an error in the myQNAPcloud screen if it cannot read the UPnP information from the router, even though it may no longer actually be a problem and connectivity will work.

You may not be able to test remote connectivity from inside the home or office using your standard internet connection, as this requires a feature called *NAT Loopback* and not all routers support it. To ensure things are working correctly, testing should be done from outside the office or home, for example by using a wireless hotspot in a coffee shop; alternatively, use a separate internet connection, such as a mobile broadband connection or a smartphone that supports *tethering*.

If you subsequently need to return to the myQNAPcloud screen, it can be found in the Main Menu.

11.3 Accessing with an Internet Browser

In the same way that the server can be accessed through an internet browser when connected locally, so it can be used remotely. When setting up myQNAPcloud in the previous section you will have received a Smart URL address, for instance *Q9999999.myqnapcloud.com* in our example. Enter this address into a browser and after a few seconds you will be presented with the login screen. Any of the QNAP features that are available through the browser as described in section **5.2 Using a Browser and File Station** will be available e.g. File Station, Music Station and so on. As this method of access is browser based, it is available to Windows, Mac, Linux, iPad and other platforms.

11.4 Qsync

Most people will be familiar with public cloud-based services such as Google Drive, Microsoft OneDrive, Apple's iCloud and others. The basic concept is that somewhere on the internet is an amount of private space for your usage, which you can think of as like a USB memory stick or hard drive in the sky. Data stored on the cloud can be accessed in two ways: the first method is by logging in to the website and working within a browser; the second method is to have a folder on your computer or device corresponding to that space, along with client software or an app. Anything you put in that folder is automatically copied ('synced') to the space on the internet and vice versa, such that whenever anything changes on one side, the change is reflected automatically on the other.

Whilst useful and popular, these public cloud services have limitations. Firstly, although they usually give some free storage space, it may not be very much and if you need more you must pay for it. Whilst these services may be relatively affordable, a regular monthly payment over several years may eventually amount to more than the cost of a NAS. Secondly, most services have restrictions on file sizes and how much data you can store on them. Finally, some people are just not comfortable with their data being held by Microsoft, Google, Apple or some other company. *Qsync* gets around all of these issues as it is free to obtain and use, there are no practical restrictions on space and usage, plus data remains stored on your own server, meaning everything is under your control. Put simply, Qsync is a *private cloud* and is particularly suitable for people who travel away from home or the office where their NAS is located, but who need to access their data.

Qsync Central

Qsync is managed using *Qsync Central*, which is downloaded from the App Center. It can then be launched from the **Main Menu** or the **Desktop**; the first time it is used it will display a short tour, followed by the *Overview* screen. The Home Folder feature within QTS needs to be enabled for Qsync to work and to check this, see section **3.4 Enabling Home Folders**. If Qsync Central is not listed on the Main Menu, locate it on the App Center, click the downward-pointing chevron and click **Display on > Administrator's main menu**.

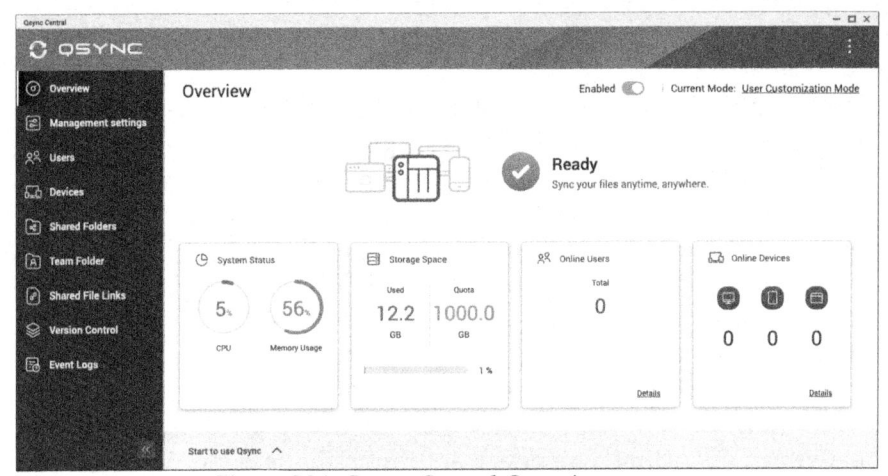

Figure 204: Qsync Central Overview screen

There are nine sections to the *Qsync Central Station* screen. Some are applicable to organizations and users with specific requirements and if you just require a simple alternative to, say, Dropbox or OneDrive for basic cloud storage, you may not even need to look at them.

Overview – provides a summary of the overall status, such as how much storage space is available and how many users are online. Towards the bottom of the screen is an expandable section labelled *Start to use Qsync*, which provides links for client apps for computers and mobile devices. At the top of the screen is a green button control, which needs to be in the **Enabled** position; if Qsync is disabled, it may vanish from the Main Menu and Desktop, in which case you will need to go into the App Center to re-enable it as described above.

Management settings – allows control over various settings, the key one being whether users can modify their own settings - *User Customization Mode* - or whether settings are always controlled centrally at the server by administrators. Known as *Central Configuration Mode*. In a business or educational setting, you might wish to use the latter to enforce standards and policies.

Users – comprises two tabs, *Online users* and *All users*. In order to use *Qsync*, users have to be given permission. To do so, click the **All users** tab. This displays a list of users; place a tick against those who should have access and remove the tick against those who should not (or use the **Action** button), plus slide the Grant switch to the right-hand position.

If required, new users can also be created from this screen, by clicking the **Create a User** link. To check the online status of users, click the **Online Users** tab.

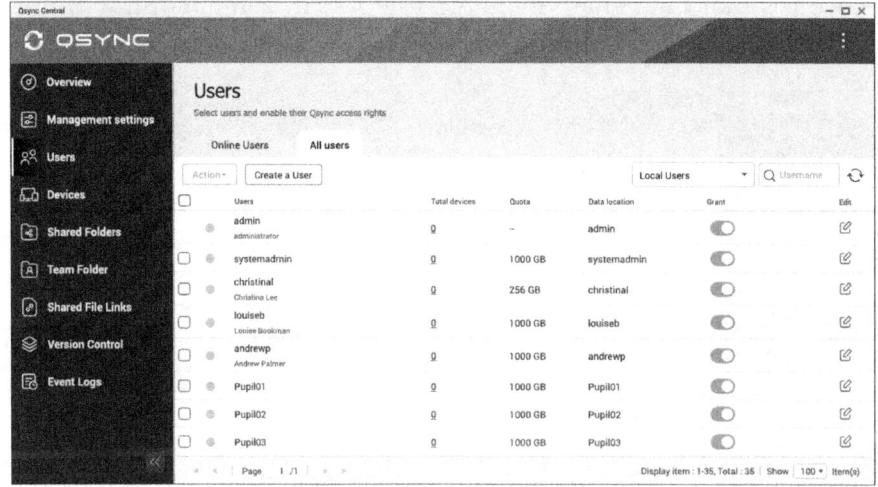

Figure 205: Users screen in Qsync Central

Devices – this tab is for monitoring the computers, tablets and smartphones that are or have been using the *Qsync* service. It can also be used for disconnecting specific devices should that be required, as well as remotely erasing a device should it ever be lost or stolen. This latter feature is an important advantage over some public cloud services.

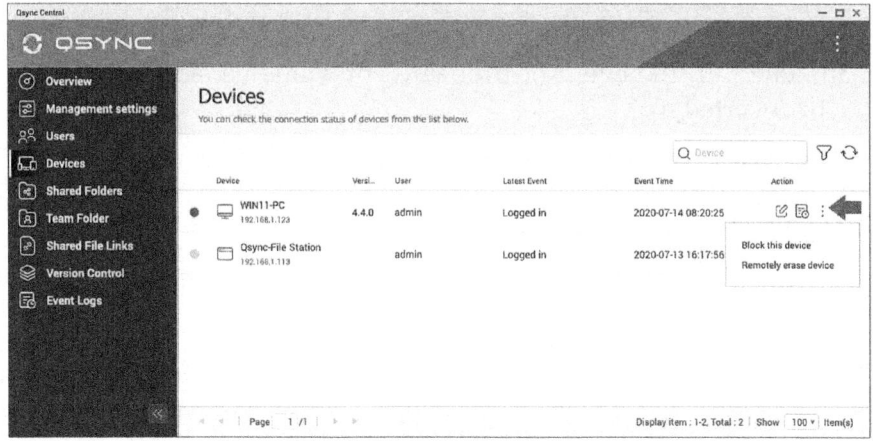

Figure 206: Online status of Qsync devices

Shared Folders – controls syncing of and access to the shared folders, such as Public and any additional ones which have been created on the server. Some thought should be given to which folders can be synced, rather than share them all. It works in conjunction with the Control Panel.

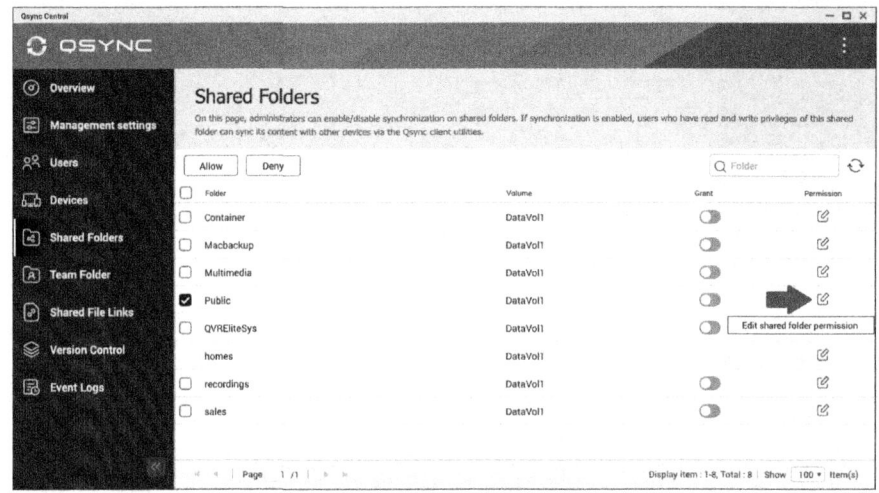

Figure 207: Control over Shared Folders

Team Folder – for creating and checking the status of sync folders that are shared between multiple users, referred to as *Team Folders*.

Shared File Links – for checking the status of files that have been shared via links.

Version Control – enables multiple versions of files can be maintained. In the event of problems, previous versions of the file can be reverted to.

Event Logs – events relating to *Qsync* (e.g. connections, disconnections) are recorded and the log files can be searched and viewed from this tab.

Installation of Qsync Client on Computers

The synchronization software – the *Qsync client* - needs to be installed on computers so they can connect to the server. It is available from the Download section of the QNAP website for Windows (8.1 and later), macOS (10.14 and later) and Linux Ubuntu (18.04/20.04). This walkthrough uses the Windows version, but all versions are largely identical in appearance and operation. If you receive a message from the computer's firewall at any stage about allowing access for *Qsync*, do so.

Upon running the *Qsync* client for the first time, a short tutorial is shown and upon completion the following panel is displayed:

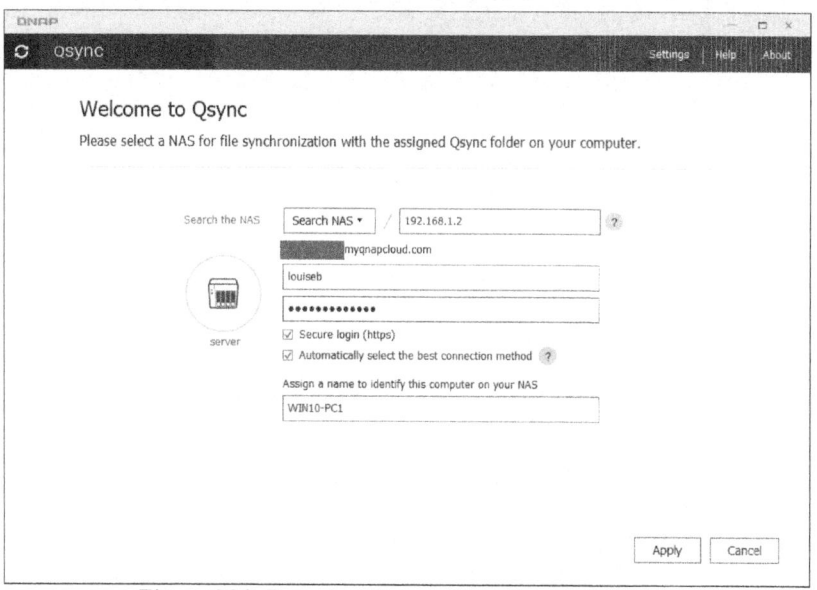

Figure 208: Running Qsync client for the first time

Click the **Search** button and the software will display a list of available NAS units (there may only be the one, of course). If the Qsync client does not 'see' the server, explicitly type in its name or IP address. If it still does not see it, it is possibly a firewall issue on the local computer. Alternatively, you can try entering the myQNAPcloud ID. Select the required NAS.

Enter the username and password. For improved security tick the **Secure login (https)** box. Unless you have some specific reason to do so, there is no need to change the name of the computer. Click **Apply**.

On the second panel you designate the *paired folders* to be synced. The basic principle here is to choose a shared folder on the NAS and one on the local computer that Qsync will then keep in sync, such that they mirror each other. For the NAS side the default is a folder called *.Qsync* in the user's home folder, whereas for the local computer it is a folder called *Qsync* in the user's main library e.g. *C:\Users\User\Qsync*. These defaults will be fine for many people so you may want to leave things as they are; however, if you wish to make changes this is done by clicking the mini icons on the right-hand side of the panel to remove or add pairings:

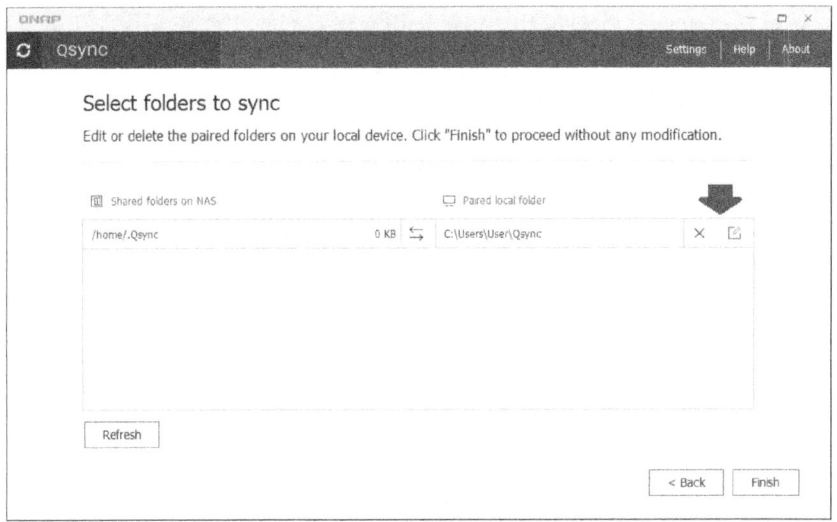

Figure 209: Select folder(s) to sync

Click **Finish** and syncing will begin. An icon for the *Qsync Client* is placed on the computer's Desktop; the screen will display a status screen along the following lines, plus provide various options that can be used to modify the behavior of the Qsync client and syncing process.

To sync files from the computer, just drag them into the Qsync folder (on Windows PCs this will have been added to the Favorites list in File Explorer/Windows Explorer) and synchronization will immediately take place. The folder can also be accessed by clicking the small folder icon within the Qsync Client, as indicated in the screenshot.

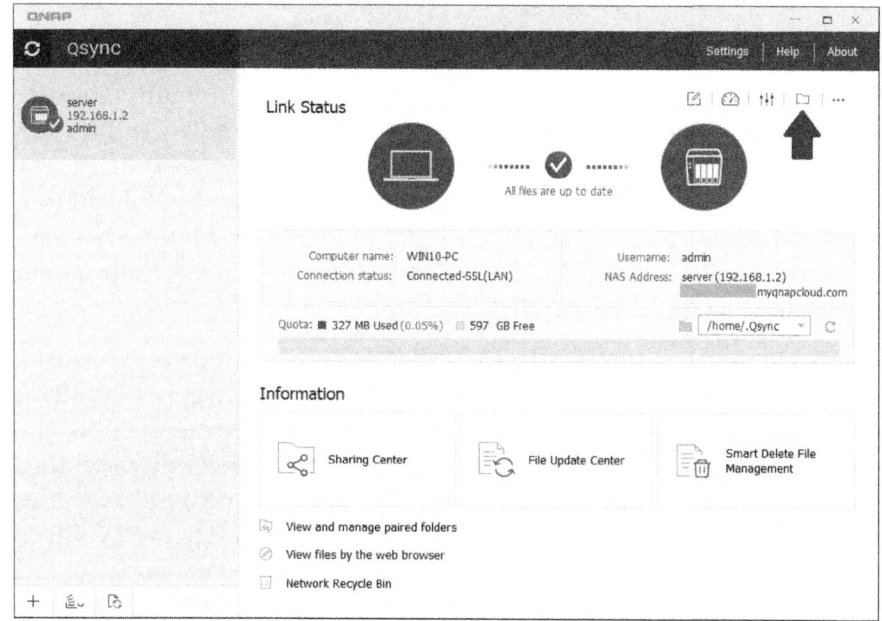

Figure 210: Qsync Link Status

11.5 HybridMount

HybridMount is a facility that integrates the NAS with many popular public cloud services, allowing you to work with folders and files in a transparent manner by blurring the distinction between them. For instance, you can access the cloud-based files from within File Station in the same way as ones installed locally on the NAS. There is no need to install additional utilities or synchronization software on the client computers, as the NAS handles everything.

HybridMount has two modes: *File Cloud Gateway* mode and *Network Drive Mount* mode. From a user perspective, they largely operate in the same way, with files accessed from File Station. Behind the scenes, the former mode caches (keeps copies) of recently used files on the server, which improves performance if the required files already happen to be in the cache, whereas the latter always goes directly to the cloud service each time. More than thirty cloud services are supported, including: *Amazon S3*; *Azure*; *GoogleDrive*; *Microsoft OneDrive* and *OneDrive Business*; *Rackspace*; *Yandex*.

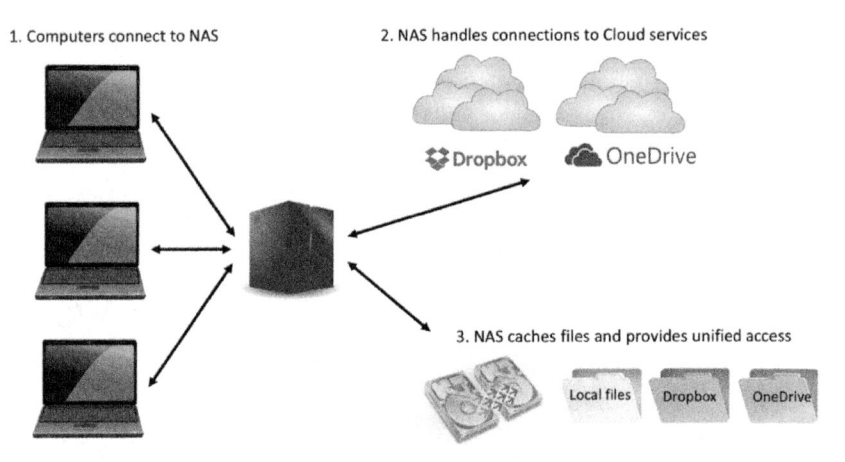

Figure 211: Overview of HybridMount

Download and install HybridMount from the App Center. Upon running for the first time it displays a Quick Start guide, which can be worked through or skipped as required. The *Overview* screen initially appears as follows:

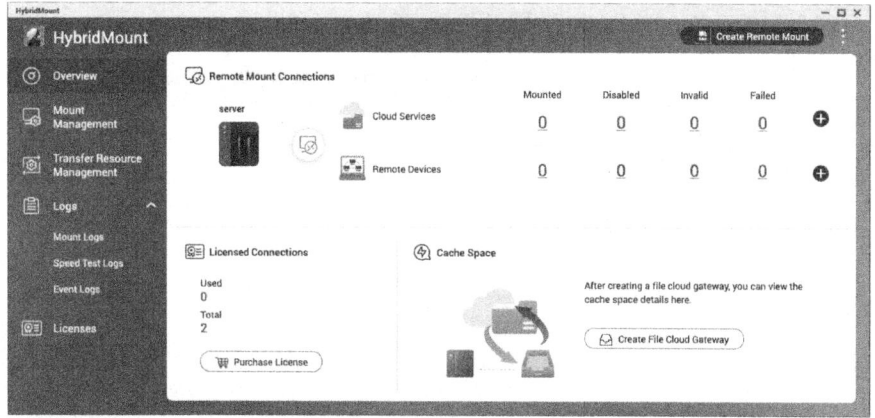

Figure 212: HybridMount Overview screen

There are five sections:

Overview - provides an 'at-a-glance' status screen, listing the current connections

Mount Management - shows the mounts (links) to the connected cloud services and the devices using them

Transfer Resource Management – enables control over the number of concurrent uploads/downloads in order to optimize performance

Logs - consisting of mount, speed test and event logs

Licenses – each connection to a cloud service requires a license. Two free ones are provided; additional ones can be purchased from QNAP as required

Begin by clicking the **Create Remote Mount** button. There are two options – *Create File Cloud Gateway* and *Create Network Drive Mount*. We are going to base our example on the latter so click **Create Network Drive Mount** and select the **Cloud Services** option on the subsequent screen. Choose your Cloud service using the dropdown. You will be taken to an authorization page generated by the provider of the cloud service, where you need to give your permission for the NAS to work with your account, the specifics of which will vary depending upon the provider. Upon selection, you will be returned to the wizard, where various parameters can be adjusted e.g. the *Connection name* can be changed. However, the defaults will be okay in most circumstances, so you only need to click **Create**:

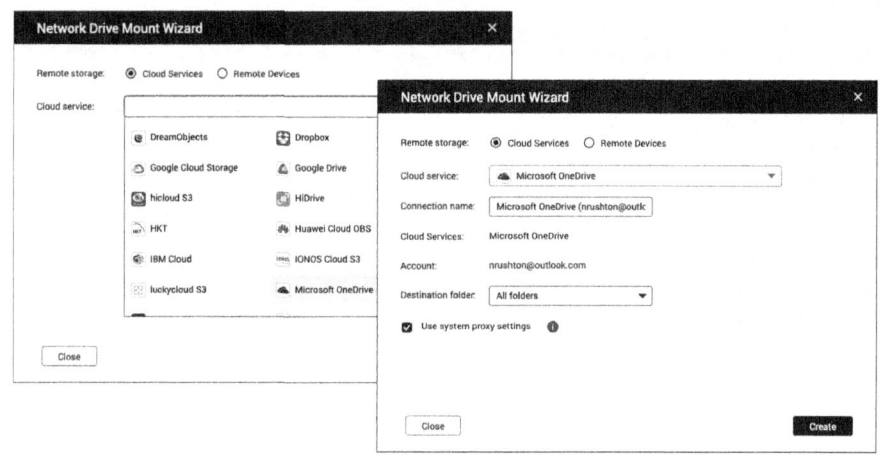

Figure 213: Network Drive Mount Wizard

A completion screen is shown; if you are finished, click **Close**. You are not restricted to a single cloud service and can create additional ones if you wish by clicking on the **Create More** button, with the proviso that additional licenses are required for more than two connections.

You can now use the **Mount Management** tab to manage the mounted cloud service(s). To temporarily disable a mount, slide its control to the left (off) position. To delete a mount, click the **More** button in the *Options* column and choose **Delete**. To test the speed of a connection, click **More > Speed Test** button:

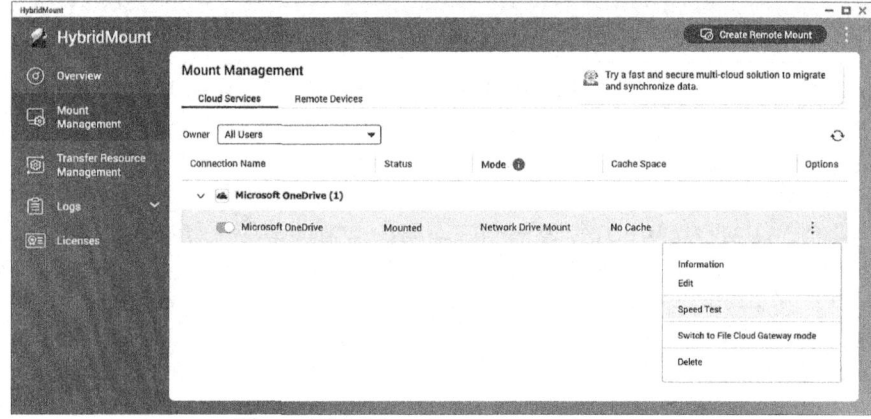

Figure 214: Mount management screen

No specific procedure is required to access the files in a remote mount; launch File Station, and the mount(s) will be listed alongside the regular folders on the NAS. The enclosed files and folders can be used in the same way as any other ones.

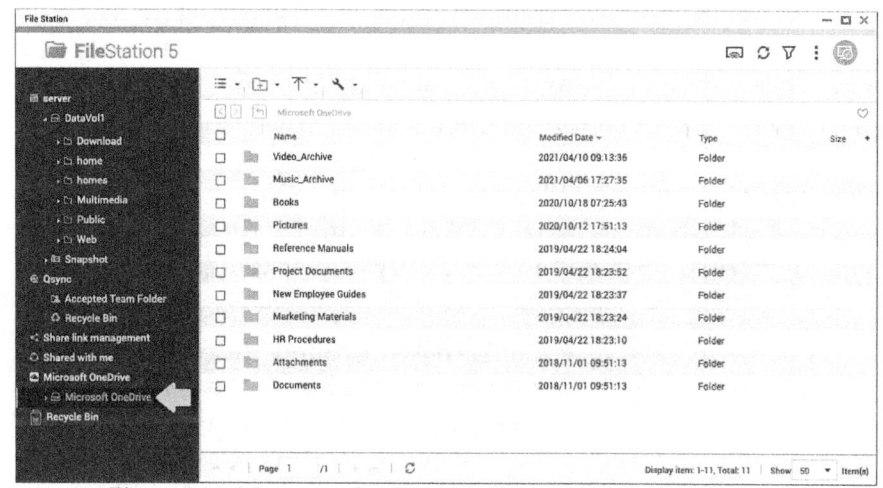

Figure 215: Mount to cloud service displayed within File Station

11.6 Virtual Private Networks (VPN)

The purpose of a *Virtual Private Network* or VPN is to securely extend a network to users who are offsite, such as home workers or those in a remote office, and you can think of it as equivalent to having a very long network cable that reaches out from the office for 10, 100, 1000 miles/kilometres or more. However, instead of an actual cable the connection goes over the internet and uses encryption and other techniques to maintain security. One advantage of a VPN is that it allows regular access to files and folders for editing, just as if in the office. The downside is that a VPN can be difficult to setup, configure and diagnose. QTS goes a long way towards making it easier and it usually works, but if it does not then be prepared for some pain.

VPNs come in several variants, based around different protocols: *PPTP*, *OpenVPN* and *L2TP/IPSec*. In addition to the three industry standards listed above, QNAP also have their own proprietary protocol, called *QBelt*. PPTP *("Point-To-Point Protocol")* is widely supported on many different types of clients but is relatively old and has some weaknesses compared to later systems. QNAP also support the new WireGuard standard. OpenVPN is popular, although requires a third-party piece of software to be installed on Windows PCs. L2TP/IPsec may be the best practical solution for many people as it is supported natively by Windows, macOS and other clients. The focus is on L2TP/IPSec in this guide, although the others are basically similar in setup and operation should you have reason to use them instead.

Note 1: some governments block VPN access, particularly to computer systems located outside of their territory.

Note 2: VPN services are also used to provide anonymous access to the internet, for instance to avoid censorship and geographical restrictions. That is a very different use of the term and NAS-based VPNs do not provide this capability.

Installing the QVPN Service

Begin by downloading and installing *QVPN Service* from the App Center. There are two variants: for x86-based servers, QVPN Service 3 is used; for ARM-based servers, it is QVPN Service 2, although the differences between them are quite minor (for instance, the latter does not support WireGuard protocol). Launch it using the resultant icon on the Desktop or from the Main Menu. All aspects of managing the VPN are controlled from this app, which initially has a spartan appearance on the Overview screen. In the left-hand panel, click the type of VPN service you will be using – which is L2TP/IPSec - in our example, to display the appropriate configuration screen:

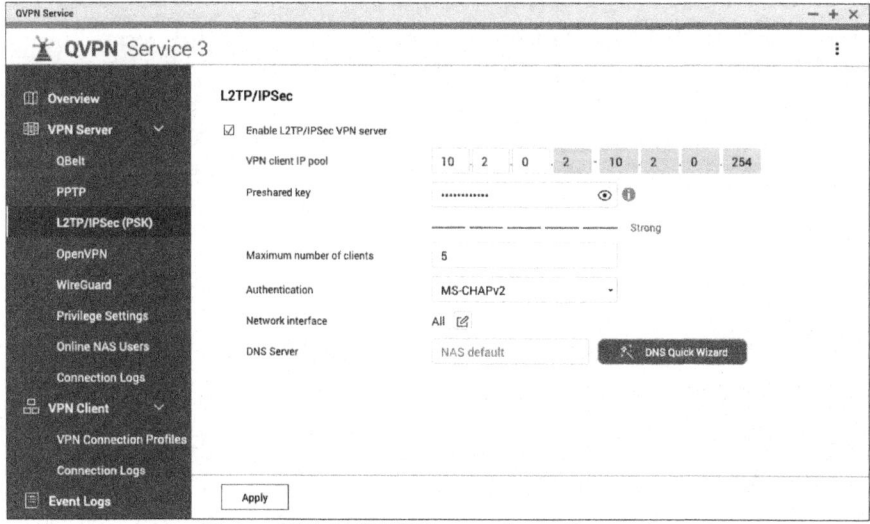

Figure 216: LP2T/IPSec configuration screen

Minimal work is required to get VPN running on the server and usually it is just a matter of ticking the **Enable L2TP/PPTP VPN server** box, or corresponding box if other VPN protocols are being used. The VPN has a range of IP addresses associated with it, called the *VPN client pool*. The key principle here is that the IP range is different from that used within the internal network so if, for example, the internal network uses the *192.168.nnn.nnn* addressing scheme, then the VPN could be set to use the *10.nnn.nnn.nnn* addressing scheme (or the other way around). In most cases, the QVPN Service will propose a suitable range, which can simply be accepted. Note the *Preshared key*, which is effectively a password, and specify something that is not obvious, involving a mixture of letters, numbers and special characters.

QVPN will advise on the strength of the preshared key as you type it in. In the case of L2TP/IPSec, *Authentication* should be MS-CHAPv2. If the NAS has multiple network cards, one can be dedicated to the VPN service using the *Network interface* option. And, to further improve performance in larger configurations with dozens or hundreds of VPN users, the *DNS Server* can be changed from the *NAS default* to a different one using the *DNS Quick Wizard* button.

Having made the changes, click the **Apply** button.

The users who will have access to the VPN need to be specified. Click **Privilege Settings**; the screen lists who has access and allows further users to be added by clicking the **Add VPN Users** button. Place ticks against the required users then click the **Apply** button (by default, *admin* receives privilege automatically). Note that we have only allowed L2TP/IPSec protocol for general users in this example. The screen will then be updated to show who has access. At this point, configuration is complete and the client computers can be connected.

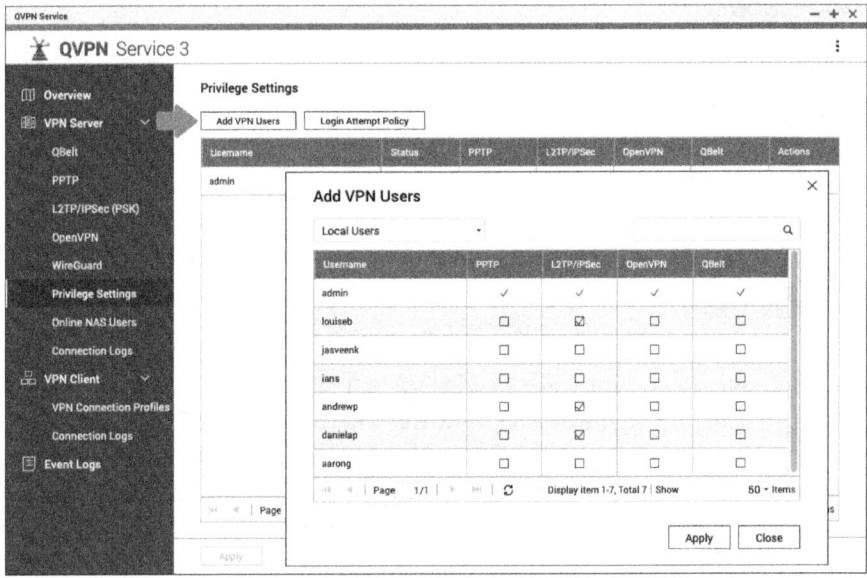

Figure 217: Adding VPN users

Configuring VPN Clients

VPN client software is available for most platforms, including mobile devices. This section covers installation on three popular desktop platforms: Windows 11, Windows 10, macOS. There may be some minor variations depending on what type of VPN you are using plus any security options you may have chosen. Here we are using L2TP/IPSec.

Windows 11 Clients

Click **Start** > **Settings** > **Network & Internet** > **VPN** > **Add VPN** to display the following panel:

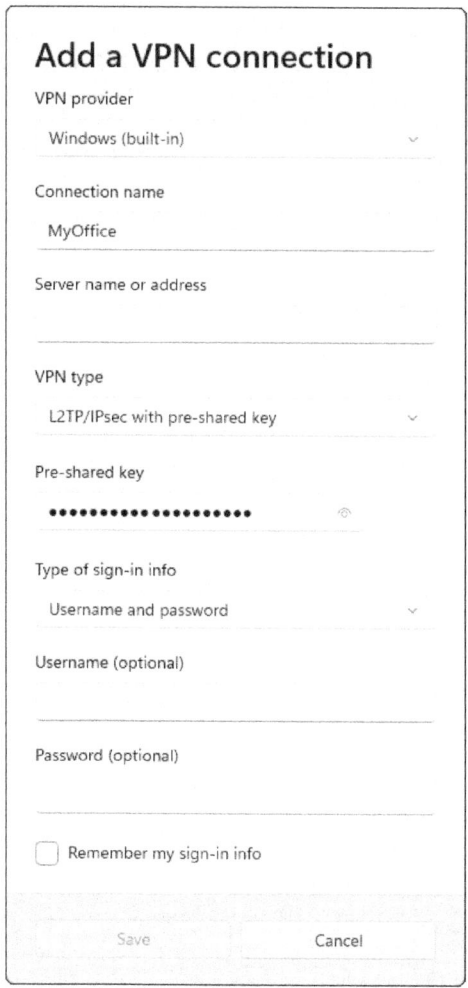

Figure 218: Adding a VPN connection (Windows 11)

Click **VPN provider** and choose *Windows (built-in)*, which will normally be the only option available. Specify a **Connection name** e.g. *MyOffice*. For the **Server name or address** enter the myQNAPcloud device name (e.g. *q9999999.myqnapcloud.com*) as discussed in section **11.2 myQNAPcloud**. Set the **VPN type** to **L2TP/Ipsec with pre-shared key** and enter the pre-shared key you specified when installing the QVPN Service. The **Type of sign-in info** should be *Username and password*. For security reasons it is suggested that you do not specify what the **Username** and **Password** are and do not tick the **Remember my sign-in info** box. Click **Save**.

The newly defined connection will now be listed on the VPN section. To use it, click the **Connect** button. You will be prompted to Sign in – enter your **Username** and **Password** as defined on the server and click **OK**. After a short while, the status will change to *Connected*.

You can now access resources on the server as though you were in the office. For instance, press the **Windows key** and the **R key** simultaneously and in the run box type *\\server\public* to display and access the shared folder.

When you have finished using the VPN, click the **Disconnect** button.

Windows 10 Clients

Click **Start** > **Settings** > **Network & Internet** > **VPN** > **Add a VPN connection** to display the following panel:

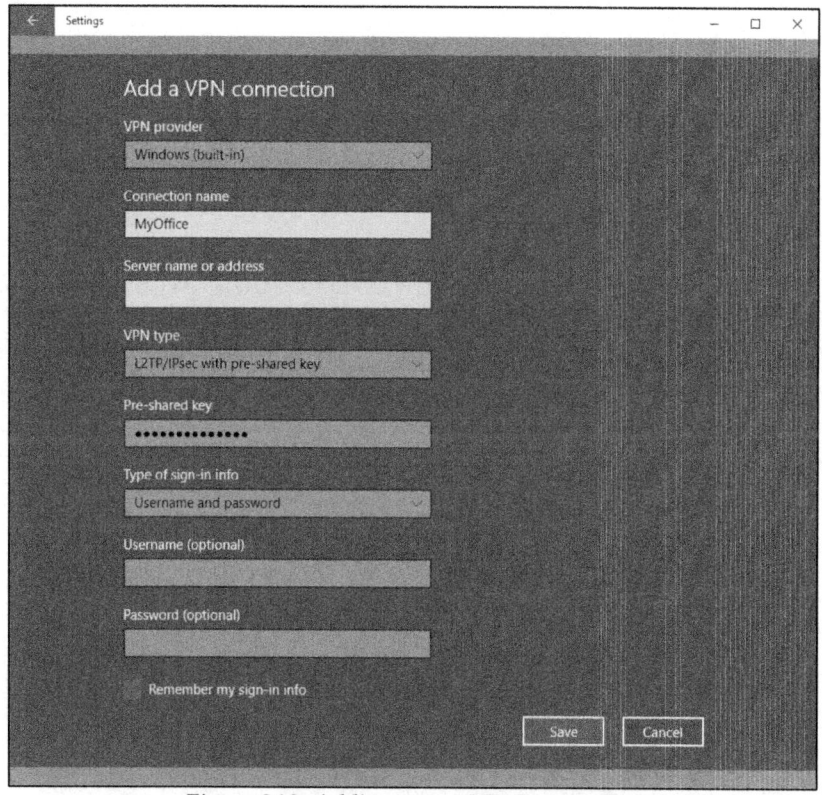

Figure 219: Adding a new VPN connection

Click **VPN provider** and choose *Windows (built-in)*, which will normally be the only option available. Specify a **Connection name** e.g. *MyOffice*. For the **Server name or address** enter the myQNAPcloud device name (e.g. *q9999999.myqnapcloud.com*) as discussed in section **11.2 myQNAPcloud**. Set the **VPN type** to *L2TP/Ipsec with pre-shared key*, then enter the pre-shared key you specified when installing the QVPN Service. The **Type of sign-in info** should be *Username and password*. For security reasons it is suggested that you do not hardcode the **Username** and **Password** do not tick the **Remember my sign-in info** box. Click **Save**.

The newly defined connection will now be listed on the VPN section within Settings. Click it and then click the **Connect** button. You will be prompted to Sign in – enter your **Username** and **Password** as defined on the server and click **OK**. After a short while, the status will change to *Connected*.

You can now access resources on the Server as though you were in the office. For instance, press the **Windows key** and the **R key** simultaneously and in the run box type *server**shared* to display and access the shared folder or *server**home* to access the user's home folder.

When you have finished using the VPN, click the **Disconnect** button.

Mac VPN Clients

Go into **System Preferences** and click **Network**. Add a new network service, with an **Interface** of **VPN** and a **VPN Type** of **L2TP over IPSec**:

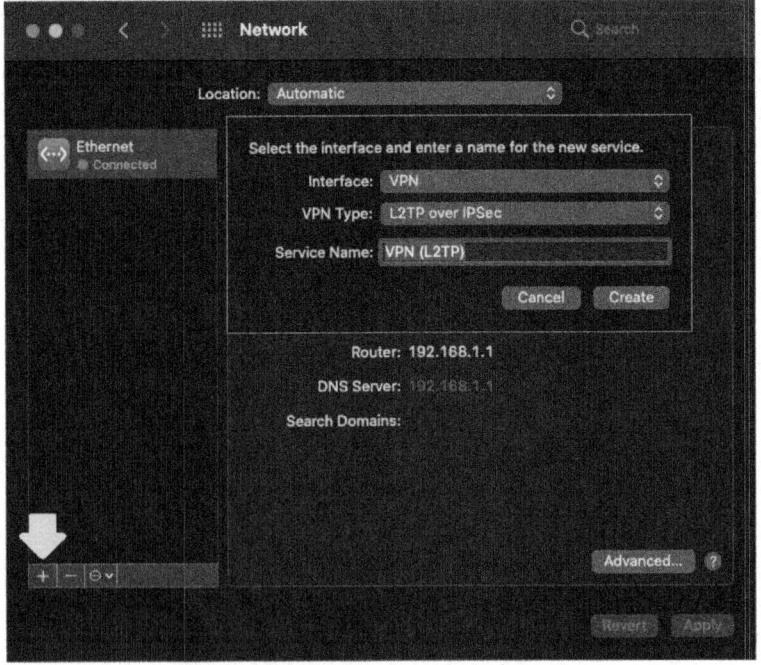

Figure 220: Add a new network service

Enter the **Server Address** (the DDNS name created in section **11.2 myQNAPcloud**) and the user's **Account Name**.

Click the **Authentication Settings** button and specify the **User Authentication Password** (i.e. the user's password on the server) and the **Machine Authentication Shared Secret** (i.e. the *Pre-shared key* for IKE authentication, which was defined during the configuration of the QVPN Service). Click **OK**. On the main screen, tick the **Show VPN status in menu bar** option, followed by **Apply**:

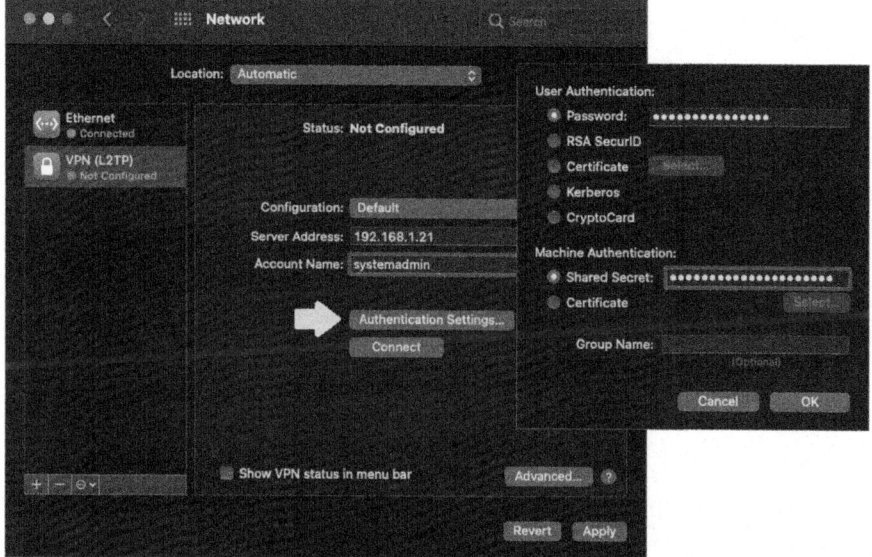

Figure 221: Configure the VPN Service

Click the VPN icon on the menu bar and choose **Connect VPN (L2TP)**. Click **Connect** and enter your user name and password when prompted.

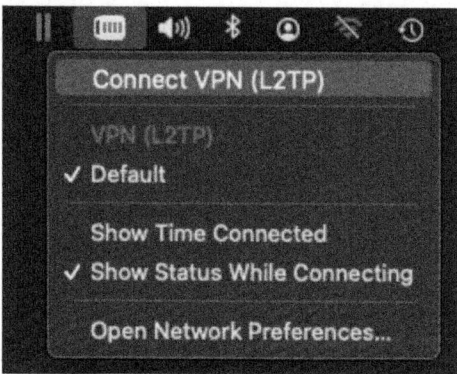

Figure 222: VPN icon on Menu bar

You can now access resources on the Server as though you were in the office. When you have finished, click the VPN icon on the Menu bar and click **Disconnect**.

Monitoring the List of Online Users

The status of the VPN and the connections in use can be monitored from the server. Within QVPN Service, click **Online NAS Users**. If required, a user can be forcibly disconnected from the VPN by right clicking their entry and clicking the **Disconnect** button.

11.7 QuFTP Service

FTP or *File Transfer Protocol* is a mechanism for transferring files between computers. It was first introduced over 50 years ago and, although now supplemented by other protocols and techniques, still remains important. It operates on a client-server model, in which FTP clients send files to and under the control of a central server. The clients run an appropriate utility or app, although some internet browsers can 'talk' FTP directly (however, support for FTP was disabled in Chrome 88 onwards and removed from Firefox 90). At the server end, QNAP offer their *QuFTP Service,* which needs to be downloaded from the App Center.

Having installed the QuFTP Service, it can be launched from the **Main Menu** or **Control Panel**. Click **System** and on the **General** tab tick the **Enable the FTP server** box. Two variants of FTP are supported: standard or original FTP, which is no longer recommended for general use, plus an enhanced and more secure version, called *FTP with SSL/TLS*, which uses SSL Certificates. For further security, *SFTP* (*SSH File Transfer Protocol*) can be used. There are configuration options on the **General** and **Connection** tabs, enabling control over the number of concurrent connections, file transfer limits and ports. Having configured QuTFP to meet your requirements, click **Apply**.

Users need to be given appropriate privileges to use FTP and this is managed by clicking on **Users**. FTP users can also be managed on a group level.

Rules can be defined to manage access to the system. Click on **Rules Engine** and click **Create**. Access hours can be controlled, along with access to folders. A useful feature for some organizations is the ability to automatically insert watermarks into uploaded pictures and videos. QuFTP can also be configured to generate Notifications.

Once QuFTP is operational, the client computers can be connected. All major operating systems have built-in FTP client software, but it is command line based. A wide range of GUI-based clients are readily available, including FileZilla and CrossFTP for Windows, macOS and Linux/Unix.

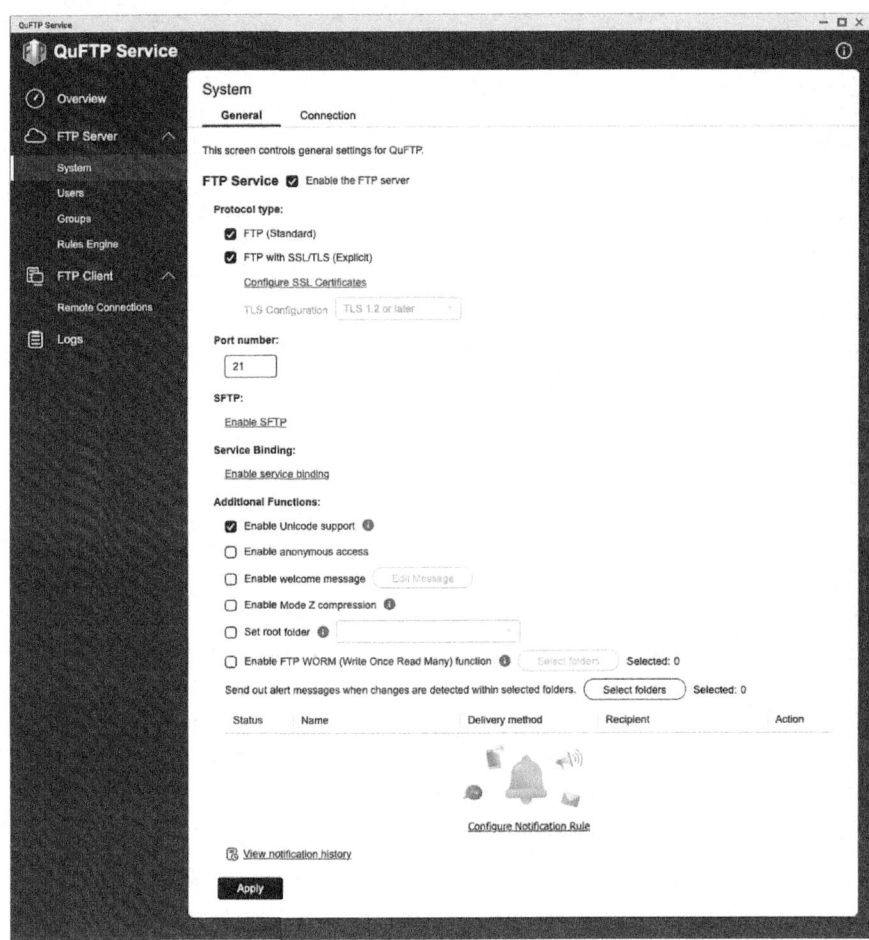

Figure 223: QuFTP Service screen

12

STORAGE

12.1 Overview

The key principles of how QTS handles storage were introduced in section **2.4 Setting up Storage**. This chapter discusses some of the more advanced storage options. The first section is an overview of RAID, whilst the remainder of the chapter explains how to configure and manage various storage options, including Snapshots, Caching and iSCSI.

12.2 RAID

The purpose of RAID - *Redundant Array of Independent (or Inexpensive) Disks* - is to improve storage reliability and performance using multiple drives that provide redundancy (protection against drive failure) and share the workload. There are various types of RAID and they referred to using a numbering system i.e. RAID 0, RAID 1, RAID 5 and so on. QNAP support many different RAID levels and depending on the model and the physical drives installed, the following RAID levels might be available: RAID 0; RAID 1; RAID 5; RAID 6; RAID 10; JBOD. When setting up RAID systems, the drives should be identical for best results i.e. same brand, same model, same capacity.

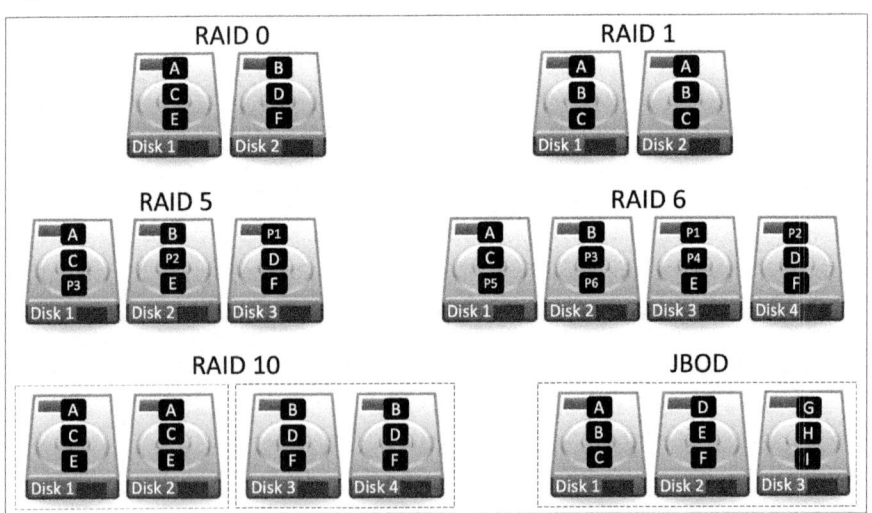

Figure 224: Commonly used RAID options

RAID 0 consists of two identical drives. When data is written, some goes on one drive and some goes on the other. As both drives are being written to (or subsequently read) simultaneously, throughput is maximized. However, as sections of files are scattered across the two drives, if one drive fails then everything is lost. Also, the speed of the disk drives may not be a bottleneck in some NAS systems. For these reasons, RAID 0 on its own is not commonly used. In a RAID 0 system, the total usable storage amount is equal to that of the total drive capacity installed. For example, if a NAS has two 4TB drives installed then the total amount of usable storage capacity is 8TB.

RAID 1 consists of two identical drives that mirror each other. When a file is saved there are physically two separate but identical copies behind the scenes, one held on each drive, even though you can only see one as the mirroring process itself is invisible. If one of the drives fails, the second one automatically takes over and the system carries on without interruption. At the earliest opportunity the faulty drive should be replaced with a new one; the system is then synced so it becomes a true copy of the remaining healthy drive in a process known as 'rebuilding the array'. In a RAID 1 system, the total usable storage capacity is half that of the total drive capacity installed. For example, if a NAS has two 4TB drives installed then the total amount of usable storage capacity is 4TB rather than 8TB.

RAID 5 needs three or more four drives. Data is written across all the drives, along with what is known as *parity information* (in simple terms, 'clues' that enable lost data to be reconstructed). The benefit of this is that the system can cope with the failure of any one single drive. RAID 5 is considered to offer a good combination of price, performance and resilience. Whereas a RAID 1 system loses half of the total drive capacity in order to provide resilience, RAID 5 loses only a third on a 3-drive system and a quarter on a 4-drive system. For instance, if a NAS has three 4TB drives installed then the total amount of usable storage capacity is 8TB rather than 12TB; if the NAS had four 4TB drives installed, the total amount of usable storage capacity would be 12TB rather than 16TB

RAID 6 needs four or more drives. It is similar to RAID 5 but uses two sets of parity information written across the drives instead of one. The benefit of this approach is that the system can cope with the simultaneous failure of two of the drives, thereby making it more resilient than RAID 5, but it loses more capacity in order to provide that resilience. There may also be a performance hit compared with RAID 5 due to the additional parity processing, but overall RAID 6 is considered superior. If a server has five 4TB drives installed in a RAID configuration, then the total amount of usable storage capacity is 12TB rather than 20TB.

RAID 10 (also known as RAID 1+0) combines RAID 1 and RAID 0 techniques. Requiring an even number and a minimum of four drives, it comprises a pair of RAID 1 mirrored drives, with data being striped across the pair in the way that RAID 0 operates. It thus combines both performance (RAID 0) and redundancy (RAID 1), making it of particular interest where high throughput in needed, for instance in demanding applications such as 4K video editing. The amount of available storage is half that of the total drive capacity e.g. a system with four 4TB drives would give 8TB of usable space rather than 16TB.

JBOD stands for *Just a Bunch of Disks* and is not actually a RAID system at all. Rather, it aggregates all the drives together to create one large volume that provides the maximum amount of storage space, but without any protection. For example, three drives of 4TB capacity each would provide 12TB of aggregated storage. In the event of a drive failure, you will lose the data stored on that drive. The drives do not have to be of identical capacities plus you can use as many drives as are in the NAS.

What to do? If you have a NAS with a single drive, then the question of RAID does not arise. If you have a NAS with two drive bays, then you should use RAID 1 if data protection is most important to you or use JBOD if you need the maximum amount of space. If you have a NAS with three or four drive bays, it should be configured as RAID 5 if protection is most important or JBOD if you need the maximum amount of space. If you have a NAS with five or more drives, it should be configured as RAID 6 if protection is most important or JBOD if you need the maximum amount of space. The maximum number of drives that a RAID group can contain is 16.

One important thing to remember is that a RAID system is **not** a backup system. Whilst it can help prevent data loss in the event of problems, it is still important to make separate provision for backup. For instance, if the server was stolen or the premises went up in flames then the data would be lost regardless of whether and whatever RAID system was used.

Note: For QuTS Hero Edition only, QNAP offer RAID Triple Parity (TP) and RAID Triple Mirror (TM). These special modes provide the ability to cope with three simultaneous drive failures, plus can work with drives of differing capacities (albeit with unused space in some configurations).

12.3 Increasing Pool Free Space

When a storage pool is setup (see **2.4 Setting up Storage**) a threshold can optionally be specified; if the amount of free space in the storage pool falls below this threshold, a notification message is generated. The first thing is to consider is whether the warning message is truly significant or just a technicality. Suppose, for instance, that the server has just been setup, that no data has been loaded or created, yet it is advising that the storage pool is already running out of space. This would suggest that the storage pool has probably been created using unsuitable capacity and threshold values and you should use the Storage & Snapshots app and File Station to confirm that the space is really being used. This can be a difficult call to make and it is best to err on the side of caution, but be aware that it is a possibility.

If it is necessary or desired to increase the amount of pool free space, do the following. Launch **Storage & Snapshots** and click the **Storage/Snapshots** section on the left-hand side of the screen. Highlight the storage pool in question and click the **Manage** button. On the screen, click **Action > Free some space**, which will cause the following panel to be displayed:

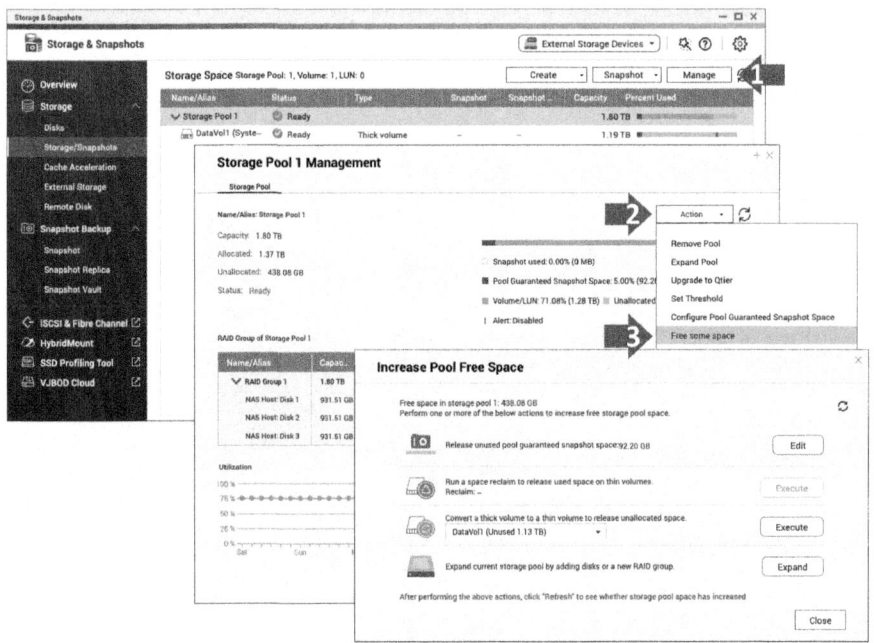

Figure 225: Options to Increase Pool Free Space

There are potentially four options available to resolve matters, depend on the configuration of the system, and any which are not applicable will be grayed out:

Release unused guaranteed snapshot space – if snapshots are used with guaranteed space, the amount of that space could be reduced. Click **Edit** to be taken to the appropriate settings.

Run space reclaim – if thin volumes are being used, click the **Execute** button to free-up some space.

Convert thick to thin volume – if a thick volume is being used, it can be converted to a thin one. Note that thin and thick volumes have different capabilities so the implications of this need to carefully be considered.

Expand current storage pool – additional disks or a new RAID group can be added to expand the capacity of the current storage pool.

12.4 Snapshots

Snapshots can be considered as a supplementary backup mechanism that allows the NAS to record the state of the data on a storage volume at a given moment. In simple terms, the system makes a note of what has been altered when a file or folder has changed, then writes away those details to a different part of the disk or to a different disk altogether. It does not make a complete copy of the file or folder, just the differences, which can then be used to restore the data should that every prove necessary. Snapshots can take place manually or scheduled to run on a frequent basis e.g. once a week, once a day, once an hour etc.

Because only changes are being recorded, the system is efficient, both in terms of time taken and disk space used. For instance, suppose you had a 10 Mbyte spreadsheet and changed a few cells; with most conventional backups the system would create a complete 10 Mbyte copy of the file, whereas with a Snapshot the backup might only be a few hundred bytes. However, although Snapshots are very efficient, they require a certain level of hardware support. All x86-based QNAP NAS boxes support it, as do recent ARM-based ones with 1GB RAM or more, but Snapshots may not be available on some older models. Snapshots are enabled by default on supported models. Using Snapshots may slightly reduce the overall speed of access to a disk or volume, although this is generally a worthwhile trade-off between performance and protection. Snapshots can be stored on volumes and/or LUNs (LUNs are discussed in section **12.7 iSCSI**).

Note: Snapshots actually operate at the block level rather than the byte level, the above explanation has been simplified to aid understanding.

Snapshots are managed from the *Storage & Snapshots* app but are also accessible from *File Station* and this is the route we will take. Launch File Station and click the blue **Snapshot** button followed by **Snapshot Manager** and the volume to be snapshotted. Exit from the *Welcome Screen* if it is shown, and the following screen is displayed:

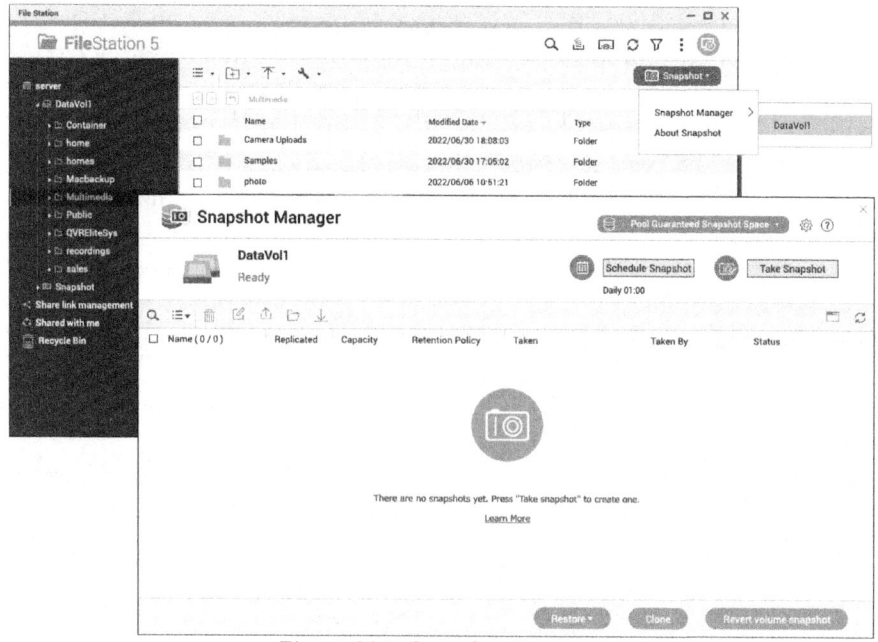

Figure 226: Snapshot Manager

Manual Snapshots

To manually take a Snapshot at any point, click the **Take Snapshot** button. If there is a message about Snapshots affecting performance, tick the **Do not show this message again** box followed by **OK**. The following panel appears:

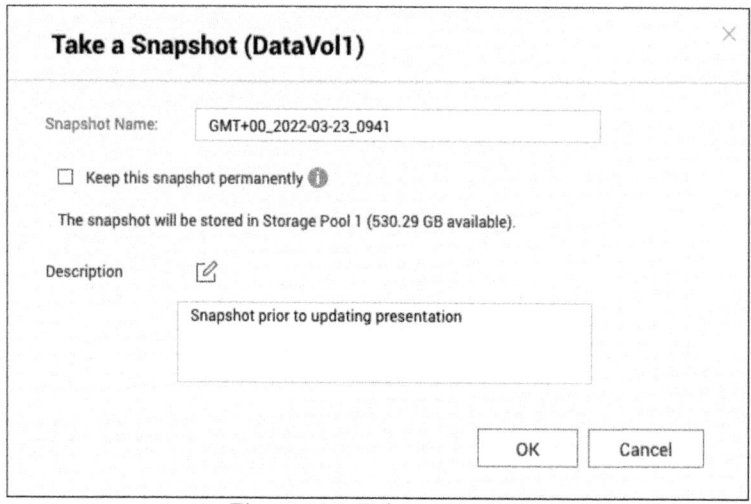

Figure 227: Take a Snapshot

At the simplest level, the only thing necessary is to click the **OK** button; however, there are several options which can be exercised. By default, the *Snapshot Name* is derived from the current date and time, which is useful but can be changed if desired and given a different name e.g. *'month_end_snapshot'*. If required, the snapshot can be kept indefinitely by clicking **Keep this snapshot permanently** box, although doing so will use up storage space and require subsequent effort in managing snapshots. Finally, the Snapshot can be given a detailed *Description* by clicking the small pencil icon. After clicking **OK**, the Snapshot is created, with the time taken depending on the amount of data that has changed.

Scheduled Snapshots

In addition to manual snapshots, scheduled snapshots can be used. By default, daily snapshots are enabled on most QNAP models, but the frequency and other parameters can be adjusted, or the schedule switched off. This is controlled from Snapshot Manager; there are two ways to access it:

File Manager > Snapshot > Snapshot Manager, click the volume to be snapshotted

Or

Storage & Snapshots > Snapshot, click the volume to be snapshotted (you have to click the text label, rather than the icon).

Click the **Schedule Snapshot** button to display the following panel with three tabbed sections:

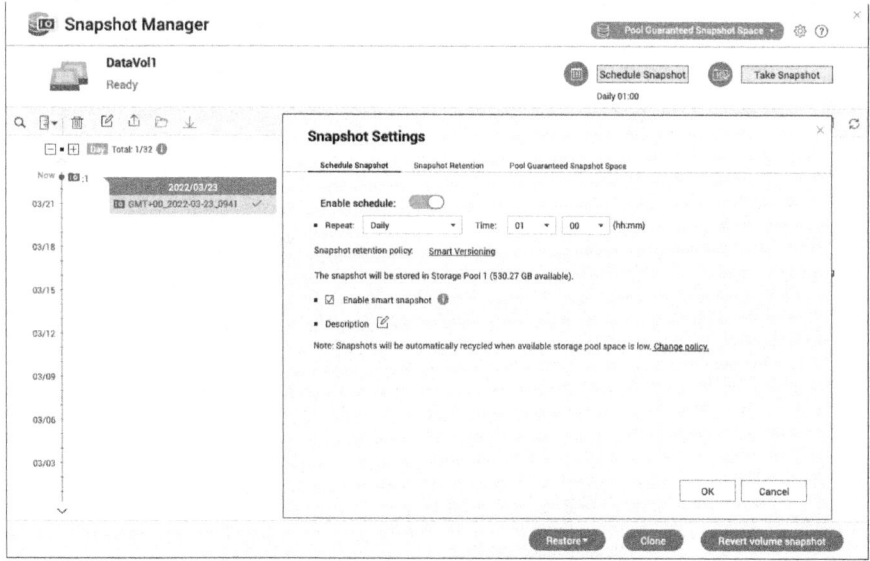

Figure 228: Schedule Snapshot Settings

On the first tab – **Schedule Snapshot** - the **Enable schedule** switch should be on the right to enable scheduling; to turn off, slide it to the left. Underneath, the *Repeat* fields can be used to specify the schedule, with Snapshots occurring at regular intervals e.g. after so many minutes, hours, days etc. or at pre-determined times e.g. a particular time each day, week etc. The **Enable smart snapshot** option can be ticked; this ensures that the snapshot is only taken if any data has changed since the last one, which can reduce the number of snapshots and the load on the NAS.

An optional *Description* can be specified. Having specified the parameters, click **OK**.

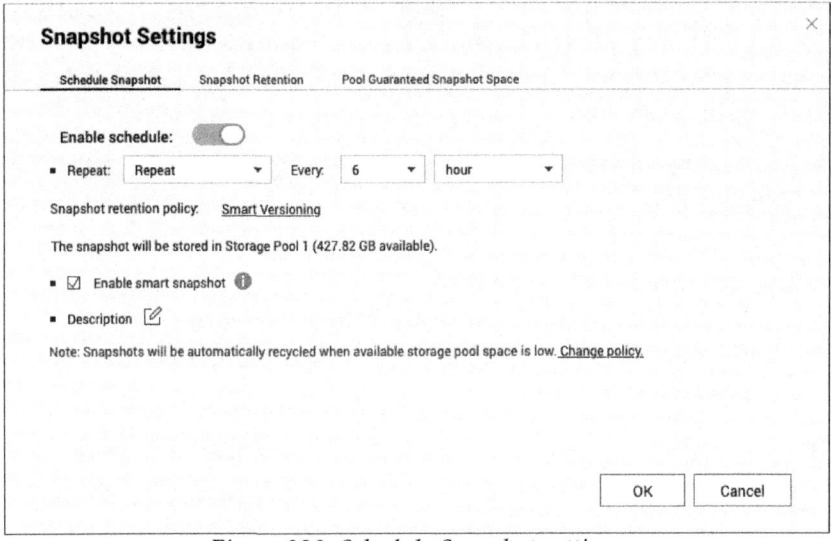

Figure 229: Schedule Snapshot settings

Snapshot Retention

By default, snapshots are kept until available storage pool space runs low, at which point they are recycled. The parameters can be adjusted from the **Snapshot Retention** tab in Snapshot Settings:

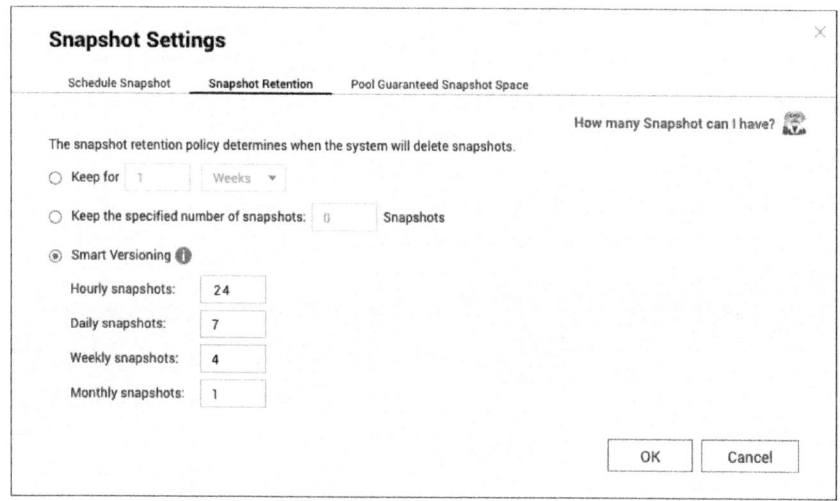

Figure 230: Snapshot Retention settings

There are three options. Firstly, the retention time can be specified as a certain number of minutes, hours, days, weeks or months. Or, the number of snapshots to be retained can be specified, up to the maximum supported for the NAS model. Finally, so-called *Smart Versioning* can be used, where different values for hourly, daily, weekly and monthly snapshots can be specified. The general principle for the latter is to have more copies of recent snapshots but less so for older ones and this is reflected in the above example.

There is a limit on the maximum number of snapshots that can be retained and this depends upon the QNAP model and amount of free storage pool space. For instance, a low-end ARM model might support 32 snapshots per volume and two volumes (or LUNs), whereas a more powerful x86 one might support 256 per volume and four volumes (or LUNs). Considering the latter case, if the repeat frequency was every hour, you would be able to 'roll back' just over 10 days, whereas with a daily snapshot you could go back more than 8 months. To find out what the maximum number of snapshots is, click the **How many Snapshots can I have?** link.

Pool Guaranteed Snapshot Space

The Snapshot Retention policy described above is based upon time or the number of snapshots. Alternatively, it is possible to exercise control by guaranteeing (reserving) a set amount of storage space for the snapshots.

On the **Pool Guaranteed Snapshot Space** tab within Snapshot Settings, slide the **Guaranteed Snapshot Space** switch to the right to display this screen. The panel displays current usage and allows you to specify the percentage of the storage pool space to be reserved for snapshots. Unless you have specific requirements, you may want to use the **Recommended** option. Click **OK**.

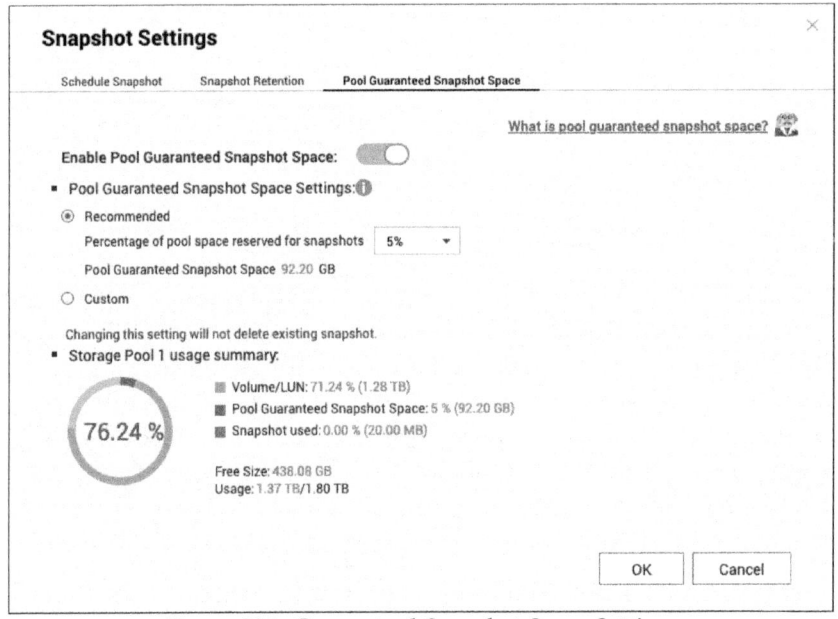

Figure 231: Guaranteed Snapshot Space Settings

Reverting a Snapshot

Should there ever be a need to recover data, this can be done as follows:

In File Station, highlight the item to be restored and click **Snapshot** > **Snapshot Manager**. Or, launch Snapshot Manager directly. On the left-hand side of the screen, highlight a snapshot from a time when the data was known to be in good condition or according to some other criterion you may have; mark the subfolder(s)/files to be restored; click the **Revert volume snapshot** button at the bottom of the screen:

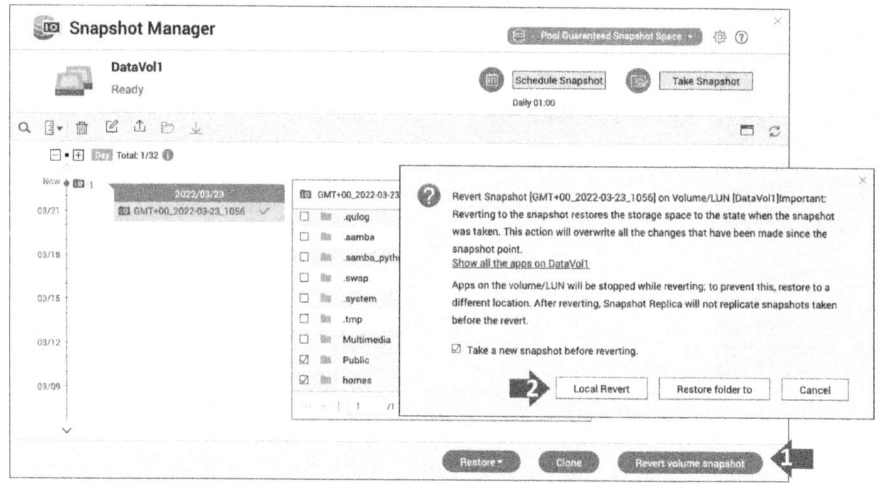

Figure 232: Reverting a Snapshot

Choose **Local Revert** to restore to the original location or **Restore folder to** for another location. If the box is ticked, a new snapshot will be taken prior to reverting to the chosen one (which can be used to undo matters should the results prove unsatisfactory). Note that in contrast to creating a snapshot, reverting the data can potentially take a considerable amount of time and disrupt the operation of the server, and a warning message to this effect may be displayed. Click **OK** to proceed.

Monitoring Snapshot Usage

Launch Storage & Snapshots and click **Snapshot** in the *Snapshot Backup* section. Click the **Show Space Utilization** link (which will toggle to 'Hide Space Utilization') and the bottom half of the screen will display utilization. Use the *Time Period* dropdown to specify the scale of the chart, ranging from the past hour through to the past year:

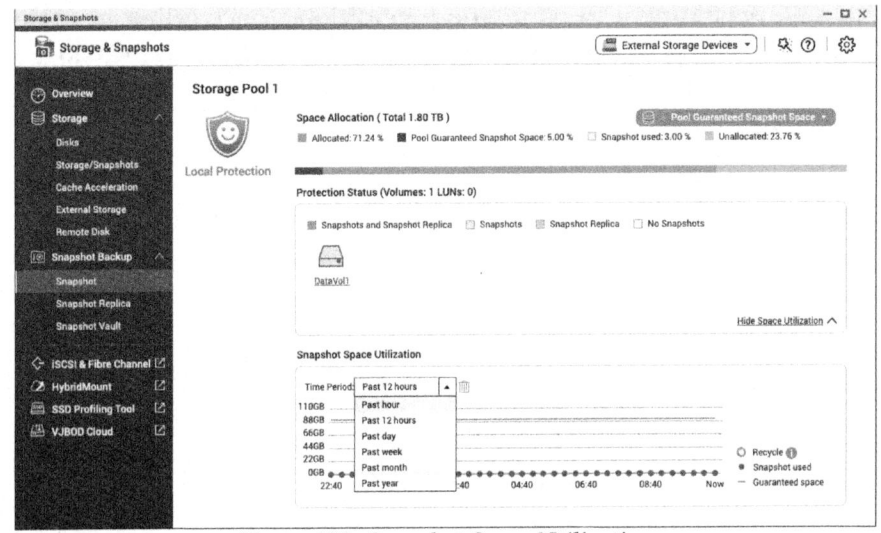

Figure 233: Snapshot Space Utilization

Global Settings in Storage & Snapshots

Options for snapshot space management and other parameters can be configured from within *Storage & Snapshots*. Click the **Cogwheel** in the top-right hand corner of the screen to display *Global Settings* and click the **Snapshot** icon:

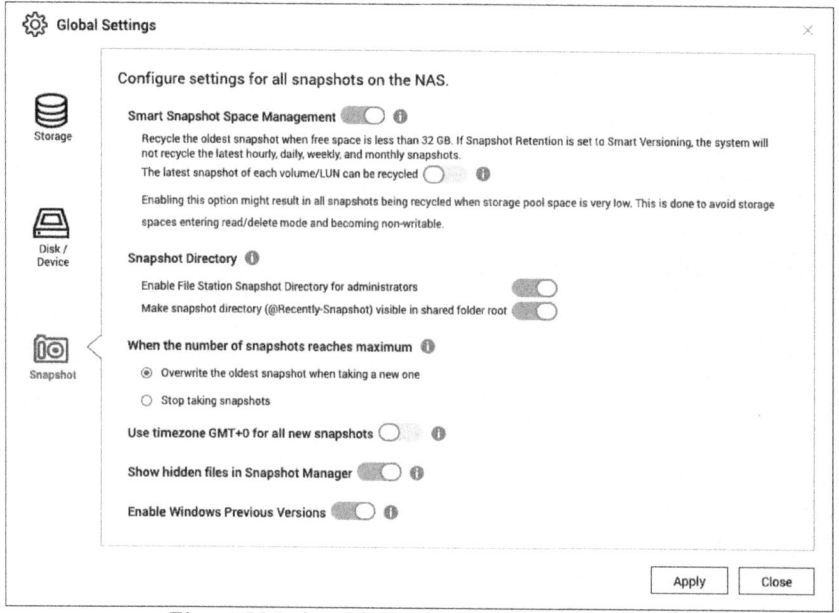

Figure 234: Snapshot options in Global Settings

Whilst the default settings will suit many users, there are some that you may wish to fine tune. The first one – *Smart Snapshot Space Management* – is usually set to the 'on' position and this causes the oldest snapshots to be recycled when free space on the volume drops below 32GB. The one underneath it controls whether the most recent snapshot can be recycled and defaults to 'off'.

Midway down is the switch that governs what happens when the maximum number of snapshots is reached. The choice here is to start overwriting the oldest ones or stop taking snapshots.

At the bottom of the panel is the option to enable *Previous Versions* for Windows users. This feature, supported by Windows 7 and later versions, allows users to restore earlier versions of files on their own computers.

Having made any changes, click **Apply** and **Close**.

Viewing Snapshots from File Station

The contents of snapshots can be accessed directly from File Station, where they appear as part of the regular file system. By right clicking a snapshot or folder or file within it, options become available to download, restore or delete it, as well as launch Snapshot Manager as described previously.

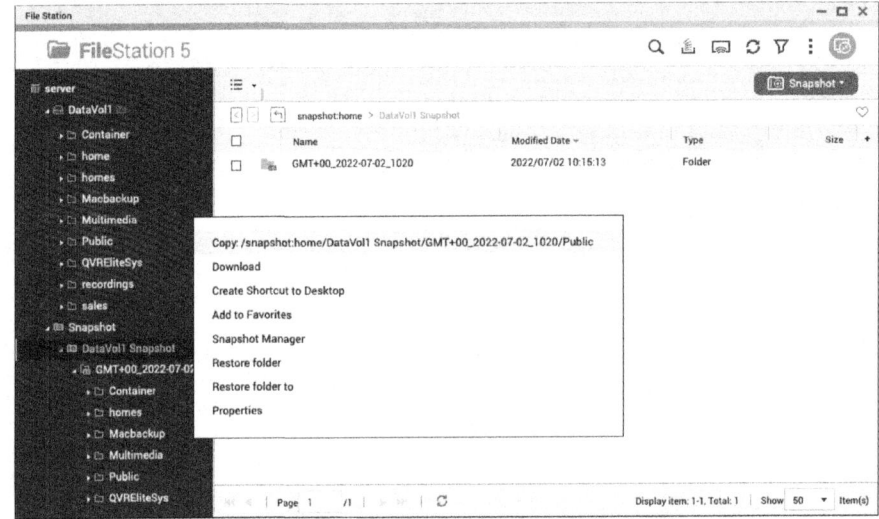

Figure 235: Accessing snapshots in File Station

12.5 SSD Caching

Solid State Drives or SSDs are very fast in operation, many times more so than traditional mechanical hard drives. However, they are also more expensive, particularly for the larger capacity ones which are of most use in a NAS. For instance, at the time of writing a 4TB SSD sells for around US $400 online, whereas a NAS-certified 4TB mechanical hard drive can be picked up for US $100 and, whilst SSD prices will continue to fall, it may be several years before they match the prices and capacities of mechanical drives. The concept of caching is that copies of frequently used data are kept on SSD, making it quickly available when required, as opposed to it being accessed each time from the much slower mechanical drives. This process happens automatically and transparently, with QTS keeping track of the data. By using a combination of lower-priced mechanical drives for capacity and SSD drives for performance, it is possible to obtain the 'best of both worlds' for a reasonable price. A suitable ratio is 10:1 e.g. if you have 10TB of mechanical storage you should aim to supplement it with 1TB of SSD as cache, although for video streaming a higher ratio rising to 3:1 is preferable.

Two types of SSD are supported. Some NAS models feature PCIe slots and can use M.2 SSD cards; these give the best results in terms of speed. However, most recent models can also use regular 2.5" SATA-format SSD drives, such as are used in laptops and, whilst these are slower than M.2 drives they still give a considerable boost to storage performance.

As with mechanical hard drives, multiple SSD cache drives can themselves be configured for RAID operation. A suitably configured RAID SSD-cache, feeding into RAID-configured mechanical drives, gives the greatest performance boost.

Setting Up Caching

To setup caching, go into **Storage & Snapshots > Cache Acceleration** and click the large blue button marked with the plus (+) sign to begin. The first screen is an introduction. On the subsequent screen, select the SSD disk(s) to be used. Specify the *Cache Type*: if a SATA SSD is being used this can be Read-Only, but with PCIe devices there are additional choices of Read-Write and Write-Only, which give better performance.

If there is more than one SSD, they can be configured for RAID operation as with regular storage drives, which further improves performance and reliability (RAID is recommended for Read-Write caches). Click **Next**:

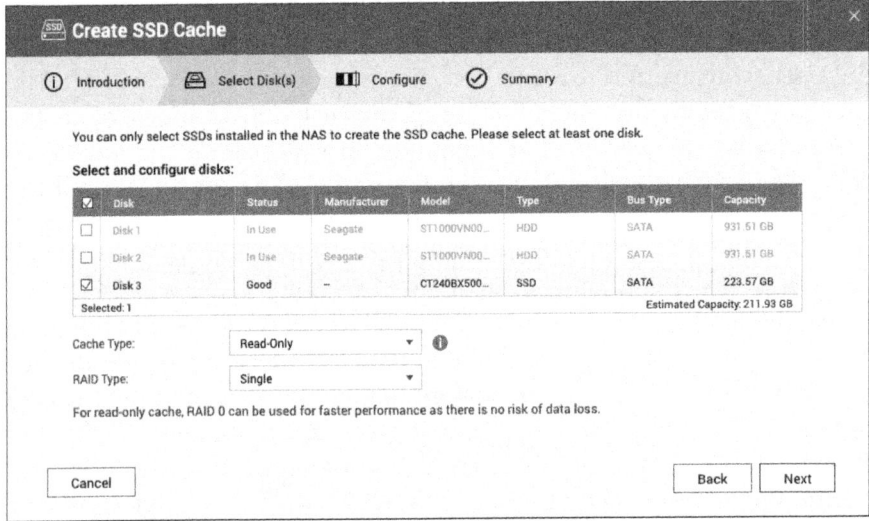

Figure 236: Select the SSD disks

The configuration screen appears, where *Over-provisioning* can be specified. This is a technique for extending the lifespan and performance of an SSD, but at the expense of reduced capacity. To determine optimal settings, QNAP have an optional SSD Profiling Tool, discussed later on, but the default is that over-provisioning is enabled and with a value of 10%, which will suit most configurations.

The *Cache Mode* should be set. In most installations, the **All I/O** option will be most suitable; however, if you are making extensive use of virtualization and/or using database applications, then **Random I/O** is recommended. The *Bypass Block Size* dropdown can be left at the default setting.

Having made your choices, click **Next**:

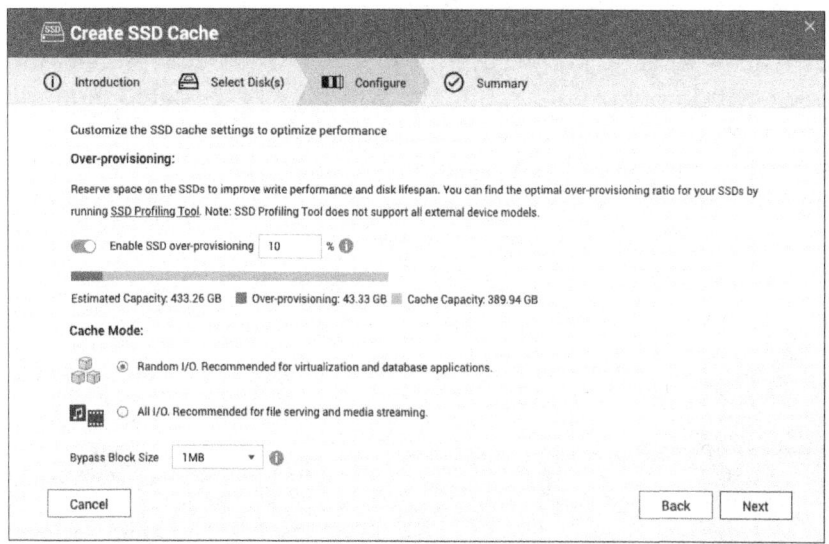

Figure 237: Configure the SSD cache

On the subsequent screen, the data volume to be cached is specified. Tick the volume to enable caching and click **Next**. Should you ever wish to stop caching the drive at some stage you would subsequently untick it.

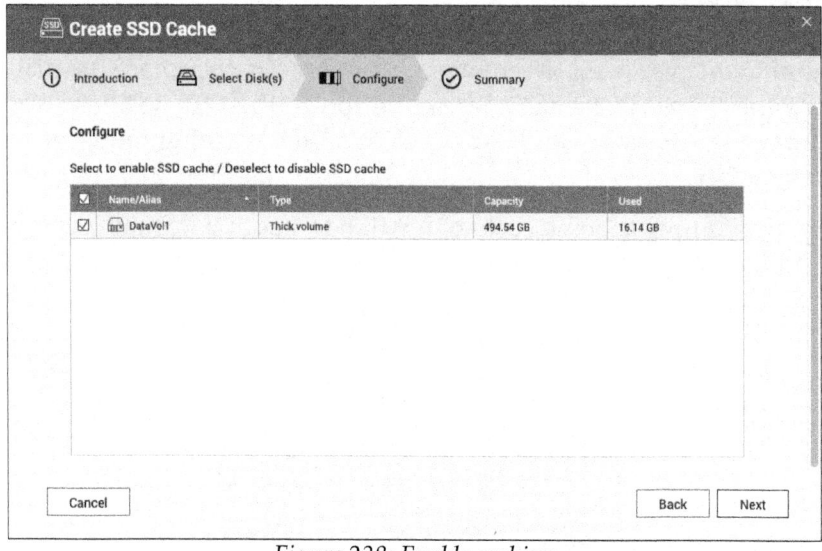

Figure 238: Enable caching

A Summary screen is displayed; click **Create** to proceed and a warning message will be displayed about data being lost if the SSD is subsequently removed without first disabling the caching function.

Note that the risk of data loss applies even if the NAS is powered down at the time. Acknowledge the message. The Cache Acceleration screen within Snapshots & Storage will now be updated along the following lines, showing that the cache is operational and indicating its performance. Note that it will take a short while for the cache to initialize, during which time the Cache Acceleration Service button will be in the 'Off' position, but it will subsequently switch itself to the 'On' position.

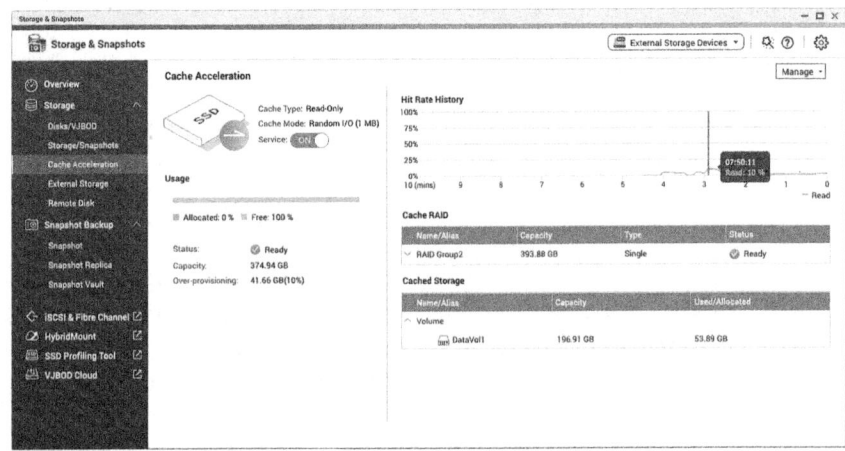

Figure 239: Cache Acceleration operational

Should you ever need to remove the caching e.g. to replace the drive, slide the *Cache Acceleration Service* button to the **Off** position. Click **Manage > Remove** and acknowledge the warning message by clicking **OK**.

Tip: if a volume is being cached, it will be listed in File Station with a small lightning bolt against it:

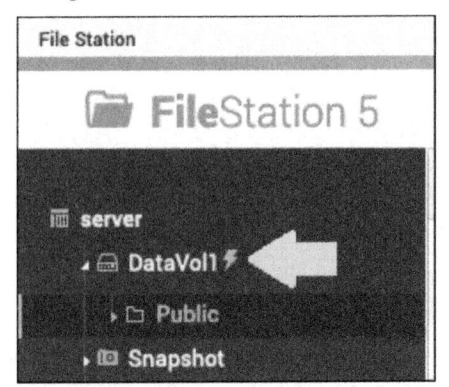

Figure 240: Cached volume in File Station

SSD Profiling Tool

Having installed an SSD, the optional *SSD Profiling Tool* can be used to test it and determine the best settings for the drive(s). There is a link to it in Storage & Snapshots; initially this to the App Center, from where it has to be downloaded. This will also place an icon on the desktop. The first time it is run, it is necessary to accept the End User Agreement, one of the provisions of which is that the tool will share test data with QNAP.

Over-provisioning (OP) is an important concept with SSDs; all SSDs feature some reserved space, which allows the drive to continue writing without affecting performance when it is running out of regular free space. If this reserved space is used up, the internal data on the drive has to be re-organized and this process affects both performance and, crucially, the lifetime of the drive. The manufacturer of the drive will have set aside some space for OP; this space is not directly visible but partly accounts for why SSDs are sold with apparently non-standard capacities e.g. 240GB rather than 256GB, 480GB rather than 512GB etc. The optimal amount of reserved space depends on how the drive is being used, but the typical manufacturer allocation of about 7% may sometimes be inadequate. The idea behind OP is that some of the regular available space can be used to supplement it and, whilst this reduces overall capacity, it can improve performance and longevity.

Click the blue **Create Test** button to run the SSD over-provisioning test. Click **Next** and choose the SSD(s) on the subsequent screen. Click **Next**. The third screen advises how long the test will take and allows some of the parameters to be adjusted. The test time varies, depending on the configuration and capacity of the drives, but is typically several hours and may take as long as 24 hours. Click **Next**, followed by **Finish** on the Summary screen, and the test will commence after advising that any existing data on the SSD will be destroyed.

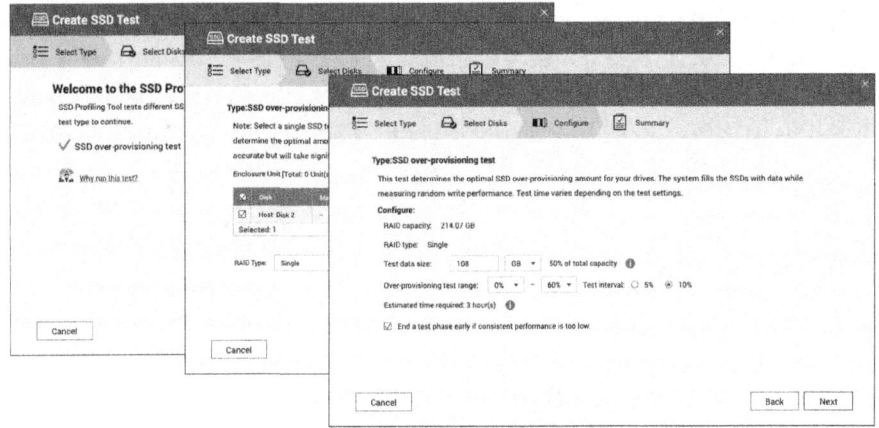

Figure 241: Creating an SSD Test

The results of the test will vary on the configuration of the NAS and the type of SSD drive(s) being used. The read and write speeds achieved by the drive(s) will be reported, along with any suggestions for over provisioning. Armed with this knowledge, the caching parameters can be adjusted.

12.6 SSD Trim

Note: this feature only applies if SSDs are being used for regular storage. It does not apply when SSDs are used for caching.

SSD Trim is an operating system feature that improves the performance and lifespan of SSD devices. QNAP recommend that it is used if any of the following conditions apply SSD-based Thin Volumes are used; VJBOD Cloud Volumes are used; SSD-based RAID 0, RAID 1 or RAID 10 groups are used.

To enable SSD Trim, go to **Storage & Snapshots** and click the **Global Settings** cogwheel in the top-right corner of the screen. Within the **Storage** section, slide the *Auto Reclaim and SSD Trim Schedule* switch to the 'On' position. Use the dropdown to specify a schedule for when SSD Trim will run e.g. Daily at 0200 (it is best performed overnight or at another time when the server is not heavily used). Click **Apply**.

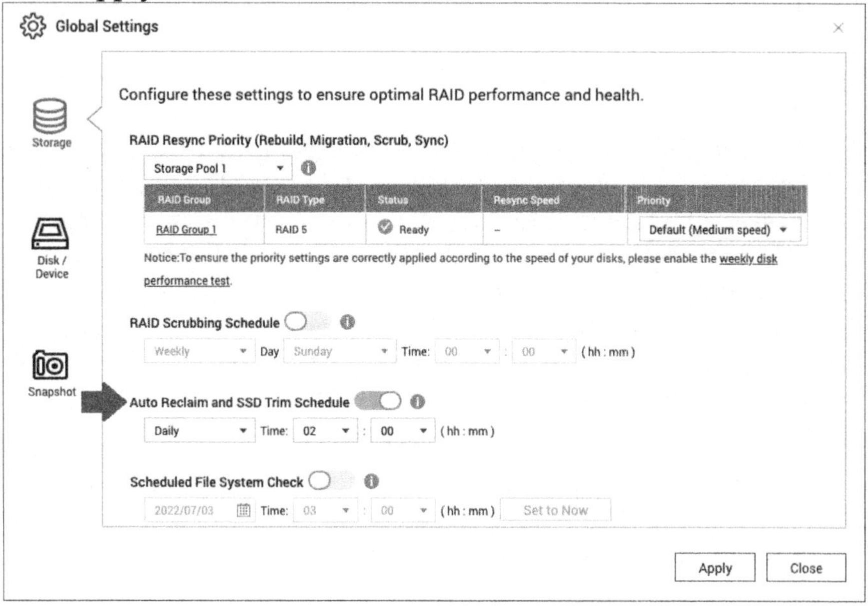

Figure 242: Enable SSD Trim

12.7 iSCSI

iSCSI - *Internet Small Computer Systems Interface* - is a standard for connecting virtualized storage to computers. Its origins lie with large computer systems and it is of particular interest to organizations that run multiple servers, have large amounts of storage and require great flexibility when it comes to managing that storage. In the following examples, we will be creating storage for use with QTS; however, such storage can also be used with popular virtualization products such as VMware ESXi Server, Microsoft Hyper-V and Citrix XenServer.

First, we need to consider how it operates. So far, we have used shared folders on the server. For Windows users, it is possible to map drive letters to shared folders, as described in section **5.4 Connecting Windows Computers**. This enables us to refer to, say, **\\server\home** as drive H, but it is not a real drive in the sense that the physical C: drive on a Windows computer is and we are simply using the letter H as a form of shorthand. With iSCSI, an amount of space is set aside on the server. The server is referred to as the *iSCSI host* and the space is known as the *iSCSI target*, which is given a *LUN* (*Logical Unit Number*) to help reference it. A computer - known as the *iSCSI client* or *initiator* - connects to the LUN (target), which it sees as a complete disk drive. This drive, to most intents and purposes, behaves like a real physical drive and can be partitioned, formatted and used in any way the user requires. It is possible to move targets from one server to another without unduly affecting the clients, hence the reason for its relevance to larger organizations with requirements for redundancy and disaster recovery.

When setting up storage volumes on the NAS, as described in section **2.4 Setting up Storage**, there was a choice of creating *Static*, *Thick* or *Thin* volumes. As LUNs cannot be created on Static volumes, it is necessary to use Thick or Thin volumes if you are intending to use iSCSI.

All aspects of iSCSI are managed using the *iSCSI & Fibre Channel* utility.

Creating an iSCSI LUN

Go to the **Main Menu** or Desktop and launch **iSCSI & Fibre Channel** (or use the link in **Storage & Snapshots** by clicking **iSCSI & Fibre Channel** on the left-hand side of the screen). The first time you do so you will receive a message advising that the iSCSI service is disabled and asked whether you want to enable it – click **OK** to do so. After a few seconds, you will be asked if you wish to run the *Quick Configuration Wizard* – also click **OK**. The *iSCSI Target Creation Wizard* will then run; click **Next** and on the second screen define the *iSCSI Target Profile Name* e.g. *LUN1*. There is usually a one-to-one relationship between a client and a target; however, if the **Allow clustered access to this target** box is ticked, then the target can be shared by multiple clients (with the proviso that the filesystems on the clients are 'cluster aware'). Click **Next**:

Figure 243: Create new iSCSI Target

The next step of the wizard can be used to specify authentication and improve security using *CHAP authentication*. This is useful within a larger organization and should be considered mandatory if the LUN is to be accessed externally, but if everything is internal and within a small organization/household you may not require the additional security, in which case you can just click **Next**.

The final screen is a summary of the settings. Click **Apply** and the LUN will be created. After a few seconds, the *Block-Based iSCSI LUN Creation Wizard* will then run:

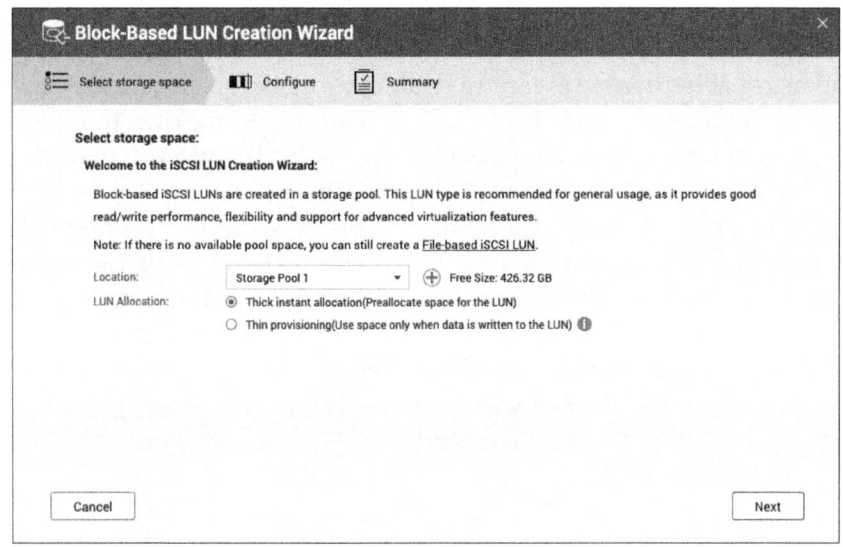

Figure 244: iSCSI LUN Creation Wizard

If you have more than one storage location on the NAS, it can be specified using the dropdown. For *LUN Allocation*, choose **Thick instant allocation** unless you understand how iSCSI works and the implications of choosing the other option. Click **Next**. On the subsequent screen, use the *LUN Capacity* field to specify how much space will be available in the LUN. There is an option to set it to the maximum available, but this can cause issues and you would only do this if the storage location had no other purpose and was dedicated to iSCSI. Click **Next**.

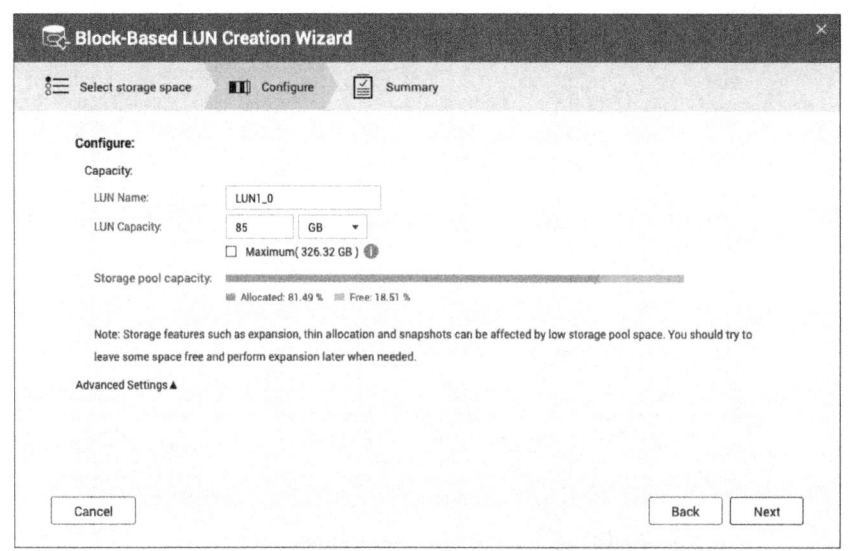

Figure 245: Configuring LUN Capacity

A Summary screen is displayed. Click **Finish** and you will be returned to the main Storage & Snapshots screen, where the details will now be listed in the *iSCSI Storage* section once the LUN is ready. This may take a short while, depending on the size of the LUN and selected options.

Connecting a Client

Having set up the LUN(s) on the server, the client computer(s) can now be connected. This section describes how to do so with modern versions of Windows. There is no built-in capability on macOS, although third party solutions may be available.

Windows 11 – click the **Search** icon on the taskbar and search for **iSCSI Initiator**.
Windows 10 - click **Start > Windows Administrative Tools > iSCSI Initiator**.
Windows 7 - go into **Control Panel** on the Windows PC, choose **Administrative Tools** and within it launch **iSCSI Initiator**.

The first time you do this you may receive a message stating that the Microsoft iSCSI service is not running – click **Yes** to start the service and it will start up automatically on subsequent occasions. In the *Target* field on the Targets tab, enter the IP address of the server and click **Quick Connect**. The target should be quickly found and a status of *Connected* shown:

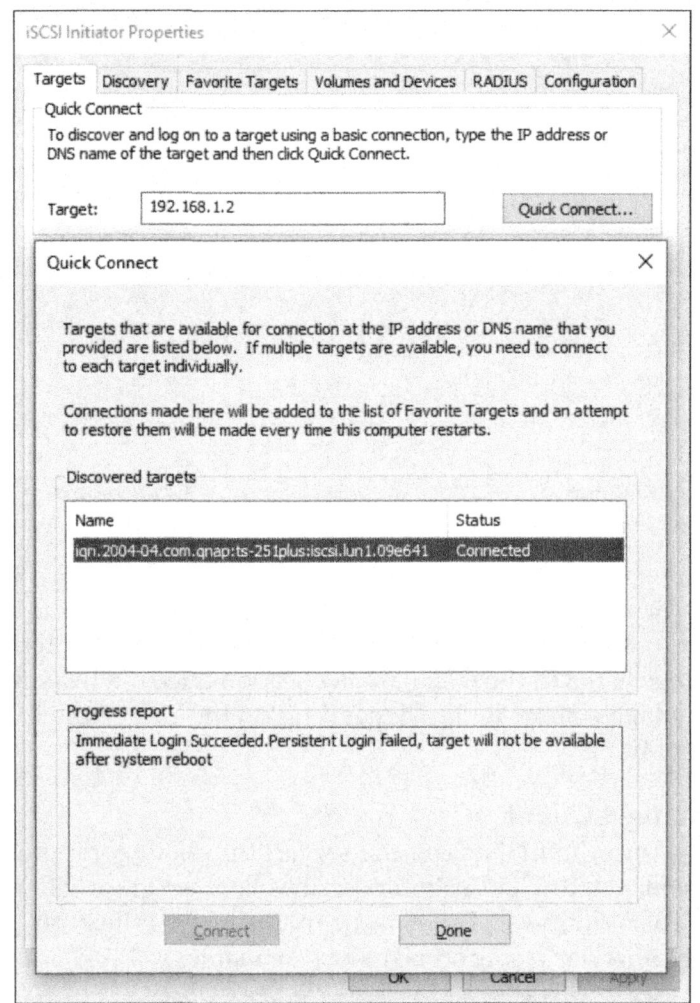

Figure 246: Connecting to the Target

Click **Done** and **OK**. Go back to **Administrative Tools** and choose **Computer Management**; within it choose **Disk Management**. You will receive a message about having to initialize the new disk. If the disk is less than 2TB in size choose MBR, if greater than 2TB you will need to choose GPT. Click **OK**.

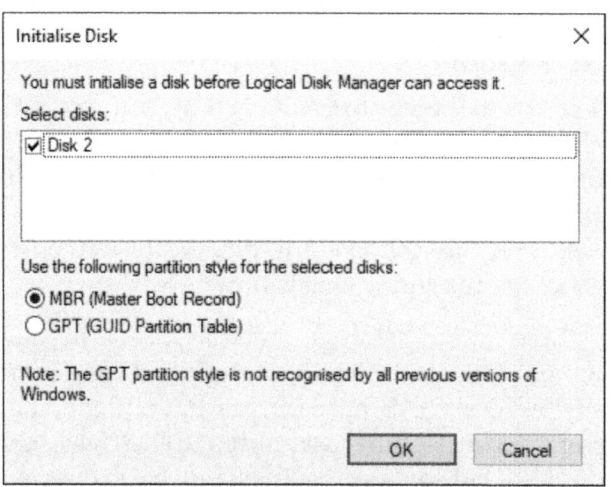

Figure 247: Disk initialization

The new disk will then be visible within Disk Management. Right-click it and choose **New Simple Volume**. Run through the *New Simple Volume Wizard* to create and format the volume and assign a drive letter to it; thereafter it can be used as a regular disk drive.

LUN Import/Export

LUNs can be exported to and imported from other locations. This provides a mechanism for transporting them to and from other NAS devices, and provides a way of backing them up (there is no explicit backup option for LUNs in Hybrid Backup Sync or elsewhere). To export a LUN, launch **iSCSI & Fibre Channel** from the **Main Menu**. Click **LUN Import/Export** followed by **Create a Job**. Choose *Export an iSCSI LUN* or *Import an iSCSI LUN* as required and select a location. LUNs can be stored on the same NAS or on a shared folder on a separate Linux or Windows server.

12.8 What is Qtier?

QNAP's *Qtier* is analogous to SSD caching but takes the concept further. With a cache, frequently used data is copied to the cache and accessed from there. However, the cache is only a copy of the original data, temporarily placed on a faster medium in order to provide quicker access. With tiering, data is physically moved to the most appropriate storage medium. This is how it works:

There are three main storage media used in large server deployments; SATA hard drives have good performance, high capacity and low cost; SAS hard drives have higher performance, slightly lower capacities but cost more; SSD drives have the best performance of all, but lower capacities and are expensive.

Data can be categorized as frequently used ('hot' data), less frequently used ('lukewarm' data) and rarely accessed (archival or 'cold' data). The principle behind tiering is that the system identifies which data is which based upon its usage and moves it automatically to the correct media. So, hot data will move to SSD, lukewarm data will move to SAS, and cold data will end up on SATA.

Tiering thus provides appropriate access to data whilst minimizing the overall cost of storage. Although most QNAP models support it, it is mainly of interest in corporate environments and data centers.

13

SURVEILLANCE

13.1 Overview

QVR Elite is an application from QNAP that turns a NAS into a fully functional CCTV surveillance system and network video recorder. It works with a wide variety of IP cameras and features include real-time monitoring, recording and playback, alarm notifications and Intelligent Video Analytics (IVA). Whether you wish to setup a single camera to monitor your home, a sophisticated system monitoring multiple business premises with dozens or hundreds of cameras, or any other monitoring requirement, then there is a good chance that *QVR Elite* is suitable. This chapter describes how to get started.

Note: the predecessor to QVR Elite was Surveillance Station. Although not supported on QNAP models manufactured from 2021 onwards, it can still be downloaded from the App Center and installed on older units. It is not covered in this guide.

13.2 Setting Up QVR Elite

Begin by downloading and installing QVR Elite from the App Center. It requires Container Station, so this will also be downloaded and installed if not already in place.

Once installed, launch QVR Elite from the **Main Menu** or by clicking its icon on the desktop. Click the **Start** button and the *QVR Elite Initial Setup* wizard will run; after it has confirmed that the NAS meets the minimum system requirements, click **Next**. Confirm that the date, time and time zone settings are correct by ticking the box and clicking **Apply**. The setup process will then continue and when it has done so, click **Finish**. The installation process creates a shared folder called *QVREliteSys* on the NAS, and this should not be changed in any way. QVR Elite will thereafter open in a new browser window, from where it may be necessary to login and you should do so as the administrator.

What you see may possibly surprise you, as it looks like a customized version of QTS specifically designed for running QVR Elite. It includes its own Main Menu, standard QTS features such as the Dashboard, Notifications and Search, along with icons for specific functions related to surveillance:

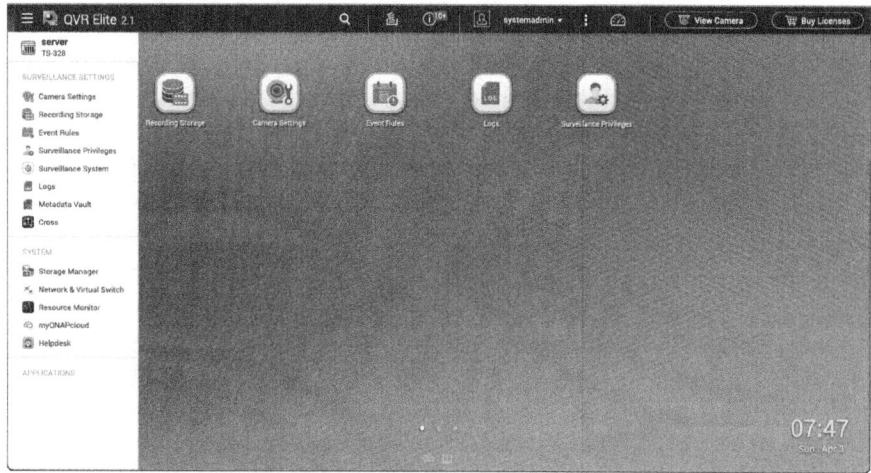

Figure 248: QVR Elite desktop screen

The Dashboard now has additional information relating to surveillance when viewed in QVR Elite, which does not show in the 'regular' QTS version:

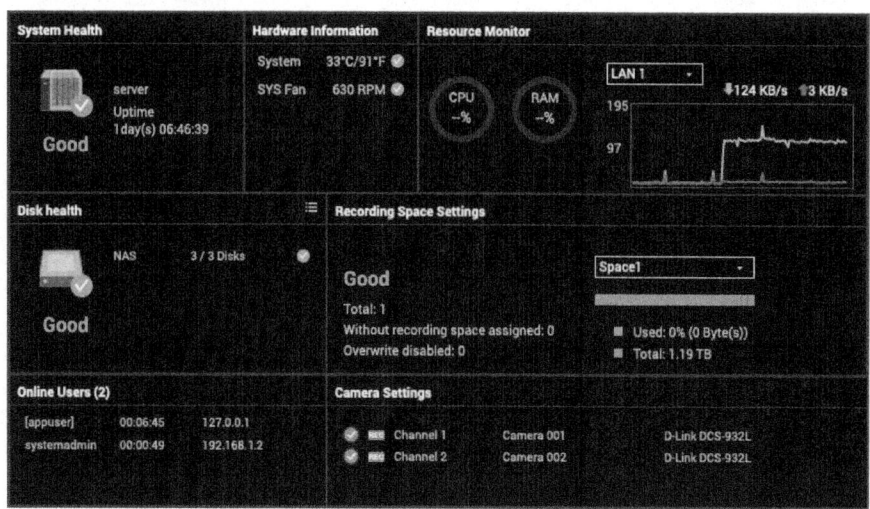

Figure 249: Dashboard in QVR Elite

313

Recording Storage

Decide where QVR Elite will store its recordings. Click **Recording Storage** from the app's **Main Menu** or its Desktop and click on the large plus (**+**) sign in the middle of the screen. Although an existing folder can be used, you may want to create a new folder specifically for this purpose (**Control Panel > Shared Folders > Create > Shared Folder**). In this example we are using a shared folder called *recordings*, to which the administrator user has full rights. A good choice is to use a dedicated volume for the recordings, should one be available. The *Maximum recording size* should be set at less than the *Current available size*, whilst the *Reserved storage space* should be set at 5% or greater. Click **Apply**:

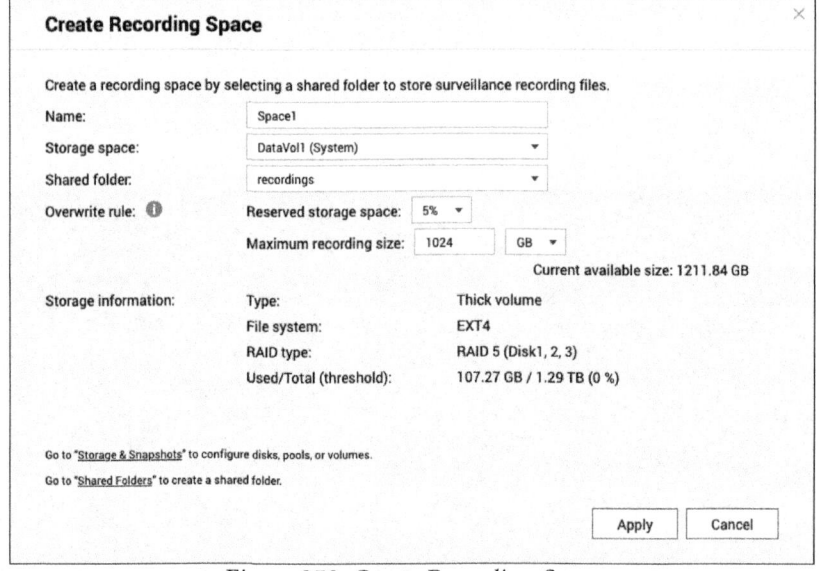

Figure 250: Create Recording Space

Camera Settings

After the recording space has been successfully added a message will appear, asking if you want to add a camera - click **Yes** and the *Camera Settings* screen is displayed. Before proceeding, note the following:

Each camera is referred to as a *channel* and requires a license. QNAP grant two free licenses and the screen will initially be listing the channel usage. If two channels (cameras) are insufficient, additional licenses can be obtained from QNAP. These paid licenses are provided on a subscription basis and up to 192 channels can be deployed, depending on the hardware capabilities of the NAS.

Prior to adding the cameras, they should first be separately configured for the local network, using the instructions and any software provided by the manufacturer. This process varies depending on the brand and model, but typically it is necessary to provide a username and password for security purposes and assign an IP address to the camera - make a note of these as they are important. All that is needed is that the camera is connected and operational; you do not want to sign-up to any services or install any other software for monitoring and recording.

On the *Camera Settings* screen, click the large plus (+) sign in the middle area of the screen.

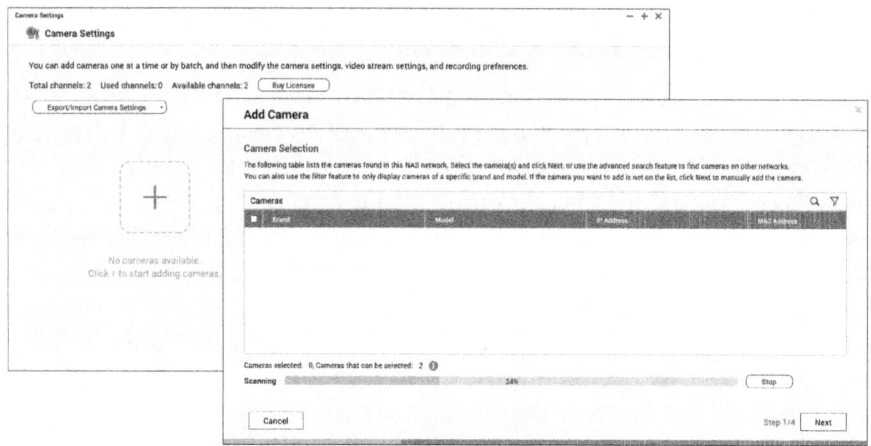

Figure 251: Camera Settings, Add Camera

The system will scan for cameras, which should be located within a short while. Click **Next**. On the subsequent screen, select the camera.

No camera found? Click **Next** anyway, click the **Add Manually** button which appears, then enter the details of the camera, choosing the *Brand* and *Model* using the dropdowns. If the exact model is not listed, choose the closest available e.g. if you had an *'AcmeCam 402'* but only the *'AcmeCam 401'* is listed, you could try that. Give it a name e.g. its location. Enter the *IP Address* and *Port* number (80). Specify the *User Name* and *Password* for the camera – these are the ones that were used whilst setting up the camera and are unrelated to any user accounts on the NAS itself. Click the **Test** button and if everything has been done correctly you will be able to see a small preview image from the camera.

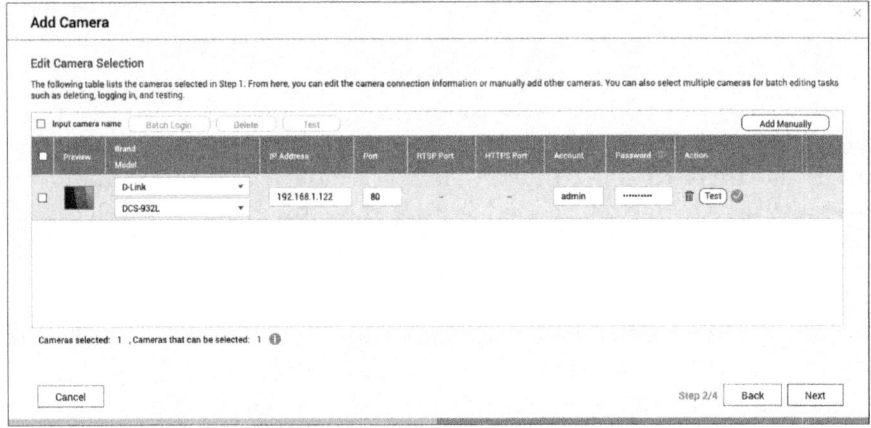

Figure 252: Edit Camera Selection

Click **Next**. A message is displayed, asking *'Do you want to modify the settings before adding the cameras to the list?'*. Choose the **Edit now** option and click **OK** to display the *Stream & Recording* panel. Use the tick-boxes to enable/disable video and audio recording as required. To adjust the video parameters of the camera (resolution, frame rate, quality), click the **Stream Settings** button. For instance, a lower frame rate might be better for some applications. Schedules can be defined for cameras. For instance, you may have premises that only need to be monitored during the night-time and at weekends, when they are unoccupied. To add a schedule, click the small plus (+) sign on the right-hand side of the screen. On the resultant panel, select the *Active* and *Inactive* boxes as required and drag the mouse cursor to 'paint' the schedule. When complete, click **Apply**:

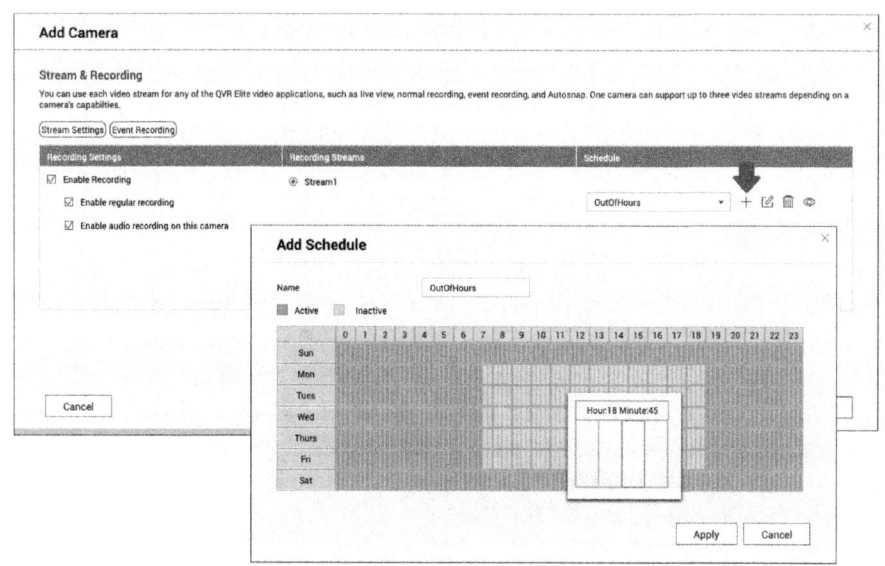

Figure 253: Stream & Recording and Scheduling options

Returning to the previous screen, click **Next**, followed by **Finish** on the one after that.

A *Confirm Settings* panel is displayed. Review the choices and click **Next**, followed by **Finish** on the next panel and you will be returned to the main screen. On the *Camera Settings* screen, the newly added camera will be listed, along with a thumbnail displaying a live feed:

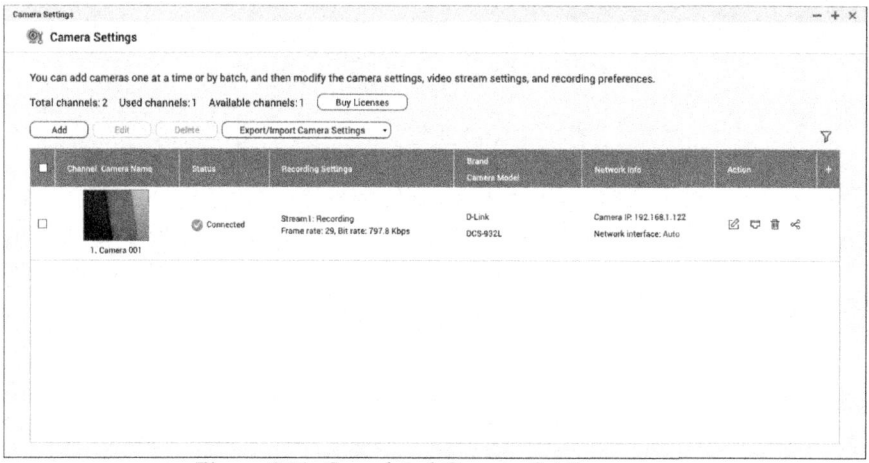

Figure 254: Completed Camera Setting screen

317

At this point the camera is operational. There are numerous options available to control cameras, recordings and how the system responds to trigger events, such as movement, and these can be explored if your requirements are more sophisticated. These options are managed by clicking the **Event Rules** icon on the desktop.

Event Rules

Event Rules define conditions under which specific actions take place in QVR Elite. For instance, rather than have a camera recording constantly, it can be programmed to only start recording when it detects motion (assuming the camera has such capability). To define a rule, click the **Event Rules** icon on the desktop, followed by the large plus (+) sign. Give the rule a *Name* and an optional *Description*. Specify a *Schedule* using the dropdown or click the small plus sign (+) icon to create a new one. Click **Next**.

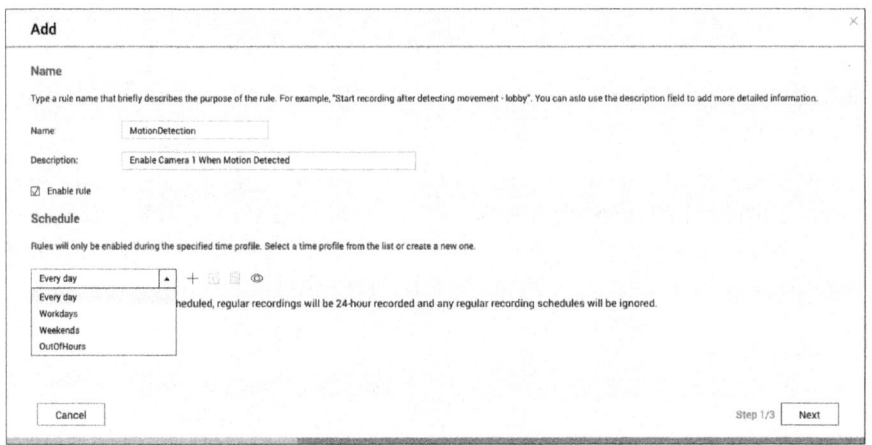

Figure 255: Adding a new Event Rule

The subsequent screen is for specifying the trigger event(s) and works on an 'If... Then' basis. Click the **Add** buttons. Upon returning to the underlying screen, make sure the boxes are ticked and click **Next**, followed by **Finish** on the third and final screen.

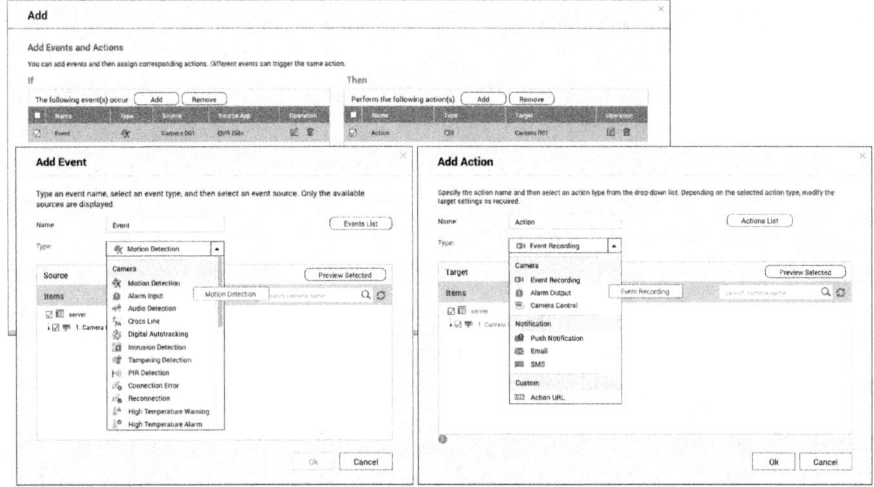

Figure 256: Specifying Events & Actions

Logs

QVR Elite generates log files containing records of the various events that take place. These can be used to help determine problems, such as non-responsive cameras, unexpected occurrences or storage-related issues. To view the log files, click the **Logs** icon on the desktop. The dropdown at the top of the screen is used to select the log to be viewed.

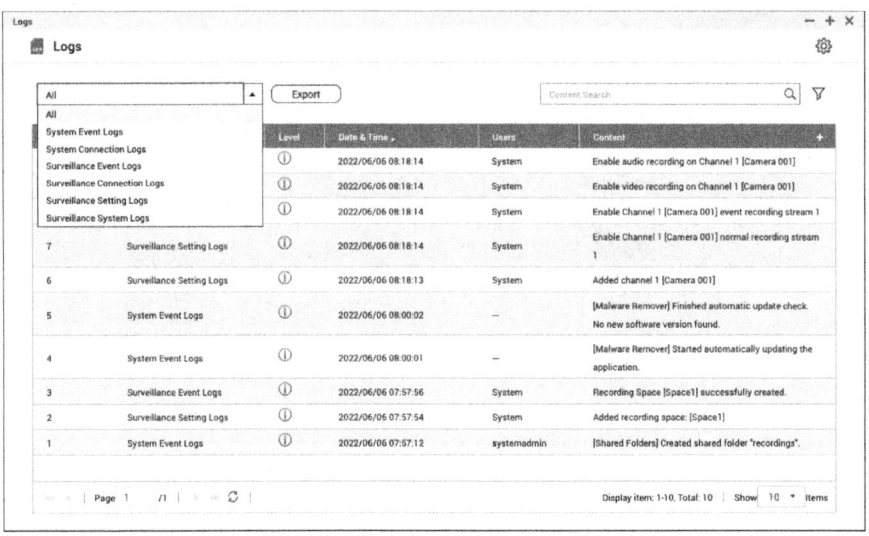

Figure 257: Viewing the Log files

319

Surveillance Privileges

Users need to be given privileges in order to use QVR Elite and this is done by clicking the **Surveillance Privileges** icon on the desktop. Privileges can be assigned on an individual or group basis, with the process being analogous to that of managing users from the Control Panel. However, one addition is that users are assigned specific *roles*. Launch **Surveillance Privileges**. The *Users* screen lists all the users defined on the NAS; to assign privileges, highlight a user and click the *Select User Role* mini icon against their name (it is the fifth one listed). On the resultant panel, choose one of the three roles (and it is possible to define further ones):

administrator-qvr – this is the default administrator of the QVR Elite system. Usually, there should only be one such user (possibly with a further backup administrator).

supervisor – a supervisor can view all cameras and recordings, but cannot change the system.

viewer – a viewer can browse the cameras, but does not have access to recordings and cannot change the system

Tick the appropriate role box and click **OK**.

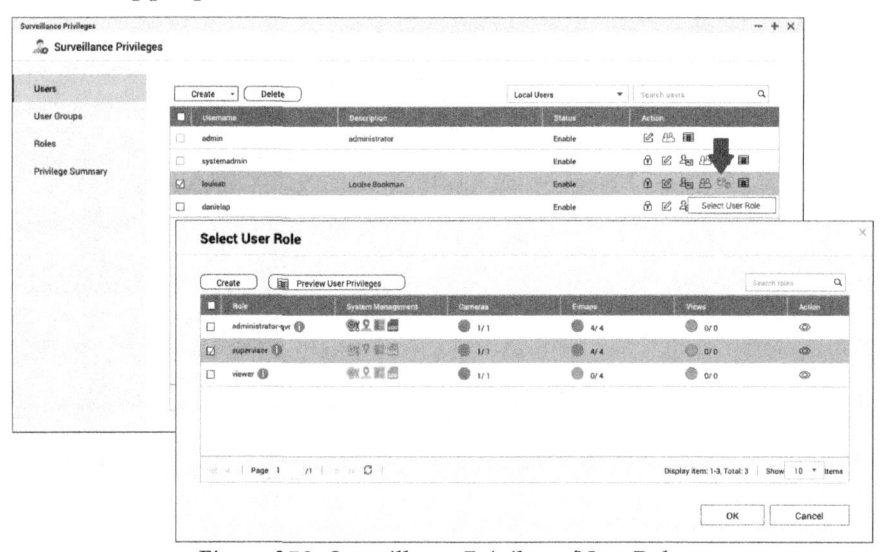

Figure 258: Surveillance Privileges/User Roles

13.3 QVR Pro Client

Viewing the cameras requires the *QVR Pro Client* app, available for macOS, Windows and HD Station from QNAP's website, and for Android and iOS from the appropriate App Stores. If the **View Camera** icon within the QVR Elite desktop is clicked, a panel with download links and QR codes is provided.

In this example, the Windows version is being used. Upon running it for the first time, choose the **QVR Pro/Elite** option and enter the details of the *Host server*, which can be in the form of the myQNAPcloud name or the internal IP address of the server, along with a *User name* and *password*. Tick the **Secure login** box and click the **Log In** button. A short introduction is displayed, thereafter the main screen appears along the following lines. Available cameras are listed on the left-hand side of the screen and double-clicking one will cause the live image to appear. The app operates in two modes, *Live* and *Playback*, controlled by the buttons towards the bottom of the screen.

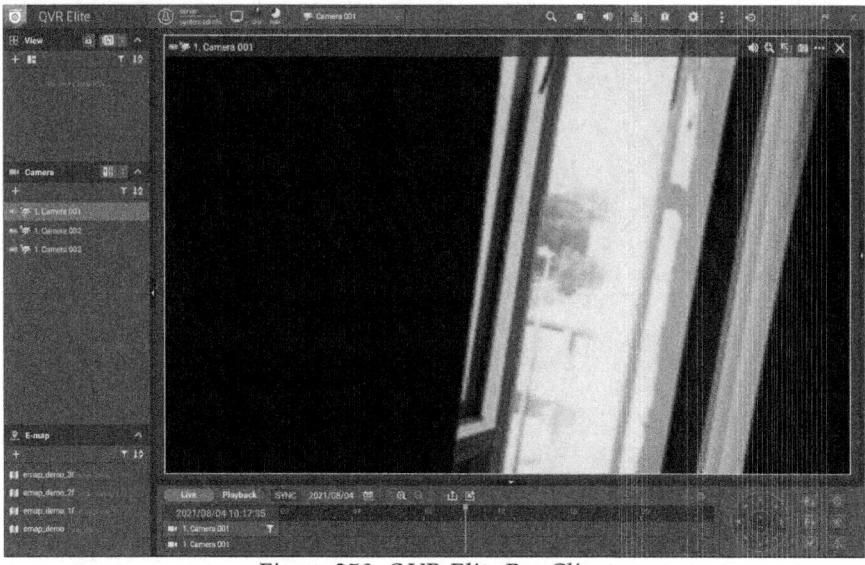

Figure 259: QVR Elite Pro Client

To control a camera, click the Live Panel mini icon in the lower right-hand corner of the screen (this icon operates as a toggle switch). The facilities available depend upon the capabilities of the camera, such as the ability to move the camera and zoom.

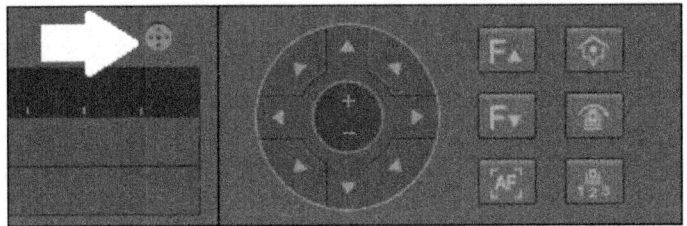

Figure 260: Camera controls

If multiple cameras are in use, different views can be selected from the View section in the top left-hand corner of the screen. A number of pre-defined layouts are provided, or you can create your own:

Figure 261: View options for multiple cameras

QVR supports E-Maps, where a plan for the premises can be overlayed with the location of the cameras. The maps can be drawings or photographs in popular graphics file formats, and the cameras are 'dragged' into position using the mouse. Once this is done, the map can be saved for future use:

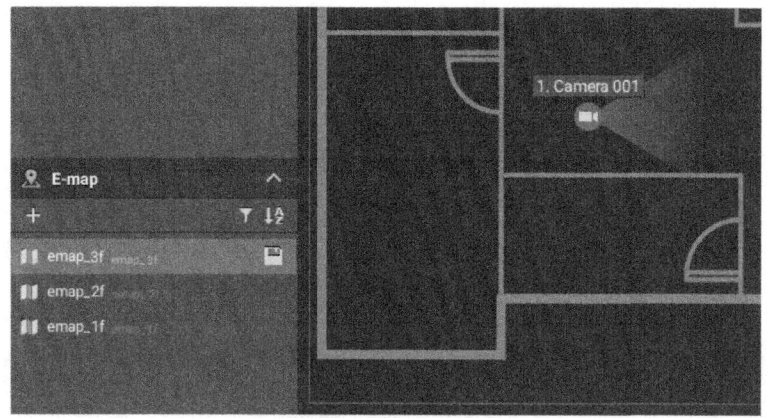

Figure 262: E-Map

Playback of Recordings

To playback videos, change mode by clicking the **Playback** mode button towards the bottom of the screen. Select the video using the timeline; as the 'cursor' is moved, a small preview is shown. The scale of the timeline can be adjusted using the small plus (**+**) and minus (**-**) icons. For earlier recordings, click the calendar icon and navigate using the pop-up calendar. Play, pause, fast forward and rewind controls are provided, plus the playback speed can be adjusted from 0.1x to 16.0x using the slider control.

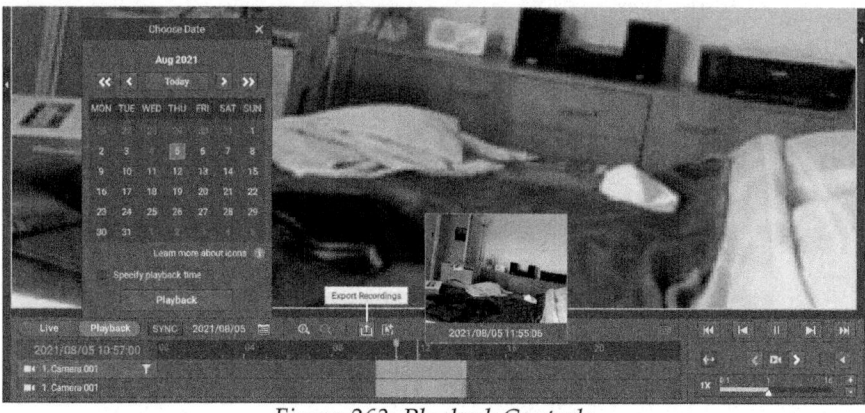

Figure 263: Playback Controls

To export a recording – for instance, so it can be kept permanently or used as evidence – click the **Export Recordings** icon. Use the panel that appears to specify the start time and duration of the video, and the storage location on the local computer. Videos are stored as .avi files on Windows computers.

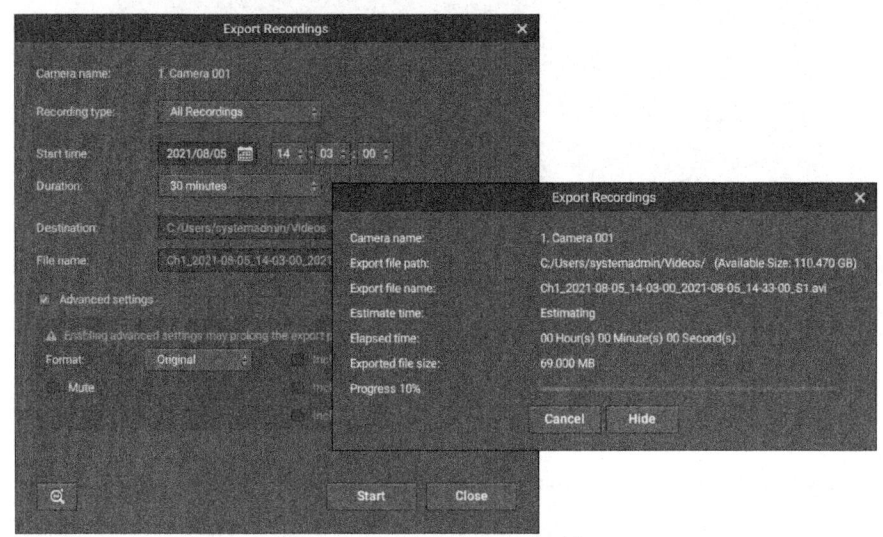

Figure 264: Exporting a video

14
VIRTUALIZATION

14.1 Overview

A number of QNAP models support *virtualization*, enabling them to run other operating systems alongside QTS, such as Windows or Linux, or multiple copies of QTS in the form of QuTS Cloud. These capabilities provide enormous benefits to corporate users, but virtualization is so accessible with QNAP that it becomes practical for small business and home users, too. Here are some practical examples of using virtualization:

- A home user can have two discrete systems running on a single NAS, one to provide multimedia and streaming capabilities to the household, the other for experimentation, testing and learning
- A school has several classes and wishes to provide totally separate networks for each of them. By running multiple copies of QuTS on a single powerful server, they can potentially reduce costs, complexity and physical space requirements
- A small business is in the progress of migrating away from Microsoft Windows Server to QNAP for general purpose use but needs to retain a copy of Windows Server in order to continue running a specialized accounting application for a small number of users. Using virtualization, they can do this on the QNAP NAS, dispensing with the old server hardware and saving on overall running costs
- Access to other operating systems, such as Windows or Linux, is required for testing and support purposes
- Running a ready-made application 'appliance' in its own secure space

The main reason that virtualization is possible is that NAS boxes, like most computers, spend much of their time doing very little. Although they may be running apps, maintaining communications and serving up files, typically they are sitting there quietly, waiting for requests. As such, they have a lot of spare time (i.e. low resource utilization) which can be put to better use, such as running additional operating systems.

QNAP support several different virtualization technologies:

Virtualization Station - this can handle many different types of operating system. It requires an x86-based system with 4GB RAM or more.

Container Station - this integrates LXD and Docker technologies to create a 'lite' form of virtualization that runs Linux-based virtual machines. It is available both for x86-based systems and modern 64-bit ARM systems with 2GB RAM or more, although capabilities may vary across models.

Note: Container Station will work with older LXC images, but it is strongly recommended that you use LXD ones. Support for LXC will be dropped in future versions of Container Station.

QuTS Cloud – can run on Virtualization Station, or on public clouds such as Amazon EC2, Azure, Alibaba Cloud, Catalyst Cloud and Digital Ocean.

The first two options are introduced in this chapter.

14.2 Virtualization Station and Installing Windows

Full virtualization on QNAP is provided by *Virtualization Station*, downloadable from the App Center. It makes use of the *Network & Virtual Switch* app, which will have been pre-loaded automatically during the installation of QTS. An icon for Virtualization Station will be placed on the desktop and it is also accessible from the Main Menu.

Launching Virtualization Station will display a *Welcome Screen*. This may advise that the virtual network adapter needs to be created – click **Finish** to do so. The Virtualization Station *Overview* screen appears as follows (there may be an advertisement for *VM Marketplace*, where ready-to-use virtual machines can be obtained):

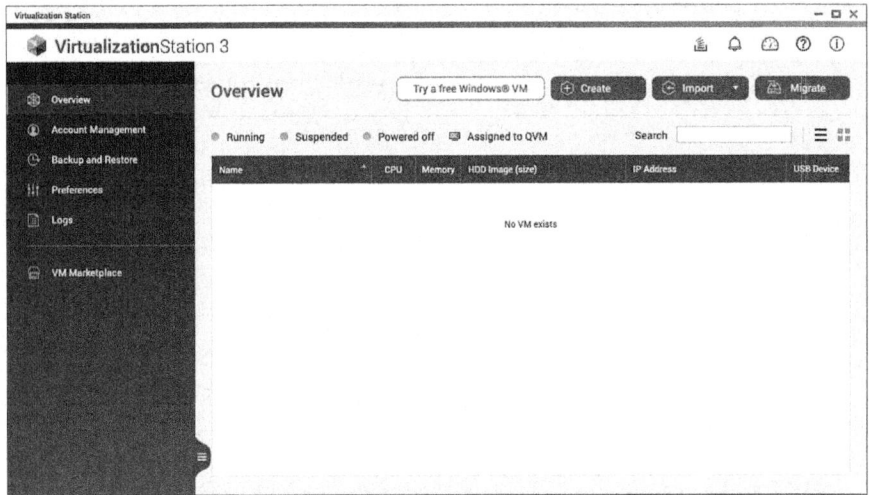

Figure 265: Virtualization Overview screen

A virtualized operating system is referred to as a *Virtual Machine* or *VM*. There are four main options from the overview screen: *Create* a new virtual machine from scratch; *Import* an existing virtual machine created previously on another computer; *Migrate* a running VM from another QNAP NAS; *Try a free Windows VM* (a time-limited, pre-built VM intended for testing different versions of Windows and different browsers). In this example we will create a new VM, as this illustrates more of what is involved with Virtualization Station. Click **Create VM** to display the following panel:

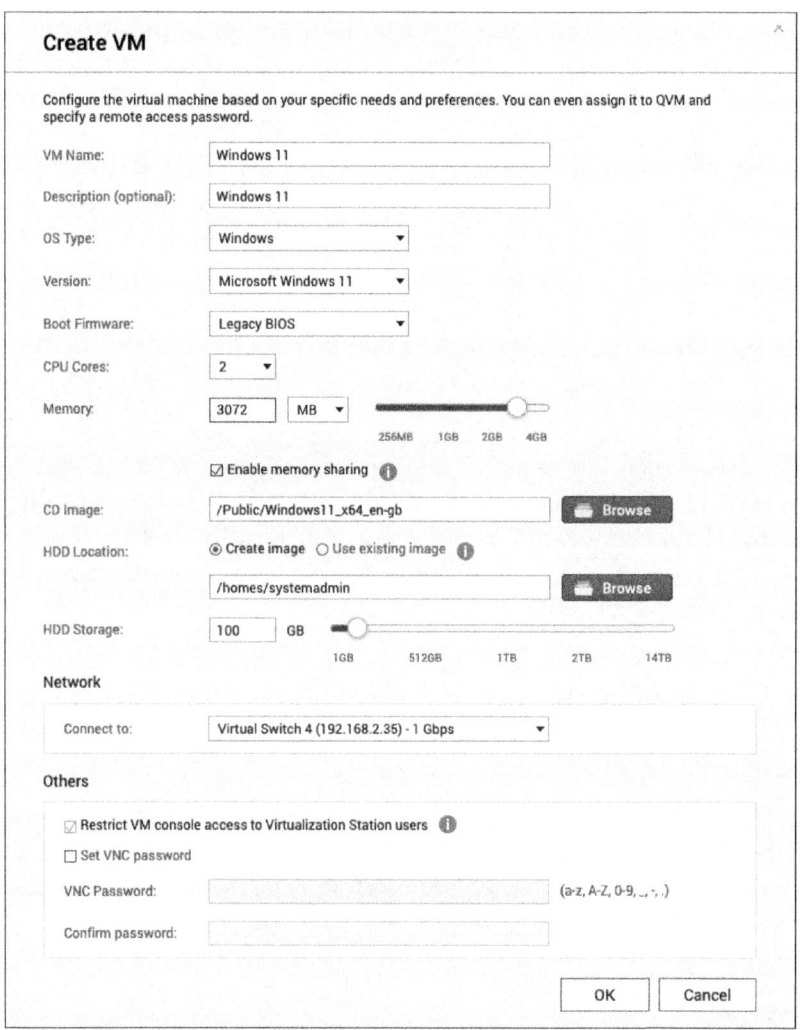

Figure 266: Create VM panel

Enter a meaningful name for the VM and optionally specify a description; Virtualization Station will use these to infer the *OS Type* and *Version*, but if incorrect you can use the dropdowns to change them. The *Boot Firmware* can be Legacy BIOS or UEFI, depending on the requirements of the operating system. Specify how many CPU cores the VM should have and how much memory should be allocated; the options and limits here depend on the specification of your NAS and requirements of the operating system, but the general principle is 'the more the better'. In this example we are running Windows 11, with dual CPU cores and 3GB of RAM.

Specify where the *CD Image* is to be found. Operating systems are usually distributed in *ISO format*, even if they are not physically on CDs or DVDs (and when the OS is not in ISO format, third-party utilities exist to convert it). It is suggested that you keep the ISO files in a suitable location on the NAS; click the **Browse** button to locate them. The *HDD Location* and amount of storage also need to be defined; this is a virtual hard disk or, in simple terms, a file masquerading as a hard drive and the storage represents the maximum size it can grow to, although in practice it only takes the space it needs. The *Network* setting can be left as is unless you have a specific requirement, such as working with a dedicated physical adapter.

In the *Others* section, a *VNC password* can be set. VNC is short for *Virtual Networking Computing* and is a utility for viewing the virtual machine. In a corporate environment you would probably want to password protect it, but in a home or small environment you may choose not to. Click **OK**.

In the case of some operating systems, Virtualization Station will detect it and offer an 'Auto Install' option to slightly simplify the installation. In this example we have declined it, in order to have full control over the process.

The Overview screen will now be updated to show the newly prepared VM. The images are 'live', with running ones showing thumbnail images of the screens and status showing the CPU and Memory utilization:

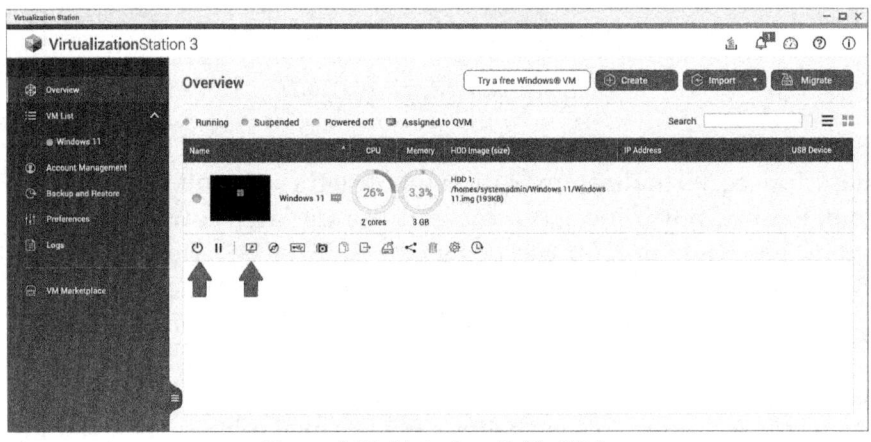

Figure 267: List of available VMs

Having done the preparation, the next step is to run the Windows installation process. On the list of mini icons, click the left-hand side one to power up the virtual machine. Then, click the third one along (it looks like a small computer screen), which will open a new tab in the browser to display the virtual machine, courtesy of the VNC viewer; alternatively, you can click the thumbnail screen. The installation and setup should now be performed in the standard manner for the specific operating system.

Upon completion, it is recommended to install *Guest Tools*, which are helper programs to assist the operating system perform better in a virtualized environment. Go into the VM and click the tab in bottom left-hand corner to expand the options; click **VM Information** followed by **Insert Guest Tools CD**:

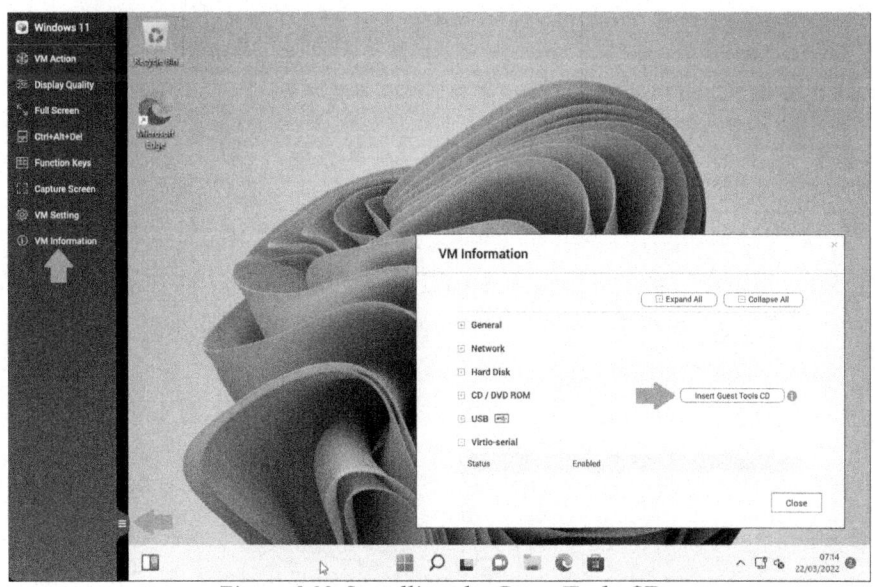

Figure 268: Installing the Guest Tools CD

Click **Close**, launch Windows Explorer, double-click the CD drive and run the *qnap-guest-tools* program. After it has completed, it is suggested that you restart Windows.

A virtualized operating system can be used in exactly the same way as a real computer, with the proviso that performance is dependent on the hardware specification of the NAS and it may be slower than an actual PC. To maximize performance, ensure that the VM has sufficient RAM allocated to it and consider storing VMs on SSDs.

If an active VM is not used for any length of time, the tab containing it will logoff, as with a regular QTS screen, although the VM will continue to run. A Virtualization Station login screen will be displayed, from where the user can login again i.e. it is not necessary for the administrator user to do anything on the server to restore the session.

14.3 Container Station

Container Station can be thought of as a 'lite' form of virtualization that runs Linux virtual machines and specific applications. It has less demanding hardware requirements than Virtualization Station and is available for both x86 and 64-bit ARM QNAP models. QNAP advise a minimum of 4GB RAM for Container Station, but in practice it may run in less, at least for less demanding tasks. If the NAS is short of memory, stop any unnecessary apps (see **15.2 App Center**) and use Qboost to free up RAM (see **8.9 Qboost**).

A *Container* is a self-contained applications environment, largely isolated from the underlying supporting operating system, which in this case is QTS. This approach offers good performance and enhanced security. A container is created using an *Image* file, which is a read-only template. The image may contain a version of Linux e.g. Ubuntu, or a specific application e.g. WordPress. Images come in three flavors: *Docker*, *App* and *LXD*. Images files can be built-in to Container Station, imported from a PC or NAS, or downloaded from a hub.

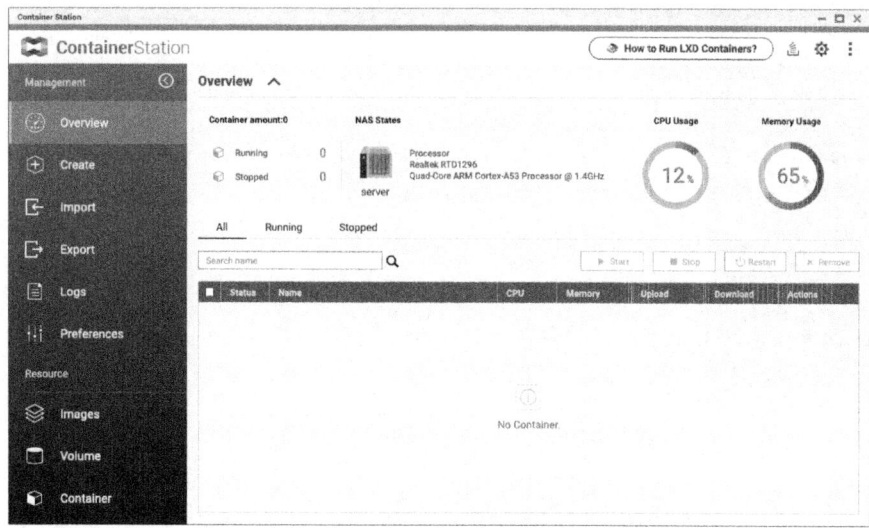

Figure 269: Container Station Overview screen

The containers that are created using the image files and can be readable, writable and executable. In simple terms, they are the things that 'do stuff'.

Multiple containers can be created by a single image. Containers come in two flavors: LXD containers are created by LXD images and Docker containers are created by Docker images.

Download and install Container Station from the App Center. Upon running it for the first time it will create a shared folder called *Container* for storing images and containers. Click **Start Now** and after a short delay the above screen is displayed:

Creating a Docker Container

Click **Create** and a list of popular images in different formats will be displayed. However, tens of thousands of other Docker images exist and the one we want, WordPress, is not shown. Type 'wordpress' in the *Search apps or images* box and hit enter. The results screen contains several categories (IoT, AI, Docker Hub etc) and we want the results from the Docker Hub section - think of it as a sort of App Center for images. Choose one by clicking **Install**. This may result in an additional dialog box with a dropdown, giving a choice of versions:

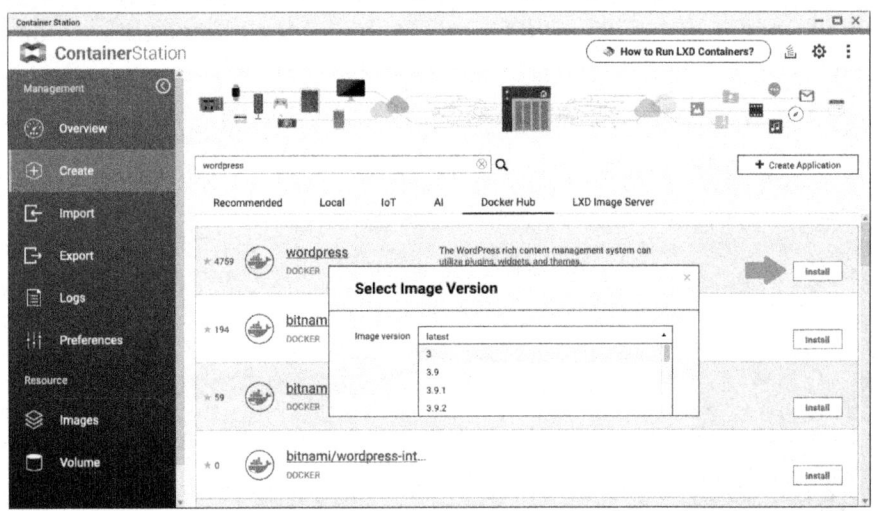

Figure 270: Searching for a Docker container

The next panel is for naming the container and specifying memory and CPU limits. Adjust if necessary and click **Create** then **OK** on the resultant summary screen:

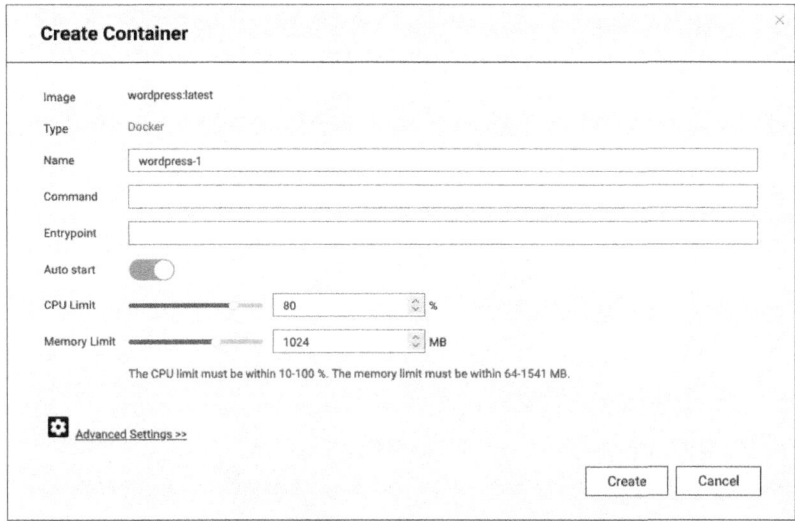

Figure 271: Creating a Container

The container will now be downloaded and created, which may take a short while, then listed on the *Overview* screen, from where it can be managed. Clicking on the name of a container will display a larger panel.

Figure 272: Options for monitoring and managing a container

If you are new to containers and Docker, you might find it slightly underwhelming as they are mostly for running 'black box' appliances and do not appear to do very much in a visual sense. However, you may have noticed when installing some QNAP applications that they also require Container Station to be installed, which illustrates what it is capable of.

14.4 Ubuntu Linux Station

Whereas Virtualization Station can run a wide variety of operating systems, *Ubuntu Linux Station*, as the name suggests, is specifically for running a popular Linux distribution and if this is your requirement, it provides a more streamlined approach. Running Linux on your NAS provides access to a wide variety of applications, including LibreOffice, Chrome, Spotify and Plex, plus is also a good option for software developers. If the NAS has an HDMI output, it can be used as a complete Linux system if a suitable screen is connected and a keyboard and mouse are plugged into the USB ports. Alternatively, Linux can be viewed in a browser tab. To run Ubuntu Linux Station, a supported NAS with at least 4GB RAM is needed. On multimedia models, HybridDesk Station and Ubuntu Linux Station cannot be used simultaneously as both require exclusive use of the HDMI port.

Download and install Ubuntu Linux Station from the App Center. It requires an additional component in the form of *Container Station*, so this will also be downloaded if it is not already installed. Upon accessing Ubuntu Linux Station for the first time, a screen with links to several Ubuntu Linux distributions from the third-party *Linux Containers* website is displayed. Choose one and the distribution will be downloaded and installed, which may take a while depending on the speed of your internet connection. Upon completion, a screen along the following lines is shown. Make a note of the remote desktop/VNC IP address for accessing it, which will have been derived from the IP address of the NAS. Check that the **Enable Remote Desktop** option is ticked.

There are some basic controls on the screen, enabling the copy of Linux to be Enabled (i.e. startup automatically), Restarted, Reinstalled and Uninstalled. In the Output Settings section, the screen resolution and audio output can be specified, along with the Network Settings, although the default values should be suitable.

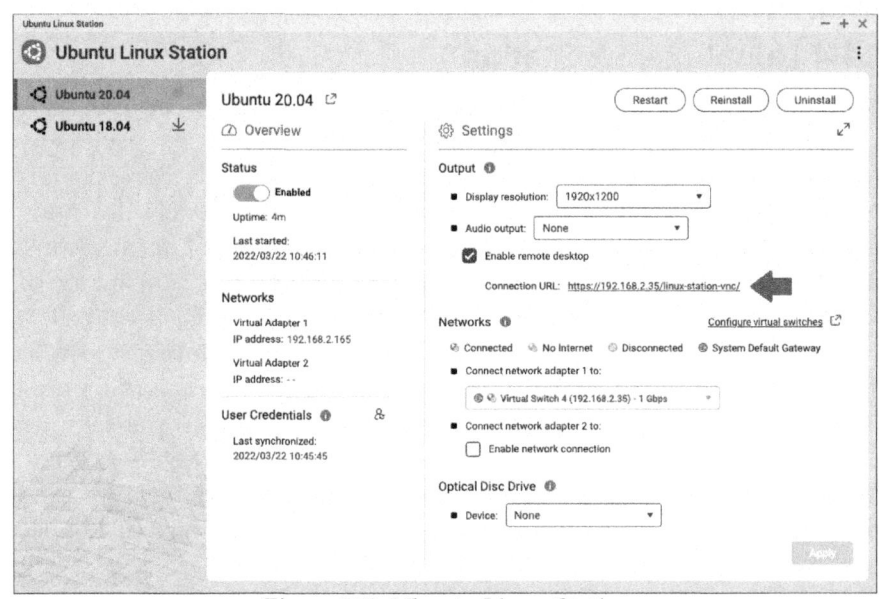

Figure 273: Ubuntu Linux Station

To access the Linux system, click or enter the URL/IP address for the remote desktop/VNC, which will cause it to be displayed in a new browser tab. It is necessary to login and QNAP have cleverly arranged matters so that the NAS admin credentials are carried across i.e. login as the administrator with the same password as QTS. When finished with Linux, logout and close the browser window.

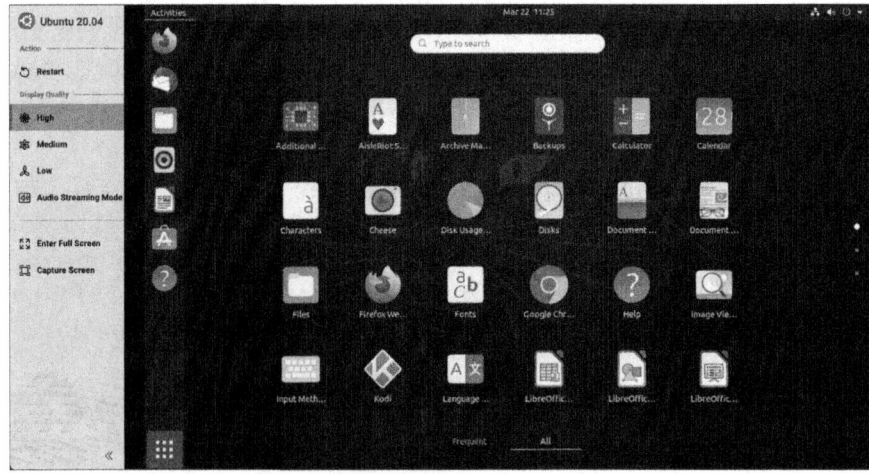

Figure 274: Linux Station running

338

15

MISCELLANEOUS & ADVANCED TOPICS

15.1 Overview

This chapter contains a selection of miscellaneous topics which do not easily fit elsewhere, along with those of a more advanced or specialized nature.

15.2 App Center

Whilst the QTS operating system has a huge amount of useful functionality built-in, it is possible to greatly extend it further through the installation of optional packages or apps, the vast majority of which are free. Some of these have already been discussed in this book, but many others are available. Some have been developed by QNAP, whilst others are supplied by third parties. Some are business focused, others are aimed more at home users, whilst some are suitable for both.

To review what is available, click on the **App Center** icon located on the QTS Desktop. The first time it is accessed, a quick tour is shown. When complete, click the **Not display** button to prevent it displaying subsequently. The App Center itself appears as follows:

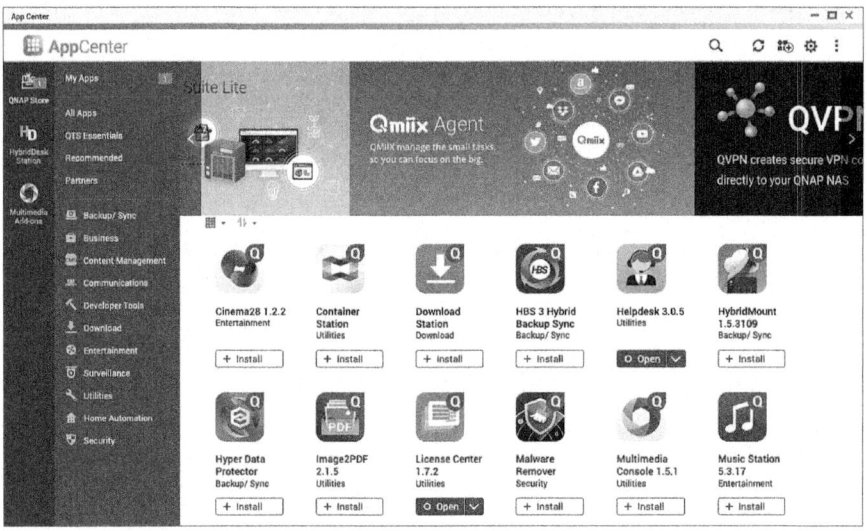

Figure 275: App Center

The apps are organized into categories such as Backup/Sync, Business, Communications, Entertainment, Utilities and so on. Not all apps are available for or suitable for all NAS models, although the majority are, whilst those unsuitable for your NAS will not be listed (there are more apps available for x86-based than ARM-based models). Besides the general purpose or universal apps, there are additional Multimedia Add-ons listed in their own section. If your NAS supports HDMI and HybridDesk Station (see section **9.10 HybridDesk Station**), then you will have a further section listing HybridDesk Station-specific apps. QNAP categorize some apps as *QTS Essentials*; this description is slightly misleading and should really be interpreted as meaning that they are official QNAP developed and branded apps (these icons are branded with the letter Q in the top-right hand corner).

Managing Apps

Apps which have been installed are listed in the *My Apps* section, from where they can be managed. Once an app has been installed, options appear beneath its entry in the App Center, enabling it to be controlled. For example, it can be used to temporarily switch off infrequently apps without necessarily having to uninstall them and will also advise of when updates are available. It is possible to control whether the app is listed on the user's Main Menu or on every user's menu, with the available options depending on the app:

Figure 276: Managing an App

Sometimes there will be a requirement to update an existing app, for instance to add features or because of a recent QTS firmware upgrade. This will be indicated by a separate message displayed on the QTS desktop, as well as within App Center. In some instances, the update may be necessary to maintain functionality.

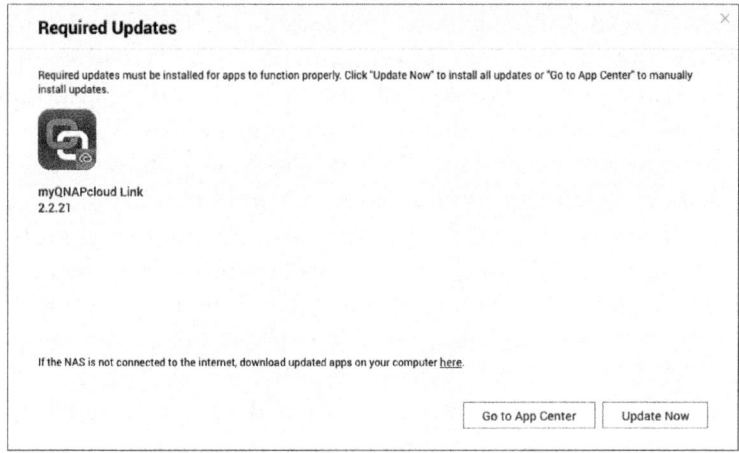

Figure 277: Required update

Manually Installing an App

Whilst apps are normally downloaded and installed from the QNAP Store within the App Center, there may be occasions when you need to do so manually, bypassing this process. For instance: QNAP may have released an early beta or test version of the app and it is not yet in the QNAP Store; you are a software developer, producing your own apps; a third-party has developed an app which is not available through the QNAP Store (you need to be careful in these circumstances as unauthorized apps may harm your data or system or leave it open to attack).

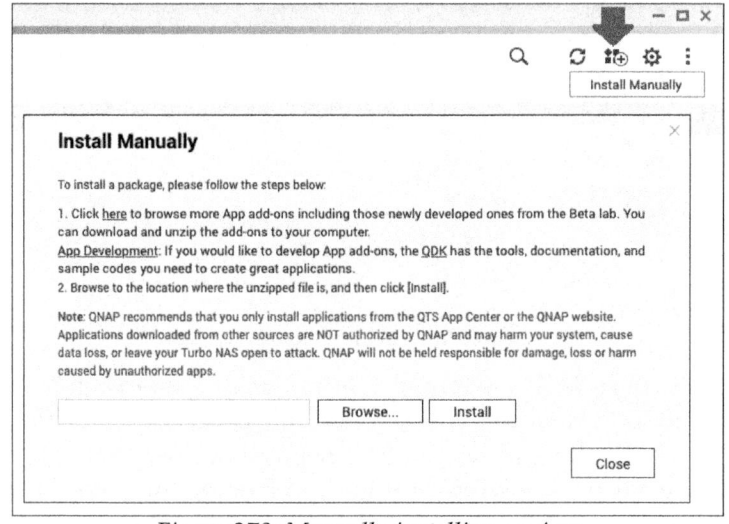

Figure 278: Manually installing an App

To install an app manually, download the packaged app onto your computer. Within App Center, click the **Install Manually** icon in the top-right hand corner of the screen, browse to the download, select it and click the **Install** button.

What Apps Are Other People Downloading?

You might have very specific ideas of how you wish to use your QNAP NAS and will choose packages accordingly. But some people, perhaps just starting out, are interested to know what other people are doing. The following statistics, derived from the App Center, show the number of downloads for some of the packages covered in this manual, as of June 2022. These numbers are not absolute – for instance, some packages may be downloaded but not subsequently used – but give an indication.

Container Station, 4.0 million. See **14.3 Container Station**

Download Station, 5.9 million. See **10.6 Download Station**

Hybrid Backup Sync, 8.8 million. See **7.2 Hybrid Backup Sync**

HybridMount, 1.7 million. See **11.5 HybridMount**

Music Station, 6.9 million. See **9.4 Music Station**

Notes Station, 0.4 million. See **10.5 Notes Station**

Photo Station, 10.7 million. See **9.6 Photo Station**

Qsirch, 1.3 million. See **10.2 Qsirch**

QuMagie, 0.8 million. See **9.5 QuMagie**

QVPN Service, 3.1 million. See **11.6 Virtual Private Networks (VPN)**

Video Station, 6.4 million. See **9.7 Video Station**

15.3 Help Center & Helpdesk

The *Help Center* provides help and assistance in the operation of the NAS and is launched from its desktop icon or from the Main Menu. There are three main sections: *QTS Manual* - a built-in reference guide covering various aspects of QTS; *Online Resources* – links to online resources including tutorials, forums, FAQ and more; *Helpdesk* – for obtaining support directly from QNAP. Clicking on **Helpdesk** displays the following screen (the first time it is accessed, a short overview is given):

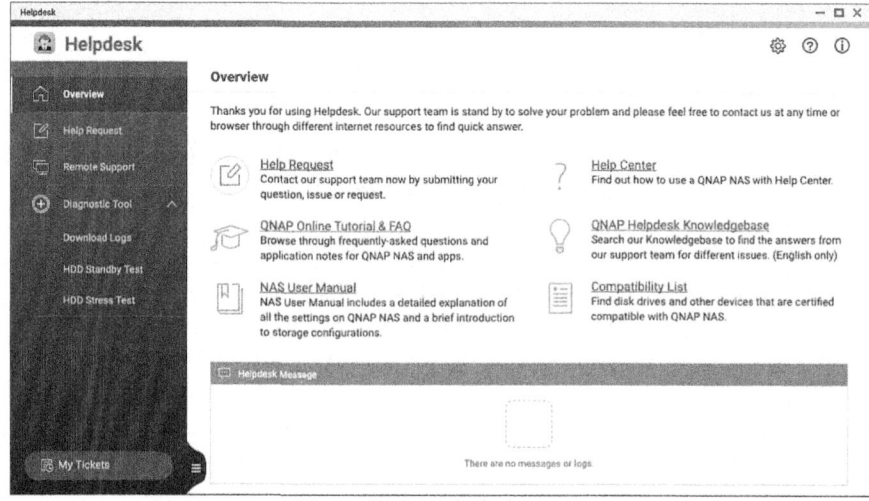

Figure 279: Helpdesk screen

The *Overview* screen within Helpdesk duplicates much of the Help Center's *Online Resources* screen. However, from here you can send support requests to QNAP, plus enable remote support so that they can, with your permission, connect to the NAS to diagnose and resolve problems. To obtain assistance, click the **Help Request** link and complete the resultant form as comprehensively as possible; if required, you can also send attachments such as screenshots. Tick the *I allow my system logs to be sent to QNAP to assist in providing support* box (it may already be ticked) then click **Submit**. Note: you need to have a QNAP ID and be signed in to use this feature.

If QNAP need to remotely access your NAS, they will email you a support ticket number or *Ticket ID*. Click the **Remote Support** tab, enter the Ticket ID and your email address, then click the **Enable Remote Support** button.

15.4 License Center

Most aspects of QTS and additional apps obtained through the App Center are completely free. In a small number of instances, additional licenses may need to be purchased and examples include commercial software such as McAfee Antivirus, additional camera licenses for use with QVR Elite, upgrades to Qfiling etc. These licenses can be purchased and managed through the License Center app, which is added automatically during the installation of QTS. Launching it from the Main Menu displays the following screen:

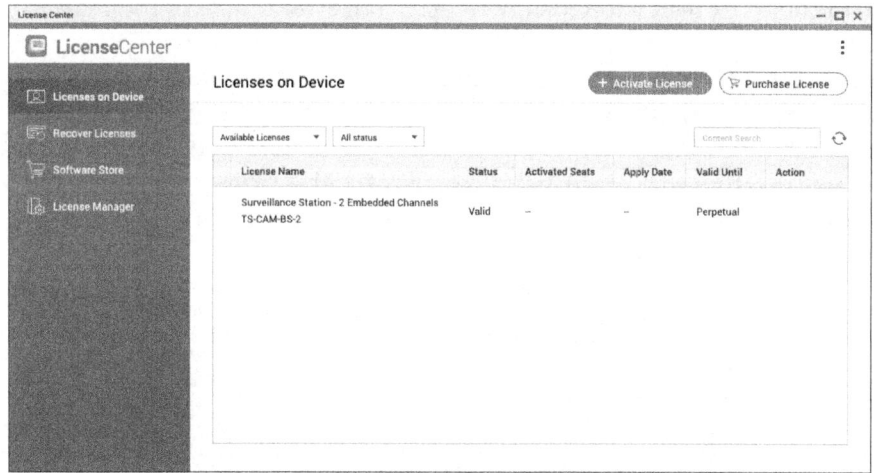

Figure 280: License Center

There are four panels within License Center:

Licenses on Device - Licenses are purchased through the *Software Store*. Their details are then added to the *Licenses on Device* screen by clicking the **Add** button, which invokes the License Activation screen. Purchasing software and licenses requires that you have a QNAP ID.

Recover Licenses - In the event of ever having to restore the NAS to factory default settings, the license information of installed apps will be lost. The Recover Licenses panel can be used to resolve this.

Software Store – This a link to the QNAP Software Store website.

License Manager – This is a dedicated website that enables licenses to be managed. It is particularly useful for larger organizations that may have many servers and many licenses.

15.5 Personalization Settings

The Desktop can be personalized by each user on an individual basis in several ways:

Icons: You can add icons that you find useful, whereas infrequently used icons can be removed. When viewing the Main Menu, drag an icon onto the Desktop to make a copy there. When using the Control Panel, right-click an icon and click **Create Shortcut**. To remove an icon from the Desktop, right-click it and choose **Remove**.

Language: A user can work with QTS in the language of their choice, regardless of what language the server is configured in. This can be useful in environments where multiple languages are used, such as English and Spanish in parts of the United States, or French and English in Canada. To switch language, click the three-dot snowman menu in the top right-hand corner of the screen, followed by **Language**. More than 20 widely used languages are available – click the desired one to switch.

Figure 281: Choosing a language

Desktop Preferences: if QTS is being accessed from a touch-sensitive device such as a tablet, rather than a desktop computer or laptop, choose **Desktop Preferences > Tab Mode (For Touchscreen)** to improve the user experience.

Wallpaper: To change the background wallpaper of the desktop, click the user name in the top right-hand corner of the screen and choose **Options** from the drop-down menu, followed by the **Wallpaper** tab.

From the drop-down there is a choice of *Dynamic, Picture* or *Color* wallpaper types; dynamic wallpapers change between daytime and night-time, with the times definable. For picture wallpapers there is a small selection of built-in wallpapers, or you can use an uploaded image of your own in JPG/JPEG format. The **Desktop icon and font size** can also be changed from here, using the dropdown. Having made a choice, click the **Apply** button:

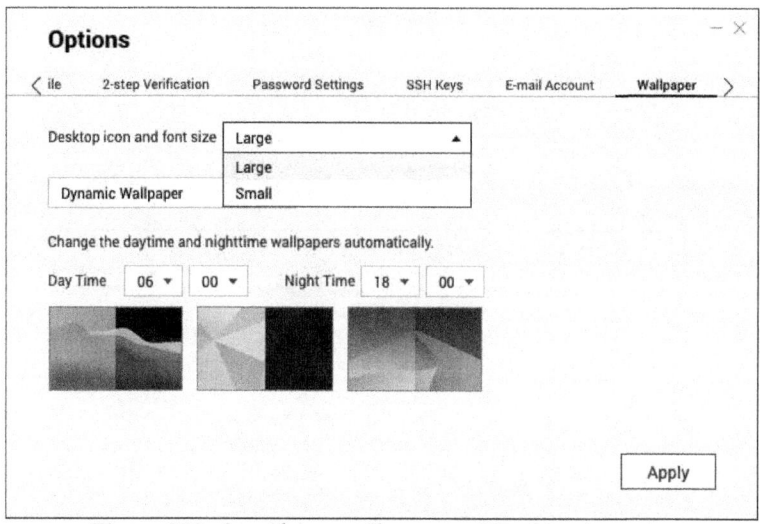

Figure 282: Specifying wallpaper and Desktop icon size

Miscellaneous Options: There are various options that can be controlled by clicking on the user name in the top right-hand corner of the screen and choosing **Options > Miscellaneous** from the resultant drop-down menu. These include displaying the time on the desktop; re-opening previously open windows when logging back into the NAS; changing the behavior of the Main Menu; setting the auto logout time (short logout times increase security but may be inconvenient). These are the options available to standard users - the administrative user has some additional ones.

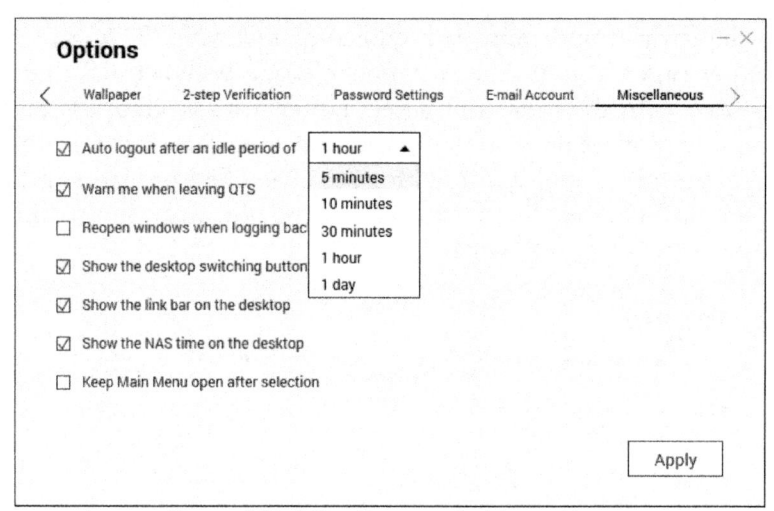

Figure 283: Miscellaneous desktop options

15.6 Customizing the Login Screen

The login screen for QTS can be changed and customized by the administrator. For instance, you might wish to do this in a business or educational setting to enforce 'branding' for the organization. Or, in a domestic setting, you might want to display a favorite family photograph.

On the **Control Panel**, click **General Settings** followed by the **Login Screen** tab. In the Background section, click **Change** and select an image or photograph from your computer. An additional small picture can also be chosen - useful for an organization's logo perhaps – plus a customized greetings message, with specified color and font size, can be added. To view the result, click **Preview**. To apply the new screen, click **Apply**.

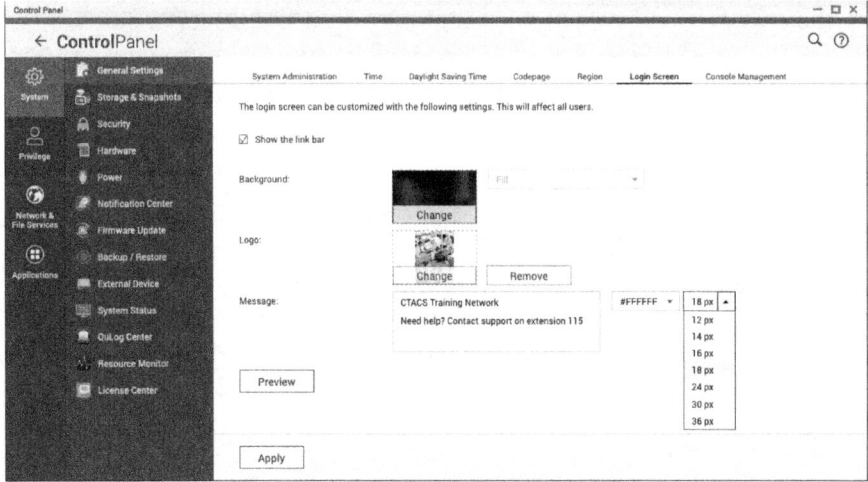

Figure 284: Customizing the login page

15.7 Printing

One advantage of networking is that it allows printers to be shared, potentially saving money as well as physical space. QTS does not have any specific features relating to printing (earlier releases did, when the ability to share USB printers was considered a useful feature). These days nearly all new printers have built-in Ethernet or wireless connections and with such printers the NAS has no significance at all and you simply follow the manufacturer's normal installation procedure on each of your computers.

The exact method of setting up any particular printer varies, but the following principles can usefully be followed:

Configure the printer with a fixed IP address. This should be adjacent to the address of the server and separate from the IP addresses used by the computers. Suppose, for instance, that the internet gateway is 192.168.1.1 and the server is 192.168.1.2; if two printers were added to the network then suitable addresses might be 192.168.1.3 and 192.168.1.4

Download the latest drivers for the printers. Consider storing the drivers on the NAS so that they can then be copied to the individual computers, rather than download them from the internet each time.
Printer manufacturers sometimes offer a choice of drivers, for instance a basic one as well as a full featured one. Use the basic one as the 'full feature' ones sometimes have superfluous features designed to capture marketing information and sell you more cartridges. However, be aware that with some multifunction devices, specifically combined printer/copier/scanners, not all functions may be available in a networked environment or may require additional software from the manufacturer to fully utilize them.

15.8 ACL (Access Control Lists)

When a shared folder is created on the NAS, the access permissions are specified as *Read/Write*, *Read only* or *Deny*, and in most home and small business environments that choice of options will be sufficient. However, in some scenarios it may not provide the necessary granularity to provide precise control over the folders and individual files. If you work in information technology and have used Windows Server, then you may have come across ACL or *Access Control Lists*, which are designed to precisely do this, and QTS also supports the ACL mechanism. The purpose of this section is not to explain ACL in detail, but to illustrate how it is implemented in QTS for the benefit of those who understand and wish to use it.

Important note: if Windows ACL support is enabled, it *replaces* the Access Permissions within Control Panel and folder and subfolder permissions can only then be edited from within Windows File Explorer for that particular folder.

Go into **Control Panel** > **Shared Folders** on the server. Select the folder you wish control and click **Advanced Permissions**. Tick the **Enable Windows ACL support** box followed by **Apply** – there will be a warning message and then a short delay.

Using File Explorer on a Windows PC, it now becomes possible to edit the permissions of shared folders to which you have access. This process varies slightly depending on the version of Windows and this example is for Windows 10/11:

Right-click the folder, choose **Properties**, click the **Security** tab followed by the **Advanced** button. On the resultant screen there are four tabs and you need to be on the *Permissions* tab. There will be several *Permission entries* – choose the user (we will assume the *administrator*) and click the **Edit** button. On the next panel, click **Show advanced permissions**. From here you can control the access attributes plus whether those rights are inherited and what they apply to. Having made changes, click **OK**.

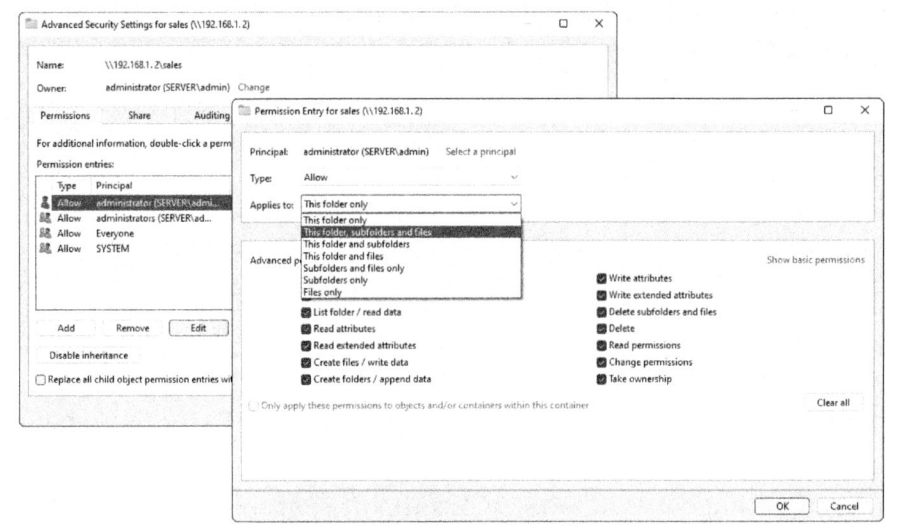

Figure 285: Advanced attributes

15.9 Internet Router Does Not Supply DHCP

In most small business and home environments, the router that connects to the internet will also provide IP addresses for the computers and other devices via its built-in DHCP server. If so QTS will use it, but if a DHCP server is not present then the NAS can be configured to act as a DHCP server itself.

Click **Control Panel > Network & Virtual Switch** icon or launch it from the Main Menu. Click **DHCP Server** on the left-hand side, followed by **Add**. If the NAS has more than one network adapter, then a separate DHCP service can be run on each one. Select the adapter from the first screen and click **Next**. On the second panel, choose an option, which is most commonly **Enable DHCP server on the current network** unless you are working with subnets:

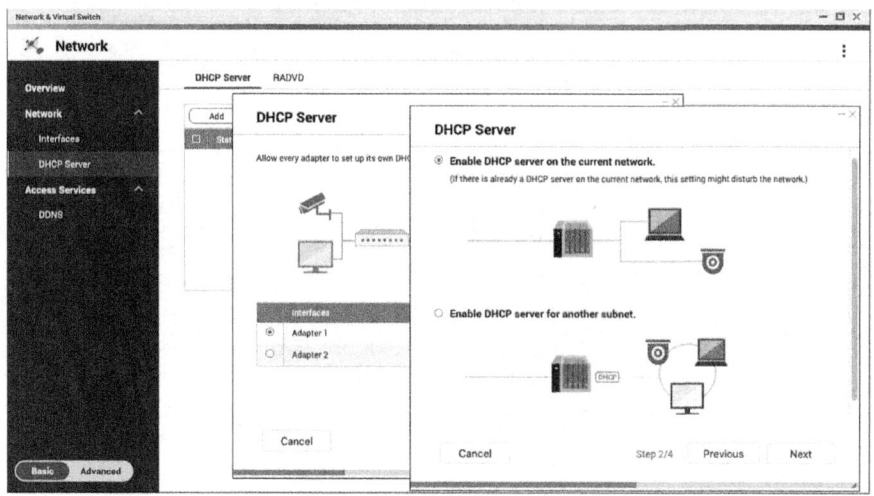

Figure 286: DHCP options

On the subsequent panel – marked as *Step 3/4* – you may receive a message stating that the DHCP client, which relates to the network adapter – needs to be changed to a static IP address, if so give it a *Fixed IP Address* within your IP addressing scheme. Change the *Subnet Mask* if required, although this is unlikely to be necessary in a small network (in this context, one with less than 255 devices). The *Default Gateway* address should correspond to the router and have been picked up automatically. *Jumbo Frame* and *Network Speed* are left as is. The *Primary DNS server* should be set to the router address, whilst the *Secondary DNS server* can be left blank. Click **Next**.

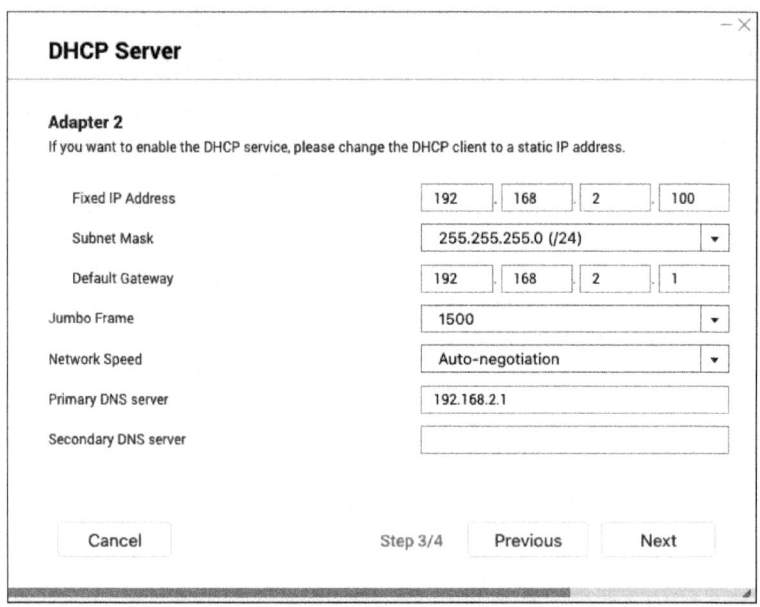

Figure 287: Change adapter to a fixed IP address

On the subsequent panel, enter the *Start IP address* and *End IP address*, although the values being proposed may already be suitable. Change the *Subnet Mask* if required, although again this is unlikely to be necessary in a small network. The default *Lease Time* will be suitable. The *Default Gateway* address should correspond to the router and should have been picked up automatically; the Primary DNS server will be set to the loopback address; the Secondary DNS server will be set to 8.8.8.8 (this is Google – it can be changed to something else if desired). Click the **Apply** button, at which point the NAS will process for a short while and may restart.

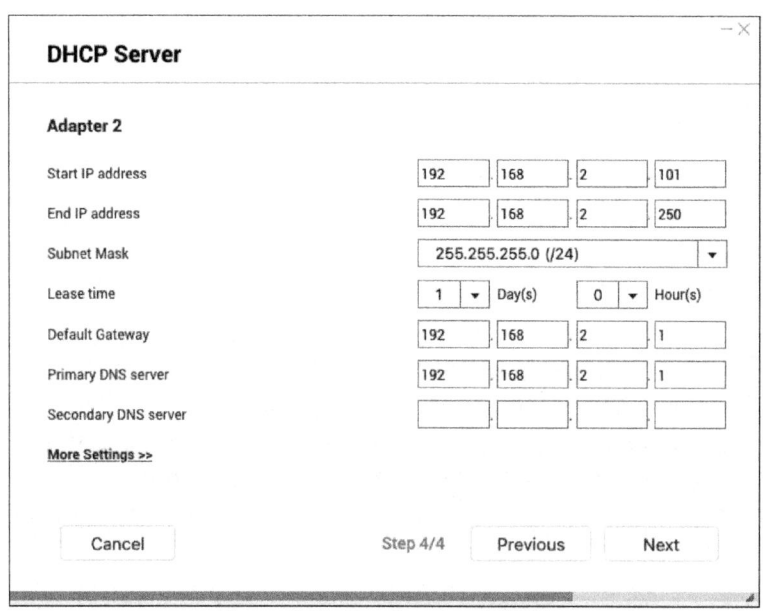

Figure 288: Configuring DHCP

Experienced IT professionals may note that the DHCP server is rudimentary - for instance, it does not provide for IP address reservations - but is generally adequate for a typical small business environment.

15.10 Internet Access Using a Proxy Server

In most organizations a router is used to connect the server and network directly to the internet. However, in some circumstances the connection might be indirect and through a *proxy server*. An example might be where managed or serviced offices are being used or in an educational establishment, in which case the NAS needs to be configured appropriately.

Click **Control Panel** followed by **Network Access**. Click the **Proxy** tab. Tick the **Use a proxy server** box and enter the details of the proxy, which will need to be obtained from the person or organization that administers the internet service. This will consist of entering an address or server name and port number, but may also require authentication (logon) details. Having provided the necessary information, click the **Apply** button.

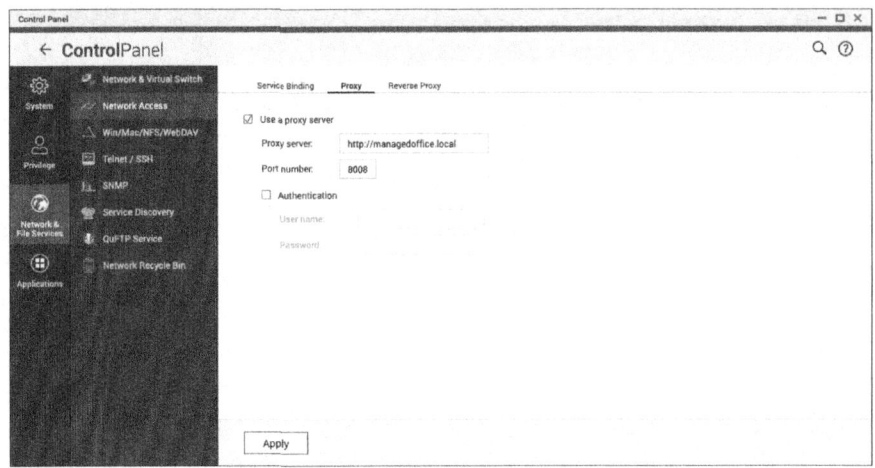

Figure 289: Example proxy server settings

15.11 Port Trunking

Many QNAP models have multiple network adapters, which can be linked together using a technique called *Port Trunking* (also known as teaming, bonding or link aggregation on other systems). This provides two benefits:

Resilience – There are several types of failure that can occur: an adapter can fail, a port on a network switch can fail, an Ethernet cable can become unplugged. These failures can be mitigated against by bonding the network adapters together, such that if one fails then another takes over.

Performance – The maximum performance of a single gigabit Ethernet adapter is 1,000 Mbits/sec, equating to around 100 Mbytes/sec of data. If there are multiple users, and especially if there are activities such as video streaming or editing, this can be a bottleneck as all network traffic must pass through it. For instance, if 5 users were simultaneously using the NAS then they would be averaging around 20 Mbytes/sec each. However, by aggregating multiple adapters, network throughput can be increased e.g. two ports can theoretically double it and four ports can quadruple it (assuming the NAS can actually deliver this amount of data from its disk drives). The following table shows the potential throughput for different numbers and type of network adapters when aggregated:

No. of Adapters	1 GbE	2.5 GbE	5 GbE	10 GbE
1	1,000 Mbits/sec 100 Mbytes/sec	2,500 MBits/sec 250 Mbytes/sec	5,000 MBits/sec 500 Mbytes/sec	10,000 Mbits/sec 1,000 Mbytes/sec
2	2,000 Mbits/sec 200 Mbytes/sec	5,000 MBits/sec 500 Mbytes/sec	10,000 Mbits/sec 1,000 Mbytes/sec	20,000 Mbits/sec 2,000 Mbytes/sec
4	4,000 Mbits/sec 400 Mbytes/sec	10,000 Mbits/sec 1,000 Mbytes/sec	20,000 Mbits/sec 2,000 Mbytes/sec	40,000 Mbits/sec 4,000 Mbytes/sec

Figure 290: Potential throughput with multiple network adapters

In this example, the NAS has two adapters and both are wired to the main network switch. Note that some modes require managed network switches that support IEEE 802.3ad Dynamic Link Aggregation.

Launch **Network & Virtual Switch** from the Main Menu or Control Panel to display the following screen. If there are multiple network adapters they will be listed and a button marked **Port Trunking** will be available:

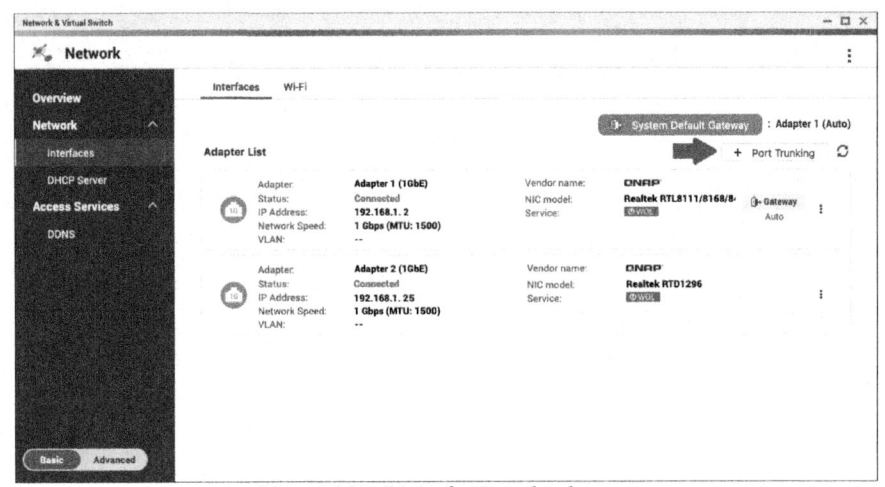

Figure 291: List of network adapters

Click the **Port Trunking** button and on the resultant panel click **Add**. Select the network adapters and click **Next**.

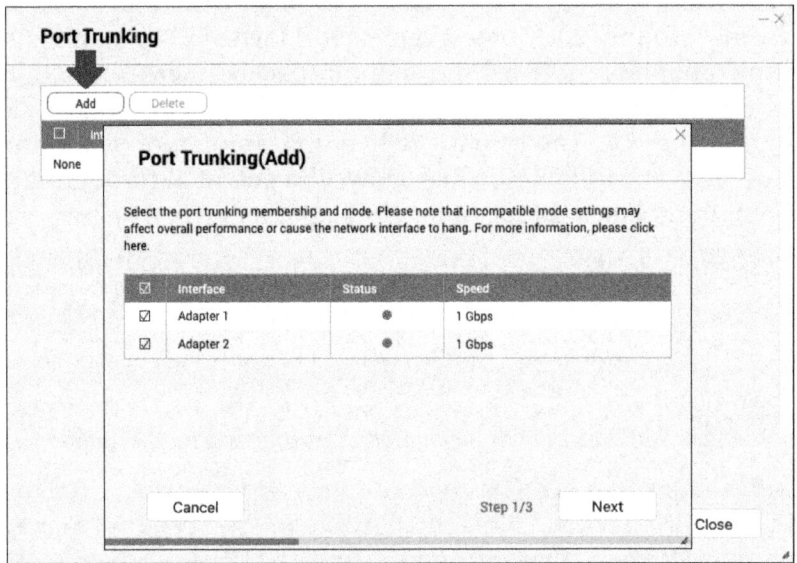

Figure 292: Choose the network adapters

On the next panel, specify the type of switch being used. In most instances, this will be **General Switch (most common)**. Click **Next**:

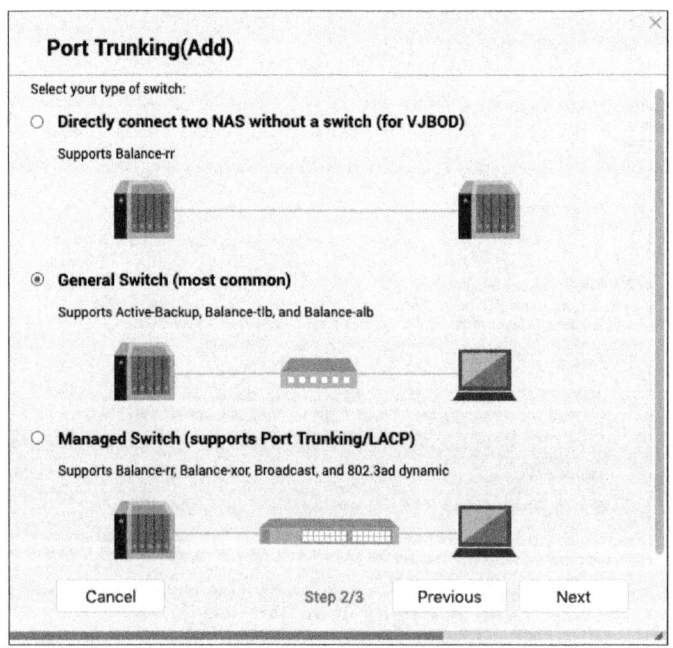

Figure 293: Specify the type of switch

On the subsequent panel, choose a trunking mode. The options available depend upon the type of switch selected, but if it was the General Switch then they are as follows: for redundancy (Failover) choose **Active-Backup**; for performance and redundancy (Load balancing & Failover) choose **Balance-tlb** or **Balance-alb**. Click **Apply**:

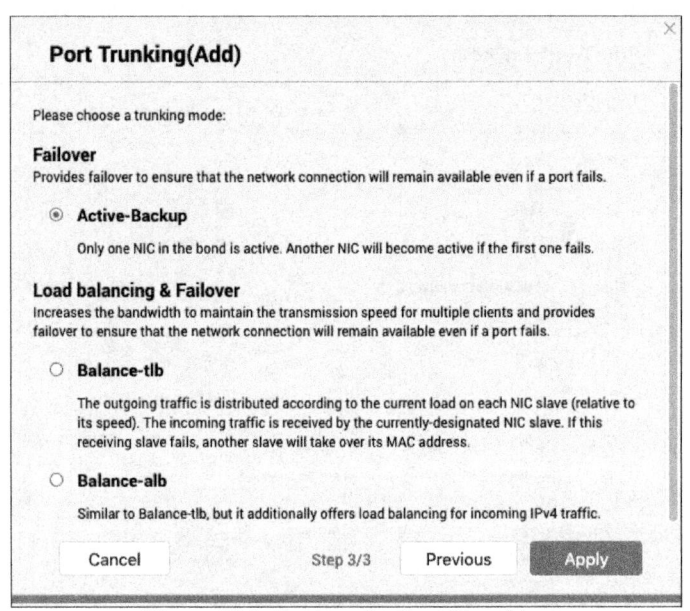

Figure 294: Options for Port Trunking

A warning message will be displayed, advising that there will be an interruption to services whilst the change takes effect and which may take a minute or two. It may then be necessary to refresh the browser, or login again to the server if the IP address has changed as a result. Go back into **Control Panel > Network & Virtual Switch** and notice how the screen has been updated. Test the trunking by unplugging one of the network cables; a warning message will be displayed after a few seconds but the NAS should remain connected.

15.12 Using an external NTP Server

The NAS can be configured to pick up the correct time from an external NTP (Network Time Protocol) server. This is recommended, especially if you are using any form of cloud file syncing service, as these rely upon accurate timestamps for keeping files in sync. It is probably the case that you chose this option during the installation of QTS; otherwise, to specify or modify an NTP server go to **Control Panel > General Settings > Time**. Click the option **to Synchronize with a time server automatically**, specify a *Time Interval* e.g. every day, then click **Update** and **Apply**. The *Time zone* and *Date and time format* can also be selected on this screen.

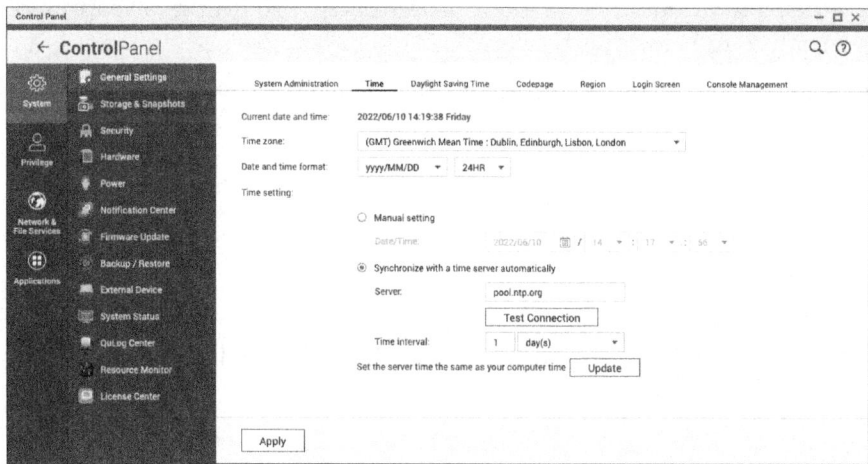

Figure 295: Specify an internet time server

The server itself can operate as an internal NTP server for the benefit of client devices on the local network, although this is not commonly done in a home or small business network. To do so, go to **Control Panel > NTP Server**, tick the **Enable NTP Server** box and choose the Operating Mode e.g. Broadcast, followed by **Apply**.

15.13 Additional Networking Features

QTS supports several additional, more specialized networking features. Some of these might not be of interest or relevance to many home and small business users, but are available if you have the requirement. They can be setup and accessed from the Control Panel.

Domain Security – a QNAP NAS can be used in conjunction with a Windows Server or other network to provide additional storage. To control access and security, QTS can work with Active Directory authentication and LDAP authentication.

Domain Controller – QTS can be figured to act as a Windows-compatible domain controller, potentially providing a complete alternative to Windows Server.

Telnet / SSH – Provides Telnet and Secure Shell (SSH - preferred) access to the server.

LDAP Server – Lightweight Directory Access Protocol (LDAP) provides directory services for authenticating clients.

RADIUS Server – Authentication system for remote users to the system.

TFTP Server – For booting devices that do not contain an operating system on local storage

15.14 The Admin Anomaly

During the installation of QTS, it is necessary to create a main, administrative account and throughout this guide we have used one we created called *systemadmin* (you may have chosen a different name). Prior to QTS 5, the built-in default administrative account was called *admin*, and could not be changed. However, as this is such a widely used name, both on QTS and other computer systems, it is an easy target for miscreants and hackers. Accordingly, QNAP have now blocked its usage, but the problem is that the *admin* account still exists within QTS, having been disabled rather than deleted.

This occasionally gives rise to the 'admin anomaly'. At the time of writing, some functions and apps require the specific use of *admin*. For instance, you may launch an app and it defaults to the *admin* user, with no opportunity to change it. It might be thought the solution to this is to re-enable the *admin* account, as described in section **4.3 Modifying, Disabling and Deleting User Accounts**. This is part of the solution, but the problem is that there is no method to view or reset the password, and without that you cannot use the account. So how do you find out what the password is?

The answer is that the default *admin* password is the 12 numbers and letters of the MAC Address of the first or only network adapter, but without the dashes. For example, if the MAC Address was 12-34-56-78-90-AB, then the password would be 1234567890AB (the letters are always upper case). There are three ways to determine the Mac Address: it can be found on a sticker on the rear or underneath of the NAS; it is displayed by Qfinder Pro; alternatively within QTS, click **Control Panel > System Status > Network Status**.

15.15 Resetting the Admin Password

If the administrative password is forgotten, lost, or otherwise unavailable, it is possible to reset it back to the factory default. On the back of the NAS is a small reset hole; the position of this varies depending on the model but it is typically towards the top of the unit. Insert a paperclip or similar object and press down for three seconds, after which the NAS will beep and you can remove the paperclip. All data on the NAS is retained, and the *admin* account is re-enabled. Wait a few minutes, and the unit will beep (if this has not happened after 5 minutes, forcibly shutdown the NAS by holding down the power button). The IP address of the NAS may have changed, in which case you can use Qfinder Pro to find it. Login as *admin* using the default password, which is derived from the MAC address of the network adapter, as explained in the previous section. You will immediately be forced to change the password, then logout and login using that the new password. Having done so, reset your preferred administrator account password e.g. for *systemadmin*, then disable the default *admin* account once you are satisfied that everything is working correctly.

If the reset button is depressed for 10 seconds rather than 3, there will be a second beep and all the settings (users, user groups, shared folders etc) will be deleted, but the actual data on the disks will still be retained.

Whilst it is clearly useful to be able to reset the NAS in this way, the security implications of this need to be considered, particularly in a business environment. For instance, the NAS could be kept in a locked cabinet or equipment rack to prevent unauthorized physical access. Or, the reset switch can be disabled altogether. To do so, go to **Control Panel > Hardware > General**, remove the tick from the **Enable configuration reset switch box**, click **Apply**.

15.16 Preparing the NAS for Disposal

If the NAS is to be disposed of, first make sure that backups of all the important data have been taken, using the techniques described in section **7 BACKUPS**.

From the **Control Panel**, choose **Backup/Restore**. On the **Restore to Factory Default** tab, click the **Reinitialize NAS** button. A message will be displayed asking whether the system should shut down or restart after the reset; make a choice and you will be prompted for the admin password as a final confirmation before the system resets, which will take a sort while.

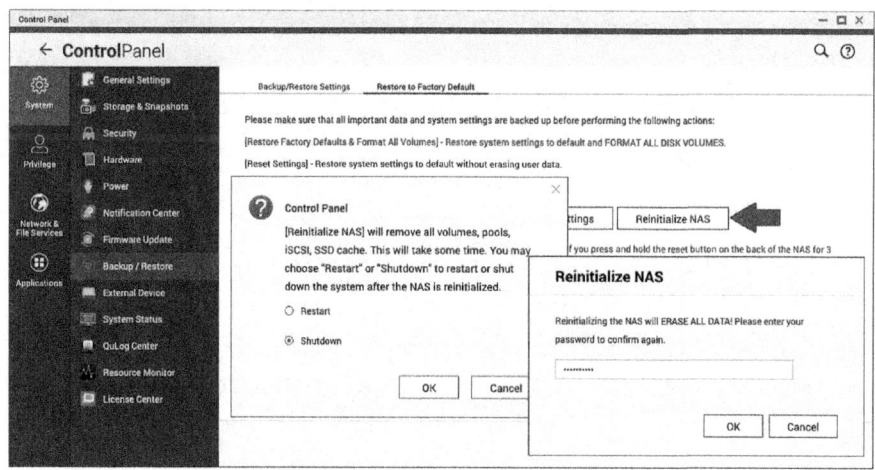

Figure 296: Reinitialize the NAS

Index

2

2-Step Verification, 39, 117, 118

A

AFP, 49, 87
Android, 16, 26, 97, 100, 186, 189, 212, 216, 220, 223, 224, 233, 238, 244, 247, 321
Antivirus, 106, 107, 345

B

BitTorrent, 235, 245, 247

C

Caching, 21, 280, 297
Certificate, 113, 114, 255
Chromebook, 26, 99, 100
Cloud, 265
Container Station, 213, 219, 239, 242, 312, 327, 333, 334, 336, 337, 343

D

Dashboard, 38, 39, 167, 170, 183, 312, 313
DHCP, 32, 33, 353, 355
DLNA, 196, 199, 200, 206, 207, 210, 227, 228
DNS, 32, 33, 270, 353, 354
Docker, 327, 333, 334, 336
Download Station, 235, 245, 246, 343
Dropbox, 14, 142, 252, 258

E

Ethernet, 13, 15, 17, 22, 25, 33, 95, 350, 357

F

File Station, 265
FTP, 111, 245, 246, 277

G

Groups, 78, 79, 164

H

HDMI, 18, 19, 37, 55, 196, 210, 227, 228, 229, 230, 337, 341
Home Folders, 66, 257
HybridDesk, 196, 227, 229, 230, 231, 337, 341
HybridMount, 41, 252, 264, 265, 343

I

Indexing, 198, 200, 201, 210, 219
IP address, 32, 33, 35, 83, 87, 89, 97, 98, 110, 111, 163, 193, 250, 256, 261, 307, 315, 321, 337, 338, 350, 353, 354, 355, 360
iSCSI, 41, 122, 280, 286, 304, 305, 306, 307, 309

L

License, 225, 345

M

Malware, 36, 108, 109
myQNAPcloud, 27, 28, 29, 84, 97, 173, 193, 212, 220, 224, 253, 254, 256, 261, 272, 273, 274, 321

N

NetBak Replicator, 154, 155, 156, 157, 159
NFS, 48, 49, 96
Notification Center, 71, 89, 107, 120, 122, 169, 171, 173, 174, 189

P

Printing, 350

Q

Qboost, 184, 186, 187, 188, 333
Qmanager, 63, 64, 72, 100, 167, 173, 189, 247
QNAP ID, 27, 28, 29, 34, 216, 225, 344, 345
Qsync, 154, 252, 257, 258, 259, 260, 261, 262, 263
QuFirewall, 103, 110, 111, 119, 120
QuMagie, 100, 196, 198, 205, 213, 214, 216, 217, 219, 343

R

Rysnc, 147

S

Security, 102, 103, 104, 105, 108, 110, 111, 112, 113, 115, 118, 119, 351, 362
Smartphones, 15, 16, 97, 221
SMB, 18, 49, 84, 89, 96, 100, 163
SMTP, 56, 71, 89, 172, 193
Snapshots, 35, 40, 41, 43, 125, 128, 129, 178, 181, 242, 280, 284, 286, 287, 289, 291, 294, 295, 296, 297, 300, 301, 303, 305, 307

T

Tablets, 15, 97
Thumbnails, 201
Thunderbolt, 13, 17, 67, 128
Time Machine, 19, 48, 62, 126, 133, 162, 163, 164, 242
Transcoding, 198, 203, 204

U

Updates, 167, 168, 169, 190
UPS, 23, 54
USB One Touch, 132, 140, 141

V

Virtualization Station, 327, 328, 329, 330, 332, 333, 337
VPN, 252, 268, 269, 270, 271, 272, 273, 274, 275, 276, 343

Printed in Great Britain
by Amazon